GERMANY'S WESTERN FRONT

TRANSLATIONS FROM THE GERMAN OFFICIAL HISTORY OF THE GREAT WAR

VOLUME II

1915

Mark Osborne Humphries and John Maker,

EDITORS

Wilfrid Laurier University Press

WLU

We acknowledge the financial support of the Government of Canada through the Book Publishing Industry Development Program for our publishing activities.

Library and Archives Canada Cataloguing in Publication

Germany's western front : translations from the German official history of the Great War, volume II: 1915 / Mark Osborne Humphries and John Maker, editors.

Translation of : Der Weltkrieg
Includes bibliographical references and index.
Issued also in electronic format.
ISBN 978-1-55458-051-4

1. World War, 1914–1918—Germany. 2. World War, 1914–1918—Campaigns—Western Front. I. Humphries, Mark Osborne, 1981– II. Maker, John, 1974– III. Title.

D531.W4513 2010   940.4'144   C2009-904030-1

ISBN 978-1-55458-259-4
Electronic format.

1. World War, 1914–1918—Germany. 2. World War, 1914–1918—Campaigns—Western Front. I. Humphries, Mark Osborne, 1981– II. Maker, John, 1974– III. Title.

D531.W4513 2010a   940.4'144

Cover design by Blakeley Words+Pictures using a photograph from the private collection of Anthony Langley. Text design by Catharine Bonas-Taylor.

This book is printed on FSC recycled paper and is certified Ecologo. It is made from 100% post-consumer fibre, processed chlorine free, and manufactured using biogas energy.

Printed in Canada

Every reasonable effort has been made to acquire permission for copyright material used in this text, and to acknowledge all such indebtedness accurately. Any errors and omissions called to the publisher's attention will be corrected in future printings.

FSC

Recycled
Supporting responsible use
of forest resources
www.fsc.org Cert no. SGS-COC-003153
© 1996 Forest Stewardship Council

CONTENTS

APPENDICES

LIST OF MAPS, SKETCHES, AND FIGURES

All maps and sketches have been translated and redrawn by Mark Humphries from the original German maps and sketches provided with *Der Weltkrieg* except where noted as follows. Maps 1 and 2 are based on maps originally printed in Frank M. McMurry, *The Geography of the Great War* (New York: Macmillan Co., 1919), figures 17 and 15. Maps 1, 2, and 3 and Sketches 11 and 20 have been adapted from larger fold-out maps from *Der Weltkrieg*. Sketch 9 is adapted from a map in Rudolf Hanslian-Bergendorff, *Der Chemische Krieg* (Berlin: E.S. Mittler & Sohn, 1925), as well as from a larger fold-out map in *Der Weltkrieg*, Volume VIII.

FOREWORD

WAR IS A REACTIVE BUSINESS, A COMPETITION WHOSE OUTCOME IS DEPENDENT not on some sort of absolute standard of excellence on the part of one side, but on the relative superiority of one side over another. It is this relationship—the dynamic between two opponents as each struggles to impose its will on the other— that should be at the heart of operational military history. But it rarely is. Military history, for all its massive progress in the past two or three decades, particularly in the English-speaking world, remains far too national—and even nationalistic—in its approach. If the serious study of military history as a self-contained subject has a significant agenda for the future, it is this—to be comparative.

For no war and no front is this injunction more important or more pressing than for the First World War and its Western Front. The cycle of reaction and reaction between two coalitions, remarkably similar in their military organizations and in the technologies they employed, produced a conflict that was not as static as suggested by the immobility of the trenches which dominated the character of the fighting. It has now become axiomatic that "modern war" was conceived and developed through the experience of this titanic fight and the lessons it bequeathed. But the military history on which such arguments rest continues to be lopsided. English-language historians, not just Britons but also Americans, Australians, Canadians, and New Zealanders, have done more than those writing in French and German to deepen our understanding of the conduct of operations on the Western Front. However, their research is too often written from the perspective of one side only. It pays little or no attention to the sources available for the Germans, for what they tell us about German intentions, German reactions, or even German perspectives on British and French efforts.

This gap is all the more extraordinary because the German official history of the war on land, *Der Weltkrieg*, is not a rare set of volumes, at least for the war up to the spring of 1917—a point it had reached with Volume XII, published in 1939. By then the pace of its authors was quickening: the events of 1914 had taken six volumes, those of 1915 three (and these are the basis for this translation), and those of 1916 two. Two more volumes appeared to take the story to November 1918. Being completed during the Second World War, Volumes XIII and XIV never gained wide circulation. Five hundred copies of each were reprinted in 1956 but did not sell out until 1975.

Such disappointing sales were themselves indications of two phenomena. First, the Second World War had made the study of the First World War deeply unfashionable throughout Europe—a trend that only changed in Britain in 1964, after the fiftieth anniversary of the war's outbreak, and in Germany not until the ninetieth anniversary in 2004—if then. Second, German military history after 1945, insofar as it survived at all, stepped away from the operational focus embraced by the General Staff historians of the Wilhelmine period, of which *Der Weltkrieg* was the final manifestation. This condition still pertains: operational military history does not have the respectability in German academic circles that it has now acquired in the English-speaking world. The British official history has been reprinted; the German has not been, despite the scarcity of Volumes XIII and XIV.

These two arguments may be sufficient explanations for the neglect of the *Der Weltkrieg* in Germany, but they do not apply to English-speaking historians. Their reasons for not consulting it more frequently are, presumably, linguistic. For monoglot scholars, this translation will be a boon beyond measure. It has been fashionable to rubbish the work of the official historians of the First World War of all languages. Sir James Edmonds, whose labours on behalf of Britain were not completed until 1948, and who has been criticized by David French, Tim Travers, and Denis Winter—to cite three historians with very different perspectives—presided over an enterprise that may not conform to current expectations of historians but that nonetheless strove hard for objectivity. As Stephen Green has shown in *Writing the Great War: Sir James Edmonds and the Official Histories 1915–1948* (2003), this was team writing *avant la lettre*. Draft narratives were compiled from the documents and then, in the search for balance, were circulated to the surviving participants for their comments. Edmonds's creation could lay much greater claim to unbiased authority than could, say, Basil Liddell Hart's *The Real War*, probably the most widely read one-volume account of the war in the English language between 1930 and 1964. Markus Pöhlmann has produced a study comparable to Green's on the writing of *Der Weltkrieg*, to which this foreword is heavily indebted. *Kriegsgeschichte und Geschichtspolitik: der Erste Weltkrieg. Die amtliche deutsche Militärgeschichtsschreibung 1914–1956* (2002) shows us that the historians of the *Reichsarchiv*—the organization established in 1919 to produce the German official history—were as thorough in their construction of the operational story. The first head of *Reichsarchiv*'s section for the collection of documents, Theodor Jochim, distinguished its work from that of academic historians, contending that "the events of the war, strategy and tactics can only be considered from a neutral, purely objective perspective which weighs things dispassionately and is independent of any ideology."

The Nazis' rise to power in 1933 would test this resolve. Volume IX, parts of which are included in the present translation, was published in 1933 and so was the last to appear under the old regime. The president of the *Reichsarchiv* that year, Hans von Haeften, resisted flying the swastika flag over the office building. In 1934 the *Reichsarchiv*, which even though staffed by former army officers had thus far remained an independent body at least in name, was subordinated to the *Wehrmacht*. It is has therefore been easy to condemn the later volumes of *Der Weltkrieg* as ideologically tainted. But this is both to exaggerate the impact of the Nazis on the writing of the history and at the same time to underplay a pre-existing issue whose roots date back not to Weimar but to Wilhelmine Germany.

After 1933, Jochim's goal remained the guiding principle for the historians of the *Wehrmacht,* as it had been for those of the *Reichsarchiv*. Their careers were formed under the Hohenzollerns, and their function within the army, as it had been for the historians of the Prussian General Staff, was not only to record but also to teach. Military history enabled officers of the future to learn from the examples of the past; they would not do so if mistakes committed by their predecessors were glossed over. *Der Weltkrieg* did not set out specifically to glorify the German soldier. His heroism in front-line combat had been the subject of a separate, more popular series edited by Georg Soldan. *Schlachten des Weltkrieges* covered individual battles in a run of thirty-six much slimmer volumes, the last of them published in 1930, three years before Hitler came to power. What did affect the writing of *Der Weltkrieg* was the course of Nazi foreign policy. The *Reichsarchiv* had established working relationships with the official historians of other powers, especially Britain. But when contacts with the Soviet Union, which had provided training areas for the *Reichswehr* in the late 1920s, were broken after 1933, the comparative input available for the earlier volumes began to wither. During the Second World War itself, Volume XIV—dealing with the events of 1918—was censored for fear of upsetting Rumania (Germany's ally in the Second World War, if not in the First) and Bulgaria (an ally in both wars). These political pressures drove the German official historians even more to a purely military narrative of events.

This focus on military history narrowly defined was a product not of Nazi rule but of a much older tradition in German military thought, to be found in the quarter-century before the outbreak of the First World War in the famous dispute between Hans Delbrück, professor of history in Berlin, and the military historians of the General Staff. Delbrück argued that Frederick the Great in the Seven Years War (1756–63) had adopted a strategy of attrition, designed to wear out the coalition of France, Austria, and Russia by manoeuvre; whereas the staff historians said that Frederick's strategy was one of annihilation, using manoeuvre to seek battle. Both were right, because for each the focus of attention was a different level of war. Delbrück was concerned to place war in its political context; the staff historians were considering the operational aspects, the relationship between strategy and tactics. So determined were they that the conduct of war could be separated from its political objectives that they could not even see the point of Delbrück's argument. Aspects of the dispute with Delbrück lingered on after the war, until his death in 1929. Delbrück was one of ten academics appointed to the historical commission to oversee the work of the *Reichsarchiv*, and the bulk of them favoured placing the war in its political context. They were not helped when the Foreign Ministry refused to co-operate, as it wanted to produce its own story, the better to rebut the terms of the Versailles Treaty of 1919. This suited the General Staff historians, who by 1923 had established virtual control of the entire project, convinced that they could produce an adequate history of the war that was almost exclusively military in its focus.

Their hopes rested on an illusion: *Der Weltkrieg* could not be apolitical. German officers—like those of many other armies—were wont to protest their political neutrality; Hans von Seeckt, the head of the surrogate General Staff between 1919 and 1926, provided a case in point. But both the German army and its Chief of the General Staff had too great a professional role in shaping German policy for that to be a deliverable aspiration. Germany had been united by war, and its subsequent history until 1945 was shaped by it. The focus on operations carried its own implications for the formulation of German strategy between 1870 and 1945: operational excellence came to be seen as the tool which could cut through Germany's problems, its encircled position in Europe, its quantitative inferiority in the First World War, and its "humiliation" at Versailles in 1919. The presumption in the didactic purpose of *Der Weltkrieg* was that there was a perfect solution to the conundrums of operations: that strategy and even policy could be subordinated to the operational level of war and that a war conducted as the military experts thought it should be waged would produce the right outcome for Germany.

Erich von Falkenhayn, the Chief of the General Staff between September 1914 and August 1916, and therefore the central character in this book, became a prime target for the historians of the *Reichsarchiv*. Having served in China before the First World War, his career had not been shaped by Alfred von Schlieffen, the Chief of the General Staff between 1891 and 1905 and the principal architect of the army's approach to the operational level of war before 1914. Falkenhayn's overseas service had convinced him that Britain's maritime and imperial strength made it the centre of gravity of the enemy coalition, and that therefore it should be the focus of Germany's war effort. In the bitter debates between "easterners" and "westerners" (to borrow the vocabulary of the British memoirs of the wars and apply it to a more apposite context), Falkenhayn focused on the West because he realized that ultimately French and Russian capacity to carry on fighting rested on British economic strength. The trouble was that there was no operational solution to this strategic conundrum, as Britain's forte was naval and Germany's military. Joint planning was in any case a casualty of institutional division, since Falkenhayn as a soldier had no leverage over the navy. The best he could hope for was to bring the war to a satisfactory conclusion before Britain deployed its "New Armies" to France. Unlike Schlieffen's, his solutions were not primarily operational, but political. He wanted a separate peace with Russia to free up the German Army so that it could concentrate on the West. This is the underlying thread of Volumes VII, VIII, and IX *Der Weltkrieg*, whose sections relevant to the Western Front are here published in English for the first time.

Falkenhayn's grasp of the wider strategy imposed on Germany was not compatible with his own staff's focus on the operational level. Even his friends, such as Wild von Hohenborn, who succeeded him as Prussian Minister of War, were not persuaded. Like the victors of Tannenberg in 1914, Paul von Hindenburg and Erich Ludendorff, they could see the opportunity for operational success in the East. Envelopment battles of the sort so strongly advocated before the war by Schlieffen (who was now dead) could be carried through against Russia. Hans von Haeften, who had played a key role in the work of the *Reichsarchiv* since its inception, was appointed its president in 1931 and oversaw the production of Volumes VII to IX of *Der Weltkrieg*. He was not as unbiased in his views as the standards demanded by Jochim suggested he should be. Heart problems had meant that he had had to forgo active operational appointments on the General Staff in November 1914. Instead he had become adjutant to Helmuth von Moltke the Younger, Schlieffen's successor and Chief of the General Staff at the outbreak of war. Moltke became the scapegoat for the defeat on the Marne in September 1914, and thereafter stirred the opposition to Falkenhayn, who had replaced him. Haeften began work on a history of the Eastern Front even while the events described in this volume were unfolding. Shuttling back and forth to the East, visiting the headquarters of Hindenburg and Ludendorff, he became such a fierce critic of Falkenhayn that he was nearly court-martialled.

The operational perspective of the official historians therefore provided the ammunition with which *Der Weltkrieg* attacked Falkenhayn. Holger Afflerbach's political biography, *Falkenhayn. Politisches Denken und Handeln im Kaiserreich* (1994), provides important correctives. Falkenhayn's operational efforts need to be set in their political context. They were accompanied by a sustained attempt to prise the Entente apart, but his efforts to persuade Russia to negotiate were incompatible with the predilections of Germany's principal ally, Austria-Hungary, and with those of Hindenburg and Ludendorff. For them, the weight applied to Russia in 1915 should be directly military, not diplomatic. Hindenburg's iconic role as a national hero created a political leverage that ultimately neither the chancellor, Theodor von Bethmann Hollweg, nor the Kaiser could resist.

It has been argued that *Der Weltkrieg* was written to glorify Hindenburg and (especially) Ludendorff, just as it has been said (wrongly, as Andrew Green shows) that Edmonds used the British official history to defend Douglas Haig. In 1917–18, Haeften had worked on propaganda in the German Supreme Command, *Oberste Heeresleitung III*. But after the war Hindenburg and Ludendorff kept their distance from the work of the *Reichsarchiv*, and *Der Weltkrieg* barely mentioned Hindenburg in its account of the events of 1918. Wolfgang Foerster, who succeeded Haeften in 1934 as director of what was now called the *Forschungsanstalt für Kriegs- und Heeresgeschichte*, was better disposed toward Ludendorff. He treated the victory at Tannenberg, whose site was both a focus for the commemoration of the First World War and a memorial to Hindenburg after his death, as a "model battle" on a par with the great German victories of Leipzig in 1813 and Sedan in 1870. But the lesson from all three cases was that the use of envelopment as an operational method had led to a decisive victory. So the real influence on Foerster was not so much Ludendorff as Schlieffen. In 1921 he had published *Graf Schlieffen und der Weltkrieg*, a book designed to show how Schlieffen's legacy had shaped Germany's conduct of the war. The combination of Ludendorff's right-wing radicalism and his mental instability increasingly alienated him from his former colleagues on the General Staff in general and from the *Reichsarchiv* in particular. The authors employed on *Der Weltkrieg* never subjected Hindenburg and Ludendorff to the sort of psychological profiling that they accorded to their predecessors, Moltke and Falkenhayn. However, in 1952 Foerster published an independent study of Ludendorff's "psychological state in the final stages of the First World War," *Der Feldherr Ludendorff im Unglück*.

Most of the papers that went into the writing of *Der Weltkrieg* were destroyed when the Royal Air Force bombed the depository in which the Prussian military archives were stored in 1945. This is the single most compelling reason for according the utmost seriousness to this book. Unlike the official histories of the other major belligerents of the First World War, that of Germany can never be written again, at least not from a comparable primary source base. However, the military papers of the other states of imperial Germany have survived, and so too have collections of private papers belonging to those involved in the writing of *Der Weltkrieg*. Most important, the papers that were still the subject of active investigation by official historians were kept elsewhere and so were not destroyed in 1945. Having been stored in Potsdam during the Cold War, they have now been united with the military archives in Freiburg. From these it is clear that many facets of Germany's war effort other than the operational level of its conduct interested the *Reichsarchiv* and its successors. Though the volumes of *Der Weltkrieg* are Eurocentric, theatres outside Europe were covered briefly and were due to be the subject of individual studies. Ludwig Boell's monumental history of the East African campaign, completed in 1944, was effectively recreated by its author after the war and then privately published. Most weighty were the projected volumes on the economic history of the war, of which only the first, prewar volumes ever appeared.

Mark Humphries, John Maker, and their team of translators, Wilhelm J. Kiesselbach, Peter Meinlschmidt, and Ralph Whitehead, are to be congratulated on a major achievement. The year 1915 marked the moment when the fighting on the Western Front adapted to trench warfare, and when the armies of all sides began what recent British military historians have described as a "learning curve." This process was of course not a uniquely British phenomenon, but one in which Germans and French also shared, and to whose development the battles at Soissons and Neuve Chapelle, the gas attack at Ypres, and the offensives in the Champagne and the Artois all contributed. This volume will transform English-speaking historians' understandings of a crucial stage in the First World War. It might even make Germans take their own operational military history seriously.

Hew Strachan
Chichele Professor of the History of War
University of Oxford

ACKNOWLEDGEMENTS

THIS VOLUME OF *GERMANY'S WESTERN FRONT*, THE FIRST TO BE PUBLISHED IN the series, is the work of many hands. This book—and series—began in 2006 with a search for existing translations of scattered German-language sources in Ottawa, Pennsylvania, Washington, Kansas, and London. In Ottawa, Owen Cooke, Sarah Cozzi, Steve Harris, Andrew Iarocci, Barbara Wilson, the staff of the Directorate of History and Heritage, the Canadian War Museum, and Library and Archives Canada were all enormously helpful in tracking down unutilized German sources and translations in Canada. At the United States Army War College in Carlisle, Pennsylvania, we were assisted most ably by the circulation and reference staffs, especially David Keough. The circulation and reference staffs of the National Archives and Records Administration in Washington, the Combined Arms Research Library at the Command and General Staff College, Fort Leavenworth, Kansas, and the National Archives, Kew, were also most helpful. Many others have contributed to this project in one way or another at conferences or in private discussion. Tim Cook especially has been a friend and has pushed us towards realizing our goals in this project—he also provided funding for translations that will appear in later volumes.

At Wilfrid Laurier University Press the editors want to thank Brian Henderson for being flexible on timelines and willing to think in grand terms, not single books. We'd also like to acknowledge the work of Lisa Quinn, Rob Kohlmeier, Penelope Grows, Clare Hitchens, Leslie Macredie, Heather Blain-Yanke, and Cheryl Beaupré. All of these people contributed to the book in one way or another.

At Mount Royal, Mark Humphries wants to thank Tom Brown, Scott Murray, Manuel Mertin, and Jennifer Pettit and to acknowledge that he was afforded more time to finish up the project during the winter of 2009 with course release funding from the Faculty of Arts. At the University of Western Ontario he would like to thank Roger Hall, Luz Maria Hernández-Sáenz, Francine McKenzie, and Robert Wardhaugh. Most of all Mark thanks Jonathan Vance, his doctoral supervisor, who gave him the confidence, time, and the financial assistance necessary to complete this book. At the University of Ottawa, John thanks Jeffrey Keshen, Rich Connors, and Galen Perras for their support and guidance. His colleagues in the Ph.D. program Nicholas Clarke, Mark Bourrie, Daniel Macfarlane, Max Dagenais, and Juraj Hochman provided support and encouragement. John also wishes to thank Brian McKillop at Carleton University. John is most grateful to Serge Durflinger, whose patient guidance, advice, and support have helped him navigate some rough waters. The Laurier Centre for Military Strategic and Disarmament Studies (LCMSDS) at Wilfrid Laurier University—home to Mark Humphries between 2003 and 2008 and to John Maker during 2003 and 2004 when both were students of Terry Copp, Roger Sarty, and John Laband—has provided the funding for the majority of the translations. A centre of excellence in the Department of National Defence's Security and Defence Forum program, the centre provides an academic home for students and researchers alike. Both editors have had the pleasure to work there with Brandy Barton, Mike Bechthold, Michelle Fowler, Geoff Keelan, Kellen Kurschinski, Kathryn Rose, Vanessa McMackin, Andrew Thompson, Jane Whalen, and Jim Wood.

Travelling, obtaining copies of the German official history, and the process of translation were costly. While Mr. Kiesselbach and Mr. Meinlschmidt were generous enough to work for a pittance, as they believed in the project, the cost was borne by several organizations and this project could never have been started (or the first volume completed) without them. Both editors therefore owe the following organizations and people a great debt of gratitude. Alexander Freund, the Chair in German-Canadian Studies at the University of Winnipeg, and the Spletzer Family Foundation provided a generous grant for translation, materials acquisition, and travel in 2007. Dr. Jonathan Vance, Canada Research Chair in Conflict and Culture at the University of Western Ontario, provided funding in the form of a graduate student research assistantship in the summer of 2007. Dr. Humphries also benefited from a Social Sciences and Humanities Research Council (SSHRC) Canadian Graduate Scholarship while completing his Ph.D.

Our families have been the only casualties in this endeavour, having been forced to discuss *ad nauseam* the finer points of the translation process and Germany in the First World War. Mark thanks his partner, Lianne Leddy, for her understanding and love. Audrey and Farley always sat quietly around (and sometimes on) the computer desk while he worked on the manuscript. John would like to thank his parents and siblings for their love and support. He thanks his wife, Tammy, for her inestimable patience, understanding, and willingness to listen attentively to discussion of the minutiae of this project and of his life as a history student in general. He also thanks his daughter, Imogen—her inspirational zest for life is a reminder that sometimes it really is all about the ABCs.

Last, but most importantly, this project and the editors owe Terry Copp, the director of LCMSDS and Professor Emeritus at Wilfrid Laurier University, more than can be expressed. Terry has been a tireless advocate for the project (and both editors' careers) and has believed in the editors' vision and provided the time, research space, and financial assistance necessary to see the project through to completion. Terry is always there to lend an ear and debate ideas great and small. He has pushed both of us to find the best evidence, to ask the most pertinent questions, and to be good historians striving for important things to say. While it is up to others to judge whether we have met his expectations, we have done our best to live up to his example. This book and the series *Germany's Western Front* are dedicated to him for inspiring Canadian students to study military history and pursue their academic endeavours.

INTRODUCTION

ON 14 APRIL 1945, A BRITISH BOMBER DROPPED SEVERAL FIVE-TON BOMBS OVER the Bauhausberg in Potsdam. They pierced the roof of the German National Archive's warehouse and fell through seven floors of documents, exploding in the basement. The combination of incendiary devices and high explosives melted the steel girders holding up the warehouse's immense collection of books and papers. As the posts fell in, the building collapsed. Germany's Great War records burned in the inferno.[1]

The quiet, tree-lined streets along the Teltow Canal had been home to the *Reichsarchiv* (Imperial German Archives) and its military historians since the autumn of 1919.[2] In November of that year, officers from the *Kriegsgeschichte des Großen Generalstabes* (War History Section of the Great General Staff) transported the Reich's war documents away from the political instability in Berlin.[3] They shepherded boatload after boatload of records down the canal, piled high atop open barges, toward the former *Reichskriegsschule*, an imposing rectangular building crowned by a distinctive tower and set next to an elegant mansion that would become the *Reichsarchiv* warehouse.[4] In these two buildings, *Reichsarchiv*

---

1 See Uwe Löbel, "Neue Forschungsmöglichkeiten zur preußisch-deutschen Heeresgeschichte," *Militärgeschichtliche Mitteilungen* 51 (1992): 143.

2 A short introduction to the history of the *Reichsarchiv* is Karl Demeter, *Das Reichsarchiv: Tatsachen und Personen* (Frankfurt: Bernard und Graefe, 1969). See also Matthias Herrmann, *Das Reichsarchiv 1919–1945* (Ph.D. diss., Humboldt Universität, 1994).

3 Markus Pöhlmann, *Kriegsgeschichte und Geschichtspolitik: Der Erste Weltkrieg. Die amtliche deutsche Militärgeschichtsschreibung, 1914–1956* (Schöningh: Paderborn, 2002), 79.

4 Alexander L.P. Johnson, "Military Histories of the Great War," *Journal of Modern History* 3, no. 2 (1931): 277.

historians—civilian in rank but officers by trade—would toil away for more than two decades on an official history of Germany's war effort. By the spring of 1945 they had produced three series of books, two popular and one academic, and assisted researchers working on hundreds of regimental histories and dozens of films.[5] They guarded access to Germany's war records and actively moulded an official memory of the war that would remain consistent in the shifting intellectual and political currents of interwar Germany. Theirs was the most comprehensive history of Germany's military effort in the Great War. It would be the only secondary source to be written with unfettered access to a long-ago destroyed documentary record.

The April 1945 bombing raid destroyed those records of the sort that British historians are accustomed to using in their studies of the Great War. War diaries, orders, operational plans, maps, ration cards, situation reports, and telegrams were all burned. But, as was revealed in the early 1990s, some of the records housed in the historians' offices in the *Reichskriegsschule* did in fact survive. In August 1945 they were confiscated by the Soviet government, some eventually ending up in Moscow, others remaining in Potsdam. All were inaccessible to Western historians until they were returned to the *Bundesarchiv* in 1990. This block of some three thousand files and fifty boxes is of great importance; note, however, that they cannot replace the papers lost in April 1945. They are the working files of Germany's official historians—that is, they are the files that were generated in the course of researching and writing the official histories.[6] As Helmut Otto notes, they are comprised of "business documents, correspondence, research notes, studies, field reports, manuscript drafts, copies of corrected drafts, galley proofs, copies of documents from military and political authorities and agencies, excerpts from officer's personal war diaries and writings with notes from the editors, and newspaper clippings."[7] As working papers they are partially digested history, closer to the raw materials than other secondary sources, but they are not a comprehensive primary archive.[8] Their greatest contribution has been to confirm the value of the official histories and the work of the *Reichsarchiv* historians.[9]

---

5 Markus Pöhlmann, "Yesterday's Battles and Future War: The German Official Military History, 1918–1939," in *Shadows of Total War: Europe, East Asia and the United States, 1919–1939*, ed. Roger Chickering and Stig Förster (New York: Cambridge University Press, 2003), 230.

6 Helmut Otto, "Der Bestand Kriegsgeschichtliche Forschungsanstalt des Heeres im Bundesarchiv-, Militärisches Zwischenarchiv Potsdam," *Militärgeschichtliche Mitteilungen* 51 (1992): 433–34.

7 Ibid., 433.

8 For a complete file list, see I. Zandek and H. Böhm, *Bestand RH 61—Kriegsgeschichtliche Forschungsanstalt des Heeres* (Freiburg: Bundesarchiv-Militärarchiv, 2002), pp. i–ii.

9 Hew Strachan, *The First World War: Volume 1: To Arms* (Oxford: Oxford University Press, 2001), xvi–xvii.

Any examination of Germany's First World War must begin with the published work of these official historians—although it certainly cannot end there. Of the three sets of official histories that were produced between 1919 and 1945, the academic series (for lack of a better term) *Der Weltkrieg, 1914 bis 1918*, is the most comprehensive. The *Weltkriegwerk*, as it is also known, provides a narrative overview of the Great War spread across fourteen volumes published between 1925 and 1944.[10] In form, *Der Weltkrieg* is typical of other national official histories of the period. It is a top-down military history of operations that rarely takes the tactical analysis below the level of the infantry division. While focusing on German military operations on land, it presents summary chapters on naval and air operations, the economy, foreign policy, the political situation, and logistics. Like other official works of the period, it ignores the social and cultural history of the war. Its greatest strength and inherent flaw is its single-minded focus on military operations.

Work on the series began early in 1919, when Hermann Mertz von Quirnheim, a Frankish general staff officer who held several important posts on the Eastern and Southern Fronts during the war, was promoted to serve as *Oberquartiermeister* of the Great General Staff's *Kriegsgeschichte* (War History) Section.[11] Military history in Prussia-Germany had always been the purview of the Great General Staff; indeed, the War History Section had already published several detailed accounts of specific battles before the war ended.[12] After the Treaty of Versailles was signed and the German General Staff system was abolished, Mertz's organization was officially disbanded on 1 October 1919.[13] The military personnel under his command were transferred to the new civilian *Reichsarchiv* in Potsdam, which functioned as the German Imperial state and military archives but was also tasked with writing a comprehensive military history of the Great War.[14] This momentous undertaking was assigned to a special subsection under the direction of Hans von Haeften, another General Staff officer, and about eighty former *Kriegsgeschichte* officers.[15] As in Great Britain, France, and Canada, the military would dominate the planning and writing of an official national history of the war.

10 The final two volumes covering 1917 and 1918 were completed in the early 1940s but were not published until 1956.

11 Pöhlmann, *Kriegsgeschichte und Geschichtspolitik*, 82–84.

12 In the incomplete series *Der grosse Krieg in Einzeldarstellungen* published by Gerhard Stalling beginning in 1918.

13 Pöhlmann, "Yesterday's Battles and Future War," 236–37.

14 Otto, "Der Bestand Kriegsgeschichtliche Forschungsanstalt," 430.

15 On Haeften's war service see Ekkehart Guth, "Der Gegensatz zwischen dem Oberbefehlshaber Ost und dem Chef des Feldheeres 1914–15: Die Rolle des Major von Haeften im Spannungsfeld zwischen Hindenburg, Ludendorff, und Falkenhayn," *Militärgeschichtliche Mitteilungen* 35 (1984): 113–39.

In theory, the *Reichsarchiv* was to be a civilian organization operating under the mandate of the Ministry of the Interior. To ensure that it remained as such, and was not unduly influenced by former officers of the General Staff's Historical Section, a *Historische Kommission für das Reichsarchiv* (*Reichsarchiv* Historical Commission) was established by order of the German president in July 1920.[16] The Historical Commission was tasked with advising the personnel of the *Reichsarchiv* in their scholarly methodology, guarding the independence of their research, and building bridges to the academic community.[17] The commission was relatively balanced, being composed of left-leaning academics such as Hans Delbrück, Friedrich Meinecke, and Hermann Oncken and right-leaning scholars like Erich Mareks, Aloys Schulte, and Hermann Schumacher. Delbrück was an especially telling choice, for he was a long-standing opponent of official military history in Germany and before the war had been embroiled in public controversy with German staff historians.[18] The academics on the Historical Commission agreed that the *Weltkriegwerk* should be a broad general history that would include the controversial U-boat war, internal and foreign politics, the economic war, and the revolutions on the home front.[19] They objected to Haeften's plan, which was for *Der Weltkrieg* to focus exclusively on the military operations of the Imperial Army.

In late 1920, Mertz announced a compromise. The main series (*Der Weltkrieg*) would comprise at least ten volumes and would focus on military operations and the broader political and strategic picture, but it would be written in the tradition of the anonymous official General Staff histories to emphasize its objective, definitive reading of the past. Delbrück, however, had reservations about this characterization of the *Reichsarchiv*'s mission. Specifically, he objected to Mertz's conception of a single, anonymous, and definitive official history. In his view, no single book or series could arrive at an overarching truth that would adequately describe the reality or complexity of the war's events. To suggest otherwise was dangerous, he said, and was simply a return to the old methodologies and reductionism of the General Staff historians to which he had always objected. Delbrück's problem was that the genre of official history would portray the *Reichsarchiv*'s findings as the only historical truth where he believed there were many. This conflict, which soon broadened out into an all-out war

---

16   Otto, "Der Bestand Kriegsgeschichtliche Forschungsanstalt," 431.

17   Pöhlmann, *Kriegsgeschichte und Geschichtspolitik,* 94.

18   For an overview, see Robert Foley, *German Strategy and the Path to Verdun: Erich von Falkenhayn and the Development of Attrition, 1870–1916* (New York: Cambridge University Press, 2005), 38–55. See also Arden Bucholz, *Hans Delbrück and the German Military Establishment: War Images in Conflict* (Iowa City: University of Iowa Press, 1985).

19   Pöhlmann, *Kriegsgeschichte und Geschichtspolitik,* 106.

between the Historical Commission and Haeften's military historians, reflected a larger disagreement about the nature of historical inquiry and the purpose of the *Reichsarchiv*'s work.[20]

Official military history as a distinct historical discipline emerged along with the General Staff system in the mid-nineteenth century in Prussia and Great Britain.[21] Voluminous campaign histories of the German wars of unification (1864–71), and of British operations in the Crimea, India, Africa, Persia, and South Africa, became textbooks for officers training for the "next war."[22] The genre of official history embodied the Victorian emphasis on acute classification and meticulous attention to detail. By creating an encyclopaedic history of past campaigns, future generals could converse with the past and learn how history might have unfolded differently—if only their objects of study had access to all the facts.[23] In this sense, every official history embodies von Ranke's claim that history must be written *wie es eigentlich gewesen.*

Most historians now agree with Delbrück, arguing that it is impossible to "see the past as it actually was."[24] The writing of any history, no matter how voluminous or seemingly objective, must necessarily omit details, ignore themes, and discard whole lines of inquiry while emphasizing others. These problems become especially acute in an "official" work that purports to contain a single, objective truth encompassing the national experience as a whole because for a time, official historians alone work from the documents and they alone control access to the archival sources needed to challenge their assertions.[25] As

20 Ibid.
21 Antulio J. Echevarria, "Heroic History and Vicarious War: Nineteenth-Century German Military History Writing," *Historian* 59, no. 3 (2007): 573–90. A good introduction to the concept of the official history is Robin Higham, ed., *The Writing of Official Military History* (Westport, CT: Greenwood, 1999).
22 See, for example, H.E. Colville, *History of the Sudan Campaign, 2 volumes* (London: Intelligence Division, War Office, 1890); Indian Intelligence Branch, *The Second Afghan War, 1878–80* (London: HMSO, 1908); War Office, General Staff, *Official History of the Operations in Somaliland, 1901–4,* 2 vols. (London: HMSO, 1907).
23 See Jay Luvass, "Military History: Is It Still Practicable?" *Parameters* (Summer 1995): 83.
24 Richard J. Evans, *In Defence of History* (London: Granta, 1997), esp. 75–102. A good discussion of academic attitudes toward official history is found in Tim Cook, "Canadian Official Historians and the Writing of the Two World Wars" (Ph.D. diss., University of New South Wales, 2005), 2–9.
25 In many countries, including Great Britain, historians had very limited access to the documents used to write the British official history until decades after it was completed. And when the first batch of files was released in the late 1960s, it was found that huge portions of the original documents had been destroyed to save storage space. The files that went into the furnace were deemed "historically insignificant," but that was a judgment based in contemporary historical proclivities as well as on the assumption that few would want to check every source consulted by Edmonds. As an official history, it was the facts, not an interpretation.

Delbrück recognized, an official history really does at once construct and guard historical memory. While aimed directly at the student of military history—the officer in training—such histories also have a profound influence on popular conceptions. As a multi-volume, definitive history, any official work automatically looms large in the literature, setting the tone of public and academic discourse for decades to come. If the official historians do their job, their work becomes the first and last word on the subject—it becomes *the* meta-narrative. Popular historians will look to the official history for their facts, a basic chronology, and an interpretive framework.[26] It will frame the questions they ask and often provide the answers as well. As Jay Winter observes, "the [popular] history of battle ... is the lens through which readers are invited to re-examine the national character of their own country."[27] In keeping with Winter's metaphor, official histories are thus meant to refract light in a specific way, highlighting portions of the past that are useful in the present while hiding others that are at odds with national aims.[28]

Official historians of the Great War were not engaged in a conspiracy to defraud the public—far from it. They were operating from the assumption that if all the facts could be elucidated and described, the truth would become self-evident. This was especially important in the postwar climate as the former belligerents refought the war on paper to validate their peculiar national interpretations of the conflict and its outcome. The assembly and deployment of facts represented a new battle of materiel. For example, the French Ministère de la Guerre's Service Historique produced a 109-volume official history of the Great War titled *Les Armées françaises dans la Grande Guerre*. In the narrative tomes, neutral statement of fact follows neutral statement of fact, each supported by footnotes not to sources buried in the archive, but to those reprinted for the reader in dozens of volumes of appendices. Indeed, the narrative volumes in the French official history serve almost as an index to the documents. Because relatively little analysis appears in the text itself, the volumes have an appearance and form which suggest objectivity—that is, they seem to ring true. After all, the sources are all there for the reader to read for themselves. Perhaps this

---

26 Tim Cook, *Clio's Warriors: Canadian Historians and the Writing of the Two World Wars* (Vancouver: University of British Columbia Press, 2006), 4–7.

27 Jay Winter and Antoine Prost, *The Great War in History: Debates and Controversies, 1914 to the Present* (New York: Cambridge University Press, 2005), 62.

28 On official history as a tool of the state, see Keith Wilson, "Historical Engineering," in *Forging the Collective Memory: Governments and International Historians through Two World Wars*, ed. Keith Wilson (Providence: Berghahn, 1996), 1–28. See also Holger H. Herwig, "Clio Deceived: Patrotic Self-Censorship in Germany after the Great War," *International Security* 12, no. 2 (1987): 14–17.

is why so few operational histories of France's Great War have been produced since.[29]

The French official history is the most extreme example of the materiel battle in words; it also best highlights the genre's shortcomings. For all its value as a source of historical facts—and it certainly is an underutilized and exhaustive history—every document reprinted in its pages appears as the result of a subjective process of selection. Historians suppressed some documents while emphasizing others in order to present a particular view of military operations. No matter how complete or voluminous their results, official historians often ask highly specific and pointed questions that are based on subjective assumptions, official purposes, and personal bias. The criticisms of James Edmonds's British official history are notorious. Historians such as Liddell Hart, Denis Winter, Tim Travers, and David French have all directly criticized Edmonds's objectivity, truthfulness, and factuality. The suggestion is always that Edmonds's history distorted the facts and thus affected the subsequent trajectories of academic inquiry and popular perceptions about the war.[30] This is not to say that official histories are useless—indeed, these historians often used Edmonds's work in their own writings. It is to say, rather, that such histories must be understood and used in a critical context that acknowledges the genre's limitations. Official histories present a subjective interpretation of events—they are intentionally constructed meta-narratives. Once this is understood, they become a useful synthesis of historical knowledge and provide insight into the legacy and meaning of the war.[31]

The *Reichsarchiv*'s Historical Commission objected most to the construction of a purely military meta-narrative, which they believed would distort the experience of the war. To them the questions raised by the war could only be answered by a holistic history. Jurisdictional disputes with the Foreign Office and Navy, and the financial constraints facing the Weimar Republic, brought the crisis to a head in 1923–24. When it became clear that sufficient resources would not be available for the type of broad history demanded by the commission, Haeften's colleagues pled for "academic freedom" to write the type of official military history that they

---

29 See Ministère de la Guerre, État-Major de l'Armée, Service Historique, *Les Armées françaises dans la Grande Guerre*, 11 vols. (Paris: Imprimerie Nationale, 1922–37). Another example is the fifty-six-book series published by the German Foreign Ministry, *Die Grosse Politik der Europäischen Kabinette, 1871–1914*.

30 A good overview of these criticisms—and a rebuttal—is provided in Andrew Green, *Writing the Great War: Sir James Edmonds and the Official Histories 1915–1948* (London: Frank Cass, 2003), 44–45.

31 Cook, *Clio's Warriors*, 4–5.

believed best fit the facts as well as their mandate as former soldiers.[32] Markus Pöhlmann contends that in the end, the Weimar government failed to support the Historical Commission and the former soldiers working in the *Reichsarchiv* were able to pursue a narrowly conceived history focused on questions "purely of a military nature."

With the debate about the series' form and purpose settled, the first two of fourteen volumes appeared in 1925. The remaining books would be written over the next two decades. Over the years, Haeften would continue to exert a dominant influence over the series as the Historical Section's director and later, after 1 November 1931, as the president of the *Reichsarchiv*. After his promotion, historian Wolfgang Foerster assumed the directorship of the War History Section. Between 1919 and 1 April 1934, when the historical section was removed from the *Reichsarchiv* and placed under the purview of the *Reichswehrministerium* (Military Ministry), the organization produced the first nine volumes of the main series and several ancillary texts. On 1 April 1937 the Historical Section became the *Kriegsgeschichtliche Forschungsanstalt des Heeres* (KGFH) and was reintegrated with the German General Staff system until the project was completed. By the time the last volume was published in 1956 by the *Bundesarchiv*, the series totalled more than 9,300 pages and was accompanied by more than 430 maps and sketches.[33]

Der Weltkrieg asks two separate but interrelated questions: What were the military lessons of the Great War? And what did the sacrifices of ordinary Germans mean? The first question was of immediate relevance to a military that was desperately trying to understand what exactly had gone wrong on the battlefield. The second was more significant to the future of Germany and to public discourse. For the *frontsoldaten* who watched comrades die on the icy passes of the Carpathians or in the mud of Ypres, there had to be some kernel of meaning and truth waiting to be discovered in the heretofore untold history of a war seemingly waged in vain.[34] To *Reichsarchiv* historians, the answer to both questions would be arrived at through the traditional methods of official history: an "objective" study of the past would let the facts speak for themselves. Seeking truth would be their objective. "No people need be less afraid of this frankness than the German people," reads the preface to the first volume of *Der Weltkrieg*. "In this most dreadful of all wars, they have, together with their allies, accomplished achievements which are among the greatest, but also fiercest in the experience of

---

32 Pöhlmann, *Kriegsgeschichte und Geschichtspolitik*, 118–19; Pöhlmann, "Yesterday's Battles and Future War," 229.

33 Otto, "Der Bestand Kriegsgeschichtliche Forschungsanstalt," 431–33; Pöhlmann, *Kriegsgeschichte und Geschichtspolitik*, 163.

34 Pöhlmann, "Yesterday's Battles and Future War," 228.

humanity. Thus the work presented here is limited purely to a description of facts so that it will become a monument to the army which fought and bled together, to those that laboured and suffered at home, and a cenotaph to the German dead resting in German or foreign soil."[35] In reaching an understanding of battlefield events, the heroism and bravery of the individual German *jäger* would be revealed. As Mertz argued in 1921, it would bring clarity to the murky personal experience of war.[36]

In pursuing its self-appointed aim, *Der Weltkrieg* is successful and is an accurate, academically rigorous, and straightforward account of military operations—at least in comparison with the other official histories of its day, which must serve as our basis of comparison. *Reichsarchiv* historians worked in teams focused on particular subject areas. They analyzed the available sources, identified gaps and contradictions, and solicited clarification from surviving participants. They worked with a precision and methodology that would be impossible for any single historian to duplicate. Their overriding purpose was to provide lessons for future soldiers and meaning for the German veterans. Both goals assumed a pursuit of truth as it would be counterproductive to intentionally mislead the reader. As a case in point, all information presented in the main text is taken directly from archival documents, whereas insights derived from personal diaries, memoirs, or correspondence with veterans are presented in footnotes—as are the sources for potentially contentious pieces of information. The purpose of this was to red-flag those parts of the narrative where personal bias and motivation could colour the analysis. Once satisfied that they had "got the facts right," these teams produced first-draft monographs, which senior historians then revised and condensed into a synthesized final text.[37]

In this narrative the facts would be allowed to speak for themselves. "The work does not claim to present a picture of the operations and their consequences brought to perfection by criticism; given the short amount of time which had elapsed since the events took place, this is not possible at present," reads the introduction to the 1925 edition of the series' first volume. "These problems can only be solved when the personal papers of army commanders and combatants become available, when works of scholarship become more readily accessible, and when the archives of our erstwhile allies and adversaries are opened up. Therefore criticism had to be restrained, but all the clues necessary to evaluate the events have been presented here, with frankness and without reservation."[38] If the intent of the

---

35 Reichsarchiv, *Der Weltkrieg 1914 bis 1918: Die militärischen Operationen zu Land, Band I* (Berlin: E.S. Mittler & Sohn, 1925), herafter cited as *DW* followed by the volume number.
36 Pöhlmann, *Kriegsgeschichte und Geschichtspolitik*, 106.
37 *DW* I, vii–x.
38 Ibid.

Reichsarchiv was to create an impression of objectivity and frankness, then we must say they succeeded—at least that was the judgment of contemporary historians. "The military historians, who remain anonymous, deserve great credit for their splendid work," wrote Alexander Johnson in a 1931 book review for the *Journal of Modern History*. "They present their story in simple, readable language that will sustain the interest of the lay reader and with a degree of fact-finding objectivity which commends itself to the military reader and student."[39] This positive reading of *Der Weltkrieg* by a contemporary historian might surprise modern readers. Some recent authors have implied that the series was heavily influenced by the politics of National Socialism or that its language is too archaic and outmoded to be easily understood today.[40] But these criticisms are baseless. Nine of the series' fourteen volumes were written and published before 1933, and even a cursory reading of the remaining five will reveal that they are hardly Nazi propaganda. As the newly available files from the KGFH suggest, much of the research for these volumes was completed well before the outbreak of the Second World War. The language is also no more archaic or outmoded than Edmonds's history or that of other works of a similar vintage. As Hew Strachan points out, "the reluctance to use inter-war German histories on the grounds that they are tainted by Nazism is not only chronological nonsense ... but also an absurd self-denying ordinance, given the destruction of the bulk of the German military archives in 1945. The Reichsarchiv historians saw material we can never see; not to refer to their output is a cloak for little more than laziness or monolingualism."[41]

Like any work of history—especially official history—*Der Weltkrieg* must be read with a critical eye. As Markus Pöhlmann notes, the series' greatest problem is that its focus is too narrowly conceived.[42] Supplementary volumes on the war economy were planned but never finished, and the series lacks any cultural or social dimension—a product of the historical conventions of the time more than short-sightedness on the part of its authors. The War History Section's interest in addressing questions of military significance led to a lopsided focus on the first year of the war (six of the fourteen volumes deal with 1914, three with 1915, two with 1916, and three with 1917–18). Perhaps most unsettling—and misunderstood—is the repetition of the stab-in-the-back myth in the final volume. The *Dolchstoß* myth was certainly perpetuated and supported by some *Reichsarchiv*

---

39 Johnson, "Military Histories of the Great War," 277.
40 See, for example, Andrew Godefroy, "The German Army at Vimy Ridge," in *Vimy Ridge: A Canadian Reassessment*, ed. Geoffrey Hayes, Andrew Iarocci, and Mike Bechthold (Waterloo: Wilfrid Laurier University Press, 2007), 225; and Robin Prior and Trevor Wilson, *Passchendaele: The Untold Story* (London: Yale University Press, 2002), 219.
41 Strachan, *The First World War: Volume I*, xvi–xvii.
42 Pöhlmann, "Yesterday's Battles and Future War," 237–38.

historians, especially at the "stab in the back" trials of the 1920s.[43] But we must be careful when accusing the German official history of contributing to attacks on the Weimar Republic or of being unduly influenced by Nazism.[44] Originally written and bound for internal military use in 1943 and 1944, the final two volumes in the series were released for public consumption by the *Bundesarchiv* only in 1956. The final volume states: "The Imperial government had paralyzed the spirit of the Armed Forces and thus dangerously weakened their strength to resist while at the same time creating the conditions for revolution. Then it quickly created a situation which culminated in unconditional surrender on 11 November. In reality it was the revolution that represented the 'thrust of the dagger' into the back of the Armed Forces which were already exhausted but not yet unable to resist."[45] Yet it is important to place this statement in context. The rest of the volume does not in fact actually support the "stab in the back" argument.[46] It instead portrays an army on the verge of physical collapse, worn out on the field of battle. In *Der Weltkrieg*'s pages it is the generals who demand an armistice because they are unable to continue with military operations. It is in apportioning ultimate blame for the army's collapse—that is, for the lost military campaign—that the history reverts to the argument that Hindenburg coined after the war. The conclusion that the army did not lose the war—that, rather, it had been betrayed by the civilian population—had been formed long before the appearance of Hitler. It had been born in the dying days of the 1918 campaign, and it should be no surprise that it is reiterated in an official history written by the men who had served under the officers in question. What is most interesting about *Der Weltkrieg* is the lack of Nazi influence, not its prevalence.

It is true that *Der Weltkrieg* is far narrower in scope than Delbrück and the Historical Commission desired; however, we must not press this point so far as to lose all perspective. As a military history written for soldiers and veterans interested in how battles are won and lost, it is narrow by the modern historians' standards. The real tragedy is that *Der Weltkrieg* had the potential to be something more— a larger holistic socio-cultural history of the war with political and economic dimensions. Had the ancillary volumes that were originally planned actually been published, we would have today a far more nuanced understanding of Germany's war. What we are left with is a remarkable work of scholarship that despite its limitations provides an impressive and relatively objective history of the war. Even with its narrow focus on military operations, the subject is not examined in a

---

43 Ibid., 230.
44 Winter and Prost, *The Great War in History*, 62.
45 *DW* XIV, 768.
46 Pöhlmann, "Yesterday's Battles and Future War," 230.

vacuum. The main narrative is supplemented by sections on the economic history of the war, naval operations, the air force, and logistics. These sections provide windows into the ancillary volumes that might have been; nonetheless, they are useful on their own. The link between the battlefield and international relations is always clear, as are the constraints placed on operations by Germany's economic situation. So are the ambitions of Germany's leaders and the shortcomings of its generals. *Der Weltkrieg* is a truly global history of the war that transcends the normal limitations of official history. It is the place where every examination of Germany's Great War must begin.

Because it is an unparalleled but underutilized source, we have endeavoured to translate a significant portion of the series into English for the first time. Over a total of four volumes, some in multiple parts, this series details Germany's war and operations in the West. The editors' aim is to use the series to emphasize the transnational nature of the First World War and to recast the British and Commonwealth experience in a global perspective. At first glance, focusing on the Western Front may seem to be an odd way of achieving this purpose, but selecting one front for emphasis was necessary given the impracticality of translating the entire series. Given the way *Der Weltkrieg* is divided into relatively self-contained analyses of particular segments of the story, we have been able to retain all materials at the operational level pertaining to the fighting in the West, while including materials that focus on politics, grand strategy, decision making at the level of the *Oberste Heeresleitung* (Supreme Army Command), and the war economy.

This volume details the German experience in 1915. By the beginning of the year, the war that both sides had expected to win by Christmas was far from over. The Russians, while suffering severe setbacks, still stood wobbling on two feet. To the south, the Dual Monarchy had yet to deal with Serbia; and despite Italy's membership in the Triple Alliance, the Italians maintained a guarded neutrality and in fact looked increasingly as if they might enter the war on the side of the Entente. Although the Ottoman Empire had joined the Central Powers, Germany and the Dual Monarchy remained without a land connection to their Eastern ally, for Rumania, Bulgaria, and Greece remained obstinate in their neutrality, blocking trade with Constantinople. For Erich von Falkenhayn and the Imperial German Army, these problems in the East were compounded by stagnation and stalemate in the West.

Strategically, Germany was a nation besieged and beholden to an unreliable ally. Germany was almost completely surrounded and often called upon to support the Austro-Hungarian Empire; thus, Falkenhayn found himself under pressure to acquiesce to his ally's plans, which did not always coincide with those

devised at the *OHL*. Economic and political pressures became ever more important in strategic planning. During the course of the year it became clear that Germany would need to wage a defensive war on most fronts while carefully
husbanding its resources in order to strike a decisive blow at some critical future—
albeit as yet undetermined—juncture. The decision of where such a blow would
fall was the subject of much heated internal debate—one that set in relief the serious internal and inter-allied divisions that existed at the highest levels of the German and Austro-Hungarian command structures. Discord and acrimony are often
evident in the exchanges between Falkenhayn and Austria-Hungary's Chief of the
General Staff, Count Conrad von Hötzendorf. Their disagreements make the relationship between Entente leaders look friendly in comparison. At the same time,
internal debate raged within the German command structure. Falkenhayn, as the
head of the *OHL*, favoured landing a blow in the West—or perhaps Serbia—while
Paul von Hindenburg and Erich Ludendorff, the German commanders in the
East (*OberOst*), desired that a decisive campaign be launched in support of Austria-Hungary and against Russia. Here the debate rested on one's appraisal of the
relative importance of the two fronts to the overall war effort.

These inter-allied and internal disagreements resulted in a potentially dam-
aging division of effort that manifested itself most seriously in the nearly constant transfer of troops back and forth between the two fronts. Strategic indecision
threatened to paralyze the Central Powers' capacity for decisive action throughout 1915. At the same time, the German soldiers fighting the war in the West successfully met numerous Entente offensives despite being virtually stripped to the
bone in terms of both manpower and materiel. The frequency and scope of the
unit transfers back and forth across Germany's Western Front highlight the seriousness of the military situation. Reserves were almost non-existent at times, and
repeated attempts by France and Britain to break through in the Champagne and
the Artois came within a hair's breadth of success.

Yet larger strategic imperatives had to take precedence over Falkenhayn's natural inclination toward the Franco-Belgian theatre of war. The Austro-Hungarian High Command emphasized that defeat of the Russians would be most
beneficial for the common cause. At times Falkenhayn was induced to agree if
only because failure to find success against Moscow's forces might force Austria-
Hungary to succumb, leaving Germany alone in Europe and even more detached
from its Turkish ally. The German General Staff Chief also recognized that victories and defeats could have a critical influence on the position of the neutral
Balkan powers, which were being courted by both sides. A successful Balkan policy promised to open up trade routes to the Middle East, whereas failure threatened to further isolate the two European Powers. Over the course of the year,

Falkenhayn came to believe that victory against Serbia held the best chance of inducing the neutrals toward the Central Powers—or at least away from the Entente. With the conclusion of an alliance with Bulgaria in late summer, this goal was accomplished in part. Italy, however, entered the conflict on the side of the Entente in the spring, though it failed in repeated attempts to break through the Austro-Hungarian lines along the Isonzo River.

While the strategic debate raged, the German nation and army struggled to provide both the manpower and the materiel required to feed the war machine. As its war planners knew, Germany was not equipped to fight a protracted war, and its economy nearly buckled under the strain of industrialized total war. One of the answers to Germany's economic woes came in the form of unrestricted submarine warfare—a topic that elicited much debate at the Kaiser's Headquarters. The other answer was to limit offensive operations. The lack of offensive spirit in the German armies in the West in 1915 sits in direct opposition to the popular image of the German army. Germany's Western Front was a defensive zone of operations in 1915. This operational imperative was made necessary by economic shortages and by the realities of multi-front coalition warfare. It also resulted in innovation. Here we find that the defence-in-depth was not a planned response; rather, it was the outcome of an evolutionary process: the relative weakness of the German army in the West necessitated the ad hoc construction of rearward defensive installations.

The material in this volume of *Germany's Western Front* is taken from Volumes VII, VIII, and IX of *Der Weltkrieg 1914 bis 1918: Die militärischen Operationen zu Land*, first published by E.S. Mittler & Sohn between 1931 and 1933. The original volumes are lengthy texts that cover the war in France, Belgium, Russia, the Balkans, Italy, the Middle East, and Africa chronologically. In keeping with our goal, all materials relating to the operations and conduct of the war in France and Belgium have been translated and are included here unabridged. The operational narratives for the other fronts have necessarily been omitted, although short summaries have been incorporated into the text at key points to bring the reader up to speed. Portions of the text pertaining to the conduct of the war as a whole, strategy, the German economy, manpower, and military organization have also been translated in their entirety. The result is a narrative that conveys the scope of Germany's war effort at the strategic level while providing new insight for English-language readers into how the war in the West was conducted on the ground in 1915.

A NOTE ON THE TRANSLATION
AND SOURCES

This volume of *Germany's Western Front* is divided into three parts, each consisting of translated material from a different volume of *Der Weltkrieg*. "Part I: Winter and Spring" is taken from Volume VII, *Die Operationen des Jahres 1915: Die Ereignisse im Winter und Frühjahr*[1] (originally published in 493 pages) and includes translations of pages 1 to 73 and 301 to 345. "Part II: Spring and Summer" is drawn from Volume VIII, *Die Operationen des Jahres 1915: Die Ereignisse im Westen im Frühjahr und Sommer, im Osten vom Frühjahr bis zum Jahresschluss*[2] (originally published in 666 pages) and includes translations of pages 1 to 24, 34 to 102, and 598 to 615 as well as Appendix 1 (reprinted here as Appendix 1). "Part III: Summer and Winter" is made up of material from Volume IX, *Die Operationen des Jahres 1915: Die Ereignisse im Westen und auf dem Balkan vom Sommer bis zum Jahresschluss*[3] (originally published in 519 pages) and includes translations of pages 1 to 133 and 486 to 495 as well as four appendices. Notably absent from Volume IX are pages 338 to 395, which examine the German war economy, financing, and manpower from the outbreak of war in August 1914 until the end of 1915. Translations of this important material are instead printed in Volume I, Part II, of *Germany's Western Front*.

---

1 Reichsarchiv, *Die Operationen des Jahres 1915: Die Ereignisse im Winter und Frühjahr* (Berlin: E.S. Mittler & Sohn, 1931).
2 Reichsarchiv, *Die Operationen des Jahres 1915: Die Ereignisse im Westen im Frühjahr und Sommer, im Osten vom Frühjahr bis zum Jahresschluss* (Berlin: E.S. Mittler & Sohn, 1932).
3 Reichsarchiv, *Die Operationen des Jahres 1915: Die Ereignisse im Westen und auf dem Balkan vom Sommer bis zum Jahresschluss* (Berlin: E.S. Mittler & Sohn, 1933).

In annotating the translated text, the editors have attempted to make themselves as unobtrusive as possible. We have not attempted to correct any errors of
fact or interpretation (except for obvious typographical errors) from the German
text and have instead tried to reproduce its content as faithfully to the original as
possible. Where points in the original text require clarification for English-language
readers, we have inserted explanations in footnotes. As this book includes both our
own footnotes and those from the original texts, the editors' comments are indicated by italics while original notes appear in normal typeface (all citations to
other sources, both our own and those of the *Reichsarchiv* authors, follow a conventional style with italicized titles and regular author and publication information). We have also felt it important to sometimes point the reader toward further
sources. In doing so we have assumed a certain familiarity on the reader's part with
the events on the Western Front, especially in the British sector. Thus our suggestions have tended to relate to those happenings on the other fronts or in the realm
of grand strategy. In addition to these sources it is assumed that readers will con-
sult the standard works on Germany in the First World War, some of which are
listed in a short bibliography of works pertaining to the events of 1915 at the end
of this volume. This bibliography contains both our suggestions for further reading as well as the relevant sources listed in the original *Quellennachweis* from Volumes VII, VIII, and IX. A larger, more comprehensive bibliography covering the
war as a whole accompanies the final volume of this series.

The utmost care has been taken in translating the German originals. The
original texts are dense volumes, written in a technical form of German that at
times makes effective—or at least elegant—translation difficult. The goal of the
editors and translators is to reproduce the meaning and form of the original German texts as closely as possible while still creating a text that is accessible to modern English readers and that conforms to accepted stylistic conventions. So, in
order to achieve greater clarity, some exceptionally long sentences have been broken into two or more shorter ones; dates have been inserted where the text is
unclear;[4] and the names of units and people have been simplified. Where such edits
would alter the tone or meaning of the original text, the phrasing or style has
been retained even though it might be awkward to the modern English ear. Para-
graphing, section breaks, and all original explanatory references remain unchanged,
though most cross-references to other points in the text have been omitted. German ranks and unique words such as *Ersatz* and *Landwehr* have also been retained
in their original form, and all expressions of time have been converted to the
twenty-four-hour clock. Generally speaking, where the German names of cities

---

4 In the original, dates were denoted in the margins.

and regions differ from those used in English, they have been translated. Many places in Europe have, of course, gone through several naming conventions since the Great War, and as a result the editors have decided to use the most common English name, not necessarily the most current.

The actual process of translation and proofing is a lengthy one. The editors are most fortunate to have worked with two skilled translators with a native knowledge of German and, most importantly, a deep technical understanding of military terminology and the conventions of military writing. Wilhelm J. Kiesselbach provided the initial translations for most of the text (all but pages 598 to 615 of Volume VIII). Mr. Kiesselbach is a professional translator who served in the U.S. Army during the early 1960s in Germany, where he acted as the translator and interpreter for the commanding officer in the U.S. Army. His first draft translations were carefully proofed against the original German by Mark Humphries, who also did some translating of footnotes and made corrections where necessary; the translations were then reworked by both editors so as to maintain a consistent, readable style. Edited final drafts were again proofread against the original German by Peter Meinlschmidt, a NATO translator working and living in Poland (who also provided the initial translation for pages 598 to 615 from Volume VIII) and Ralph Whitehead. Mr. Meinlschmidt is a native German speaker, while Mr. Whitehead is native to the English language; in combination they provided important insights into the nuances of the translation process. Translations housed at the U.S. Army War College in Carlisle, Pennsylvania, were used to double-check some sections of the text, including pages 1 to 15 and 301 to 345 of Volume VII and 35 to 48 of Volume VIII. Any errors remain the editors' responsibility, and they would welcome suggestions for improvement.

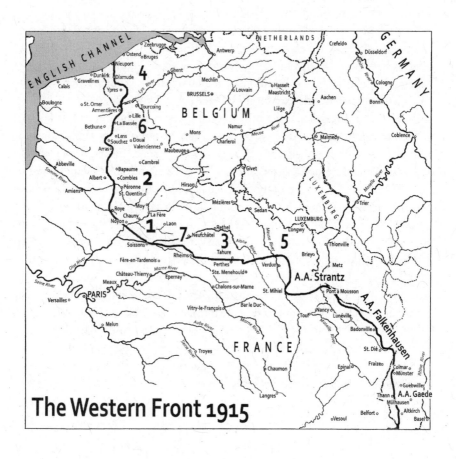

The Western Front 1915

The Eastern Front
May 1915

BALTIC

SEA

Libau

Memel

NIEMEN

Königsberg

Danzig

GERMANY

Tannenberg

12

9

Lodz

WOYRSCH

WARSAW

Ivangorod

1

4

Krakow

Tarnow

11

Gorlice

3

Kaschau

2

SUD

Kovno

Vilna

Grodno

Bielostok

Brest-Litovsk

Pinsk

RUSSIA

Minsk

Bobruisk

Dubno

Rovno

Zhitomir

Przemysl

LEMBERG

CARPATHIAN MOUNTAINS

Kamianets-Podolsk

7

Czernowitz

Botosani

Budapest

Debreczyn

AUSTRIA-
HUNGARY

Jassy

Botosani

TRANSYLVANIAN ALPS

Galatz

RUMANIA

Belgrade

Vitebsk

Dvina River

Mogilef

Dniester River

Gomel

Bug River

Vistula River

Niemen River

Pripet River

Kiev

Berdichef

Dniester River

Sereth River

Pruth River

Kischenef

Danube River

Tisza River

Danube River

0   100   200   300

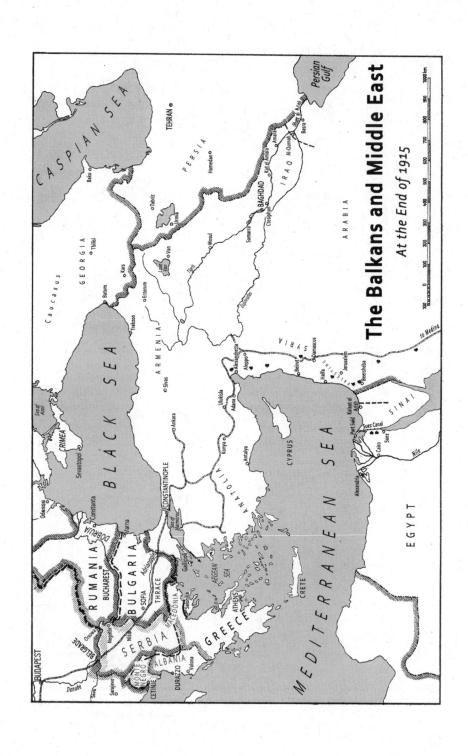

The Balkans and Middle East

At the End of 1915

PART I

Winter and Spring

1

THE QUESTION OF THE WAR'S CENTRE
OF GRAVITY IN JANUARY

AT THE BEGINNING OF 1915, THE WAR IN THE EAST WAS NOT GOING WELL FOR *Germany or Austria-Hungary. Despite victories under Paul von Hindenburg and his Chief of Staff Erich Ludendorff at Tannenberg and the First Battle of the Masurian Lakes in August and September, the situation was far from stable. To the south, Count Conrad von Hötzendorf's Austro-Hungarian armies had failed to defeat the relatively small Serbian Army in the summer and autumn of 1914; indeed, they had been driven from the southeastern Balkans while Russian forces pressed deep into Austrian Galicia from the northwest. At the end of September the Russians laid siege to the fortress city of Przemysl; by year's end they had caused 1.25 million Austro-Hungarian casualties.[1] Austria-Hungary was threatened with collapse. Conrad told Austrian Foreign Minister Leopold von Berchtold that unless drastic action was taken, the Dual Monarchy "could no longer master the military situation."[2]*

---

1   Norman Stone, *The Eastern Front 1914–1917* (New York: Penguin, 1998), 122.
2   Franz Conrad von Hötzendorf, *Aus meiner Dienstzeit 1906–1918*, 5 vols. (Vienna: Rikola, 1925), V:753, translation quoted in Robert Foley, *German Strategy and the Path to Verdun: Erich von Falkenhayn and the Development of Attrition, 1870–1916* (New York: Cambridge University Press, 2005), 128.

The failures of 1914 and Austria-Hungary's weakness had significant political as well as strategic consequences for Germany. An undefeated Serbia meant that Germany remained separated from its Ottoman ally and thus cut off from the trade in weapons, food, and raw materials that was necessary to sustain them both. The Dual Monarchy's obvious vulnerability threatened to persuade the neutral Balkan powers (especially Bulgaria, Rumania, and Greece) to join the Entente. Italy, once a partner in the Triple Alliance but now neutral, also seemed to be making moves toward the enemy, which raised prospects of a third front in Southern Europe.

In the West, Germany's offensives had also failed to secure a victory, but there the front was stabilizing, with trench warfare becoming the norm from Belfort near the Swiss border to Nieuport on the English Channel. Falkenhayn's attempts to capture the Channel Ports and then the city of Ypres with a late-autumn Flanders offensive resulted only in disappointment and heavy casualties. By new year, Germany was faced with a war on two European fronts, a struggling ally in the East, and an ominous political situation in the Balkans, all of which threatened to turn the war's tide against the Central Powers.

NO DECISION WAS REACHED IN THE SUMMER AND FALL CAMPAIGNS OF 1914, ON either the Western or Eastern fronts. The initial war plans of both the Central Powers and their adversaries came to naught. A balance of power was reached on all fronts and operations stood at a halt. Although the German armies managed to liberate the soil taken by the enemy (except for small areas in southern Alsace and in Eastern Prussia) and to carry the war far into enemy territory—conquering commercially valuable areas—this advantage was offset by the extremely grave danger posed by the blockade that was closing in around the Central Powers. Although Turkey entered the war on the side of the Central Powers,[3] the problem of establishing a secure link to this new ally was still awaiting a solution: Serbia

---

3 *Turkey entered the war on 29 October 1914 after signing a secret pledge to do so on 2 August 1914. A good survey of the circumstances surrounding Turkey's entry into the war is* Ulrich Trumpener, "The Ottoman Empire," in *The Origins of World War I,* ed. Richard F. Hamilton and Holger H. Herwig (Cambridge: Cambridge University Press, 2003), 337–55. *A more complete overview is* Ulrich Trumpener's *Germany and the Ottoman Empire, 1914–1918* (Princeton: Princeton University Press, 1968).

had not been defeated, Bulgaria had not been won over to the Central Powers, and Rumania was not willing to allow ammunition transports destined for Turkey to pass through its territory.

Considering the situation, the behaviour of the neutrals was of vital importance. In his letter of 14 December 1914 to Erich von Falkenhayn, Chief of the General Staff of the Field Armies, Generalfeldmarschall Baron von der Goltz (the German general who had been seconded to the Ottoman Emperor) emphasized that the decision now "rested in the hands of the small Balkan powers." By committing their not inconsiderable military forces they could sway the balance of power to one side or the other. The leaders of the Central Powers, like those of the Entente, were well aware of this. Therefore it was understandable that all the warring parties struggled for the Balkan states' favour, for the Entente's success would threaten the collapse of Austria-Hungary. The Balkan states' decision making would be influenced not only by the war's status but also by the increasingly questionable position of Italy, which more and more insistently was approaching Austria-Hungary with claims for considerable territorial concessions.[4]

While the Central Powers' efforts to create a "Balkan Bloc" against Russia had favourable prospects at the beginning of the war, they had deteriorated despite Turkey's entry into the conflict. Now the Central Powers would have to consider it a success if they managed to convince Italy and the Balkan states to remain neutral.[5]

---

4 *Der Weltkrieg* (hereafter *DW*), VI:412, *reads*: "Despite the declaration of neutrality, Italy's position had become doubtful. On the strength of Article 7 of the Three Party Agreement, the Italian government had—before the outbreak of war but right after the Austro-Hungarian Ultimatum to Serbia—already raised demands for substantial concessions in territory. [*Article 7 called for compensation to be paid to the other country if either Italy or Austria-Hungary were to occupy parts of the Balkans or the Turkish Islands in the Adriatic or Aegean Seas*] The diplomatic war over this demand had since made slow progress. The exchange of views between Rome, Berlin, and Vienna up until the end of the year demonstrated that without transfers of Austrian territory, Italy could hardly be satisfied. Italy also proved that it aspired to further territorial expansions in Albania, where, on 30 October, Italian troops hoisted the Italian flag and, on 25 December, occupied Valora [in present day Albania]." *On Italy's neutrality, territorial demands, and gradual entrance into the war, see* William A. Renzi, *In the Shadow of the Sword: Italy's Neutrality and Entrance into the Great War, 1914–1915* (New York: P. Lang, 1987). *Regarding Italy's demands at the end of 1914, see especially* 167–68.

5 *At the outbreak of war, some Turkish and German policy makers thought that an alliance of Bulgaria, Rumania, Greece, Albania, and Turkey could be brought together against Serbia and Russia. This would have not only provided an important land link between the Central Powers and Turkey, but also shifted the balance of forces in the East in favour of the Triple Alliance. For a succinct discussion of Germany and Balkan politics, see* Hew Strachan, *The First World War: Volume I: To Arms* (Oxford: Oxford University Press, 2001), 668–80. *On German strategy in the Balkans in the years before the Great War, see* Bernd F. Schulte, *Vor dem Kriegsausbruch 1914: Deutschland, die Türkei, und der Balkan* (Düsseldorf: Drost, 1980); *and* Fritz Fischer, *Krieg der Illusionen: die deutsche Politik von 1911 bis 1914* (Düsseldorf: Drost, 1969), which was translated into English as *War of Illusions: German Policies from 1911 to 1914* (New York: Norton, 1975).

As well, at the turn of the year, political issues began to assume an ever stronger influence over the conduct of military operations. Around Christmas 1914, during a conference in Teschen, Count Czernin, the Austro-Hungarian envoy in Bucharest, advised the Commander-in-Chief of the Austro-Hungarian Army, Conrad von Hötzendorf, that Italy and Rumania would enter the war unless the Central Powers achieved a major success by the spring. Rumania, it seemed, was making its decisions conditional on those of Italy, which had "ever more aggressively asserted her old claims for the surrender of Austro-Hungarian territories."[6] This conference prompted Conrad's telegram to Falkenhayn of 27 December 1914,[7] in which he reiterated his earlier thoughts, "[that] a complete success on the Eastern Front would still be crucial to the overall situation and therefore was of the utmost importance." He believed that only with the commitment of new units, or additional German forces from the West, could he attain such success:

> A fast decision and quick implementation are absolutely necessary in order to pre-empt the neutrals' entry into the war, which can be expected [to occur] by the beginning of March at the latest. Under the prevailing circumstances, I consider that hopes of dividing the Entente diplomatically with special treaties with one or the other party to be totally hopeless without a decisive success on our part.

This telegram proved to the Chief of the German General Staff that the conference at Opole on 19 December 1914 had not resolved disagreements about the

---

6 DW VI:412, reads, "The dispatches from Rumania were still hardly favourable. The views in Bucharest varied depending on the situation in the different theatres. The government did not reject the enticing requests of the Entente to join the war against Germany and Austria-Hungary, but a connection between Rumania and the Central Powers was now thought impossible. [Above all else], Rumania sought to maintain its freedom of action." *A good overview of Italy's position in the autumn of 1914 is* Richard F. Hamilton and Holger Herwig, "Italy," in *The Origins of World War I*, ed. Richard F. Hamilton and Holger H. Herwig (Cambridge: Cambridge University Press, 2003), 356–89. *A survey of the situation in the Balkans as a whole is provided in the same volume*, Richard C. Hall, "Bulgaria, Romania, and Greece," 389–414.

7 *Conrad's telegram to Falkenhayn summarized the military situation on the Eastern Front and pointed out that the Austro-Hungarian forces were overstretched and faced superior Russian numbers. Conrad argued that* "Given this situation, a decisive success against Russia can hardly be obtained without the deployment of new forces … To me, complete success on the Eastern Front appears still to be crucial for the overall situation and is greatly urgent, especially considering the approaching spring and the impending shift in the balance of power that will come with the intervention of the neutrals, which only a success against Russia can safely avert. The consequences of such an intervention for the military situation of the [Austro-Hungarian] Monarchy, and concomitantly for Germany, are incalculable." *See DW VI: 360–61.*

conduct of the two-front war but had only set them aside temporarily.[8] Falkenhayn's thoughts now moved in an entirely different direction.

From the beginning of the war until the end of mobile warfare, the Supreme Army Command (*Oberste Heeresleitung*, hereafter *OHL*) regarded achieving a decision in the campaign against the French and British on the Western Front to be its primary task and one to be achieved as quickly as possible. For this reason, it assumed immediate operational command in the West, while operations in the East were largely left to the discretion of the Commander-in-Chief of the Eastern Front (*Oberbefehlshaber Ost*, hereafter *OberOst*)[9] in direct consultation with the Austro-Hungarian Army High Command (*Armeeoberkommando*, hereafter *AOK*). After the transition to static warfare in the West, Falkenhayn persistently clung to this assessment of the relative importance of the theatres of war. He saw every transfer of power from West to East as dangerous because it strayed from the guiding strategic principle that had been formed for the conduct of the war.[10] Therefore the military forces in the East were to be supported—if at all—only by necessity, for a short time, and within minimum parameters. By virtue of the fact that General Headquarters (GHQ) remained on the Western Front, the attention of the *OHL* was occupied primarily by events there. Because Falkenhayn's thoughts were dominated by the objective of mounting a major offensive against the French and British, he was incapable of objectively judging the overall situation of the Central Powers, which had been changed fundamentally by the onset of static warfare and the evolving political situation. In his eyes the East was and remained a secondary theatre of operations. Because he was skeptical of the possibility that a final decision could be reached in the East,[11] Falkenhayn found himself in sharp

---

8 *At a meeting between Falkenhayn and Conrad on 19 December 1914, in Opole, the Chief of the Austro-Hungarian General Staff argued against committing forces to the northeast corner of Serbia because he believed that "by thrashing Russia, the Balkan question would be solved." Encouraged by private statements by Generalfeldmarschall von der Goltz that were relayed to Conrad by the Austro-Hungarian military attaché in Constantinople that "without endangering the situation on the Western Front, 500,000 men could be pulled out of France and sent to the Eastern Front," Conrad argued for a new and stronger commitment of German forces to the East. In contrast, Falkenhayn regarded such a shift in his forces as impractical. The meeting was ultimately inconclusive. See DW VI:354 and 419.*

9 *On 1 November, Hindenburg was made Commander-in-Chief of the Eastern Front (OberOst) and Erich Ludendorff was appointed his Chief of Staff. OberOst was thus in command of the Eighth and Ninth Armies. While this reorganization was intended to simplify the command structure in the two-front war, it quickly created tensions between the OHL and OberOst.*

10 *Falkenhayn believed that the war would ultimately be won or lost in the West.*

11 *DW VI: 423–24 reads:* "Falkenhayn wanted to strike at the enemy, but aspired only to temporary and localized objectives. In the West he wanted to initially hold the line which had already been achieved. In the East he wanted the German commanders 'to expel the Russian forces from East Prussia as well as those facing West Prussia, as quickly as possible.' He also

opposition to the opinions of the German Chancellor Bethmann Hollweg, *OberOst*, and the *AOK*.

On 27 December, the same day that Conrad explained his point of view regarding the further conduct of the two-front war to the Chief of the General Staff, the latter expressed his point of view in a letter directed, but never sent, to Generalfeldmarschall von Hindenburg.[12] The letter demonstrated without a doubt that the next offensive was not planned in the East, but in the West, and was to take place at the end of January at the latest. To this end, Falkenhayn planned to deploy to the West the new units about to be formed (XXXVIII through XXXXI Reserve Corps and the Bavarian 8th Reserve Division, in total four and a half corps). He also planned to transfer one or two corps from the Eastern Front. However, nothing definite had been articulated about the objectives of this new operation in the West. On 25 December, Falkenhayn approached his trusted

---

wanted the AOK to throw back the Russians in Galicia and to capture Serbia. He further believed that the roles should be exchanged no later than the end of January when the East would pursue defensive and delaying actions, while the army in the West would 'go over strongly to the offensive.' But the ultimate goal had yet to be defined. Apparently General von Falkenhayn initially intended to mount attacks that would revive the troops' dwindling offensive spirit which had been consumed by positional warfare. Evidently, he did not envision reaching an ultimate decision in the campaign in the West. In his memoirs he wrote, '[the OHL] was convinced that reinforcement by the accumulation of new divisions alone—even with their most careful preparation—would not be sufficient to bring about a real decision in either the West or East.' Between the leaders of the Central Powers, an unbridgeable contrast in outlook developed. General von Falkenhayn was in the end firmly determined to assert his point of view in all circumstances. With that the conduct of the two-front war threatened to result in indecision."

12 *Falkenhayn's letter, marked "Done—do not send," disclosed that he was in disagreement with Conrad as to how the two-front war should be conducted. While Conrad wanted to mount a simultaneous strike toward Siedlce (to the east of Warsaw and north of Lublin) with German forces from Western Prussia and Austro-Hungarian forces from the San River, Falkenhayn believed that the Austro-Hungarian army was incapable of such an attack as it would be occupied with fighting enemy forces in Galicia and in Serbia. Falkenhayn's priority was instead to throw the Russian forces out of Eastern and Western Prussia, behind the Vistula, and then to go over to the defensive. He wrote to Hindenburg:* "I could not convince General von Conrad of my opinions; or, at least he did not admit it. He did seem to understand the *OHL's* position in this— at least now he is aware. We cannot deviate from this position; the situation in the West demands that we go over to a strong offensive stance towards the end of January at the latest. I cannot imagine asking those troops to endure life in the trenches and this passivity any longer. I ask Your Excellency to permit the above comments to be the criteria for your decisions of the near future. The sooner that Your Excellency is able to transfer forces to the *OHL* for deployment in the West, the better will be the general situation. The stamina of our troops in the West is drawn down by the debilitating trench warfare that they continuously have to endure. It would be irresponsible to permit this situation to continue any longer than is made absolutely necessary by the situation in the East without providing appropriate relief." *See DW* VI: 421–23.

colleague, Quartermaster General Generalmajor Wild von Hohenborn, as well as Fifth Army's Chief of Staff, Generalmajor Schmidt von Knobelsdorf, to request that they present operational concepts for a new offensive in the West with the condition "that in addition to the forces tasked with holding the frontlines, six corps with a generous supply of ammunition would be available for a deployment at any desired location." No start date was indicated for such an operation.

These plans were unexpectedly thwarted by Conrad's demand that the war effort's centre of gravity be immediately be shifted to the East. In order to find a compromise between these fundamental differences of opinion, Falkenhayn proposed a new discussion to be attended by the Chiefs of the German and Austro-Hungarian General Staffs. This was set for 1 January 1915 in Berlin.

In the meantime, Falkenhayn received the operational drafts he had requested for his proposed offensive in the West. Even though it had not been asked of him, Wild responded in depth to the question of whether the war's centre of gravity should be placed in the West or the East, and came to the following conclusion:

> It is impossible to reach a decision in the West, but in the East ... where an operational opportunity is still available, as well as by virtue of the fact that there freedom of movement [still] exists on both flanks—especially on our primarily important northern flank[13]—and during the transition of our forces into a defensive mode, the ability would exist to withdraw forces for new operations, which is obviously not the case on the Western Front. Furthermore, in the West each operation must begin with a difficult penetration, whereas in the East the space for a new deployment is available. Finally, despite good soldierly attributes and despite numerical superiority, the Russian [soldier] is a better objective for us than the superbly tenacious French and British soldiers who, in the defence, have proven themselves to be very respectable adversaries. Additionally, our use of the railway system provides us with predominance over the Russians in the East, as opposed to the situation in the West where the circumstances are reversed. Therefore, at this time, the East is militarily more viable than the West.

He added that the perseverance of Austria-Hungary and Turkey, as well as the development of the situation in the Balkans, depended on positive military developments in the East; furthermore, "in the East it seems to be militarily easier—and more compelling politically—to reach an early decision as opposed to the West." Wild acknowledged that a massive spring reinforcement of the Franco-British

---

13 In his memorandum General Wild added the following annotation: "It is questionable whether this will remain the case for long. The recently reported fortification of the line Pułtusk–Płotzt would be quite disruptive."

Army was to be expected, "while Russia is not going to become militarily stronger in the foreseeable future"—a fact that seemed to favour first attacking in the West; nevertheless, he argued that the military and political considerations in the East were so compelling that the deployment of the soon to be available four-and-a-half corps—"so far as the present situation can be judged"—should occur there as soon as possible. Therefore, all considerations regarding potential operations in the West were "of a more academic character."

From Falkenhayn's notes in the margins of this memorandum, it is evident that he still adhered to his initial opinion "that we shall never accomplish Russia's total military defeat."[14] Wild remarked to a General Staff officer on 30 December "that prior to proceeding on his trip to Berlin, Falkenhayn had practically decided to conduct the next attack in the West." In order to provide the new units with some time for training, the offensive was planned for February.

After Falkenhayn's departure for Berlin, the German Chancellor Bethman Hollweg learned of his intention to mount an offensive in the West following the deployment of the newly formed GHQ Reserve (*Heeresreserve*). For the same reasons as the commanders in the East—and being mindful of the positions of Italy and Rumania—Bethmann Hollweg considered it most urgent that an early decision be reached in the East. At a briefing attended by the Kaiser on 2 January 1915 at GHQ, he referred to the judgment of the commanders in the East and requested that the Supreme Warlord[15] remove Falkenhayn from his position as Chief of the General Staff of the Field Army, to be replaced by Generalleutnant Erich Ludendorff. The Chancellor added that it was necessary to settle a staffing matter of this importance for constitutional reasons, as the combination of the offices of the Chief of the General Staff and the War Minister in one person, with the latter having responsibilities to the *Reichstag*, could lead to operational conflicts.[16] The Kaiser, who had received advice to the contrary from the Chief of the Military Cabinet General der Infanterie Baron von Lyncker, rejected the Chancellor's request.[17]

IN THE MEANTIME, ON 1 JANUARY 1915, THE CONFERENCE IN BERLIN HAD TAKEN place. Initially it was attended only by the Chiefs of the German and Austro-

---

14 See Erich von Falkenhayn, *Die Oberste Heeresleitung 1914–1916* (Berlin: E.S. Mittler & Sohn, 1920), 50.

15 *Kaiser Wilhelm II.*

16 *Falkenhayn was both Chief of the General Staff of the Field Army and War Minister, having been appointed head the* OHL *following Moltke's collapse after the Battle of the Marne.*

17 *On the relationship between Falkenhayn and Bethmann Hollweg, see* Karl-Heinz Janssen, *Der Kanzler und der General: Die Führungskrise im Bethmann Hollweg und Falkenhayn* (Göttingen: Musterschmidt, 1966).

Hungarian General Staffs and their closest staff officers. At the beginning of the meeting, Falkenhayn stated that it was impossible to further weaken the Western Front in favour of the East as the German army already faced a supremacy created by two powerful enemies on the Western front. He stated that the new units would not be ready for deployment until February, at which point he intended to employ them in the West. A lively discussion followed between the two General Staff chiefs regarding where the war's centre of gravity would be in the future, but a compromise could not be reached between their opposing positions. During a lunch break, Falkenhayn had a brief conversation with the Chief of Staff of *OberOst*, General Ludendorff, who had also been called to Berlin.[18] During this conversation, Ludendorff argued on behalf of General Hindenburg in favour of deciding the war in the East by means of an offensive from East Prussia, for which he requested the deployment of not only the new units, but also all expendable forces in the West.[19] Falkenhayn replied that moving any forces from the Western Front to the East was out of the question. After this, the discussion between the Chiefs of the German and Austro-Hungarian General Staffs continued, this time in the presence of Ludendorff. Conrad brought the conversation around to specifically whether the newly formed German units should be deployed in the East or the West. Falkenhayn at that point declared that he could not make a decision in the matter at the present time, stating that it would be a matter for discussion in approximately three weeks, when, based on the demands of the then prevailing circumstances, he would just as gladly deploy the new units "in one direction or the other." Regarding the discussion's outcome, in a letter to the *Reichsarchiv* dated 12 June 1930, Ludendorff mentioned the meeting and his inability to bring Falkenhayn to a decision about whether the reinforcements should be deployed in the East or the West:

> As I remember it, I did not receive a clear response and even later on in the presence of Conrad, Falkenhayn deferred everything. The entire discussion was unpleasant and insignificant. It was a fight against preconceptions. Since the conversation lacked clarity, it is possible that Conrad misunderstood Falkenhayn.

In a telegram to the Chief of the Austro-Hungarian General Staff dated 2 January 1915, Falkenhayn summarized the result of the discussion in Berlin as follows:

---

18 *It does not appear that General Ludendorff attended the earlier meeting.*
19 *On the relationship between Ludendorff and Hindenburg, see* Robert B. Asprey, *The German High Command at War: Hindenburg and Ludendorff and the First World War* (New York: Warner, 1994). *Though it begins in with their appointment in 1916 to the head of the OHL, see also* Martin Kitchen, *The Silent Dictatorship: The Politics of the German High Command under Hindenburg and Ludendorff, 1916–1918* (London: Holmes and Meier, 1976).

His Majesty consented to my position which I had already verbally presented to your Excellency. Release of forces from the West to the East
presently impossible. Whether the new units that are presently being formed
can be deployed to the East in February cannot be decided at this time. The
decision in about three weeks depends on the prevailing general circumstances then.

The next day, a telegram with the same tenor was dispatched to *OberOst*, in which
Falkenhayn elaborated on his position:

Sight cannot be lost of the fact that a transfer of the new units to the East
amounts to abandoning any offensive operations in the West for the foreseeable future with all the serious consequences that that would entail. On
the other hand, it is possible that it might be necessary to support the Austrian Army with German forces in the centre or on the right flank. However,
according to General von Conrad's assurances and agreements, this necessity does not presently exist and without persuasive reasons, no one is going
to make that decision.

On his return to Teschen, Conrad relayed the outcome of these debates to
his friend Baron Bolfras, Aide-de-Camp to Emperor Franz Joseph and Chief of
the Military Cabinet: "Falkenhayn stated that it made no difference to him
whether success would be achieved in the East or the West, just as long as it was
achieved at all. He was entirely prepared to also deploy the new units in the
East, and even in the Carpathians, should the situation require it."[20] The letter
continued:

The rivalry between the Kaiser and Falkenhayn as commanders in the West,
and Hindenburg and Ludendorff as commanders in the East represents a
major problem. If the Kaiser were in Berlin, the entire matter would be
much easier. However, I believe that all personal aspirations should be
repressed during a serious time such as this. I would consider it beneficial,
if it appeared to be possible, to bring Kaiser Wilhelm to Berlin as the head
of the Western and Eastern Armies.

At the same time, Conrad made clear the special position of Germany's ally:

The Austro-Hungarian Armies can never be subordinated to [the Kaiser], this
would be totally inappropriate not only for national and dynastic reasons,

---

20 This indicates a misunderstanding by Conrad. If it were necessary to insert German forces
    into the Carpathian front, General von Falkenhayn did not have the newly formed German
    forces, or forces from the Western Theatre of Operations, in mind, but expendable forces
    from *OberOst*'s sector.

but for political and operational reasons as well. In such a case we would lose all freedom of action and would be at his mercy.

The next day, 4 January, Conrad received a report from the Austro-Hungarian military attaché in Rome which revealed that Italy was making all preparations for entering the war against Austria-Hungary and Germany. The report stated that Italy's mobilization would reach its peak by the end of March; however, the standing army would be prepared by the end of January. At almost the same time, Conrad received a telegram from Count von Berchtold, the Austro-Hungarian Foreign Minister, which confirmed the military attaché's information and which pointed to the immense impact that military successes could have on this situation. The serious news regarding Italy's posture helped Conrad decide to mount a major offensive out of the central Carpathians. On 6 January, after a detailed presentation regarding the situation, Conrad requested that the *OHL* and *OberOst* transfer four or five German divisions to the Carpathians. Initially Falkenhayn disagreed with Conrad's assessment. The response he directed to Teschen on the same day again illustrated the immense difference of opinion between the two General Staff chiefs where grand strategy was concerned: the content of Falkenhayn's wired response dealt instead with "Rumania's position." It read: "Bulgaria's attack and the supremely important establishment of a connection with Turkey depends exclusively on the situation in Serbia. If one would make the decision to detach forces from Ninth Army, would it not for this reason be prudent to deploy them against Serbia rather than in the Carpathians?" His wire contained another important advisement: "According to the opinion of German diplomats, Italy can only be kept quiet by immediately satisfying her demands, and not by pushing the Russians back from the Carpathians into Galicia."[21]

These statements provoked a spirited response from Conrad, which was wired to German GHQ in Mézières on 7 January:

> Satisfaction of Italy's wishes, in large measure, cannot be considered. In my opinion, France's gratification in the destruction of her enemy's alliances is much more important. [The] entire political situation particularly in the East and in the Balkans is entirely dependent on the military situation with Russia. Without a decisive success against Russia, even a major success in Serbia will be ineffective.

---

21 General von Moltke had already refused Conrad's request for German forces to be made available for border security against Italy on 19 August 1914, and referred Austria-Hungary to diplomatic negotiations to satisfy Italy's demands.

In the meantime, having been informed by Conrad about the *AOK*'s intentions, *OberOst* proposed to send German units into the Carpathians in accordance with Conrad's plan.

The same day, 7 January, Falkenhayn asked Quartermaster General Wild for his opinion regarding the war's centre of gravity. Wild supported the Eastern commanders' proposals and in a written analysis of the situation suggested that Ninth Army's operations in Poland had bogged down and that additional major successes could not be expected there. He suggested that it would be expedient to

> resolve such a fruitless situation … It is certain that we can inject life into the situation in the East. By going onto the defensive we could withdraw considerable forces from the Ninth Army and use them elsewhere. The only question is which option to take?
>
> 1. The offensive into Serbia, with all its known consequences, would be the most effective … However, we do not have sufficient forces available for Serbia and do not want to gamble with insufficient forces. Thus this operation must be abandoned …
> 2. Acceptance of the proposal by *OberOst* … I believe that this operation can be conducted as a surprise, that it will be politically very effective in more than one respect and, most important, that it could lead to a military reversal. It is not impossible that it would force the Russian flank across the Weichsel …
> 3. The utilization of the forces made available by Ninth Army in Eastern Prussia. It is certain that we can liberate the East Prussian lands and this success would be enormous … However, this operation requires more strength.
> 4. First East Prussia, but no further pursuit of other objectives there except mopping up, followed by the commitment of the expendable forces to the Carpathian operation as per option 2 …
>
> Another point of view must be considered when deciding upon the operation: I am firmly convinced that the new corps must be deployed in the East, even if we do not like it … Which one of the operations discussed above will best employ the new corps after their deployment? In my opinion, [it is] the Carpathian operation because it … will draw Russian forces to the South, divert the attention of the enemy from Eastern Prussia, and accordingly will make the best use of the new formations.

These remarks by Falkenhayn's trusted adviser, coupled with the extremely determined opinions of Hindenburg and his Chief of Staff regarding the Austrian plan of operation, seem to have convinced Falkenhayn to agree, albeit with inward reluctance. In any case, *OberOst* had already promised Conrad reinforcements for the Carpathian Front without waiting for Falkenhayn's approval. During a briefing on 8 January, the Kaiser decided in favour of Conrad's proposals and orders were issued for the formation of a new German *Südarmee* to be created from forces on the Eastern Front. Its newly nominated commander, General der Infanterie von Linsingen, was assigned Ludendorff as his Chief of Staff, and *OberOst* was notified of the change in a special letter:

> Generalleutnant Ludendorff, who will temporarily be replaced in his responsibilities at *OberOst* by the longest-serving officer on the General Staff, Oberstleutnant Hoffmann, joins this *Südarmee* as the first Chief of its General Staff. His Majesty expects that Generalleutnant Ludendorff regards this choice as a special indication of [His Majesty's] supreme faith and that with his proven abilities he will invest everything to help and guide this creation, in which he has been involved from its inception, to a positive conclusion; additionally His Majesty expresses His conviction that Generalleutnant Ludendorff especially, given his rich experience in dealing with allied troops, would be able to maintain good relationships even under difficult circumstances.

As much as military necessity justified Ludendorff's reassignment, Hindenburg could not misunderstand the fact that the detachment of the *Generalleutnant* had been precipitated by the difference of opinion between Falkenhayn and the Eastern commanders regarding how the two-front war should be conducted. Moreover, it was not only their different assessments of the whole situation, but also the fact that Hindenburg enjoyed a phenomenal reputation with the people owing to his military achievements, that made Falkenhayn's position extremely precarious as soon as their differences of opinion became known. In order to protect himself from future surprises by the commanders in the East, Falkenhayn intended to secure more influence over the operations there for himself in case the employment of the new corps in the East became necessary after all.[22] There is no doubt that this was made undeniably easier by the separation of Hindenburg from his previous Chief of Staff.

Ludendorff's new assignment with *Südarmee* generated serious objections from Hindenburg. On 9 January he sent a report to the Kaiser in which he offered his opinion about the status of the war as well as his reasons for releasing forces to Germany's allies. He suggested that in a few weeks a success could be expected on the Carpathian Front due to the employment of German forces there, which, in his opinion, would still not be sufficient given the precarious situation of the allied powers. His letter continued:

---

22 See Falkenhayn, *Die Oberste Heeresleitung 1914–1916*, 50.

[This operation] must be connected with a decisive attack in Eastern Prussia. In the beginning of February four newly formed Corps will be ready for deployment. Employing these new forces in the East is a necessity. With them it will not be difficult to inflict a decisive, probably devastating, defeat on the adversary in Eastern Prussia, to finally liberate that badly ravaged province and to advance with full force upon Bialystok. When the Russians are strongly attacked on both flanks, an impact on their centre cannot fail to result. The final victory over Russia will have an influence on the situation in France. I visualize this operation with the commitment of all newly formed units to the East, as decisive for the outcome of the entire war, while their commitment in the West will merely result in the strengthening of our defensive power or, as with Ypres, lead to a frontal assault with high casualties and little chance for success. Our army in the West ought to be capable of holding its position in tiered and fortified positions without reinforcements from the new corps until the final decision in the East is achieved—Your Imperial and Royal Majesty has most graciously ordered that Generalleutnant Ludendorff be transferred from me to *Südarmee*. Due to the fact that the senior serving general staff officer has been designated as his replacement, I believe to be permitted the assumption that the Generalleutnant's reassignment is meant to be temporary. Since the days of Tannenberg and the Masurian Lakes, since the operations against Ivangorod and Warsaw and since the breakout from the Wreschen–Thorn line, I have been closely attached to my chief. He has become my faithful adviser and a friend who has my complete confidence and who cannot be replaced by anyone. From the history of war, your Majesty knows how important such a happy relationship is for the state of affairs and the well-being of the soldiers. Additionally, his new and so much smaller area of responsibility does not do justice to the General's comprehensive capabilities and great competence. Furthermore, I am afraid of certain difficulties caused by his subordination to Conrad with whom, and while on equal terms, he had numerous disagreements regarding strategic and tactical questions, which always represented a justified criticism of the Austrian actions. In addition to this, the longest serving General Staff officer on my staff, Oberstleutnant Hoffman, despite his competency, cannot be expected to have the necessary authority which is essential in the course of a longer official relationship with the Chiefs of the General Staff of the armies which are subordinate to me. For all of these reasons, I dare to submit this reverential appeal to return my comrade in arms to me as soon as the operations in the south have been put into action. It is not personal ambition that motivates my submitting this plea at the feet of your Imperial and Royal Majesty. That thought never crossed my mind. Your Majesty has overwhelmed me with grace that far exceeds my accomplishments and after the conclusion of the war I shall gladly, and with a happy heart, return into the background. Therefore, I only consider it my duty to express this most respectful plea.

These professional and personal differences of opinion caused Falkenhayn to again travel to the East for a personal conversation. On 11 January he held a conference in Breslau regarding the formation and employment of *Südarmee* with Conrad in the presence of the new army's commander, General Linsingen, and his Chief of Staff, General Ludendorff. In a general way, consensus regarding the Carpathian Front was reached. During the further course of the meeting, the Italian issue was again discussed. Falkenhayn explained that Austria-Hungary would have to be willing to relinquish territories to Italy; Conrad firmly rejected acquiescence to Italy's demands, for political reasons of both a foreign and domestic nature. He instead hoped to influence Italy by achieving a success in the Carpathians. Following the meeting, a conversation between Falkenhayn and Ludendorff regarding the latter's new responsibilities failed to create an understanding; instead it led to a deepening of the existing disagreement.

The next day, 12 January, Falkenhayn travelled to Posen,[23] where he had a private conversation with Hindenburg, followed by a larger conference with Ludendorff (who had temporarily returned to Posen), Oberstleutnant Hoffman, and select generals. This conference was quick and formal. The generals conducted a briefing about the situation on their fronts; the deployment of the new corps and the operation from Eastern Prussia planned by *OberOst* were not mentioned at all. Immediately afterwards, however, Falkenhayn had Hoffman brief him privately in his office regarding *OberOst's* planned offensive to be launched from Eastern Prussia.[24] The conference in Posen did not yield specific results. Falkenhayn refused to give Hindenburg, Ludendorff, or Hoffmann any assurances regarding the utilization of the new corps or Ludendorff's reassignment. Later the same day, Falkenhayn travelled to Berlin and Ludendorff returned to the Carpathian Front.

Falkenhayn's trip to the Eastern Front aggravated existing antagonisms. Given the emotional strains caused by the temperaments of the personalities involved, it was only natural that a difference of opinion regarding an issue that could decide the outcome of the war was developing more and more into a severe crisis. At this point, in a telegram to Falkenhayn on 16 January, Conrad urgently requested the deployment of the new formations to the Eastern Front. Only after

---

23 *Posen was the headquarters of* OberOst.
24 Max von Hoffmann, *Die Aufzeichnungen des Generalmajor Max von Hoffman, Band II* (Berlin: Verlag fur Kulturpolitik, 1929), 91.

hard-fought battles, which included the reiteration of demands by the German Chancellor—and then by Hindenburg—that Falkenhayn be removed from his post as Chief of the General Staff of the Field Army, were the differences temporarily alleviated by way of a compromise. Falkenhayn resigned his position as War Minister but stayed on as Chief of the General Staff of the Field Army. His trusted colleague, Wild von Hohenborn, became War Minister and was succeeded as Quartermaster General by Generalleutnant von Freytag-Loringhoven, previously the German general assigned to the *AOK* (his successor became Oberst von Cramon). According to the Kaiser's decisions of 20 and 21 January, the deployment of the new units (four corps) was to take place in the East and Ludendorff was to return to his old assignment as soon as the deployment of *Südarmee* was complete. On 23 January, Falkenhayn advised the War Ministry that Tenth Army, which was in the process of being activated and consisted of XXXVIII, XXXIX, and XXXX Reserve Corps as well as XXI Corps of the Western Army (after having been replaced by XXXXI Reserve Corps), was to be employed in the East. He requested the formation of the appropriate Tenth Army Headquarters and the Tenth Lines of Communication Inspectorate (*Etappen-Inspektion*) by 1 February. The XXXXI Reserve Corps and Bavarian 8th Reserve Division had been assigned to the Western Front on 16 January; their transfer was to begin on 21 January. With that, the immediate and vital question of the war's centre of gravity was decided in accordance with the wishes of the commanders in the East. Certainly it must have been questionable from the beginning whether the four newly available corps would be sufficient to force a decision in the Eastern campaign.

FALKENHAYN HAD GIVEN HIS APPROVAL TO THE DEPLOYMENT OF THE GHQ RESERVE in the East with "a heavy heart,"[25] as commitment there meant that "any active conduct of the war in the West on a major scale [had to] be abandoned for an extended period." Additionally, he felt that it was scarcely to be hoped that the commitment of forces there would be sufficient "to wrest from the enemy an advantage that would be truly important to the general situation ... especially since it was improbable that the natural obstacles, caused by the weather of the season, especially in the mountains, would permit taking advantage of any initial successes."[26] He doubted whether "it was possible that two operations, for which there were limited forces available and which were separated by 600, weakly held kilometres, could be brought to a successful outcome when the advantage of the interior line

---

25 Falkenhayn, *Die Oberste Heeresleitung 1914–1916*, 49.
26 Ibid., 46–47.

belongs to the Russians." Contradicting the commanders in the East, who believed that with a sufficiently strong commitment of forces these operations would bring about a decisive change in the general situation, Falkenhayn expected merely "substantive local successes" on the Carpathian Front and in Eastern Prussia. Despite this, when Falkenhayn gave his approval to the operation in Eastern Prussia anyway, he claimed that his decision was dictated by the circumstances that he thought necessitated the relief of the Austro-Hungarian Carpathian Front due to "the incessant influx of the Russians."

Because of fundamental disagreements between Falkenhayn and the commanders in the East, the former suggested that he naturally had to consider it important "that the direction of the war in the East ... be conducted with a continuous consideration for the overall situation."[27] He felt that this could only be guaranteed if he assumed leadership of the operations on the Eastern Front himself, but "because of the enemy's enormous attack preparations in the West," he was temporarily compelled to forgo assumption of command in the East.

Whether it truly was the situation on the Western Front that was the decisive factor, or rather that he came to realize the difficulties inherent in limiting the independence of *OberOst*, Falkenhayn did not pursue the ever vital questions of *where* the GHQ Reserve should be deployed or *whether* he could exert his personal influence over the conduct of the war in the East. All told, however, the fact that he remained Chief of the General Staff of the Field Army had grave consequences for his future activities.[28]

---

27 Ibid., 50.
28 When DW VII *was written, the* Reichsarchiv *was headed by Hans von Haeften, a former aide-de-camp of Moltke. In January 1915 he was at the centre of the intrigues within the German General Staff, touring the Western Front to garner support for OberOst and the other "Easterners." Haeften's efforts rallied many senior officers—even the German Crown Prince—to the cause but ultimately he failed to win the Kaiser over to OberOst's side. Haeften was working on behalf of OberOst to get Falkenhayn removed from his position as Chief of the General Staff of the Field Army and to reorient the war effort toward the Eastern Front. In the above description, while the acrimony felt between OberOst and Bethman Hollweg on the one hand and Wilhelm II and Falkenhayn on the other is clear, the role played by the Reichsarchiv's director is left out of the story. See* Holger Herwig, The First World War: Germany and Austria-Hungary 1914–1918 (London: Arnold, 1997), 130–35; and Foley, German Strategy and the Path to Verdun, 109–24. See also Ekkehart Guth, "Der Gegensatz zwischen dem Oberbefehlshaber Ost und dem Chef des Feldheeres 1914–15: Die Rolle des Major von Haeften im Spannungsfeld zwischen Hindenburg, Ludendorff, und Falkenhayn," Militärgeschichtliche Mitteilungen 35 (1984): 113–39.

2

The Western Front to
the Middle of April

Decision Making at the *OHL*

In the last days of 1914, when the deployment of the corps that had been newly formed in Germany was still undecided, Falkenhayn hoped that the Eastern Army would be able to supplement the newly activated four and a half corps—which were still intended for the West—to a total of six. The question was: Could a successful and decisive victory be achieved on the Western Front with those resources? Falkenhayn had asked generals Wild and Knobelsdorf; neither could respond in the affirmative. Both were of the opinion that deploying six new corps in the Champagne, or on both sides of the Argonne, might make it possible to push the French front back to the Marne, resulting in the capture of Verdun; however, neither general thought that more would be attainable. Wild also contemplated a breakthrough to Amiens, pointing out that the separation of French and British forces there held great promise; however, he did not believe that the six available corps could guarantee the success of such an operation. In conclusion he explained: "In February it would hardly be possible to clear the way in the West with six corps, but rather this might be possible with twelve corps in March, despite all of the new French and British formations." Falkenhayn agreed, adding: "Totally correct—it is just that in March we'll never have twelve corps in the West. The East is not going to return anything, except in pieces. Anyway, I too consider an attack on Amiens to be important." While both Wild and Knobelsdorf agreed that limited successes in the Champagne and against Verdun could be attained, Falkenhayn was not sufficiently certain.

With that, the possibility of conducting major operations on the Western Front faded, which meant that the West again had to be left to its own devices for an extended time, a prospect that caused Falkenhayn to take new precautions. As early as 2 January he demanded a report from the armies in the West regarding the orders that had been given, or were intended to be given, for the installation of positions in the rear; he found the results to be unsatisfactory. Thus on 7 January he issued a directive to all the armies in the West in which he emphasized that the goal of "consolidating positions in such a manner that, if necessary, they could be held by small elements against vastly superior forces for an extended period of time," had only been accomplished in a few places. "Only when this is ensured, will it be possible to provide the forces in the rear with true rest and recuperation and, on the other hand, to occasionally place major forces at the disposal of the *OHL*, which is necessary for obvious reasons." Holding the first line, as well as upgrading the positions located closest to the enemy, was still his first priority. Additionally, he demanded the construction of "installations that guarantee the interception of the enemy, in case he manages to overrun the first line of defence in one place or another."

On 25 January Falkenhayn complemented these orders with an instruction[1] sent to all army headquarters on the Western Front demanding that every soldier tenaciously defend the foremost defensive line in the event of an enemy attack: "Even the tiniest success" was "immediately" to be wrested from the enemy. Because he knew it had to be anticipated that the enemy would manage to break through in isolated places, he ordered that rear fortifications be expanded. Nevertheless, he explained: "Under no circumstances is it intended that a vast occupation of the expanded rear positions will take place, but instead only in the isolated local positions where the enemy manages to break through [the front line]. The connection between this small part of the rear position and the part of the frontlines not taken by the enemy, should, if at all possible, be immediately re-established so that the result would be a mere 'bulge' in the main line."

He further precluded the interpretation of these orders as being the preliminary step in a voluntary withdrawal of major units from the front lines: "Should a withdrawal for operational reasons by one or more armies into positions towards the rear ever be necessary, the requisite orders will be dispatched in a timely

---

1   This provision was issued because of a difference of opinion between the Army Group commanders Crown Prince Rupprecht of Bavaria and General von Heeringen. In early January, in the case of Crown Prince Rupprecht, Falkenhayn appears to have requested the construction of a continuous rear position and mentioned small sacrifices of territory "between Lys and the Atlantic." Heeringen, who had not received a similar suggestion, maintained that all strength should be directed toward upgrading the forward positions.

manner by the *OHL*; the expansion of the rear positions by the army has not been made in anticipation of such a case."

In his own memorandum, Wild pointed to the necessity of having the *OHL* construct extensive and connecting rear positions; he even advocated fortifying along the Meuse. That said, it was apparent that one of the most important problems yet to be resolved was the procurement of the necessary labour, given that the armies were not capable of solving the problem from within their own strengths. Initially, the labour units allocated to the armies in the West were completely inadequate, since the additional manpower required could not be recruited from the field armies. Despite this, wherever the location and topography permitted, the advanced positions were arranged in multiple trenches, one behind the other, connected by access routes and with the appropriate distribution of dugouts and flanking defences in which to take cover. However, forces for the defence had not been freed up to the degree expected, and only the Fourth and Sixth Armies were able to allocate complete divisions to the reserves in accordance with Falkenhayn's requirements of the previous November.[2] The structuring of the armies in the West into army groups (*Heeresgruppen*)[3] had indeed allowed the armies to assist one another temporarily without necessitating interference from the *OHL*. Nevertheless, none of the group commanders was in a position to form any army group reserves of significant strength.

It could not be known how effective the facilities constructed in the recent months would prove in the battles that were anticipated. It was improbable that the ease with which enemy attacks had been repulsed in December 1914 could be used as a reliable benchmark. In all likelihood it could be assumed that if the Western Front remained on the defensive, while the armies in the East attacked the Russians, the French and British would make the utmost effort to exploit the situation to achieve a success in the West. At the beginning of January the *OHL* ordered a count of the number of enemy and friendly artillery rounds discharged; this appeared to show a considerable preponderance of the former. How far such an increase would force the infantry to protect itself in the course of serious

---

2 See Appendix 5, Falkenhayn's Orders for the Defence in the West.

3 *DW* VI: 372 *reads in part:* "Following a reorganization of the armed forces, on 25 November Falkenhayn issued orders to the army in the west for the period of defence. First the army was arranged into three army groups. The right group consisted of Fourth, Sixth, and Second Armies, under the Crown Prince of Bavaria, the middle group was comprised of First, Seventh, and Third armies, under Generaloberst von Heeringen, the left group, commanded by the German Crown Prince, consisted of Fifth Army, and, through to the Swiss Border, Armee-Abteilungen *Strantz, Falkenhausen,* and *Gaede.* The commanders of these army groups still retained command of their own armies. Meanwhile they were to separate mobile GHQ reserves that were to then be available for relief."

combat operations either through the excavation of deeper, more innovative installations or by a greater dispersion of the cover in the rear, would have to be determined by the experience of the troops, for the *OHL's* attempts to develop consistent guidelines and specifications for the construction of fortifications had not yet been initiated. In his instructions of 7 January, Falkenhayn wrote: "Protective trenches in which the occupants can take cover in the case of heavy artillery fire must be created behind the first line of defence, as lately the enemy tries to prevent the advance of the supporting forces in critical moments by laying an artillery barrage behind the forward trenches. Thus it is necessary to provide for covered connections from the position of the supporting forces to the front." However, Falkenhayn's provisions did not extend beyond these general directions.

Falkenhayn believed that, faced with the uncertainty created by the expectation of forceful and well-prepared attacks, he could not deprive the West of any significant forces by transferring them to the East and that he had to refuse all demands to that effect. The possibility of shortening the front through a voluntary retreat—which had been entertained in the fall of 1914[4]—was not revived, and it was to be expected that remaining on active defence, without the possibility of transferring troops to the rear for rest and recreation, would exert a negative influence on the troops.

On the other hand, the situation on the Western Front had solidified considerably compared to the autumn of the previous year, mainly because the railway system had been entirely rehabilitated. By the spring of 1915 the railway network's most important lines had been finished to such an extent that the High Command's demand for faster supporting movements could be wholly satisfied. To allow for the immediate introduction of reinforcements in the event of enemy attacks, standby trains were positioned at the ready in each army's sector near the reserve billets, as well as all along the Western Front for the transporting of units withdrawn from the front lines. By allowing for expedited evacuations, the railway network facilitated not only greater flexibility, but also a constant ability to resist and—through its improved performance—an increased defensive capability at

---

4 *DW* VI: 9 *reads:* "In a long distance call on the morning of 9 November with Generalleutnant von Kuhl, the Chief of Staff of First Army, Falkenhayn considered the possibility of a withdrawal on the Western Front in order to create reserves. He said that it could become necessary that 'in the West we would have to go over to the defensive in order to supply the East.' Then we would have to shorten the positions in the West in order to extract corps [from the front]. The new positions would not lie too far to the rear, as otherwise such a large retreat would become equal to a defeat. Everything will depend on how the situation develops on the outermost right wing. Only after that could we determine the [new] line of defence." *Falkenhayn ultimately decided against the withdrawal when events in the East and West changed his considerations.*

the front. Static warfare, by virtue of its constant need for building materials and the growing logistical requirements of the armies, placed increasing demands on the railways that led to the creation of the then unknown concept of supply via mass freight transportation. More than before, the army depended on the home front and efficient connections to it.

Falkenhayn expected that in the coming months the enemy would grow considerably stronger in the West. A memorandum dated 25 December 1914 by the Intelligence Assessment Division (*Nachrichtenabteilung*) of the *OHL*[5] estimated that the enemy forces would "by the spring of 1915" have twenty-one to twenty-two new divisions. On the French side, the memorandum estimated the expected gain to be approximately seven divisions, on the British side, twelve to thirteen. The Belgians, it was thought, could raise two additional divisions. According to intelligence, it was not likely that the Entente's forces intended to wait for the arrival of their reinforcements. In the last days of December, in agreement with agents' dispatches, Third Army reported that all indications pointed to a massive new attack in the Champagne. At the same time, news arrived that attacks in the area of Soissons seemed to be in the works for around the middle of January, a few days prior to the convening of the French Parliament on 12 January. It also seemed that in co-operation with the British fleet, the British High Command intended to break through the German positions near the coast.

The British Army had been reinforced. An agent's report received in late January indicated the disembarkation of the entire 28th Division between 15 and 20 January, which, together with 27th Division, constituted British V Corps; both formations were comprised of yet uncommitted active units.

In a memorandum dated 21 January, the Intelligence Assessment Division of the *OHL* assumed that the first Kitchener army of six divisions would appear in February; the second (with the same strength) was expected to arrive in France in April. A third, formed by 21st through 26th Divisions, was not thought to be available for operations on the continent for the foreseeable future. A strong Canadian Division was still in England, but it could be expected to arrive in France in the near future. The five British and one Indian corps already in France had apparently been recently reorganized into two armies. An agent's dispatch, which reached Falkenhayn on 27 January, reported that the prevailing opinion on the British home front was that it was only a matter of buying time in order to develop the

---

5   *The* OHL *had two Intelligence Departments:* Sektion *(later* Abteilung IIIb*) was the Secret Intelligence Department, while* Nachrichtenabteilung *(later renamed* Fremde Heere*) performed intelligence assessment. For a discussion of German intelligence, see* Markus Pöhlmann, "Towards a New History of German Military Intelligence in the Era of the Great War: Approaches and Sources," *Journal of Intelligence History* 5, no. 2 (2005): 1–8.

British military forces "before they would win." This report also suggested that the appearance of Zeppelins over London would have a sobering effect on British public opinion.

The Belgian Army was being rebuilt; however, it had not sufficiently progressed to consider the possibility of their participating in an offensive.

On the whole, the opinions expressed in December by the *OHL* regarding the projected growth of the French and British armies up to February 1915 seemed to be coming true. Even though initially there were no discernable indications of the anticipated seven newly activated French divisions, two new and previously uncounted for British divisions had appeared.[6] Thus a major offensive that promised success against the enemies in the West had become increasingly difficult.

On 28 January the Kaiser, accompanied by Falkenhayn, departed for home and then went to the Eastern Front. Even from there, Falkenhayn personally maintained control over the Western Army.

Operations on the Western Front to the Middle of February

Fourth Army, commanded by Duke Albrecht von Württemberg (Chief of Staff, Generalmajor Ilse), was responsible for the Ypres Salient. The towns from Westende to Zeebrugge on the North Sea coast remained the focus of daily firefights and minor operations. Enemy warships of all kinds—including submarines and torpedo boats—often appeared off the coast while aircraft bombed the occupied towns and fortifications. German air force squadrons and the coastal batteries of the Naval Corps conducted the defence without difficulty. The Germans also launched remote operations against the enemy's interior: bomber squadrons attacked the staging area of Dunkirk a number of times, while German aircraft patrolled the sea all the way to the British coast. Around the same time, German submarine activity out of Zeebrugge began.

Except for a partially successful attack by 53rd Saxon Reserve Division in the sector southwest of Passchendaele, and the successful repulse of a Moroccan attack in the Nieuport sector, nothing of real importance occurred.

---

6 *The 27th and 28th (British) Divisions likely went uncounted because they were formed in December 1914 by assembling the regular British battalions that had returned to England from garrison duty elsewhere in the Empire.*

On 17 DECEMBER 1914, BRITISH AND FRENCH FORCES LAUNCHED ATTACKS BETWEEN
Armentières and Arras against Sixth Army, under Crown Prince Rupprecht of
Bavaria.[7] By 20 December the attack had bogged down, but its after-effects smoul-
dered for weeks. Flashpoints remained around Neuve Chapelle, La Bassée, Carency,
and Ecurie. On 1 January 1915, Sixth Army Headquarters instructed XIV Corps "to
initially gain sufficient ground for the establishment of a stronghold at the Lorette
Chapel[8] thus eliminating the enemy's ability to use the heights for artillery observation." The VII and XIV Corps were directed to then conduct a joint attack on
Givenchy-lez-la-Bassée–Cuinchy on both sides of La Bassée Canal. On the Lorette
Spur, because means for the attack were lacking, the efforts of the Baden regiments resulted only in a back-and-forth battle that produced high casualties from
artillery fire and hand grenades. As with the attacks of VII and XIV Corps west
of La Bassée on 25 January, by the beginning of February this attack had produced no noticeable successes.

IN GENERAL, THE FIRST MONTHS OF 1915 WERE A TIME OF RELATIVELY QUIET,
static warfare in the sector of Second Army, under the command of General von
Bülow.[9] On 27 January, Second Army was combined with First Army to form a new
army group. Only in the sector of XIV Reserve Corps did the enemy launch a
number of small attacks, around Beaumont, Thiepval, and La Boiselle. In the
middle of March the Guard Corps (corps headquarters and 2nd Guard Division),
which until then had been under Sixth Army, joined Second Army.

The Battle of Soissons

While at GHQ on 27 December 1914, Seventh Army's Chief of Staff Generalleutnant von Haenisch was advised that as a result of Joffre's attack orders of 17 December,[10] and their consequences for the area of the centre army group (First, Seventh,
and Third Armies) in the Champagne and Artois, the *OHL* desired that an operation be mounted to contain the opposing forces. Since appreciable reinforcements

---

7   At the same time, Crown Prince Rupprecht of Bavaria commanded the Right Army Group
    consisting of the Fourth, Sixth, and initially Second Armies. At Sixth Army his Chief of Staff
    was Generalmajor Krafft von Dellmensingen.
8   *Notre Dame de Lorette.*
9   On 27 January, Bülow was promoted to Generalfeldmarschall. At Second Army, his Chief of
    Staff was Generalmajor von Zielen.
10 *On 17 December, Joffre issued an order of the day which pointed out to the troops that the soil
    of France had to finally be released from the clutches of the enemy and that, more than ever,
    the Motherland counted on their will to win. See DW* VI: 385.

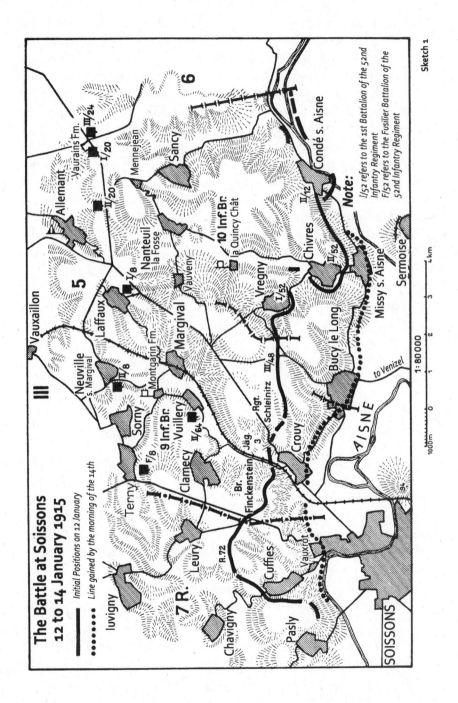

The Battle at Soissons
12 to 14 January 1915

—— Initial Positions on 12 January

•••••• Line gained by the morning of the 14th

Note:

I/52 refers to the 1st Battalion of the 52nd Infantry Regiment

F/52 refers to the Fusilier Battalion of the 52nd Infantry Regiment

1 : 80 000

1000m 0 1 2 3 4 km

Sketch 1

could not be expected, large-scale plans had to be postponed. It was only possible to consider a local attack, which III Corps had already prepared in the area of First Army on the Vregny Plateau northeast of Soissons. The objective of the operation was to throw back the enemy across the Aisne between the Terny–Soissons road and Missy-sur-Aisne.

First Army, commanded by General von Kluck (Chief of Staff Generalmajor von Kuhl), held a sector about 70 kilometres wide on both sides of Soissons immediately north of the Aisne, across which strong, bridgehead-like French positions extended. By shortening its front, First Army had been able to form a reserve of one infantry brigade, which was to assist in the attack planned for the middle of January. Command of the operation was given to the commanding general of III Corps, General der Infanterie von Lochow, but soon after beginning preparations for the attack, First Army had to relinquish its newly formed reserve to Armee-Abteilung[11] *Gaede* on the orders of the *OHL*. Nevertheless, the headquarters of First Army and III Corps stood by their decision to attack. Only by radically stripping the remainder of the front could III Corps be provided with weak reinforcements totalling nineteen and a half infantry battalions and thirty-two and a half field and heavy batteries with ammunition for only one day of battle.

During the preparations for the attack, on 8 January at 10:00, the enemy launched an attack against the positions at Clamecy, north of Soissons.[12] After several days of fighting, and despite their valiant resistance, the Brandenburgers deployed in that sector were pushed out of some of their trenches and the reinforcements intended for the attack north of Soissons had to be used for their relief. On 11 January, because of additional fierce enemy attacks south of Clamecy, Lochow decided to postpone the planned offensive action. Instead he deployed all available forces for a counterattack on the threatened right flank. The reinforced 5th Infantry Division, commanded by Generalleutnant Wichura, was tasked not only with pushing the enemy back again, but also with wresting from him the commanding heights north of Soissons. Fortunately, plans for such an operation had already been in the works for some time; therefore, only minimal new reconnaissance and troop movements were necessary.

---

11 An "Armee-Abteilung" *(Army Detachment)* was a formation, usually named for its commanding general. It was slightly below the strength of an army but larger than a corps. On the Western Front, while Armee-Abteilungen functioned in much the same way as an army, they were usually subordinated to them.

12 They were French Sixth Army's 5th Reserve Division Group consisting of the 55th Reserve Division and the mixed "Brigade *Klein*." According to information provided by the French, the offensive had already begun on 7 January.

At 11:00 on 12 January, a combined assault regiment moved against the heights east of Crouy, which harboured artillery observation posts. The operation was successful, and prisoners of war later reported that it had come as a total surprise to them. As a result, enemy artillery fire immediately became less noticeable. An hour later, after heavy fighting, an attack under the command of Generalmajor Count Finck von Finckenstein (9th Infantry Brigade) by two other combined assault regiments and a Jäger battalion took the French trenches north and north-west of Crouy, as well as the northern edge of the village. The neighbouring 7th Reserve Division joined the attack on its left flank with a regiment and advanced up to the southern edge of Cuffies.

Because of this success, Lochow decided on the afternoon of 12 January to launch the carefully prepared attack west of Vregny on the following day. After an urgent request, the *OHL* approved the issuance of ammunition for one more day of combat. The attack began in limited visibility early on a rainy afternoon. Despite the sodden clay terrain, three combined regiments under the command of Generalmajor Sontag (10th Infantry Brigade) seized the positions at Vregny in a pincer movement: one attacked from the front and the other two from each side. Again, the enemy was surprised because it had concentrated its reserves against the point of attack at Crouy. By evening the enemy remained only in the wooded ravines that descended to the Aisne. Generalleutnant Wichura contemplated an immediate push through to the Aisne. Owing to the dangers of a reverse in the approaching darkness, and considering that the attacking units were exhausted—not to mention that they had become intermingled and that it was impossible to move sizable artillery units forward in the almost bottomless terrain—he decided to cease operations.

On 13 January the French launched strong counterattacks on both sides of the Soissons–Terny road, but they failed without exception. In addition to the French 55th Reserve Division and a brigade formed from six reserve *Chasseurs* battalions and a Moroccan light infantry regiment, regiments of 14th Infantry Division participated in the fight. On the evening of 13 January, First Army Headquarters had to expect that the enemy would make more counterattacks; therefore it brought forward the last two available battalions of IX Corps and IX Reserve Corps in trucks to Terny, north of Soissons. Their deployment, however, became unnecessary since on 13 and 14 January the enemy withdrew its main forces across the Aisne, which had become severely swollen by rains, which had also destroyed the pontoon bridges near Missy and Venizel.

On 14 January, following rearguard actions, the units on IV Reserve Corps' left flank managed to take Vauxrot and the northernmost foothills near Soissons. Afterwards, Lochow's forces reached the approximate line of Crouy–Bucy-le-Long–Missy and pushed outposts forward to the Aisne. With that, the objective of the attack had been achieved. The German losses amounted to 169 officers and 5,360 enlisted men; approximately 5,200 prisoners, 35 guns, and 6 machine guns had been captured. Joffre was so upset by this defeat that he relieved all the divisional commanders who had participated in the action.

THE GERMAN VICTORY AT SOISSONS WAS PRIMARILY DUE TO THE COMMANDERS' meticulous preparations, the systematic coordination of all weapons, and the bravery of both the infantry and the pioneers. The artillery and *Minenwerfer* proved themselves totally equal to the difficult task of quickly transitioning from defence to counterattack and then going on the offensive in another location. The practice of pooling field and foot artillery batteries in groups suited to each specific mission also stood the test of battle extremely well.[13] The experience gained from this attack had a stimulating and significant impact along the entire Western Front; for a long time, "Soissons" was viewed as an exemplary attack in a confined space in positional warfare.

ON 16 JANUARY, FALKENHAYN ORDERED THE NEWLY ACTIVATED XXXXI RESERVE Corps to move to the Western Front, where it was to relieve XXI Corps west of St. Quentin on 21 January. Even though major military operations in the West had had to be postponed for the foreseeable future, the *OHL* was not willing to give the enemy the upper hand by going entirely over to the defensive. On 17 January, Falkenhayn questioned First Army Headquarters regarding whether a further "promising operation of a lasting value" could be conducted in its sector between 25 January and the first part of February, for which it was proposed that one corps[14] and the necessary ammunition could be allotted.

At the same time, Falkenhayn informed Armee-Abteilung *Gaede* that Bavarian 8th Reserve Division, a new division that had been raised in the homeland,[15] would arrive there on the 21st, but that the actual deployment of the new division, and the

---

13 *A foot artillery battery comprised between two and four tubes with calibres varying from 10 cm field guns to 24 cm howitzers. A field artillery battery comprised four to six guns, often of a 10.5 cm calibre.* See Hermann Cron, *Imperial German Army, 1914–18: Organization, Structure, Orders of Battle* (Solihull: Helion, 2002), 271–72; *and* Donald Fosten, D.S.V. Fosten, and Robert R.J. Marrion, *The German Army, 1914–1918* (Oxford: Osprey, 2005), 13–15.

14 Which Corps had been designated for this is unknown.

15 *Before the war there were five classes of service in the German Army: the regular army, the reserves, the* Landwehr, *the* Landsturm, *and the* Ersatz *reserve. At age seventeen, a healthy German male would serve in a* Landsturm—*or home defence—unit. At twenty he would be called up for service in the regulars for a period of two years as an infantryman, or three years in the artillery or cavalry. Following his regular service he would spend four or five years in the*

extraction of Division *Fuchs*, which had been seconded to the Armee-Abteilung, were still to be decided. First Army, however, believed that if it was issued sufficient ammunition, and if the infantry brigade it had given up earlier in the month to Armee-Abteilung *Gaede* was returned, it could expand on the victories it had recently won at Soissons in a westerly direction. In such case, a fresh corps would not be necessary. However, in order to mop up the right bank of the Aisne in Seventh Army's sector, stronger forces would be needed. At first, Falkenhayn said that he was willing to satisfy First Army's demands; but he then changed his intentions, presumably because it was more important for him to achieve a success in the Vosges and Upper Alsace, thereby liberating German soil from the enemy, than it was to capture French territory in the sectors of First and Seventh Armies. Thus on 22 January he requested proposals from Armee-Abteilung *Gaede* for "a major offensive operation in the Upper-Alsace to take place in the near future" in which Bavarian 8th Reserve Division, as well as the remainder of the forces presently attached to Armee-Abteilung *Gaede*, including the elements of the First and Third Armies combined in Division *Fuchs*, were to be deployed. On the 24th, the proposals of Armee-Abteilung *Gaede* were approved. With that, the return of the elements of both other armies was postponed until further notice.

CONSEQUENTLY, IN MID-JANUARY A PERIOD OF QUIET RETURNED TO FIRST ARMY'S front. During the attacks in the Champagne, its positions frequently came under strong diversionary artillery fire, but for all that, the enemy did not conduct an attack anywhere along its front. Because it possessed insufficient forces, First Army was in no position to provide relief by mounting the attack near Nouvron that had been planned since the middle of January.

Seventh Army

Since the beginning of the winter battle in the Champagne, Seventh Army, under command of General von Heeringen (Chief of Staff Generalleutnant Haenisch)

---

reserves and a further eleven years in the Landwehr. *He would complete his compulsory military service by returning to the* Landsturm *until the age of forty-five. The* Ersatz *reserve comprised healthy males who were excused from regular service for a variety of familial or economic reasons. Ersatz reservists were required to attend training camps three times per year for twelve years before being transferred to the* Landwehr *and* Landsturm, *though few ever completed their training as prescribed. German military units were subsequently designated by class of service. See* Alan Allport, "Germany, Army" in *The Encyclopaedia of World War I*, ed. Spencer C. Tucker (New York: ABC-Clio, 2005), Vol. 2, 474–77. *For a more thorough description of the organization of the German infantry, see* Cron, *Imperial German Army, 1914–18*, 109–20.

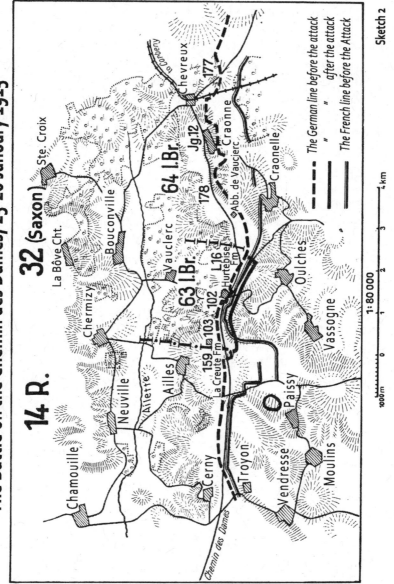

The Battle on the Chemin des Dames, 25-26 January 1915

14 R.

32 (Saxon)

Chamouille

Ste. Croix

La Bôve Cht.

Chermizy

Bouconville

Neuville

Ailette

Ailles

63 I.Br.

64 I.Br.

Vauclerc

La Creute Fm.

159 I

103 I

102

L16 I

Hurtebise
Fm.

178

Jg.12

Craonne

Abb. de Vauclerc

Craonelle

Chevreux

177

Cerny

Troyon

Vendresse

Moulins

Paissy

Vassogne

Oulches

Chemin des Dames

The German line before the attack
"   "   "   after the attack
The French line before the Attack

1 : 80 000

1000m   0   1   2   3   4 km

Sketch 2

was frequently required to support the hard-pressed Third Army. For this reason, Seventh Army was preparing to relieve XII (Saxon) Corps by mounting an attack on the French positions on the heights of the Chemin des Dames in the sector La Creute Farm–Hurtebise (west of Craonne). The well-prepared operation was launched on the afternoon of 25 January under the command of Generalleutnant Edler von der Planitz, Commander of 32nd Saxon Infantry Division. His right-flanking brigade, supported by a composite infantry regiment, advanced with a forceful assault in the centre and on the division's right flank. Although the main attack initially broke down in the face of machine-gun fire near Hurtebise, the infantry reached their assigned objectives on the morning of the 26th by employing hand grenades. All the enemy's immediate counter-attacks failed.

The French positions north of the swollen Aisne also invited further German attacks. However, VII Reserve Corps' preparations for an offensive in the direction of the high ground near Paissy set for the beginning of February were not realized because insufficient forces were available. Also, in mid-February, in connection with the battle in the Champagne, unsuccessful French holding actions were launched against the positions of XII and X Corps between Berry-au-Bac and Loivre.

ON 25 JANUARY, FALKENHAYN ORDERED SEVENTH ARMY TO WITHDRAW X RESERVE Corps from the front. That corps was then to be broken up and assembled as the *OHL's* reserve, with one infantry brigade, reinforced by the other arms of service, behind First, Seventh, Third, and Fifth Armies. This task was to be completed by early February. These brigades would then be available to relieve units of comparable strength in the army opposite their position. First Army was permitted to make use of the reinforced brigade arriving behind its front for as long as the elements it had sent to Alsace (to Armee-Abteilung *Gaede*) were not returned. However, at the same time it received an order to shift its boundary against Second Army up to the Avre. These measures again placed a reserve—although minimal compared to the enormous front—at the disposal of the *OHL*. Its disposition indicates that the Champagne was considered to be the sector on the Western Front in most urgent need of protection.

The Winter Battle in the Champagne

The battles in the Champagne, which would tie up the forces of the armies in the West again and again throughout 1915, had already begun by the last weeks of 1914, when they were almost exclusively conducted by Third Army under the command of General der Kavallerie von Einem (also known as von Rothmaler).[16] With seven and a half divisions,[17] Third Army had to cover an area of about 55 kilometres between Reims and the Upper Aisne. Because sufficient reserves for support or relief were not available, initially assistance had to be provided by one division to the other, or by one corps to the other; later, however, the commander of the centre army group and the *OHL* allocated reserves to the endangered part of the front.[18]

Especially lively enemy activity had been noted on both sides of the Souain–Somme Py road for quite some time. Saps had been pushed out from the French front lines, their heads had been connected, and new positions had been created in closer proximity to the German trenches. Underground mining activities also commenced.[19]

The French mode of attack remained essentially the same for the duration of the battle in the Champagne. Warnings of an attack were indicated by lively activity in and behind the enemy lines. This was followed by artillery, infantry, trench mortar, and heavy howitzer fire that lasted several days, pausing intermittently but eventually increasing to a *Trommelfeuer*,[20] which was followed by French infantry attacks from positions that had been driven as close to the German lines as possible. Because the German ammunition shortage had still not been rectified, effective countermeasures were unavailable. In spite of all that, attacks during December 1914 between Souain and Massiges failed in the face of German rifle and machine-gun fire.

On the Champagne Front, 1915 began with clear indications that more forceful enemy attacks were in the works. The French were increasingly concentrating their resources in front of both Rhenish corps. Meanwhile, XII Saxon Reserve Corps was kept occupied with feints and diversionary fire; combat, however, was

---

16   He was promoted to General on 27 January. His Chief of Staff became Generalmajor von Hoeppner.

17   The 12th, half of 11th, 23rd (Saxon) Reserve, and 24th (Saxon) Reserve, 15th, 16th, 16th Reserve, and 15th Reserve Divisions.

18   *For more on the battle in the Champagne, see* Arndt von Kirchbach, *Kämpfe in der Champagne, Winter 1914–Herbst 1915 (Der grosse Krieg in Einzeldarstellungen, Heft 11)* (Oldenburg: Gerhard Stalling, 1919); and *the French official history,* Ministère de la Guerre, État-Major de l'Armée Service Historique, *Les Armées Françaises dans la Grande Guerre* (Paris: Imprimerie Nationale, 1930), II: 410–81 *(hereafter* French Official History*).*

19   *On 30 November 1914, Joffre ordered his army commanders to push their trenches forward to within 150 metres of the German positions in order to get the attacking infantry closer to their objectives. See* Robert A. Doughty, *Pyrrhic Victory: French Strategy and Operations in the Great War* (Cambridge, MA: Harvard University Press, 2005), 128.

20   Trommelfeuer: *Literally translated as "drum-fire," it refers to an intense hail of heavy-calibre shells.*

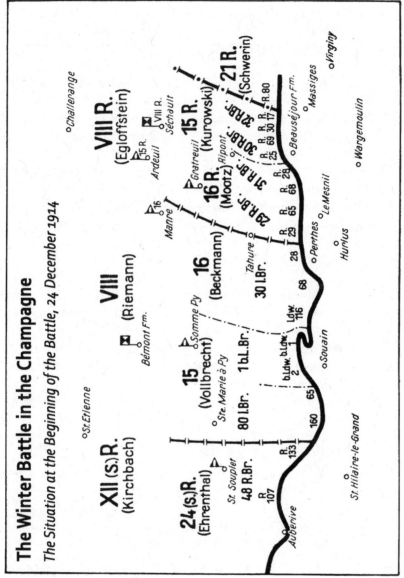

The Winter Battle in the Champagne

The Situation at the Beginning of the Battle, 24 December 1914

Sketch 3

mostly limited to raids and artillery duels of varying intensity. With the trenches badly shot up by shellfire and crumbling due to heavy rainfall, the strength of the German combat forces was barely sufficient to maintain the lines in a defensible condition. Those forces were also barely able to begin work on the newly ordered defensive network in the rear, which was to be located, on average, 3 kilometres behind the front lines. The condition of the soaked and damaged roads was so poor that trucks frequently got stuck even on the paved roads. On the front lines, the thick, heavy mud made all movement difficult. The horses were mostly unprotected from the weather, and both the animals and their effectiveness suffered severely. These conditions greatly impeded leadership, combat effectiveness, and supply.

On 1 January, approximately five French infantry regiments, including artillery, were reported to be advancing from Wargemoulin on Le Mesnil. Both VIII Corps and VIII Reserve Corps Headquarters were initially of the opinion that these movements were being made merely so that elements of French I Corps could relieve the battle-weary XVII Corps.[21] An attack launched against VIII Reserve Corps' centre at 18:00 on 2 January disabused them of this opinion, but it floundered in front of the remnants of the dilapidated German positions.

Following numerous French forays between Perthes-lès-Hurlus and Beauséjour Farm, on 9 January at 11:15, a strong attack was made east of Perthes-lès-Hurlus in the sector of 16th Infantry Division (which since 25 December had been commanded by Generalmajor Prince Heinrich von Reuß), but this attack again collapsed after suffering heavy losses. Starting at 16:00, the enemy inundated the German positions west of Perthes-lès-Hurlus with *Trommelfeuer*, but the infantry attack that followed was repulsed there as well. On 8 January the enemy occupied Perthes, which was situated on low ground and had heretofore been between the two opposing lines.

The VIII Reserve Corps, which had been commanded by Generalleutnant Fleck since 2 January, came under attack in the morning and again in the afternoon. South of Ripont, the enemy entered the German trenches on a narrow front and, thanks to well-placed artillery fire, was able to hold on.

The next day, elements of the Guard Corps commanded by Generalleutnant von Winckler[22] and a Saxon reserve regiment were brought up for the relief of the badly hammered Rhenish regiments around Perthes-lès-Hurlus and south of

---

21 *XVII (French) Corps had attacked Fourth Army in combination with colonial troops beginning on 20 December. The attack had been unsuccessful, and French I Corps, which had originally been held in reserve to exploit a breakthrough, was partly committed to the battle. See DW VI: 386 and* French Official History, II: 205–20.

22 Staff of 2nd Guard Infantry Division, 1st Guard Infantry Brigade, and 1st and 5th Squadron 2nd Guard Ulan Regiment.

Ripont. South of Tahure, French soldiers had been taken prisoner from XVII Corps. According to their statements, the detraining of IV Corps northeast of Châlons near Somme-Tourbe meant that further breakthrough attempts could be expected.

General der Infanterie[23] Riemann, the commanding general of VIII Corps, intended to make a foray west of Perthes, but the incessant and wearing French attacks against his left flank meant that this idea had to be abandoned. On the other hand, the plan for a relieving attack near Massiges by elements of VIII and XVIII Reserve Corps, which formed the right flank of Fifth Army, had begun to take shape by early February. On the morning of 3 February the artillery found its range and began a continuous fire for effect. In their access routes, trenches, and saps, the assault troops had been at the ready since dawn. At noon, mines (which had been prepared beforehand) were exploded and intense German artillery fire commenced against the main enemy positions; infantry from the left flank of 15th Reserve Division and the right flank of 21st Reserve Division formed the first wave of the attack. By around 12:30 the main French positions on the two ridges and at Hill 191 north of Massiges were in German hands. In the afternoon the French brought up a division near Virginy, apparently for an immediate counterattack, and their artillery fire increased from one hour to the next. The assault itself had resulted in minimal casualties; now, the numbers of dead and wounded began to steadily increase. The expected counterattack did not materialize until 04:40 on 4 February and could only be repelled after fierce hand-to-hand combat. Thus the German successes at Massiges were limited to those made during the initial surprise attack.

In the meantime, the elements of 11th Infantry Division (the divisional staff and the reinforced 21st Infantry Brigade) that had remained in XVIII Reserve Corps' sector since September 1914 had almost entirely returned to VI Corps on the right flank of Third Army. By 1 February, Third Army's right flank had been extended to the Bazancourt–Reims railway. There, 19th Reserve Division, which had become available after the extraction of X Reserve Corps from Seventh Army, was partially transferred to VIII Corps. On 5 February the staff of 19th Reserve Division and 39th Reserve Infantry Brigade relieved the staff of 2nd Guard Infantry Division (at Perthes)[24] and 1st Guard Infantry Brigade respectively, which then departed for Sixth Army on the 9th.

In the second week of February, indications mounted that a major attack was imminent near Perthes-lès-Hurlus, at least against the sector of 19th Reserve

---

23 Elevated to this rank on 25 January 1915.
24 Which had been assigned in place of the acting staff of the 16th Infantry Division since 11 January.

Division, commanded by General der Infanterie von Bahrfeldt. Since 10 February, fierce artillery fire had covered the area as far as the left flank of the XII Reserve Corps and VIII Reserve Corps. On 12 February, at 07:30, the French moved against the forested position east of Souain and managed to break through Bavarian 1st Landwehr Brigade's left flank. By evening, however, the Bavarians had regained most of their former position by mounting a quickly organized counterattack, supported by elements of the Hessian Landwehr Regiment, which had also been attacked and which neighboured the Bavarian position to the east. East of Perthes, German artillery broke up another French attack before it began. After the forces of XVIII Reserve Corps had finally taken possession of the hotly disputed Hill 191, in front of the leftmost flank of Third Army, the French vacated the slopes of both outcroppings north of Massiges, which until then had remained in enemy hands.

Thanks to the unswerving conduct of the soldiers, and despite heavy losses and the greatest demands on its resources, Third Army had successfully fought its way through the Battle of the Champagne up to that point.

Fifth Army

The fierce battles of XVI Corps continued in the sector of Fifth Army, commanded by the German Crown Prince (Chief of Staff Generalleutnant Schmitt von Kno-belsdorf), who also commanded the left army group, which was comprised of Armee-Abteilungen *Strantz, Falkenhausen,* and *Gaede.*[25] After repelling a fero-cious attack on 5 January, 33rd Infantry Division attacked in the eastern section of the Argonne, where it vanquished the enemy. By 11 January it had taken 17 offi-cers and 1,600 men prisoner and captured various war materiel as well. On 22 January, 34th Infantry Division gained some ground northwest of Le Four de Paris, and on 29 January, 27th Infantry Division, with a regiment of 11th Infantry Division on its right, successfully attacked the western part of the woods and moved its positions a few hundred metres forward. During January, in total, XVI Corps captured 34 officers, 2,849 men, and a number of close-range guns. In the first half of February the corps continued its slow advance.

Five battalions (mostly *Landwehr*) replaced those elements that departed VI Corps, and the 9th Landwehr Divisional Staff was reorganized. Since Fifth Army had no reserves worth mentioning, at the beginning of February the *OHL* provi-sionally assigned a reinforced brigade of 2nd Guard Reserve Division from X Reserve Corps.

---

25 Abteilungen *is the plural of* Abteilung.

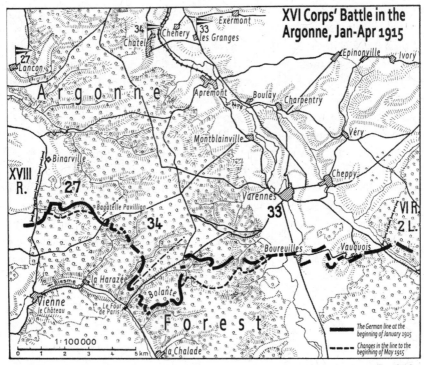

XVI Corps' Battle in the Argonne, Jan-Apr 1915

Sketch 4

Except for skirmishes between patrols sent out by both sides in January, relative quiet reigned on the northern flank of Armee-Abteilung *Strantz* which was commanded by General der Infanterie von *Strantz* (Chief of Staff Oberstleutnant Fischer). However, in the beginning of February, enemy artillery fire increased along V Corps' entire front, although it was concentrated against the positions of 33rd Reserve Division on the Combres Heights.

Vicious close combat took place at the centre in the Bois d'Ailly, in which the Bavarian Ersatz Division held its positions. Meanwhile, in the Forêt d'Apremont, Bavarian 5th Infantry Division gained ground.

Since the beginning of the year, French activity across from 8th Ersatz Division, in the western part of the Bois-le-Prêtre, had become much livelier. After an unsuccessful attack on 8 January, the French managed to take a stronghold there on the 17th. It was not until 20 January that part of the stronghold could be regained with the help of reinforcements, dispatched by Fifth Army Headquarters from 33rd Reserve Division. On 16 February the enemy renewed its attacks, with only temporary success. An attack was launched on the same day against positions of the Guard Ersatz Division between the railway and the Essey–Flirey road; it failed, with heavy casualties.

On 21 January the *OHL* temporarily seconded the Bavarian Cavalry Division to Armee-Abteilung *Strantz* as an army reserve.

UNTIL THE SECOND HALF OF FEBRUARY, ARMEE-ABTEILUNG *FALKENHAUSEN*, commanded by General Baron von Falkenhausen (Chief of Staff Oberst Weidner), was only involved in minor combat activities. Repeated raids were encountered only in the outpost positions on its northern flank. On 27 January a French foray against XV Reserve Corps' 30th Reserve Division failed. Nevertheless, on 9 February at Ban-de-Sapt, both 30th Reserve Division and 39th Reserve Division (operating south of Lusse and belonging to the same corps) achieved success. Also, the subordinate Armee-Abteilung *Gaede*,[26] commanded by General der Infanterie Gaede (Chief of Staff Oberstleutnant Bronsart von Schellendorff), had to be supported at the beginning of January with the addition of a few battalions and a number of heavy batteries.

To put a halt to the continuous enemy forays against Armee-Abteilung *Gaede* at Cernay, the *OHL* brought up a combined infantry brigade (commanded by Generalleutnant Dallmer) with a strength of six battalions and three field batteries from First Army to make an attack of its own. At first the new Brigade *Dallmer* was part of Division *Fuchs*,[27] where it relieved the exhausted 29th Infantry Brigade. Meanwhile, Army Headquarters *Gaede* began to plan an attack that was intended to bring the heights west of Wattwiller–Steinbach into German hands. In preparation for this, the summits west and southwest of Rimbach–Zell were occupied on 4 January. However, an attempt to take the Vieil Armand[28] failed. Farther south, between 3 and 7 January the enemy continued its attacks. In the end, Steinbach remained in enemy hands. There could be no doubt that stronger German forces would be necessary to throw the enemy back into the mountains.

The operation near Wattwiller was launched on 18 January. In the meantime, Division *Fuchs* was ordered to capture the line Vieil Armand–Herrenfluh Ruins–Wolfskopf–Amselkopf (west of Steinbach). The attack began between 18 and

---

26 *On 30 December, Army Headquarters* Gaede *was detached from the acting headquarters of XIV Corps. General der Infanterie Gaede retained command of Armee-Abteilung* Gaede *and its control of the fortifications on the Rhine.*

27 Division *Fuchs* now consisted of the Staff of 16th Infantry Division, 29th Infantry Brigade, Brigade *Dallmer*, and 42nd Cavalry Brigade as well as the allocated light and heavy batteries, pioneers, signal groups, etc. See *DW* VI: 391.

28 *In German the peak is known as the Hartmannsweilerkopf.*

21 January with the capture of the Vieil Armand and the Hirzstein feature, situated to the south. In subsequent days, the Vieil Armand was held against fierce, prepared French counterattacks. On 23 January the main attack near Wattwiller began, but after initial success it bogged down in front of the strong French fortifications.

During January, Armee-Abteilung *Gaede* received a few mountain units from the *OHL*, including 8th Reserve Jäger battalion. Between 21 and 24 January the newly activated 8th Bavarian Reserve Division, which was to be utilized in offensive operations together with Division *Fuchs*, also arrived. Armee-Abteilung *Gaede*'s forces were restructured on 29 January.[29] Three reinforced *Landwehr* brigades (only the 51st remained independent for the time being) served as the nuclei of 6th Bavarian, 7th Württemberg, and 8th Landwehr Divisions.

The unexpected resistance faced by Division *Fuchs* in the struggle for Wattwiller revived a plan that had first been considered at Army Headquarters *Gaede*, which was to attack not at Wattwiller but rather to push into the Thann Valley on the line Grand Ballon[30]–Sudelkopf–Molkenrain. Such a combined attack by Division *Fuchs* and Bavarian 8th Reserve Division conformed to the general intentions of the *OHL*. However, this plan had to be abandoned when Bavarian 8th Reserve Division reported that it would not be operational until the middle of February. As a result, Army Headquarters *Gaede* reverted to its former limited objective, ordering Generalleutnant Fuchs to continue the operation aimed at capturing the line Herrenfluh–Wolfskopf–Amselkopf. On 4 February, 29th Infantry Brigade attacked with limited success west of Wattwiller–Uffholtz.

At the beginning of February, Army Headquarters *Gaede* decided to deploy Bavarian 8th Reserve Division (which became operational in the middle of the month) for mopping-up operations in the Munster and Guebwiller Valleys. No major battles had taken place north of the Grand Ballon for months. There the enemy was relatively weak; only a few mountain passes usable in winter were at its disposal. The attack began on 8 February with the advance of 51st Landwehr Brigade, which began to push its right flank ahead through the Lauch Valley. On 13 and 14 February, elements of the brigade, reinforced by the Bavarian Reserve Regiment, took the line Le Hilsenfirst-Sengern in light combat. With that, the brigade's rear was secured, thus facilitating Bavarian 8th Reserve Division's main encircling attack on the strong French positions west of Munster.

---

29 On 24 January, Army Headquarters *Gaede* moved from Freiburg to the Château de Hombourg, 10 kilometres east of the town of Mulhouse.

30 *In German the peak is known as Großer Belchen—the apex of the Vosges Mountains.*

The French and British High Commands at the Beginning of the Year

The enemy offensive that Joffre had launched at the end of 1914[31] in the Artois had to be quickly abandoned on 20 December owing to strong German resistance, the weather, and the condition of the ground.[32] By the end of the year, no appreciable successes had been achieved in the Champagne and expectations for the continuation of the offensive were unfavourable. The replacement units and depots were barely sufficient to replace the losses incurred. The 1915 age group of recruits, which had been called up in 1914, were in training and would not be ready for operations prior to 1 April, while only minor new deployments from Africa could be expected. Thus, the units required for an offensive could only be obtained by withdrawals from quiet fronts. Because the Russians threatened to go over to static warfare unless the Germans were tied up by operations on the Western Front, the general situation forced a continuation of the offensive.[33]

General Joffre therefore decided to continue the offensive in the Champagne with Fourth Army and to tie up the enemy with minor operations on the rest of the front; otherwise, he planned to rest the troops if possible. Accordingly, Fourth Army was reinforced by I Corps on 8 January, followed by 8th Cavalry Division,[34] while IV Corps, which had arrived in an area east of Châlons-sur-Marne on 24 December 1914, was retained as a reserve; for the time being it was placed at the disposal of the Supreme Command.

In order to relieve Fourth Army Headquarters of additional responsibilities, Joffre ordered the Argonne Sector, between the Aire and the Aisne on the army's right flank, transferred to Third Army. Meanwhile, II Corps, which was deployed there, was withdrawn and kept at the disposal of the Army High Command. In return, Third Army relinquished the sector north of Verdun between St. Mihiel and the Meuse to First Army. This restructuring had the advantage of placing the defence of the Meuse Heights south of Verdun into one set of hands. As had been done with Provisional Army Group *North* (under Foch), which had already been created on the front's left flank, on 5 January 1915 Provisional Army Group East

---

31 *In early December 1914, Joffre had decided on a two-pronged offensive in the Artois and the Champagne. The attacks in the Artois were directed at Vimy Ridge, north of Arras. The ridge was one of the most important tactical features in the northern part of the Western Front as it commanded the Douai Plain and the important coalfields of Lens. See DW* VI: 384.

32 See ibid.

33 See *DW* VI: 383 and 392. *The French situation at the beginning of 1915 is described in* French Official History, II: 328–64.

34 It arrived on foot from French Third Army and its elements were committed to French XII Corps on 12 January.

was created on the right and placed under the command of General Dubail.[35] The Supreme Commander reserved control of Second, Fourth, Fifth, and Sixth Armies, which were all deployed in the centre of the front.

On 27 December 1914, Joffre had an extensive meeting with Field Marshal Sir John French, Commander of the British Expeditionary Force (BEF), at the French *Grand Quartier Général* (GQG) in Chantilly. In response to the British government's question about whether the Germans could strike a decisive blow in the East, which would then allow them to renew the offensive in Flanders, Joffre replied that he did not regard the situation in the East as being that serious and that the French General Staff was prepared for every eventuality. He was certain that the war's outcome would be decided in the West, and he considered events in all other theatres to be of lesser significance.[36]

In a secret dispatch of 19 January,[37] Joffre informed the army commanders about the state of affairs and his intentions. He pointed out that, so far, the offensive in the Champagne had not yielded a decisive success, nor had peripheral operations shown any appreciable results. The Germans, he warned, would potentially be able to return several corps from Russia to the West in the near future and were also in the process of activating several new corps in Germany. Nevertheless, the French leadership intended to continue the offensive in the Champagne to the desired end. Joffre's dispatch then delineated his plans: Army Group *East* was to continue its operations in the Vosges. With a view toward a major offensive on the Woëvre Plain, First Army was to continue its attacks against both flanks of the German St. Mihiel positions. In order to relieve Fourth Army, Third Army was to resume its forays in a northerly direction as soon as the condition of the troops and the reinforcement situation in its sector permitted. Fourth Army was to continue its offensive as energetically as possible and could expect further support in the event of success. Tenth Army was to make all preparations for the resumption of its postponed offensive. Using saps and mines, its units were to work themselves closer to the enemy; the Supreme Command would give the

---

35 The Army Group consisted of Army Detachment *Vosges* and the Two Group Reserve Divisions, as well as the First and Second Armies. Their sector extended from the Swiss Border to the western slope of the Argonne. *See the French Official History*, II: 408–9.

36 *On Anglo-French Strategy in 1915, see* David Dutton, *The Politics of Diplomacy: Britain and France in the Balkans in the First World War* (New York: Tauris, 1998); Elizabeth Greenhalgh, *Victory through Coalition: Britain and France during the First World War* (Cambridge: Cambridge University Press, 2006); and William Philpott, *Anglo-French Relations and Strategy on the Western Front* (New York: St. Martin's, 1996). *On French strategy and politics, see* Jere Clemens King, *Generals and Politicians: Conflict between France's High Command, Parliament, and Government, 1914–1918* (Berkeley: University of California Press, 1951).

37 Note sur la situation générale à la date du 19 janvier.

order for the resumption of the offensive as soon as circumstances permitted. On the army's far left flank, near Nieuport, the attack was to be continued as a diversionary manoeuvre.[38] All other armies[39] were to reinforce their front lines and their secondary lines; and, while providing as much rest as possible for the troops, they were also to form reserves that could be deployed to exploit a success in the Champagne or for the execution of other operations. Overall, three infantry divisions and one cavalry division from Army Group *East*; five and a half infantry divisions, two territorial divisions, and three cavalry divisions from the centre; and two infantry divisions, two territorial divisions, and three cavalry divisions from Army Group *North*, were to be detached and placed at the disposal of the Supreme Commander. In the event of a dire emergency—and only if operations on their respective fronts were discontinued—an infantry and a cavalry division from Army Group *East*, I Corps from Fourth Army, and one infantry division from Army Group *North* could be made available. In that case, the total strength of all available forces would amount to fourteen and a half infantry, four territorial, and eight cavalry divisions. Should British reinforcements arrive from the homeland to relieve French forces on their northern flank—except for the British 28th Infantry Division—then XX Corps and IX Corps as well as the remainder of 87th and 89th Territorial Divisions would also become available. The reserves would be designated as army group reserves, but in reality they were at the disposition of the High Command and would generally be made available evenly behind the front between Bar-le-Duc and the Channel Coast. The sector between Oulchy-le-Château and Montdidier, which especially had to be protected at all times, constantly required specific attention. Further planning for major operations included a resumption of Tenth Army's offensive in conjunction with the British right flank as well as First Army's concentric attack on the Woëvre Plain. In the event of a renewed German attack in strength, transportation arrangements would have to be determined with precision in order to bring the army group reserves up to any place along the front.

In a communication to the British Supreme Commander on the same day, 19 January, Joffre placed special emphasis on an expected German offensive. The Franco-British front, he wrote, had to be fully secured against such an attack. He pointed out that an enemy breakthrough at Montdidier would have the most serious consequences and that in order to be protected from such an attack, as well as to go over to the offensive, army reserves were required. These reserves could only come from the northern flank just as soon as French forces were replaced there

---

38 The attack at Nieuport concluded on 28 December 1914, with the occupation of St. Georges. See *DW* VI: 387. *See also* French Official History, II: 264–73.

39 Including Fifth, Sixth, and Second Armies.

by British forces. Joffre stressed that considering the German threat, this replacement had to take place quickly. This in turn meant that the offensive on
Ostende–Zeebrugge, which in all likelihood would be effective, had to be postponed
for the time being.

Despite the French Supreme Commander's resistance, Field Marshal Sir John
French would not give up the December 1914 plan to attack Ostende–Zeebrugge
along the Channel Coast. This attack was to be launched in conjunction with elements of the British fleet. The sinking of the British battleship *Formidable* in the
Channel by a German submarine on 1 January 1915 had caused the First Lord of
the Admiralty, Sir Winston Churchill, to send a telegram to Lord Kitchener, which
he was to pass on to Field Marshal French. In that telegram, Churchill pointed to
the great danger that the German occupation of Zeebrugge posed to British troop
transports crossing the Channel, a threat that would only be terminated after the
Germans had been driven off the Flanders coast. The British Commander-in-
Chief, who was of the same opinion, believed he could successfully conclude the
operation provided that Great Britain was able to send him fifty territorial battalions, a number of heavy guns, and an adequate supply of field and heavy ammunition. However, the British Cabinet did not believe the operation to be practical.
In the beginning of 1915 there was disagreement within the British government as
to how operations were to be continued. At the turn of the year, a variety of proposals were made by influential personalities, all of them based on the premise that
decisive operations on the Western Front could no longer be expected, and that
this required the commencement of new operations in other theatres of war.[40]

On 29 December 1914, Churchill presented Prime Minister Asquith with a
plan that proposed a naval thrust into the North and Baltic Seas. After one of the
Frisian Islands[41] was taken by force, the German fleet was to be trapped in the
Bay of Heligoland, the Kaiser Wilhelm Channel[42] was to be blocked, and Den-
mark was to be forced into joining the war by way of a landing on the coast of
Schleswig-Holstein. Once the Baltic was open to the British fleet, a connection
could be established with the Russians that would enable them to land on Germany's northern coast with the help of the British Navy. The First Sea Lord, Lord

---

40 *For a good overview of the British strategic debate in 1914–15, see* David R. Woodward, *Lloyd
George and the Generals* (London: Frank Cass, 2004), 15–73. See also David French, *British Eco-
nomic and Strategic Planning, 1905–1915* (London: Routledge, 2006); idem, *British Strategy
and War Aims, 1914–1916* (Oxford: Oxford University Press, 1995); John Gooch, *The Plans of
War: The General Staff and British Military Strategy, 1900–1916* (London: Routledge and Kegan
Paul, 1974); and Paul Guinn, *British Strategy and Politics, 1914–1918* (Oxford: Clarendon, 1965).

41 The island under primary consideration was Borkum in the North Sea, due north of the
Netherlands.

42 *Now the North Sea Channel.*

Fisher, wholeheartedly agreed with the proposal where it concerned advancing against the German Navy. Sir John French, whose opinion had been requested on 3 January 1915, responded that operations in other theatres of war would be extremely difficult, whereas a penetration of the German Western Front was entirely possible and was only a question of munitions. His proposed attack on the Channel Coast promised success, and until a penetration on the Western Front was proven to be impossible, he argued that the initiation of new operations elsewhere should be out of the question.

After receiving the communication from Joffre on 19 January, Field Marshal French visited the French Supreme Commander in Chantilly one more time on 21 January in order to again present his plan for attacking the Belgian coast. However, he allowed himself to be persuaded otherwise. In the presence of Foch, both commanders came to an agreement. Sir John declared that he was prepared to replace French IX Corps, and afterwards XX Corps, as soon as reinforcements arrived from England, which were expected in the beginning of March. After that, the French were to release British I Corps. Before the gradual withdrawal of elements of IX Corps, the British were to provide Foch with cavalry; Joffre was to leave equally strong forces on the British left flank in the sector presently occupied by XX Corps.[43]

THE FIGHTING ON THE WESTERN FRONT REMAINED QUIET UNTIL THE END OF January. As Joffre had expressly ordered, only the French offensive in the Champagne was continued, with the deployment of further elements from I Corps. By the end of the month, except for negligible gains at Massiges and Beauséjour, no significant successes had been achieved. Fighting continued in the Vosges, at Bois-le-Prêtre, on the Meuse Heights south of Verdun, and in the Argonne, where Third Army's left flank got into a dangerous situation.

On 25 January a German thrust was launched toward the southern flank of the BEF sector on both sides of La Bassée Canal, which led to the loss of a few trenches before the attack was repulsed. In the middle of January, 28th Infantry Division arrived behind the BEF, but it would not be deployed until the end of the month.[44]

There were no significant combat operations on the Belgian Front.

---

43 Meeting at Chantilly of 21 January 1915.
44 On 25 January 1915, Lieutenant General William Robertson replaced Lieutenant General Archibald Murray as Chief of Staff of the British Expeditionary Force.

IN THE BEGINNING OF FEBRUARY, AFTER CONSIDERING THE SITUATION ON THE
Russian Front, Joffre did not rule out the possibility that the Germans would shift
the emphasis of their war effort to the East. Having already ordered an offensive
in the Champagne, he decided to utilize his numerical superiority (la supérior-
ité numérique actuelle) on the Western Front to mount another offensive in the
Artois designed to cut off the German defensive salient located in between. To
this end, he planned for Tenth Army to attack in the Artois in order to take the
commanding heights at Vimy, Lens, and Pont à Vendin. At the same time, an
attack out of Arras would be made. The reinforcements necessary for these operations were to be obtained by extracting the French corps located north of the
British Expeditionary Force. However, considerable time was to pass until then;
for the immediate future, only the offensive in the Champagne could be executed.

The Apex of the Winter Battle in the Champagne from
the Middle of February to the Middle of March

French Intentions in the Champagne

Joffre ordered that the offensive be resumed on 19 January; however the Commander of Fourth Army insisted that any such a resumption must wait for the
return of dry weather.[45] Because the army was not ready for a major offensive, he
demanded fourteen days' preparation time. By economizing on the rest of the
front, it was possible to supply a considerable amount of munitions for the offensive. In particular, the heavy artillery was reinforced: by 10 February a total of 837
guns—including 109 with a calibre larger than 10 cm—had been made available.[46]
The strength of the air forces had been increased to five squadrons; on the other
hand, the infantry—which had been under fire since the beginning of the battles
in the Champagne—had suffered severely. The trenches were badly damaged,
material to fortify the positions was insufficient, and the ground was "a sea of
mud." The lines of communication behind the front were barely passable.

The French army commander intended to launch methodical attacks to create several breaches in the German front, which would then be expanded into a
larger breakthrough. However, the Supreme Commander demanded that preparation time for the attack be shortened and that a quick, surprise artillery bombardment be followed by a forceful attack. The main thrust was to be made by I
and XVII Corps across an 8 kilometre front between Beauséjour Farm and the

---

45 *Fourth Army was commanded by General Fernand de Langle de Cary until 11 December 1915.*
46 *On the reorganization of the French artillery, see* French Official History, II: 391–93.

The Winter Battle in the Champagne
The Situation between Perthes and Beauséjour Farm on 24 February 1915

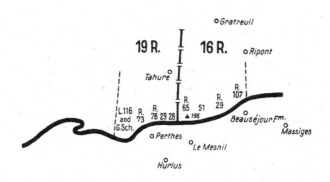

Sketch 5

The Winter Battle in the Champagne
The Situation on 11 March 1915

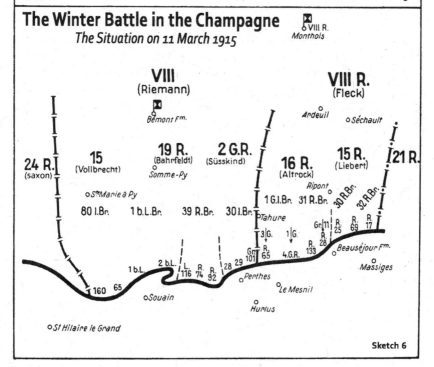

Sketch 6

forest west of Perthes; meanwhile, 60th Reserve Division was to make a second-ary attack east of Souain. The offensive was scheduled to begin on 6 February; how-ever, the weather necessitated another postponement. On 8 February the Supreme Commander made one division available from II Corps as reinforcements; on 12 February, he added I Cavalry Corps.

The remainder of the French armies in the centre received orders to divert the enemy's attention by increasing their artillery activity; at the same time, Third Army was to attack in and east of the Argonne as soon as it was able. Fifth Army was to be ready to advance in the event of success.

On 16 February, Fourth Army launched its attack, which made a recent com-munication from the Russian High Command redundant. The communiqué, sent to Joffre through diplomatic channels, had demanded the opening of a new offensive to relieve pressure on the East—a demand precipitated by the Russians' severe defeat on the Masurian Front. The new offensive meant that no further actions were required in this regard.

The German Defence

On 14 February at 17:40 the following report from the OHL arrived at Third Army Headquarters[47] in Vouziers: "A general French offensive is planned for 15 Febru-ary. The public is fasting and praying for it in the French churches." However, 15 February passed with remarkable quiet. But it was the calm before the storm.

On Tuesday, 16 February, at 08:00, the first wave of large-scale attacks marked the beginning of the French winter offensive in the Champagne. Furious artillery fire rained down between Souain and Beauséjour Farm on the positions of VIII Corps and VIII Reserve Corps. The weather was bleak and stormy, rendering any air reconnaissance impossible. The artillery fire wandered from east to west, into the adjoining divisional sectors, but gradually weakened in both directions. It lasted approximately two hours with unrelenting vehemence and ground the remaining German wire and trenches to pieces. Casualties were considerable. At about 10:00 the barrage was abruptly directed onto the rear trenches, lines of communication, and reserve billets. Simultaneously, French I and XVII Corps began their attack against 19th and 16th Reserve Divisions.

On the front of 19th Reserve Division, commanded by General der Infanterie von Bahrfeldt, the enemy was able to penetrate the trenches, which had been breached by mines. By evening, however, reserve forces had launched organized

---

47 At Third Army Headquarters, Generalleutnant Ritter von Hoehn had replaced Generalma-jor von Hoeppner as Chief of Staff.

counterattacks that had almost entirely cleaned out the sector of the eastern infantry brigade. West of Perthes, it was impossible to wrest all of the captured trenches from the French despite the utmost valour of the infantry; there, bitter close combat lasted for three days and three nights without interruption. General der Infanterie Riemann, in command of VIII Corps, initially made two infantry regiments and a few batteries and battalions of 15th Infantry Division available to 19th Reserve Division and requested the immediate transfer of additional reinforcements from army headquarters. He summarized his overall impression of the offensive by saying that the enemy's forays had far exceeded all previous attacks in terms of extent and ferocity and that the enemy artillery had increased exponentially.

In 16th Reserve Division's sector, which since 2 January had been commanded by Generalmajor von Altrock, the French attacks were directed primarily against the division's centre and left flank. With their first push, the enemy broke through in a number of places, but again all the penetrations could be cleaned up except for a French pocket in the centre of the division's sector. Captured French prisoners reported that all of I Corps was ready for the attack and that strong reserves were still standing by south of the Ruisseau de Marson. That evening, VIII Reserve Corps Headquarters ordered that two reserve infantry regiments staged in rest areas be prepared to move out on 17 February at 07:00. Generalleutnant Fleck, the commanding general of VIII Reserve Corps, described the situation as serious and requested reinforcements.

In response, the *OHL* made larger amounts of munitions available to Third Army; it also, from Fifth Army, freed up an infantry brigade with a field artillery detachment.[48] Third Army Headquarters ordered XII Reserve Corps to threaten the enemy with an attack on 17 February in order to draw its forces away from VIII Corps. Meanwhile, VI Corps was to place an infantry regiment at the disposal of Third Army, and composite Cavalry Division *Count Lippe* was prepared for deployment around St. Etienne à Arnes.

On 17 February, French attempts to penetrate from an approximate line west of Perthes-lès-Hurlus to Beauséjour Farm continued with unabated ferocity. In most cases it was possible to repel them; only on the Arbre Hill (Hill 193) west of Perthes did further portions of the trenches fall into their hands.

In consideration of the critical situation, the Army Commander, General der Kavallerie von Einem (also known as Rothmaler), concentrated all available

---

48   This brigade was composed of the staff of 38th Infantry Brigade with 144th Infantry Regiment and a second composite infantry regiment, as well as one detachment of 20th Reserve Field Artillery Regiment.

reserves behind the threatened front. In the meantime, the newly arrived 38th Reserve Brigade was made available to VIII Corps between Somme Py and Tahure while an infantry regiment from VI Corps was transferred via rail to VIII Corps at St. Marie à Py. The XII Reserve Corps had to relinquish a reserve infantry regiment and heavy artillery as well. In the afternoon the *OHL* approved the exchange of the badly mauled 39th Reserve Infantry Brigade for X Reserve Corps' 37th Reserve Infantry Brigade, which was coming up from Seventh Army.

The VIII Corps Headquarters deployed both its newly received regiments southeast of St. Marie à Py. In the event of an enemy breakthrough, headquarters intended to use these regiments as an attack formation in conjunction with 38th Reserve Infantry Brigade, which was located west of Butte de Tahure.

On 18 February, French efforts across from 16th Reserve Division weakened, because on the previous day the enemy had suffered a particularly large number of men killed, wounded, and taken prisoner.

The VIII Corps could not, however, discern a reduction in the enemy's efforts. Consequently, a German attack was ordered against the "Arbre Position" west of Perthes-lès-Hurlus at 07:00, but it collided with a French attack and therefore was unable to attain its objective. Around 10:00 the intense artillery fire resumed, and from then until 17:00, six attacks were launched against 19th Reserve Division's centre and left flank, all of which were repulsed, resulting in heavy French casualties. General Riemann expected a continuation of the enemy attacks as, according to prisoner statements, behind French I and XVII Corps not only IV Corps but also II Corps stood at the ready.

After detraining in Challerange during the night of 17 and 18 February, 37th Reserve Infantry Brigade was transferred to VIII Corps' forest encampment northwest of Tahure. The *OHL* ordered 39th Reserve Infantry Brigade to remain in the Third Army's sector after it had been released from the front.

On 19 February the enemy's attempts to achieve a breakthrough on Third Army's left flank were renewed with full force.

During the night of 18 and 19 February, despite considerable difficulties, fresh units relieved the badly mauled infantry on VIII Corps' front. The enemy then launched repeated attacks in strength on both sides of Perthes-lès-Hurlus starting at 09:30; these were repulsed through the exemplary coordination of infantry and artillery. In the few places where the enemy had breached the line, close combat continued through the night.

From 16:00, the enemy attacked in waves against the positions of 16th Reserve Division. Alarming reports from VIII Reserve Corps reached Third Army Headquarters: the French had broken through, a reserve regiment was in retreat, and the howitzer ammunition had been expended. In response, 38th Reserve Infantry

Brigade was made available to VIII Reserve Corps at around 17:00, but by then 16th Reserve Division no longer required its support. The French attack had stalled on both flanks in the face of the German defensive barrage, and a Rhenish Reserve Regiment, which had been pushed back significantly southwest of Ripont, was able to stop the enemy on its own. Generalmajor von Altrock was provided with a further reserve regiment and a reserve *Ersatz* regiment for support. However, in view of the dangerous situation, Third Army Headquarters did not consider these reserves to be sufficient. Therefore, it requested and received command over three Fifth Army battalions deployed near Bouconville and ordered XII Reserve Corps to concentrate all available troops in St. Souplet. The XII Reserve Corps Headquarters believed that the release of additional forces was risky as the enemy had attempted to launch an attack against the Aubérive position in the afternoon. Even though the attack had failed, the strong artillery bombardment that continued to fall in 24th Reserve Division's sector indicated that further attacks were possible.

According to the statements of prisoners taken during the four days of fighting, it had been French I and XVII Corps that attacked on 16 and 17 February, with elements of IV Corps participating in the fighting on 18 and 19 February. Behind them, II Corps[49] also stood at the ready.

During the days that followed, the conviction hardened at Third Army Headquarters that the "enemy attacks had only temporarily been suspended while the build-up of enemy forces continued." On the afternoon of 20 February, Sixth Army's 1st Guard Infantry Division arrived in Third Army's sector. Because of this increase in strength, Third Army's left flank appeared to be sufficiently protected against further attacks.

On 22 February, French offensive activities flared up again, but VIII Corps Headquarters did not attribute any significance to these limited thrusts and instead leaned toward the opinion that the enemy was merely attempting to conceal the failure of its primary offensive. The commanding general of VIII Reserve Corps had arrived at a similar appraisal of the situation. It is probable that this impression led to the early partial release of the reserves that had assembled behind Third Army's left flank on 22 February.[50]

The continued fighting and the nerve-racking bombardment had badly sapped the strength of the soldiers. In some areas the combat and communication trenches

---

49 Since 8 February, II Corps' 3rd Infantry Division had been attached to Fourth Army. The remaining units and corps headquarters were put at the disposal of the army on 20 February.

50 The 38th Reserve Infantry Brigade was returned to Fifth Army, 73rd Fusilier Regiment and the artillery to Seventh Army. On 24 February, 73rd Fusilier Regiment had to be requested again.

had been almost levelled, the wire mostly wiped away. The dugouts, most of which had no protection against artillery fire, were already destroyed. The combat units had to make do with shelters of the simplest type and holes in the breastworks. Efforts to repair the destroyed trenches continued day and night. The enemy barrage did not pause even in the darkness, which impeded the movement of replacements and supplies as well as the repair of the trenches. Telephone land lines were shot up again and again; dispatch runners were often wounded or killed; and the first messenger dogs to arrive from the homeland were of limited effectiveness, especially under heavy fire. The weather was mostly bleary and rainy and often stormy. The defenders were freezing in their soaked, filthy uniforms and received mostly cold and stale food that had been carried to the front lines by ration carriers under perilous and difficult circumstances. In the inadequate shelters and muddy trenches, the soldiers were unable to get the sleep they desperately needed. Because of the considerable numbers of killed and wounded, the combat strength of the regiments had been reduced to half or less. Reserves were brought up to repair the rear trenches day and night. It was emphasized again that the front trenches were to be held, and retaken if lost.

After 22 February, Third Army Headquarters gained the impression that the enemy was growing weaker and was pulling the artillery back from its front. Then suddenly, on 23 February at around 15:00, heavy artillery fire commenced against both corps on the left flank. During the heavy fighting that ensued, the enemy artillery fire continued with unabated ferocity. On the other hand, the enemy was no longer making homogeneous infantry attacks across a broad front. Yet according to all observations and prisoner statements, these attacks were intended to be coherent, and the fact that they disintegrated into individual thrusts was mainly a result of the German field and heavy artillery. These enemy attacks were generally conducted in the afternoon and evening hours; this was probably in order to provide the infantry with more favourable conditions for holding the newly occupied trench sections with the aid of approaching darkness.

The German commanders had learned from the previous battles. The artillery entirely gave up on combatting the enemy artillery—a science that was especially uncertain in those days—and instead mostly limited itself to subjecting enemy trenches to heavy fire as soon as an attack seemed imminent. As a result, in many cases the enemy assault troops often did not even advance out of their trenches, or they evaded the German barrage by moving toward the rear. In order to assist in this defensive battle, batteries belonging to neighbouring sectors that were not under attack were frequently called upon to support the defence with flanking fire. From this defensive artillery activity developed what would come to be called "harassing fire" (*Störungsfeuer*), "annihilating fire" (*Vernichtungsfeuer*), and "curtain fire" (*Sperrfeuer*).[51] Individual German batteries and battery groups were deployed in advance positions, which benefited the defence and facilitated communication between infantry and artillery. In all other situations, where the topography or lack of visibility precluded direct observation, the frequent failure of the land telephone lines meant that reliable cooperation between infantry and artillery was based largely on specifically prearranged flare signals, which the combat troops used in order to request the commencement or discontinuation of supporting fire.

Countermeasures against bothersome batteries based on aircraft or balloon observation could take place only rarely, on the few clear and quiet days. Aerial photographs, whose technology had greatly advanced, began to provide a valuable supplement to written and oral reports. German artillery resources, however, were scarce. For example, during the French attacks in the middle of February only twenty-two field and ten heavy batteries, with just a single mortar battery among them, were available along VIII Corps' 13 kilometre front line. The firing of the artillery pieces was hampered in particular by the inferior quality of the makeshift (cast-iron) ammunition, which tended to scatter, burst in the barrel, and generally produce poor results.[52] Owing to equipment breakdowns and enemy fire, the number of operational guns varied considerably. In 19th Reserve Division's sector, at times only one-quarter of the field guns were operational. In early March the *OHL* again requested—in a secret communiqué—that ammunition be economized, especially that of the mortars. In contrast, it appeared that the French had access to inexhaustible supplies of ammunition. According to the calculations of German observers, the French had expended approximately 60,000 rounds prior to the offensive on 16 February around Perthes-lès-Hurlus in the sector of 38th Reserve Division alone. Even the arrival of the new *Minenwerfer* detachments provided only a minor increase in firepower as these weapons were also considerably short of ammunition.

---

51 Vernichtungsfeuer, *or annihilating fire, refers to indirect fire targeted deep into the enemy's rear areas of concentration, while* Sperrfeuer *has a more ambiguous meaning. It can refer to a generic barrage but can also describe a curtain of direct fire against targets immediately in front of the main line of resistance. See Robert Michael Citino,* The Path to Blitzkrieg: Doctrine and Training in the German Army, 1920–1939 *(London: Lynne Reinner, 1999), 19–20.*

52 *In the autumn and winter of 1914–15 the German army suffered a shell shortage. The crisis was made more acute by the British blockade, which created shortages of the raw materials necessary for the manufacture of shells. The initial solution was to produce shells from cast iron instead of brass or steel. These "makeshift" shells increased barrel wear and had a higher rate of failure. The first shipments to the front began in October 1914 but did not peak until months later. See Strachan,* The First World War: Volume I: To Arms, *1009–49; See also DW V: 561 and VI: 428–29.*

As of mid-February the main front in the offensive lay between Perthes-lès-Hurlus and Beauséjour Farm. By the end of February the focus of the offensive was on the area north of Le Mesnil; however, separate forays were made against the German position in the forest west of Perthes. Third Army's other divisional sectors remained almost entirely unaffected. Therefore, Third Army Headquarters was able to move stronger forces to the front that was under attack and to exchange fresh for exhausted troops. Additionally, neighbouring armies and the OHL provided assistance by transferring the necessary reserves.

Even in the beginning of March, despite mostly stormy weather, the enemy attacks on Third Army's front did not let up. They were directed with special emphasis against Hill 196 north of Le Mesnil on the right flank of VIII Reserve Corps, where Silesian, Rhenish, and Guard Troops (from 1st Guard Infantry Division) of Division *Hutier,* which had been deployed there since the end of February, repelled a number attacks in bitter fighting. Because of a lack of sufficient reserves even at this location, replacements—which were requested often and urgently—could only be approved after the soldiers were totally exhausted. Owing to the interspersed "French pockets," the incessant bombardment, and frequent rain showers, the combat and communications trenches became ever more dilapidated. However, the adverse weather conditions also hindered the attacking potential of the enemy, who was constantly trying to force a decisive success by deploying fresh troops.

Fresh *Landwehr* and *Landsturm* units were brought up to work on the defences, roads, and newly constructed transportation systems in the rear of both besieged corps. The German system of fortifications was deepened more and more. During the nights, tangential trenches (*Sehnengräben*), switch trenches (*Riegelgräben*), flanking trenches (*Flankierungsgräben*), and temporary rallying trenches (*durchlaufender Aufnahmegräben*)[53] with bombproof shelters were constructed. Because these works were vitally important, it was often unavoidable that newly relieved but exhausted soldiers were called on for assistance. The scattered villages in the rear were under almost daily long-range enemy fire, and in order to avoid unnecessary casualties, these villages had to be evacuated of their French inhabitants, who desperately clung to them.[54]

---

53 *The temporary rallying trench* (durchlaufender Aufnahmegraben*) was* different from the British concept of a "reserve" trench in that it was a liminal space—that is, a support trench designed to receive either retiring troops or advancing reserves but not a position to be permanently maintained.

54 *The German treatment of French and Belgian civilians in the First World War is a contentious subject. See* Margaret Lavinia Anderson, "A German Way of War?" *German History* 22, no. 2 (2004): 254–58; John N. Horne and Alan Kramer, *German Atrocities 1914: A History of Denial* (New Haven: Yale University Press, 2005); and Larry Zuckerman, *The Rape of Belgium: The Untold Story of World War I* (New York: New York University Press, 2004).

On his return from the Eastern Front on the evening of 3 March, General von Falkenhayn arrived at Third Army Headquarters in Vouziers for a conference. He emphasized that it was vital that Third Army not relinquish even the tiniest part of its positions. In this he was in complete agreement with Einem.

By the beginning of March, preparations for a French attack in the area of Souain had become apparent, which suggested that the offensive was to be expanded westward. The advance of saps and the increase in artillery fire were both aimed primarily at the "Balcony Position," Windmill Hill west of Souain, and "Bavarian Tip" east of Souain.

Indeed, the French intended to continue the offensive with renewed vigour by expanding it into the sector of Perthes-lès-Hurlus–Souain. The command of the area west of Perthes-lès-Hurlus was given to General Grossetti, who had taken over a newly formed group on 27 February.[55] The attacks near Souain commenced on 7 March. After temporarily breaching the German line, they were repelled thanks to the valour of the troops.

On 8 March, Einem requested and received the cooperation of Fifth Army Headquarters for an attack intended to relieve VIII Reserve Corps' left flank. Besides this, Fifth Army wanted to use a forward attack to put an end to the enemy's crushing superiority in materiel. Generalmajor von Altrock, commander of the embattled 16th Reserve Division, mentioned the following to an officer of the General Staff who had been dispatched to his sector from GHQ:

> The French are worn down, but that does not make a difference because they constantly commit new forces to the fight. A voluntary retreat and surrender of the German positions is out of the question as that would cause an increase in the enemy's confidence and would hurt the morale of our troops. So we must hold out and, therefore, it cannot be avoided that the French will gain an advantage in one place or the other. An offensive on our part with the available forces is out of the question; however, with sufficient reinforcements—and if we could manage to deal with the enemy's artillery— it would be possible.

It seems that in light of the failure of their attacks at this point in the battle, the French began to seek other ways to continue the offensive. General de Langle de Cary proposed a surprise attack by XVI Corps north of St. Hilaire-le-Grand; however, Joffre decided to continue the offensive with fresh forces at Le Mesnil. He ordered that command be given to General Grossetti, who in addition to XVI

---

55 The French XII and XVI Corps and 60th Infantry Division. In the French Army the differentiation between infantry and reserve divisions was eliminated as of 19 February. *See French Official History* II: 384–87.

Corps (31st, 32nd, and 48th Infantry Divisions) was given elements of I and II Corps as well as all the artillery deployed in the sector. The commencement of the offensive was set for 12 March at the latest.

AROUND THE MIDDLE OF MARCH, THE FRENCH OFFENSIVES BEGAN AGAIN. GIVEN the deployment of four fresh regiments on 12 March, Generalleutnant Fleck, commanding VIII Reserve Corps, despite the precarious situation decided not to limit himself to defensive operations; instead he ordered the disruption of the enemy's offensive activities and the systematic mopping up of all remaining "French pockets."

On 13 March the enemy launched numerous extended attacks against VIII Corps' front—which on 10 March had been divided into three divisional sectors—as well as on the right flank of VIII Reserve Corps. Both attacks were repelled.[56] Army headquarters assumed that five and a half enemy corps were involved in the attack.[57] The primary thrust continued to be against the heights north of Le Mesnil, where the bodies of fallen soldiers accumulated in front of and within the shot-up German positions. Most of the fallen could not be recovered or buried.

On 16 March the main offensive began at 04:45 with a failed enemy foray against Hill 196 north of Le Mesnil. During the day, the areas surrounding both Rhenish corps' headquarters were subjected to strong artillery fire.

In the command area of Generals von Bahrfeldt and Baron von Süßkind (19th Reserve and 2nd Guard Reserve Divisions respectively), the Hanoveranians and Rhinelanders defended themselves in the afternoon on both sides of Perthes-lès-Hurlus against strong enemy attacks. The enemy was able to hold on in just one of the breaches, on VIII Corps' left flank.

The heaviest attacks were again directed against the right flank of VIII Reserve Corps. There, beginning at 09:25, large numbers of assault troops were observed massing ahead of the front; these were disrupted as much as possible with an artillery bombardment. However, German countermeasures were too weak to prevent a massed attack by the Turcos,[58] which followed a fierce barrage at 14:00.

---

56   The 15th Infantry Division, 19th Reserve Division, and 2nd Guard Reserve Division had been deployed in the meantime.

57   In fact, French 60th Infantry Division, French XVII Corps (with four divisions), and XVI Corps (with four divisions) were located there.

58   "Turcos" (German: Turkos) *was the nickname given to French colonial infantry from Algeria during the Crimean War. In the French Army they were also known as Tirailleurs Algériens. Though the term "Turcos" was used by the British as well, "Zouave" is often used interchangeably, though incorrectly, in English.*

Nevertheless, the attack collapsed in the face of German defensive fire. At 17:30 the soldiers of 1st Guard Infantry Brigade—which had been subordinated to 16th Reserve Division—fired flares to request the strongest possible artillery support. Soon afterwards the neighbouring 2nd Guard Reserve Division reported that according to information received by an artillery observer, French skirmish lines had reached Hill 196. Generalmajor von Altrock immediately dispatched all available reserve battalions to his threatened right flank. Not until 19:40 did he receive more specific information from the front line, which informed him that his right flank had been enveloped and pushed back to the Perthes–Cernay road.

In the meantime, army headquarters had dispatched an infantry battalion via rail to Manre for support, and VIII Reserve Corps Headquarters had made a reserve regiment available to 16th Reserve Division and agreed to mount a prepared counterattack.

BETWEEN 17 AND 19 MARCH, THE BITTER FIGHTING FOR THE HEIGHTS NORTH OF Le Mesnil continued in overcast weather that impeded all observation. The counterattack launched by 16th Reserve Division on 17 March at 04:45 failed because the period allotted for preparation had been too short. French attack preparations and the increased employment of trench mortars led VIII Corps Headquarters to believe that new attacks were imminent. The VIII Reserve Corps saw the situation the same way. On 17 March, 56th Infantry Division (112th Infantry Brigade), armed with Russian rifles, arrived at the army's rear in OHL reserve. On the evening of the same day, an order from Third Army demanded that the lost territory around Hill 196 be recaptured—this time after "thorough preparation." Generalleutnant Fleck gave command of the attack to Generalmajor von Altrock, and by 18 March four infantry battalions had been staged behind 16th Reserve Division. The attack was planned for 19 March at 19:10 and was to be preceded by a ten-minute artillery bombardment. The enemy, however, made note of the preparations for the attack and brought up more and more infantry to the forward trenches while covering the German units with artillery and flanking machine-gun fire. Indeed, the German soldiers who launched the attack came to believe that the enemy itself was about to attack, for their own broke down on the French wire before it even reached the enemy's heavily manned trenches. Likewise, an infantry regiment from VIII Corps attacking to the west suffered such severe casualties that it was almost unable to move forward. A Saxon reserve regiment, however, was able to take a French trench south of Ripont, where it captured 300 prisoners from XVI Corps. This regiment did not owe its success to a massed attack, but rather to well-led, tough bombers. While throwing their grenades, these troops, advancing from traverse to traverse in the remnants of the approach and fire trenches, and attacking from both sides as well as from the front, took the remaining pockets of French troops. The enemy was pushed into a corner and was compelled to surrender or flee.

In the last third of March the winter campaign slowly abated. As soon as the German commanders noted the easing of enemy pressure, they switched to the offence. On 20 March, Army Headquarters ordered the erasure of the French pockets on VIII Corps's left flank and VIII Reserve Corps' right flank.

On 24 March, Third Army received an order from the *OHL* that transferred 56th Infantry Division to VIII Reserve Corps; at the same time, VIII Corps (including Bavarian 1st Landwehr Brigade and a Hessian Landwehr Regiment) was to be replaced by 50th and 54th Infantry Divisions under the command of X Reserve Corps Headquarters. It was also announced that 4th Ersatz Division would arrive later from Flanders. Furthermore, 1st Guard Infantry Division was ordered to assemble on 28 March along the Amagne–Mohon railway to be transported elsewhere. On 1 April a further directive from the *OHL* was received that ordered the extraction of X Corps (from the left flank of Seventh Army) and a consequent expansion of Third Army's sector to the west—a task for which 117th Infantry Division was attached.

In the meantime, Joffre had ordered the cessation of the French offensive on 17 March, although attacks would continue for a number of days. On the German side, this change in the intentions of the French was not immediately recognized. At the end of March the higher local commands, wanting to be prepared for further attacks, warned the *OHL* against the premature removal of the reserves it had made available. Not until 30 March did aerial reconnaissance clarify the situation for VIII Reserve Corps. On the first nocturnal reconnaissance flight, heavy rail traffic in the area of Suippes–Ste Ménehould was noticed, which was interpreted to mean that the enemy was removing its forces. This dispelled all doubts: the winter campaign in the Champagne was over.

The total losses of the winter campaign in the area of Third Army were assessed at approximately 1,100 officers and 45,000 men. The French losses were estimated to be 240,000 men.

IN RETROSPECT, THE WINTER CAMPAIGN IN THE CHAMPAGNE WAS AN ALMOST four-month bitter struggle by the French to achieve a breakthrough in the direction of Attigny. The first attack of 20 December 1914—and the subsequent attacks, which accelerated in January—were followed by offensive waves in mid-February and mid-March. In the weeks before and in between, the defenders were hardly allowed a day of rest. They were covered with a hail of iron, their trenches were blown up, and minor offensive thrusts were made along a narrow sector of the front at any time of the day or night. On this battle front, which consisted of the sectors defended by VIII Corps and VIII Reserve Corps, the almost uninterrupted combat, which was intended to achieve a breakthrough, served only to slowly plough the German positions into the ground and put the defenders' endurance to a harsh test. The defenders threw back the first major breakthrough attempt by the French. The only successes the enemy had to show for its efforts were insignificant territorial gains between Perthes-lès-Hurlus and Beauséjour Farm.

Owing to the deployment of its reserves in the East, the *OHL* was unable to respond to the threatened French breakthrough in the Champagne with a major counteroffensive. The local commands were unable to provide effective support to the sectors being attacked from their own strengths and were further limited by the *OHL*'s orders to economize on the already sparse supplies, especially ammunition. It was a discouraging time characterized by makeshift measures. Army and corps headquarters were constantly striving to bring relief through diversionary manoeuvres and minor forays. The thrust at Massiges on 3 February worked and brought temporary relief; otherwise, the planned operations did not get off the ground because they were thwarted by enemy attacks, or they failed because of the lack of war materiel. As to the enemy's intentions, the Germans naturally had to grope about in the dark. Following the major attacks in February, the commanders initially believed that the French attempts at a breakthrough had come to an end; then, at the end of March, they doubted for quite some time that the end had been reached. In any case, the danger threatening the German Western Front had been recognized in time, and both the commanders and the troops had exerted all their strength to repel the attacks. The fact that they managed this by conducting a tenacious, grinding defensive battle against vastly superior forces, and despite heavy losses, indicates that the winter campaign in the Champagne was one of the more remarkable feats of German arms on the Western Front.

Operations on the Remainder of the Western Front from the Middle of February to the Middle of March

In the beginning of February, Fourth Army received a newly developed artillery projectile (15 cm shell 12 T) filled with a chemical agent to irritate the eyes. A few days later another chemical weapon arrived: chlorine gas. It was intended that the gas be blown out of the front trenches during favourable weather, thus forcing the enemy to vacate its positions. Fourth Army Headquarters considered the

The Battle for the Combres Heights, February–April 1915

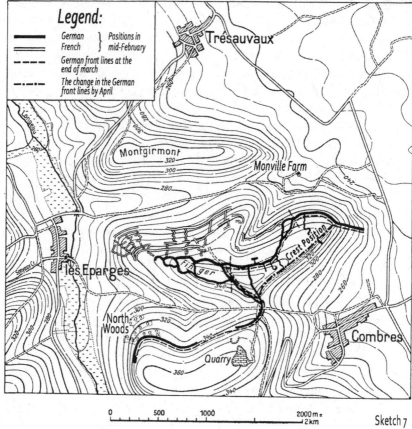

Legend:

▬▬▬ German	Positions in
▬▬▬ French	mid-February
▬ ▬ ▬	German front lines at the end of march
▬ ∙ ▬ ∙ ▬	The change in the German front lines by April

Trésauvaux

Montgirmont
320
300

Monville Farm

280

Crest Position

les Éparges

finger
340
280
260

North Woods
300
320

342

Combres

Quarry
360

340

| 0 | 500 | 1000 | 2000 m = 2 km |

Sketch 7

front-line positions northwest of Gheluvelt suitable for such an experiment. The technical leadership for the preparations was in the hands of Privy Councillor Dr. Haber, the Director of the Kaiser Wilhelm Institute for Physical and Electro Chemistry and the scientist behind the new weapon, and Oberst Peterson, the commander of the newly formed gas units. In the middle of February the plan took shape and the required preparations were initiated. It was intended to launch the attack in the sectors of 54th Reserve and 39th Infantry Divisions at the beginning of March; however, it had to be repeatedly postponed owing to unfavourable weather.

Since the middle of February there had been repeated rumours of an early British landing and an encircling attempt through Dutch territory. The knowledge that Holland was taking its own defensive measures provided some measure of reassurance.[59] Nevertheless, Fourth Army Headquarters had to be prepared for such eventualities, and on 22 February it reported to the *OHL*: "In the event of a British landing in Holland, two mixed marine brigades, the Guard Cavalry Division, the army reserve (a mixed infantry brigade) and possibly ten battalions of Rear Echelon Troops would immediately and concentrically cross the border." At the beginning of March, on the occasion of a meeting between Falkenhayn and Fourth Army's commander, General Duke Albrecht of Württemberg, the war diarist of Fourth Army[60] recorded that Falkenhayn conveyed

> the Kaiser's opinion to the effect that Holland would probably energetically defend itself against a British invasion and that Germany must scrupulously avoid any breach of neutrality. Because the entry of British vessels into the Scheldt in itself does not warrant border violations, the Commander-in-Chief consequently directs that the border is only to be crossed on his specific orders. However, in the case of a British landing, all designated units are to assemble close behind the border.

General der Kavallerie von Werder, Commander of 4th Ersatz Division, was designated the collective commander of these units. He established the required liaison with the Governor of Occupied Belgium.

In the first days of March, Sixth Army Headquarters had to withdraw Bavarian 6th Reserve Corps to Tourcoing and into the *OHL* reserve; Bavarian II Corps's sector was enlarged accordingly.

On 3 March, XIV Corps launched its carefully prepared attack against the French positions on the Lorette Spur. At 07:00, following large mine detonations, companies from three infantry regiments began the attack. With effective support from their own artillery, the units from Baden advanced across the enemy's front trenches and established themselves there. The enemy artillery was evidently surprised, because fire on the new German positions did not increase until about 11:00, whereupon German casualties, which had initially been very light, increased. In the course of the afternoon, 28th Infantry Division had to deploy its reserves. Thereupon it was sent both *Jäger* battalion from the army reserve in motor trucks. Days of bitter counterattacks followed, which brought the usual gains and losses. More than 800 French prisoners were taken; however, the German losses were high as well, amounting to 1,800 dead, wounded, and missing for the period 3 to 6 March alone.

---

59   *During the First World War, the Netherlands adopted a position of armed neutrality.*
60   *In the original this was denoted in a footnote; however, for the sake of clarity it has been included here in the text. The war diary entry is from 2 March 1915.*

The Battle at Neuve Chapelle

To ensure British cooperation in the attack planned for the Artois, on 16 February Joffre requested that Field Marshal French order the BEF to simultaneously take the heights at La Bassée and, thereafter, advance on Warneton–Messines in order to capture Lille. If French agreed, Joffre wanted British I Corps to stay at La Bassée; XX Corps would remain in its sector to the north of the British until further notice.[61] The French Supreme Commander reminded Sir John that the immediate relief of IX Corps by British forces was vital because it was to collaborate with Tenth Army in the upcoming operations.[62]

At the same time, London advised Sir John that he could no longer count on 29th Infantry Division, which had been earmarked for the Dardanelles, and that a territorial division would be dispatched instead. As a result of this information, on 18 February the Field Marshal informed Joffre that, while he agreed with the proposal for a combined attack at the beginning of March, he had some reservations. Specifically, if I Corps remained at La Bassée, and if in place of 29th Infantry Division an inadequate territorial division arrived (which would not even appear until the beginning of March), then he could not manage the requested relief until after the offensive. This response deeply disappointed Joffre. On 19 February he turned to the French Minister of War to request that he use diplomatic channels to obtain the immediate deployment of 29th Infantry Division to France, for otherwise, the planned offensive in the Artois would be jeopardized. On the same day, the French Supreme Commander wrote to Sir John to emphasize that Lord Kitchener had expressly agreed to expedite the planned attack. Even without 29th Infantry Division, he wrote, and considering the strength of the BEF, it ought to be possible to relieve IX Corps. On 23 February, however, Sir John again responded in the negative. He advised Joffre that 46th Territorial Division would not arrive before 28 February, at which point it would require further training; thus the relief of the units in question would only be possible by 1 April at the earliest. It seems that the French presentations in London had left at least some impression, for the deployment of 29th Infantry Division to the Dardanelles was postponed. Nevertheless, the War Office was not willing to make the decision to deploy it to the Western Front.

At this point the French plans were being placed in serious jeopardy. If the offensive in the Artois did not take place soon, it would not be able to perform its

---

61 In accordance with the meeting at Chantilly, British I Corps was supposed to have been replaced by French XX Corps.

62 *On French efforts to find Anglo-Belgian relief for Eighth Army, see French Official History* II: 335–65.

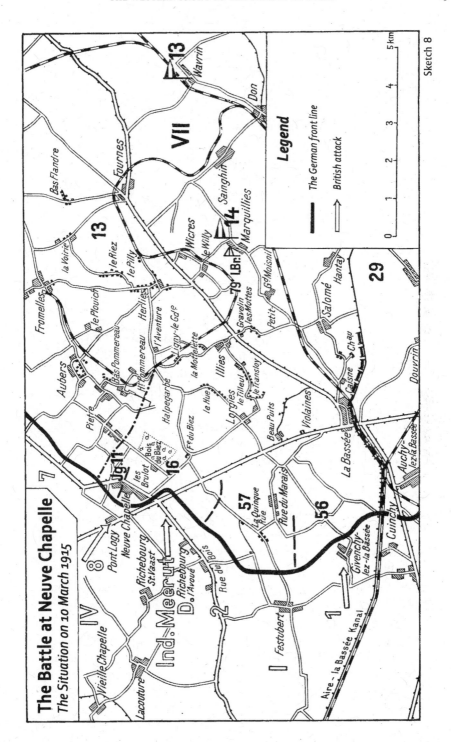

The Battle at Neuve Chapelle

The Situation on 10 March 1915

Legend

—— The German front line

→ British attack

Sketch 8

designated role in conjunction with the Champagne offensive. On 1 March, Joffre once more requested the intervention of his government in order to direct the British War Office's attention specifically to the fact that, at that point, all French reserves had been committed to the offensive in the Champagne, the overriding purpose of which was to divert enemy pressure from the remainder of the front. The offensive effort to which the British commander had agreed could only be conducted with the help of IX Corps, which was to be relieved by the British; otherwise the plans would have to be abandoned.

Apparently this appeal was unsuccessful, for on 7 March the French Supreme Commander advised the British commander that Tenth Army's attack could not be executed for the time being.

Consequently, Field Marshal French decided to launch an independent offensive operation within his sector. He ordered an attack on Neuve Chapelle, which began on 10 March.

ON 10 MARCH, IV CORPS, THE INDIAN CORPS, AND ELEMENTS OF I CORPS UNDER the command of General Sir Douglas Haig attacked the sector held by VII Corps' 14th Infantry Division at Givenchy-les-la-Bassée and Neuve Chapelle. Apparently it was their goal to break through in the direction of Lille. While all the enemy attacks at Givenchy were repelled, the British managed to break through the German lines at Neuve Chapelle, seizing the village at 11:00 after an extensive artillery preparation. Since the army reserves were no longer available, Sixth Army Headquarters moved up two reserve battalions of XIX (Saxon) Corps via rail to Don,[63] where they were placed at the disposal of VII Corps. In the afternoon, VII Corps' commanding general, General der Infanterie von Claer, reported additional enemy forces advancing on Neuve Chapelle and Richebourg-l'Avoué, adding that he expected these stronger forces to effect a breakthrough and requesting at least a division from the GHQ reserve. As it happened, at 15:30 fresh troops launched a renewed attack along a wider front. Consequently, and despite reports of strong enemy fire on the fronts of both Bavarian II Corps and XIX Corps that evening, the *OHL* approved the move of Bavarian 6th Reserve Division to Don and of four batteries from XIX Corps' reserve, which were sent to Fournes. Fourth Army was also to send 86th Reserve Infantry Brigade (which was in reserve at Roulers) to Don via rail, where it was to be placed at the disposition of army headquarters for the time being.

At 07:00 on 11 March a renewed British attack was launched against 14th Infantry Division; it floundered in the German infantry fire. By evening, reports

---

63   *About 10 kilometres southeast of Neuve Chapelle.*

indicated that the German line of defence between Neuve Chapelle and the intermediate position was unprotected and hanging out in the open. On the evening of 11 March the enemy again attacked at Neuve Chapelle. This attack was repulsed as well, with the support of a few companies of Bavarian 6th Reserve Division.

On 12 March at 06:00 the German counterattack on Neuve Chapelle began, which had been in preparation as other events unfolded. The Westphalians, Saxons, and Bavarians attacked in unison and initially retook the trenches northeast of the village; but owing to the weakness of the German artillery, casualties were so severe that a strong enemy counterattack that was launched at noon succeeded in pushing them back to their start positions. Around 20:00, Sixth Army Headquarters advised Mézières: "The British attack was conducted with two full corps which are still completely in place. Considering this superiority, the continuation of our attacks with the forces available carries no expectation of success. Therefore the army will order current positions to be held while retaining further options." After a telephone conversation between Falkenhayn and Sixth Army's Chief of Staff, General von Krafft, the *OHL* made XVIII Corps' reinforced 42nd Infantry Brigade available; it arrived at Don on 13 March. The combat units, which had been badly mauled by the additional attacks on Neuve Chapelle, were able to hold their new positions and were relieved by the mixed 42nd Infantry Brigade and 86th Reserve Infantry Brigade on 14 March. To further strengthen the front, Bavarian 6th Reserve Division was inserted between XIX and VII Corps. The planned British breakthrough to Lille was thus unsuccessful. German losses between 9 and 20 March amounted to almost 10,000 men; the British counted theirs to be 12,892.

On the fronts of second, first, and seventh armies[64] no combat activities worth mentioning occurred.

In Fifth Army's sector, the right flank—in particular, the elements fighting in the Argonne—bore the brunt of the fighting. On 17 February the French strengthened their attacks against XVI Corps' front; these were intended to relieve the German pressure that had been increasing steadily since January. Their main thrust was at 33rd Infantry Division, but the enemy gained only a momentary foothold in Vauquois. On 28 February the enemy renewed its attacks toward Vauquois, only managing to hold its ground in the southern part.

---

64 In the beginning of March, at the headquarters of Seventh Army, Oberst Tappen temporarily replaced Generalleutnant von Hänisch as Chief of Staff.

After repelling a French attack east of Vauquois, on 26 February VI Reserve Corps managed to take portions of an enemy position in the forest southwest of Malancourt by employing flame-throwers for the first time.[65] An attack by V Reserve Corps' reinforced 77th Infantry Brigade led to the seizure of several French trenches in the Bois de Consenvoye.

Armee-Abteilung Strantz

Armee-Abteilung *Strantz* had to fend off ferocious attacks on the Combres Heights. They were repulsed mainly by 33rd Reserve Division,[66] assisted by elements from 9th Infantry Division. Nevertheless, after bitter fighting that lingered on between 17 and 20 February, the mountain outcrop of the Combres position—the so-called "Finger"—and a small part of the northwest slope of the heights, remained in enemy hands; the Germans lost approximately 2,000 men. In front of Bavarian Ersatz Division in the centre of the *Abteilung*, the mining war continued. A stronger enemy foray in the Bois d'Ailly and the Forêt d'Apremont on 22 February was partially repulsed by an immediate counterattack. In the beginning of March, French combat activity also increased in the Bois le Prêtre on the *Abteilung's* southern flank. Through the extensive use of mine explosions, 8th Ersatz Division attempted to prevent the enemy from advancing any further.[67]

ON THE FRONT OF ARMEE-ABTEILUNG *FALKENHAUSEN*, FIGHTING ALSO INCREASED toward the end of February. An order issued on 21 February directed the left flank of 19th (Saxon) Ersatz Division and the right flank of XIV Reserve Corps to advance to the approximate line Domèvre–Montreux–Les Collines (west of Bionville). This operation, launched on 27 February, achieved complete surprise, as a result of which, on the first day alone, it was possible almost everywhere to reach the objective. Multiple French counterattacks by 2nd Cavalry Division from the evening of 27 February to 7 March, which focused on Hill 542 north of Les Collines,[68] collapsed with heavy losses. Further enemy attacks against the positions of 19th Ersatz Division in the second half of March failed as well. By the end of the month, the Germans had also taken the village of Parroy in front of the left

---

65 Flame-throwers were normally used to roll up enemy personnel in the trenches. They consisted of installed containers carried on the back, which threw a white-hot jet flame out of steel pipes at the target to a distance of 20 to 30 metres.

66 The 33rd Reserve Division consisted of the 66th Prussian Reserve Infantry Brigade and Bavarian 8th Infantry Brigade.

67 *On French First Army's attacks around* Éparges, *see* French Official History, II: 492–93.

68 In the area of 84th Landwehr Brigade, XV Reserve Corps.

flank of Bavarian 1st Landwehr Division. The elements positioned on the northern flank of the detachment received orders from headquarters to expand their outpost lines into a main line of resistance.

ARMEE-ABTEILUNG *GAEDE* STARTED ITS MAIN OFFENSIVE ON 19 FEBRUARY WEST of Munster. It was led by the Commander of Bavarian 8th Reserve Division, Generalleutnant Baron von Stein, who had also been assigned Bavarian 6th Landwehr Division and additional elements from the *Armee-Abteilung*. The staging was accomplished during the night of 18 and 19 February, but in the mountainous, snow-covered terrain the attack encountered major difficulties, especially for the Bavarian battalions that were advancing on Sondernach–Metzeral out of the Lauch Valley. The going became extremely difficult for these battalions in the deep snows of the Hilsenfirst Plateau. Despite this, with heavy fighting between 19 and 23 February, they reached the line Barrenkopf–Reichsackerkopf–Hilsenfirst. Since fresh reserves were unavailable to continue the fight, headquarters ordered the farthest line of advance to be expanded into a main line of resistance. By 6 March, Bavarian 8th Reserve Division had been withdrawn from the captured positions and had been replaced with elements from the reinforced Bavarian 6th Landwehr Division. On the afternoon of 6 March, the enemy, which had been relatively quiet in the Munster Valley since 24 February, suddenly launched a powerful counterattack against the line Barrenkopf–Reichsackerkopf. The enemy succeeded in capturing the Reichsackerkopf and Mönchberg west of Munster, where *Landsturm* battalions had been deployed following the withdrawal of Bavarian 8th Reserve Division. From 6 to 8 March, Bavarian 8th Reserve Division, which had immediately been brought up, pushed the enemy back—except on the summit of the Reichsackerkopf. The complete removal of the enemy from the summit was only achieved after painstaking preparations on 20 March. As a result, Bavarian 8th Reserve Division had to remain in the Munster Valley for the time being . It was assigned the sector adjoining Bavarian 6th Landwehr Division, north of Stosswihr as far as Hilsenfirst.

During these events in the Vosges, heavy fighting took place in the sector of 51st Landwehr Brigade as well as in the sector of Division *Fuchs* north of the Grand Ballon. Between 11 and 17 February the French pushed back the left flank of 51st Landwehr Brigade on the Sudelkopf. Division *Fuchs* also managed to repel strong enemy attacks on the Vieil Armand between 19 and 27 February, but on 5 March in this area, the enemy captured a portion of the front line from the division. Because the fighting on the Vieil Armand was costly for both parties, the German offensive at Wattwiller–Steinbach stalled entirely. All of the forces of Division *Fuchs* were needed to repel these enemy attacks in the difficult mountainous terrain.

Therefore, on 17 March, Falkenhayn ordered the transition to defensive operations in Alsace, as the execution of further attacks by Armee-Abteilung *Gaede* did not provide for an expectation of success, largely because of the troops available and because additional forces could not be assigned. The Guard Corps, stationed between Molsheim and Sélestat—and later X Reserve Corps, which replaced it—were put at the disposal of the *OHL* in case of a major French offensive in Alsace.

The *OHL*'s Return to the Western Front

Following the Kaiser's return to headquarters in Mézières on 1 March, in the first days of the month Falkenhayn undertook a tour of each of the Army Headquarters on the Western Front. The arrangement of the Western Army into army groups, which had been ordered prior to the Kaiser's departure for the East, was reversed on 6 March so that each Army Headquarters on the Western Front again became immediately subordinate to the *OHL*.

According to the information available in the beginning of March regarding the enemy's strength and intentions, the transfer of the first Kitchener army—Third Army—to the continent was believed to have already begun; however, this could not be confirmed. Its strength was estimated at 140,000 to 200,000 men; also, fifty to sixty British batteries were said to be located near Orléans. It was apparently intended that these armies would be deployed only after spending a period of time in transit camps in France; the completion of these transfers was not expected before the end of March. No significant strengthening of the British forces as a result of the arrival of 27th and 28th Infantry Divisions on the front of V Corps was evident. At the beginning of March the deployment of a Canadian Division was confirmed.

The French only seemed able to augment their forces in a minor way. It was believed that in February the Ministry of War had ordered the creation of a considerable number (eighty-four) of personnel replacement transfer battalions (*Marsch-Bataillonen*);[69] however, many of these had to be used to satisfy the need for replacements of front-line units. In June the 1916 age class would also be called up. In conclusion, the *OHL* considered the addition of major new formations, except for colonial units, to be a small possibility. A memorandum from the *OHL*'s

---

69 *These battalions were temporary and conducted replacement troops from the military district where they were raised to the theatre of operations. See* French Official History II: 382–87.

Intelligence Division stated: "The huge effort of the French Forces indicates that the military strength of France will have been expended by midsummer 1915 at the latest."

The Belgian Army was in the process of rebuilding and was not thought able to field more than 40,000 usable soldiers.

The Western enemy's strength was apparently not sufficient to mount a major breakthrough offensive. For the time being it was considered unlikely that the British would want to get involved in major military operations outside France. However, a number of reports indicated, with increasing credibility, that both Western Allies intended to link up with the Serbian Army—in concert with the Greeks—or to undertake an attack on Constantinople.

The Defensive Battles from the Middle of March to the Middle of April

Initially the German High Command had not intended to launch major offensive operations in the West except for Fourth Army's planned but not yet executed gas attack. The novelty of this new weapon of war and the complexities involved in calculating both its effectiveness and the proper timing for its use prevented its deployment in connection with other planned operations.

BY THE END OF MARCH, FOURTH ARMY HEADQUARTERS HAD COME TO BELIEVE that the enemy had gotten word of the planned gas attack. The enemy had moved reinforcements into the area of Ypres and had moved more men into the trenches. The installation of the gas cylinders could not have gone unnoticed by the local population, and the proximity to the Dutch border facilitated espionage of all kinds.[70] As a result of the ever-increasing artillery fire, some of the already installed gas cylinders had been destroyed, and gas had escaped into the trenches, causing casualties among the German soldiers. Initially the preparations for the attack had been made in the sectors of XXVII Reserve Corps and XV Corps around Gheluvelt. However, on 25 March, after weeks of demoralizing waiting in anticipation of favourable weather, Fourth Army Headquarters decided to deploy the as yet uninstalled gas cylinders in the sectors of XXVI

---

70 French Tenth Army had first been informed of the installation of the gas canisters in the German positions by prisoners of war on 30 March. The British first received notice on 15 April. Since no attack was launched, this information appears not to have been taken seriously; the French interpreted these reports as attempts at deception.

Reserve Corps and XXIII Reserve Corps' 46th Reserve Division. Considering the prevailing winds in Flanders, it was expected that those locations would provide a more favourable opportunity to release the gas. Army orders dated 8 and 14 April identified XXIII and XXVI Reserve Corps' mission as "the capture of the heights north of Pilkem and the adjoining areas to the East." It was expected "that the enemy would find it impossible to stay in the salient around Ypres. Another of the attack's objectives was the capture of the Yser Canal up to and including Ypres."

On 10 April, Fourth Army's Chief of Staff, Generalmajor Ilse, was ordered to attend a conference in Mézières. Since he planned to extract XV Corps and XXVI Reserve Corps, as well as 4th Ersatz Division, Falkenhayn insisted on getting the gas attack out of the way at the earliest opportunity. The XXIII and XXVI Reserve Corps headquarters urgently requested sufficient time to prepare the attack. They designated the middle of April as the earliest possible date for its implementation as, at that time of year, weather conditions would likely improve. However, on the morning of the planned attack (15 April) the winds remained totally calm and the attack had to be postponed yet again.

IN THE MEANTIME, BETWEEN 2 AND 17 APRIL, BRITISH FORCES HAD BEEN REOR-ganized. Following the assignment of the Canadian Infantry Division and two British Territorial Divisions (46th and 48th), on 17 April, Second Army took over the French sector northwards to the Ypres–Poelcappelle road. The II Corps (46th Territorial Division and 3rd and 5th Infantry Divisions) was deployed between Messines and the Ypres–Comines rail line, with V Corps (Canadian, 27th, and 28th Infantry Divisions) adjoining to the north up to Poelcappelle.

At 20:00 on 17 April the staff of German 30th Infantry Division received notice that the British had blown up[71] and taken the position on the dominating Hill 60 near Little Zillebeke. On the morning of 18 April, the Saxon Regiment that was deployed there, supported by elements from neighbouring regiments, retook the hill after bitter fighting—except for the blast craters. The attempt on 20 April to take the crater position was unsuccessful because the artillery fire was insufficient and because the new T-shells (*T-Geschosse*) harassed the German troops.[72] Fierce close combat continued on Hill 60 into early May until, on 5 May, it was again entirely in German hands.

---

71 The British 5th Infantry Division had deployed newly formed sapper detachments, which prepared the attack.

72 *The "T-Geschoss," named for its inventor, Dr. Hans Tappen, was a 15 cm high explosive shell filled with the chemical xylyl bromide. The shell had first been used in January 1915 on the Eastern Front,*

ON THE FRONT OF SIXTH ARMY, TENSION HAD MARKEDLY INCREASED OVER THE first months of the year. By the middle of March, despite the mostly rainy weather, relatively intense fighting had been taking place without much break around St. Eloi, Neuve Chapelle, La Bassée, the Lorette Spur, and Carency. The XIV Corps lost 5,000 men, mainly on the Lorette Spur, during the month of March alone. To continue holding this commanding position, it requested that Bavarian I Reserve Corps attack the heights of Mont St. Eloi to eliminate the French artillery observers who were operating there. This attack would have required considerable reinforcements, which were unavailable, so the request could not be granted. However, after a reversal at the "pulpit"[73] on the bitterly contested Lorette Spur in mid-April, and after intense discussions, the Commander of 28th Infantry Division decided to launch a counterattack on a wider front past the pulpit position up to the Bouvigny Heights. For this purpose, the *OHL* promised to commit an infantry brigade and preparations for the attack began.

IT WAS ESPECIALLY QUIET ON THE FRONTS OF SECOND, FIRST, AND SEVENTH Armies[74] along the centre of the Western Front from south of Arras to the Champagne. Fighting in the area of Third Army also abated in the second half of March.

Second Army's commander, Generalfeldmarschall von Bülow, had to return home for health reasons at the beginning of April. The previous commanding general of XXI Corps, General der Infanterie Fritz von Below, succeeded him. At the end of March, General von Kluck, in command of First Army, was severely injured by an enemy shrapnel round while visiting III Corps. General der Infanterie von Fabeck, the former commander at Eleventh Army Headquarters, assumed control of the army in his place. The offensive that had been planned since the middle of March for the area near and south of Vailly ultimately had to be abandoned. As specified in a telegram from Falkenhayn dated 17 April, no major ventures were planned for First and Seventh Armies for the immediate future.

---

where the intense cold nullified its effects. It is not clear from the original text whether the "T-Shells" were used in trying to retake the craters and proved dangerous, or were not used at all because they were dangerous. For more on the early use of gas, see Wolfgang Wietzker, *Giftgas im Ersten Weltkrieg: Was konnte die deutsche Öffentlichkeit wissen* (Ph.D. diss., Heinrich-Heine-Universität, 2006); and Ulrich Trumpener, "The Road to Ypres: The Beginnings of Gas Warfare in World War I," *Journal of Modern History* 47, no. 3 (1975): 460–80.

73 *The "Pulpit" was a bulge along the southern slope of the ridge that overlooked the village of Ablain and commanded the approaches to that part of the heights.*

74 On April 1, Oberst von Borris replaced Oberst Tappen as Chief of the General Staff at Seventh Army Headquarters.

On Fifth Army's front, the enemy attacked XVI Corps on 14 March after several hours of artillery preparation and mine detonations on the Bolante Plateau and west of Boureuilles in the Argonne. The next day, following intense shelling, enemy attacks were launched on Vauquois as well. However, the enemy did not achieve any noteworthy successes; over the following days the fighting continued without results and without changing the overall situation. Between 4 and 11 April the enemy renewed the attacks, apparently in connection with the offensive against Armee-Abteilung *Strantz;* again the attackers were unable to obtain any results even though all three of the corps' divisions were under continuous heavy artillery and mortar fire. At the same time, on 5 and 6 April, the left flank of V Reserve Corps was attacked in the area of Etain, where the enemy managed to push the German outposts back a short distance west of Warq.

In accordance with orders from the *OHL,* on 5 April, Fifth Army had to return the reinforced 38th Reserve Brigade (formerly of XVI Corps) to X Reserve Corps. Meanwhile, 56th Landwehr Regiment joined Armee-Abteilung *Gaede.* Events on the front of Armee-Abteilung *Strantz*—which was subordinated to Fifth Army—forced the deployment of troops at the end of March and the beginning of April.

Armee-Abteilung Strantz

On 17 March, the same day Joffre ordered the cessation of the Champagne offensive, he gave an extensive briefing to the French War Minister on the state of affairs and his future intentions.[75] Joffre stated that a continuation of the offensive in the Champagne would be possible and pointed out that even the soldiers wanted it. Nevertheless, he believed that a change in fighting methods was required. Because the enemy had brought up considerable reinforcements, and because the incessant fighting was placing great demands on the strength of the soldiers and their supplies of materiel and ammunition, the commitment of considerable reserves and further materiel would be required to mount decisive operations in the future. He reported that all preparations had been made to hold on to and expand the gains made in the Champagne, which would remain the basis for future operations. Reserves had yet to be formed; however, Joffre believed that if the strictest secrecy was maintained, and if the fastest modes of transportation were utilized, successful operations would ultimately follow. Until that point was reached the lull would be interrupted only by a series of individual, unconnected operations

---

75   *Alexandre Millerand served as War Minister until October 1915. Until his departure he staunchly supported Joffre's conduct of the war, often at great political risk.*

of limited scope intended to maintain troop morale as well as contain the enemy and prevent him from taking the initiative.

For the first of these individual operations, Joffre chose Provisional Army Group *East*'s sector (which included Army Detachments *Vosges* and *Lorraine*[76] as well as French First and Third Armies). On 14 March the commanding general of Provisional Army Group *East*, General Dubail, received preliminary notice that a major attack was planned against the German positions in the St. Mihiel Salient, for which the Supreme Commander would provide three corps and one cavalry division as reinforcements. To divert the enemy's attention prior to the main attack, Dubail was to launch forays between the Vosges and Nancy (with Army Detachment *Lorraine*) and west of Verdun near Vauquois (with Third Army). Without interfering in First Army's ongoing battles, Dubail thus began the necessary preparations. On 18 March, Grand Quartier Général (GQG) advised that this advance on both sides of St. Mihiel on the Woëvre Plain was gaining in priority and inquired as to when the offensive would begin. Dubail stipulated that the offensive's start depended on the arrival of the reinforcements that had been promised. On 23 March he was personally informed in Chantilly that XII Corps would be deployed between the Moselle River and St. Mihiel on 4 April and that I and II Corps, as well as Cavalry Corps *Conneau*, would also then be deployed north of St. Mihiel. Joffre desired that the operation be conducted as a *coup de force* over a period of three to four days. If a breakthrough was achieved and the enemy was dislodged from the Meuse Heights, XVII Corps would be brought up (although not before 15 April). If there was no breakthrough, the positions gained in the attack were to be held and reinforced, and the units that had been provided for the offensive were to be returned to GQG's reserve little by little.

The preparations for the attack on the Woëvre Plain unfolded under the strictest secrecy and were concluded by 4 April. Pursuant to Dubail's request, that same day a division of XVII Corps was ordered to deploy as it arrived in Givry-en-Argonne. The elements of First Army already in place between the Moselle and St. Mihiel were to attack Thiaucourt; Army Detachment *Gérard*[77]— formed by I and II Corps and Cavalry Corps *Conneau* and headquartered south of Etain—was to attack Lachaussée. The operation began during foggy and rainy weather on 5 April.

---

76 Army Detachment *Lorraine* was formed on 3 March.
77 French I and II Corps, the Division *de Morlaincourt*, and Cavalry Corps *Conneau*.

LONG BEFORE THE BEGINNING OF THE FRENCH OFFENSIVE, THE COMMANDERS of Armee-Abteilung *Strantz* had come to believe that the enemy was attempting to create the best possible jumping-off positions for a major offensive by mounting a series of individual operations. On 18 March the French again attacked up the Combres Heights, penetrating the German positions on the northwest slope. The counterattack launched by elements of 33rd Reserve Division late on the morning of 19 March regained much of the lost ground. Nevertheless, it was clear that the situation was becoming precarious. So on 21 March, General der Infanterie von Oven, in command of V Corps, personally reported to the Commander of Armee-Abteilung *Strantz* that the battles for the Combres Heights had already used up considerable forces. He proposed to alleviate the troubles at Combres with a relief attack on the Grande Tranchée de Calonne in 9th Infantry Division's sector, but General von Strantz was obliged to reject this idea because the necessary forces were not available. On the afternoon of 27 March the enemy managed to take most of the German position on the northwest slope of the Combres Heights, although by the evening of the same day it had all but been thrown back down again. In consideration of the soldiers' exhaustion, 33rd Reserve and 10th Infantry Divisions received orders to switch their sectors. At the same time, the enemy launched vicious attacks against 5th Landwehr Division's adjoining position to the north at Marchéville (northwest of St. Hilaire) on 18 and 27 March; these were repelled after close combat. The attacks on the Combres Heights and the Woëvre Plain did not result in a decisive success for the enemy. However, the defenders expended considerable strength.

A general lull developed on Armee-Abteilung *Strantz*'s northern flank from the end of March until 4 April (except for a strong artillery bombardment of the Combres Heights on 3 April). Meanwhile, intense fighting flared up on the southern flank in the sector of 8th Ersatz Division. After strong artillery preparations, the enemy launched a number of attacks, taking the villages of Fey-en-Haye and Regniéville, penetrating the German position in the Bois-le-Prêtre, and occupying a portion of the rearward positions in the western part of the forest. General von Strantz reinforced 8th Ersatz Division with units from other sectors of the front and, from Metz, brought up eight battalions (mostly *Landwehr*), one machine-gun company, one company of combat engineers, and heavy artillery. On 4 April a combined division under Generalmajor von Stumpff was formed from the Armee-Abteilung's reserves and from reinforcements transferred from Fifth Army. This combined division was assembled for a counterattack at Thiaucourt in case the enemy repeated its attack on 8th Ersatz Division in full force.

The enemy extended the scope of its attacks with a large and well-conceived operation beginning late in the morning of 5 April. From then until 8 April it launched a number of strong thrusts between Etain and the Moselle.

The enemy failed to gain ground despite determined attacks against 5th Landwehr Division—reinforced by units from V Corps—mainly between Maizeray and Marchéville (and northwest of Harville–St. Hilaire). Even on the Combres Heights, the enemy managed only temporary successes owing to the strong and immediate counterattacks of 10th Infantry Division, which drove it back. Attacks originating from the Bois de la Selouse (southeast of Seuzey) against 33rd Reserve Division's position suffered a similar fate. However, on 8 April the situation on the Combres Heights became even more precarious. The next morning, under cover of extremely intense fire, the enemy took trench sections at the centre of the heights position as well as at the Crest Position on the northwest slope.

On 5 April, following massive explosions in the sector of Bavarian Ersatz Division in the Bois d'Ailly, the enemy penetrated parts of the German positions, but were able to hold these gains only in the southern part of the forest. At first, Bavarian III Corps Headquarters saw the fierce close combat, which continued on 6 and 7 April in the Bois d'Ailly (occasionally spilling over into the sector of Bavarian 5th Infantry Division), as a diversionary tactic.

On the southern flank, the enemy's attacks were directed against the positions of Guard Ersatz Division between the railway tracks and the Essey–Flirey road, and to the east against a line running from north of Regniéville through to the Bois-le-Prêtre in 8th Ersatz Division's sector. The enemy kept introducing fresh regiments into the attack between 5 and 7 April but remained unsuccessful.

Under pressure from the French attacks taking place along a wide front, on 6 April General von Strantz ordered that Division *Stumpff* be dissolved and that some of its constituent parts be returned to both Bavarian III and V Corps. The remainder were to be divided among 8th Ersatz and 5th Landwehr Divisions. Generalmajor von Stumpff then assumed command of 8th Ersatz Division. On 7 April, General von Strantz had only one reserve battalion available even though he had requested additional forces from the *OHL* on 4 April. Falkenhayn had left the task of supporting the besieged sectors to the Armee-Abteilung's headquarters and to Fifth Army Headquarters, which had used forces from other sectors for this purpose. However, he understood that these measures were insufficient, and on 8 April he put 113th and 121st Infantry Divisions at General von Strantz's disposal. Both were newly formed divisions, each consisting of three infantry regiments. Guard and 8th Ersatz Divisions received one infantry regiment each from 121st Infantry Division, which was to arrive in Gorze on 8 April. The 113th detrained a day later near Conflans.

On 9 April the enemy repeatedly attacked 5th Landwehr Division on the Armee-Abteilung's northern flank to the south of Marchéville. Although the enemy was repelled, the defenders suffered considerable losses because of the continuing fighting. The divisional commander, Generalleutnant Auler, urgently requested reinforcements. For V Corps, the back-and-forth battle for control of the Combres Heights continued unabated. In the early-morning hours of 10 April it successfully regained the Crest Position on the hill's northwest slope. Nevertheless, there could be no doubt about the gravity of the situation as 33rd Reserve Division again repelled an attack out of the Bois de la Selouse.

In the Bois d'Ailly the situation remained unchanged.

On the morning of 9 April a strong attack developed from the line Regniéville–Fey against 8th Ersatz Division on the Armee-Abteilung's southern front. At noon the attack broke down in the face of German defensive fire. With that, the fighting in this area gradually abated, while in the western part of the Bois-le-Prêtre and in the sector of Guard Division, serious combat continued with varying results.

Also on 9 April, Strantz ordered 121st Infantry Division to move the remainder of its infantry into army reserve at Thiaucourt and ordered 113th Infantry Division to move behind 5th Landwehr Division's sector. At the same time he filed a detailed report about the situation with Fifth Army Headquarters and the *OHL*. His report described the situation on the Combres Heights as precarious. The loss of the hill, he wrote, would have the most serious consequences, as the French would be able to subject the plain's access roads to artillery fire. He believed that relief could only be obtained by moving the positions on the Meuse Heights forward along the Grande Tranchée de Calonne. For this purpose, he required an additional division.

Despite a number of attacks over the following days (10 to 14 April), the enemy did not succeed in gaining ground against 5th Landwehr Division. Two attacks on 11 April against the Combres Heights were repelled as well. After 12 April, fighting declined. The heights' left and right flanks were in German hands, while the centre remained contested territory.

The fighting in the Bois d'Ailly declined as well, and for the time being, a major German offensive was not being considered.

On the Armee-Abteilung's southern flank—where the Guard and Ersatz Divisions had retained their positions—the fighting ended around the 14th.

In the meantime, Falkenhayn had acceded to the numerous reinforcement requests. On the morning of 11 April the newly formed 111th Infantry Division arrived in Conflans. Meanwhile, Strantz had to deploy most of the two divisions that had been put at his disposal for the relief of the exhausted elements of Guard Ersatz, 8th Ersatz, and 5th Landwehr Divisions. The 121st Infantry Division remained on the southern front in a supporting posture during the following days; 113th and 111th Infantry Divisions, whose combat readiness was to be preserved for a planned German counterattack, were used only sparingly for the relief of units requiring rest.

It can be said that the French offensive against both flanks of Armee-Abteilung *Strantz* in mid-April had failed despite the commitment of considerable forces. The minor successes that the enemy had achieved had apparently come with heavy casualties. Only on the Combres Heights did the situation grow so precarious that the relief of the division deployed there became critical. This relief could only be achieved through German offensive operations, and after the allocation of 111th, 113th, and 121st Infantry Divisions, the forces for such an operation were available. Planning for a counterattack on both sides of the Grande Tranchée de Calonne began immediately.

IT WAS COMPARATIVELY QUIET ON ARMEE-ABTEILUNG *FALKENHAUSEN*'S FRONT, but the enemy was pushing against the Vieil Armand in Armee-Abteilung *Gaede*'s sector. In repeated attacks between 23 March and 6 April, the French eventually took the summit piece by piece. This allowed it to lay down observer-directed artillery fire on the Colmar–Mulhouse railway line. On 17 April the enemy launched a new action using superior forces, attacking Bavarian 8th Reserve Division in the Fecht Valley. The enemy took the Schnepfen-Riethkopf and forced the defending division to withdraw its left flank. Further enemy attacks over 19 and 20 April were repelled.

On 24 March a telegram from Falkenhayn ordered the final removal of the units belonging to Division *Fuchs*. As of the beginning of April the *OHL* intended to allocate other units to the Armee-Abteilung as replacements.

ON THE FRENCH SIDE, SOON AFTER THE INITIAL ATTACKS ON THE WOËVRE PLAIN, the Supreme Commander had concluded that a major success could not be expected. The goal of eliminating the German forces between Metz and St. Mihiel, as directed by Dubail in an order of the day dated 5 April,[78] had not been achieved. On 8 April, Joffre ordered that more "methodical" attacks be used from then on. Of the allocated reinforcements, one to two corps were to be staged behind the army group's front line to form a reserve; the daily ammunition shipments would from then on be considerably reduced. On 14 April the French Supreme Command stated that First Army's primary mission would be to push forward northeast of Regniéville and near Marchéville (northwest of St. Hilaire). Ancillary operations

---

78 A copy of the order was captured by soldier serving in Armee-Abteilung *Strantz*'s front lines.

were to be conducted in the Bois de Mort Mare (north of Flirey) and the Bois d'Ailly. The XVII and I Corps, as well as Cavalry Corps *Conneau* (less one division), were to be available for further orders. The II and XII Corps and one cavalry division would remain at the disposition of the Army Group. On 23 April, Army Detachment *Gérard* was disbanded and its constituent elements joined First Army.

In the Vosges, the attacks on both sides of the Fecht River from 17 to 19 April had achieved no appreciable results. Although 66th Division had been able to take the Schnepfen-Riethkopf, 47th Division had made no substantial progress. On 19 April, Joffre declared that he required two additional corps from Army Group *East* to be deployed elsewhere. As a result, all fighting in the Vosges was reduced considerably for the time being.

3

The Change in Falkenhayn's Plans

FORTUNES SLOWLY CHANGED IN THE EAST DURING THE WINTER OF 1915. *The joint operation in the Carpathians, which had caused so much controversy between OberOst and the OHL earlier in the month, was launched on 23 January. Conrad's plan called for the new Südarmee to seize passes through the centre of the mountains while an Austro-Hungarian army did the same to the West and another struck the Russians in the East. The goal was to get beyond the peaks and relieve the besieged city of Przemysl. The battle conditions were unimaginable: rifles locked up in the cold, shells bounced off icy glaciers, and whole units froze in the mountain passes. It took more than a week for Südarmee to reach its objectives for the first day. Although the Austro-Hungarian armies initially did better, the battle soon evolved into a series thrusts and retreats through frozen peaks and valleys. By the beginning of March, the offensive had already cost more than 800,000 Austro-Hungarian and German casualties. In March alone, Südarmee lost two-thirds of its strength. On 22 January, Przemysl fell and 120,000 men trapped inside surrendered to the Russian Armies.*[1]

---

1 Stone, *The Eastern Front 1914–1917*, 109–16; *DW* VII: 74–152.

Meanwhile, the German Armies to the north met with more success as Luden-
dorff launched a separate attack in Eastern Prussia. On 7 February, General von
Below's Eighth Army made a surprise assault in a blinding snowstorm and within
a week had advanced more than 110 kilometres against the Russian Armies.[2] A sec-
ond attack by the newly formed Tenth Army under General von Eichhorn led to the
surrender of an entire Russian corps. Between 7 and 22 February the Germans cap-
tured 92,000 prisoners—including nine Russian generals, 295 guns, and 170 machine
guns. In comparison, they lost only 120 officers and 5,600 men.[3]

Thus in the winter of 1915, Falkenhayn faced an improved albeit still ominous
strategic situation. While all fronts were more stable than they had been in Decem-
ber, the question of whether the war would be won in the East or in the West had
yet to be settled. Ludendorff's offensive at the Masurian Lakes had achieved suc-
cess, while Südarmee's joint attack resulted in disaster. As Falkenhayn had warned,
the Russians were battered but remained far from beaten while Austria-Hungary's
situation grew worse. In what Norman Stone called "the Austro-Hungarian emer-
gency" in the spring of 1915, the Dual Monarchy lost more than two-thirds of its
August 1914 strength, was having difficulty replacing casualties, and could not sup-
ply its guns with ammunition.[4] The loyalty of ethnic minority groups in the army
was also becoming increasingly questionable.

The possible collapse of Germany's closest ally weighed heavily on the Chief of
the German General Staff. At the same time, Serbia had yet to be defeated and a
land connection to Turkey had not been secured. In the Mediterranean, Entente
forces were poised to exploit Turkey's isolation with a naval attack in the Dardanelles.
As at the beginning of the year, the attitudes of the neutral Balkan powers and
Italy remained at the forefront of German strategic thinking. A Balkan Alliance

---

2 *DW* VII: 172–238; Stone, *The Eastern Front 1914–1917*, 116–21; see also Hans von Redern, *Die Winterschlacht in Masuren (Der grosse Krieg in Einzeldarstellungen, Heft 20)* (Oldenburg: Gerhard Stlling, 1918).

3 *DW* VII: 237.

4 Stone, *The Eastern Front 1914–1917*, 122–23.

against the Central Powers could now, more than ever, turn the war's tide against Vienna and Berlin. While storm clouds continued to gather in the East, in the West the German defences were holding. The French had failed to break through in the Champagne in January; the British had been rebuffed at Neuve Chapelle in March. When a late-winter proposal for the reorganization of the German Army promised to create a new strategic reserve, the question of its deployment took centre stage at the OHL. The decision would determine the emphasis of the war effort for the coming months and perhaps its final outcome.

The Creation of a New GHQ Reserve

In January, circumstances compelled Falkenhayn to allow the new formations raised in Germany to be deployed to the Eastern Theatre. Yet apparently he still desired to stage his planned offensive in the West as soon as possible. On 19 February—before the Second Battle of the Masurian Lakes had ended—he sent a request to *OberOst* from Berlin (to which he had returned following a visit to the Eastern Front) asking for its future plans. His request read:

> No matter how important it is to exploit the victory gained during the winter battle in Masuria as much as is possible, we must not lose sight of the fact that efforts in that direction are subject to certain limitations because of our military and political situation. The *OHL* will probably be compelled, perhaps as early as the second half of March, to transfer a very significant number of forces currently committed in the northeast to other theatres of operation. A reduction in replacements and of ammunition supplies for the East will have to take place even sooner. Before then, it is therefore important to put the Russian armies in such a position that they will not again become a menace to us for the foreseeable future.

The plans that precipitated Falkenhayn's request—as would become apparent in a subsequent telegram of 9 March from the General Staff Chief to *OberOst*—pertained to the "continuation of the campaign in the West" and the "opening of a route to Turkey." Both objectives presupposed that in the near future Russia would be weakened to such an extent that it would "no longer be able to pose a risk" along any segment of the front—neither on the Carpathian Front nor in Poland or East Prussia. Because the potential impact of the operations then underway could not be fully assessed, it seemed doubtful that such circumstances would arise. Even more doubtful—given the fact that Falkenhayn had neither a GHQ

Reserve at his disposal nor any prospect of procuring one by the middle of March—
was whether it would be possible to transfer such strong forces from the East to
the other theatres of war. These transfers would be necessary, however, if Serbia
was to be defeated or if a decision was to be reached on the Western Front. Both
tasks appeared equally urgent.

The political situation and the need to establish a secure link with Turkey
required Serbia's defeat, or at least the seizure of the Negotin District.[5] On the
other hand, there were many urgent reasons why a military decision in the West
needed to be reached during the approaching spring if at all possible. First of all,
there was no doubt whatsoever that this objective would become increasingly difficult once British reinforcements, the so-called Kitchener armies—which were
expected to arrive in early summer—became operational on the continent. During the winter of 1915 the balance of power in the West continued to favour a German offensive in the near future: in the second half of February about ninety-two
German divisions were facing the Entente's ninety-seven (according to estimates
made by the *OHL*'s Intelligence Division). To bring about a military decision in
the West, however, a significantly larger allocation of forces and materiel would
be required than in the East. This was because the Western Front had stabilized,
making it necessary to carry out a successful breakthrough along a comparatively
wide portion of the front before there could be any hope to launch an actual
offensive. The initial breakthrough would require a large number of forces; the
ensuing offensive would require even more, for it would require constant reinforcements until victory was achieved. Moreover, the prerequisite for success in such
a breakthrough was an especially large number of heavy artillery pieces and an
extraordinarily large supply of ammunition. When Falkenhayn sent his telegram
to *OberOst* on 19 February, he must have been aware that these requirements—
at least in terms of reserves and materiel—could hardly be obtained from the
East. So he was probably not contemplating an operation that would decide the
war in Serbia and in the Western Theatre, but rather short, sharp thrusts on both
fronts. In Serbia these thrusts would be intended to capture the Negotin District,
thereby establishing a link with Turkey; in the West they would raise the morale
of the troops, who for months had been exhausting themselves in a war of
attrition. It appears that Falkenhayn envisioned such an objective when he first

---

5 *The Negotin District is an area of northeastern Serbia bordered in the north by the Iron Gates,
a rugged, meandering stretch of the Danube between the Carpathians and the Balkans. The
area was strategically significant because it was bordered on three sides by Austria-Hungary,
Rumania, and Bulgaria. If it were captured, the Central Powers would thus secure a direct land
connection to Bulgaria and the Ottoman Empire. See* Trumpener, *Germany and the Ottoman
Empire, 1914–1918*, 82–83.

considered launching an offensive in the West in the second half of January, at a time when he still had new formations at his disposal. However desirable these two objectives might have been, the question remained whether it was not more important to first employ all available forces to reach an easier and more quickly obtained decision in the East. Only in this way would it be possible to release sufficient forces to defeat Serbia and then achieve victory in the West. As the commanders in the East stressed time and again, the prerequisite for such operations was the defeat of Russia. Thus it seemed risky to shift the war's centre of gravity again to the "other theatres of war" before a decision in the East had been achieved.

At this juncture, only a few days after the inquiry of 19 February had been sent to *OberOst*, a proposal was unexpectedly submitted to Falkenhayn that offered the prospect of procuring a new, strong GHQ reserve without concurrently weakening the Eastern Front. It also offered an entirely new basis for future decision making. On 22 February the Chief of the Army Section of the Ministry of War, Oberst von Wrisberg (who had already distinguished himself by earlier raising the new formations), recommended to Falkenhayn, who at that time was in Berlin, that new divisions be formed by detaching each existing division's fourth infantry regiment.[6] He proposed to initially introduce this plan on the Western Front and to pattern the new divisions on the ones organized in January, which had included only three infantry regiments each. In order to compensate the existing divisions in the West for the loss of their fourth infantry regiments, it was proposed that 2,400 trained replacements and two machine-gun platoons, equipped with three machine guns each, be sent to each division. The infantry replacements were to be distributed to the remaining infantry regiments so that each company would contain, on average, sixty-six more enlisted men than before.

---

6 *At the beginning of the war each regular infantry division normally consisted of four regiments, each of three battalions, assigned to two brigade headquarters. The infantry was supplemented by four machine-gun companies, three to four squadrons of cavalry, twelve field artillery batteries, one to two pioneer companies, the divisional pontoon train, and two medical companies. Reserve divisions sometimes did not have machine-gun companies, never had more than one medical company, and only had six field batteries instead of twelve.* Ersatz *divisions had three brigades for a total of thirteen to fifteen battalions, six machine-gun companies, twelve batteries, and two pioneer companies.* Landwehr *divisions were composed of twelve battalions, lacked machine-gun companies, and had only two field artillery batteries. During the reorganization in March of 1915, new divisions were created with only one brigade headquarters and three infantry regiments. The brigade headquarters was eventually scrapped to form divisional staffs and the three-regiment division became the norm across the German army for all regular, reserve,* Ersatz, *and* Landwehr *divisions. For more on the organization of infantry divisions, see* Cron, Imperial German Army, 1914–18, *95–99.*

The number of infantry rifles and machine guns along the front would thus remain the same. The field artillery, engineers, cavalry, and other arms required by the divisions would be obtained by reducing the number of guns in each battery from six to four, by downsizing the cavalry units assigned to the existing divisions, and by creating a limited number of new units.[7] Falkenhayn immediately agreed to the proposal, obtaining the Kaiser's consent on the very same day. It was anticipated that Wrisberg's plan would make a considerable number of divisions available behind the Western Front in about one and a half months' time; these would then be at the *OHL*'s unrestricted disposal. This would largely—or even completely—free the *OHL* from having to redeploy troops from the East.

Accordingly, preparations were immediately made for the reorganization of the Western Army. On 25 February, Falkenhayn issued a directive to the Western field forces, the lead paragraph of which announced that the *OHL* intended to gradually organize new units in rear of the Western forces, which were to constitute a GHQ reserve. To begin with, six infantry divisions (including 50th, 52nd, 54th, and 59th from Saxony and Württemberg, as well as Bavarian 10th Division) were to be formed and readied for service during the second half of March. In addition to three regiments of infantry united under a brigade headquarters, each division would include one field artillery brigade, one foot artillery battalion with two batteries of heavy field howitzers, and two pioneer companies, as well as ammunition columns and supply trains. Thus each division would be self-sufficient. At the same time as this directive was issued, a request was transmitted to the Ministry of War for the organization of a new army headquarters—Eleventh Army Headquarters—which was to be made ready at Cassel and was to proceed to its destination no later than 11 March.

On 3 March, Falkenhayn requested the organization of additional divisions:

> The objective to be reached during this very month, requires us to convert all line and reserve divisions of the western forces into units containing only three infantry regiments, and to organize from the supernumerary regiments thus obtained new divisions comprising likewise three regiments. Should it prove impracticable to furnish all the necessary components to the divisions under consideration, I would be satisfied if they consisted only of infantry and field batteries in the beginning. Even in this shape they will prove very useful as reserves for special missions, and it will be possible to gradually assign to them their full complement.

---

7 *This meant that each division would be equipped with forty-eight instead of seventy-two guns.*
Ibid., 99.

Because the Western Army was comprised of thirty-six infantry and thirty-seven reserve divisions, they were bound to yield, after the reorganization had been completed, twenty-four new divisions, which the OHL could keep in reserve behind the front. The prospect of achieving a military victory in the West before the effects of the British reinforcements could make themselves felt had brightened unexpectedly.

Thus Falkenhayn's intention of shifting the war's centre of gravity to the Western Theatre began to crystallize. He now regarded the proportion of strength in the West—at least as far as the German side was concerned—as being so favourable that at times he contemplated staging simultaneous decisive operations both in Serbia and on the Western Front—something that ran contrary to his previous views. To allow for this, he hoped to forgo the retransfer of any large forces from the Eastern Theatre. The idea began to take hold that the Eastern forces would be able to carry out their mission using their own resources and that they would thereby safeguard the Western Front's rear. As early as 5 March, even before it could known for certain whether the expected number of newly organized units would actually be obtained, Hindenburg announced that "a retransfer of forces from the Eastern Front to the West was, for the time being—that is during the month of March—no longer being contemplated."

Yet the reorganization of all line and reserve divisions on the Western Front, which Falkenhayn had requested, soon proved impossible. On 11 March the War Minister informed the Emperor that only a further eight additional divisions could be organized. The formation of these units was ordered on 16 March. Of these divisions, the 111th, 113th, 119th, and 121st were to be ready for service at the beginning of April; 115th, 117th, 123rd, and Bavarian 11th Divisions were to reach this stage eight to fourteen days later. These units, however, could only be supplied with six field batteries and one battery of field howitzers each; only one engineer company was assigned to each division, and the ammunition and supply trains were correspondingly reduced.

These divisions having been organized, the possibility of forming new units from surplus forces on the Western Front was exhausted, at least for the time being. Aside from difficulties with armaments, the replacement situation alone rendered it impossible to create twenty-four new divisions by reorganizing the Western forces in accordance with Falkenhayn's original request. While this reorganization was going on in the middle of March 1915, a number of men were made available for replacement purposes in the replacement units and recruit depots. These amounted to some 163,000 non-commissioned officers and men whose training was completed, and as many as 515,000 men who were still undergoing training.[8] The field forces' monthly requirements for replacements averaged 180,000 men in round numbers, whereas some 175,000 additional replacements were required in order to make up for the infantry that the existing divisions had been required to transfer during the reorganization. When projected over a protracted period of time, however, the replacement situation posed few difficulties, for apart from the recruit class of 1915, there were still a substantial number of men available from the *Landsturm* category who had never received any training at all.

By the middle of March, Falkenhayn understood clearly that until the beginning of April he would have only fourteen divisions at his disposal behind the Western Front and not the twenty-four he had expected. Nor was he able to count on any additional increases in strength for the foreseeable future because of the acute replacement situation precipitated by the difficulties experienced in meeting armament requirements. To draw from the German Eastern Front for additional troops was out of the question, considering the situation in that theatre. Neither was such action necessary, since the offensive in the West could not begin until the middle of May at the earliest. So on 20 March he wired Generalfeldmarschall von Hindenburg that a retransfer of forces from the Eastern Front to the West would not be contemplated until after the end of March. "Should the necessity arise, however," the telegram continued, "for such a transfer or if those units in the south that have been attached to Your Excellency are required elsewhere, timely advice will be sent."

Toward the middle of April, Falkenhayn also suggested that new German divisions be organized on the Eastern Front. Although considerable time was to pass before this plan could be realized, it was initially thought that three infantry divisions (101st, 103rd, and 105th Divisions) could be formed from the Eastern forces; however, it was not expected that they would be ready for service prior to the second half of May.

IN ADDITION TO THE ISSUE OF REPLACEMENTS, THE AMMUNITION QUESTION became a matter of great importance. Everyone agreed that a war-winning offensive in the West would require enormous supplies of ammunition. At the same time, it had to be anticipated that the Eastern Front would need an increased amount of ammunition, since a German offensive in the West would probably lead to a Russian attack in the Eastern Theatre.

---

8   It has been impossible to ascertain the number of men undergoing training that might have been sent to the front during March because they were considered fit for field service.

The Plan to Mount a Decisive Breakthrough Operation in the West

On 1 March, Falkenhayn returned to the Western Front, where two important tasks awaited him: the Western Armies needed to be reorganized in order to create a new GHQ reserve—something that was becoming more and more important because of the threat of a new enemy offensive; and the difficult problem of staging a breakthrough operation in the West had to be solved. To deal with.the second task, first it was necessary to ascertain the part of the Western Front along which a breakthrough and subsequent offensive would more likely result in victory. Second, it was necessary to determine the size of the force and the amount of materiel—especially heavy artillery and ammunition—that would be required.

Two plans for a war-winning offensive, both involving an initial breakthrough,. had already been worked out independently after comprehensive study at the headquarters of Sixth and First Armies. On 4 March the Commander of Sixth Army submitted his study, which had been prepared by Generalmajor Krafft von Dellmensingen. After investigating all possible directions for an attack, the general had chosen the northern wing of the enemy front (just as Wild had done at the end of December 1914) as the location for the operation; the intent in this was to separate the British forces from those of the French and then destroy them. However, he did not believe he could count on German numerical superiority; in his view it would not be possible to obtain such supremacy before Russia had been defeated. Superiority would instead have to be sought in the efficiency and technical skill of German officers and soldiers. As it was thought that the transfer of fresh troops from Great Britain to the continent might increase the number of British troops by the end of March to fifteen corps—doubling their strength—the army commander concluded: "It is therefore incumbent upon us to consider very carefully whether we are not approaching a task that might prove too great for our strength." He also pointed out that it was not merely a question of piercing the enemy's fortified front, for the victorious troops—after they had finally broken through during a battle that would continue day and night—would then be required to fight their way forward from position to position in frontal attacks that would have to be renewed again and again.

Regarding the premise that the advance should pass close to Amiens, Krafft did not consider it advisable—however desirable it might be—for the Germans to protect their left flank with the lower Somme. If this were done, the forces needed for the operation would increase greatly even while the principle objective remained the separation of the British forces from the French. The offensive would have to be directed against the French forces adjoining the British right wing, and for this reason he believed that a breakthrough on both sides of Arras was required, with a subsequent advance following the range of hills extending northwest toward the coast between Boulogne and Calais. Farther to the north, around Mount Kemmel, a secondary attack would hold the enemy. To cover the main offensive to the south, he planned to detach suitable forces as necessary to ward off any enemy attempts to interfere with the offensive along the line Albert–Doullens–Authis River, because the more preferable defensive line formed by the Somme could hardly be gained.

Sixth Army's study further recommended that the first step—breaking through the enemy's fortified front—be effected with full force, "crushing everything before it." It was proposed that during the initial artillery preparation, each high-angle battery be assigned a target not exceeding 150 metres in width. The main attack's front, the entire width of which comprised the breakthrough (exclusive of the city of Arras, which was to be pinched out), was to measure 26 kilometres. In all, in preparation for the main attack, 160 heavy and 374 field batteries were to be employed. The breakthrough would be launched with six corps. Seven additional corps, together with two cavalry divisions, were to follow the main attack, tasked with enlarging the gap in the enemy's line and acting as supports and reserves. Of these thirteen corps, three would already be at the front and ten new ones would have to be brought up for the attack. The study also stipulated that the secondary attack near Mount Kemmel would require 38 heavy and 143 field batteries, and it was here that the three new corps were to enter the line. In addition, considerable auxiliary forces would be needed: engineers, *Minenwerfer* units, aviation units, dirigibles, and so forth.

This study strongly emphasized ammunition supply. During the fighting near Ypres in the fall of 1914, the Commander of Sixth Army had found that sometimes the heavy batteries (in the majority of cases) were unable to bring their full firepower to bear because ammunition was lacking. A similar shortcoming could not be repeated, even though there had been a significant increase in the number of guns assigned to the large-scale breakthrough attempt compared to the number of pieces that had been used in the battles of the previous autumn. The entire operation would be possible only if:

> First, the heavy artillery is without exception provided with draught animals or motorized transport, and second an enormous amount of ammunition is placed in readiness; [this stockpile needs to be] large enough to enable the artillery pieces to develop their full firepower throughout the operation. The attack's success is dependent first and foremost on this prerequisite. There could be no greater mistake than to permit the attack to stall before the completion of the operation because of an inadequate ammunition

supply. For this reason, the stocks of ammunition to be kept on hand must be sufficient for at least one month of fighting—preferably for a longer period, during which time the troops that are to bring about the decision will be expected to be engaged in battle every day; or a continuous supply of ammunition to replenish expenditure must be assured.

This study was the first to thoroughly examine the question of how a large-scale strategic breakthrough on the Western Front might be achieved. The document demonstrated clearly that such an operation would need to employ a good portion of the German forces and an even greater part—comparatively speaking—of available war materiel, especially as far as the heavy artillery was concerned. Moreover, it highlighted the important problems that would arise with respect to command; the difficulties inherent in launching a surprise offensive; the requirement of placing a special mass of manoeuvre in readiness behind the units that were to break through the enemy front; and the need to assign missions to specially selected leaders for the operations that would follow the initial breakthrough, which would require the troops to advance in several directions at once. At the same time, the enemy's reserves would have to be immobilized by attacks in force along the remainder of the front.

General von Falkenhayn's comments written on Sixth Army's proposal indicate that he took very seriously the warning against mounting an offensive that would exceed the bounds of German strength. Yet there can be no doubt that he viewed the mutual proportion of forces in a more favourable light and was of the opinion that the proposed operation could be launched with fewer resources than the report suggested. Indeed, Sixth Army's proposal was similar to the one that he himself had envisaged in December. When examining the recommendations of Generals Wild and von Knobelsdorf, he had written below the former's estimate: "I certainly regard the offensive in the direction of Amiens as sound." In making this statement, he was voicing his opposition to an operation along the Aisne or in the Champagne.

The extraordinary requirements in men and materiel that the Commander of Sixth Army considered necessary gave rise to the suggestion that perhaps a breakthrough could be effected at some other point along the front—one that required the commitment of fewer resources. On 2 March, when Falkenhayn briefly visited St. Quentin, Generalmajor von Kuhl, First Army's Chief of Staff—who was accompanying Falkenhayn—pointed out to him that another study was being prepared at First Army Headquarters. This study was detailing an offensive operation to be launched across the Aisne to the east of Soissons subsequent to an initial breakthrough. Just a few hours before, Falkenhayn had voiced his doubts at Sixth Army Headquarters as to the advisability of gathering the strength of the Western forces for an offensive in the direction of the Channel Coast, reasoning that the French would then probably make extraordinary efforts toward achieving a breakthrough in the Champagne. Therefore, First Army's proposal fell on fertile soil. A number of days were bound to elapse before that proposal could be completed. So on 7 March, Falkenhayn detached Oberst Tappen, Chief of the *OHL*'s Operations Section, for duty as Chief of Staff of Seventh Army until the end of the month so that he could examine independently the prospects for an offensive across the Aisne. By now he understood that a major March offensive in the West was out of the question.

Meanwhile, the organization of new divisions in the West had not at all met the expectations voiced at the beginning of the month: the total number of new divisions amounted to fourteen instead of the anticipated twenty-four. Although it would be possible to slightly increase this number by making use of men who could be dispensed with at the front, it was quite evident that the forces considered necessary to implement Sixth Army's study would not be forthcoming. Yet this did not cause Falkenhayn to abandon the idea of staging a large-scale breakthrough operation on the Western Front. On the contrary, on 11 March he informed Oberst von Seeckt (who had been appointed Chief of Staff of the newly organized Eleventh Army) that he planned to return to a war of movement in the West by means of a breakthrough along a wide front and to thus bring the war to a decision.[9]

On 13 March, Falkenhayn received First Army's study, which had been completed by Kuhl. It suggested that a breakthrough in the area of Roye was no longer advisable as such an operation would merely push the British back along a more or less extended semicircle in the direction of Dunkirk, Calais, and Boulogne, whereas the French would withdraw their left wing to the line Boulogne–Dieppe or Rouen.[10] In such an event, two new frontal attacks would then become necessary. The study correctly emphasized that above everything else the breakthrough itself had to succeed:

> The point where the breakthrough is to be made must be selected in such a manner as to favour the attack tactically, and to guarantee that considerable elements of the enemy forces are either defeated or driven off. It is important to prevent the enemy from renewing his resistance in prepared rear positions. The breakthrough operation must be prepared in such a manner and executed with the aid of such strong forces that its success—

---

9 This is according to General Seekt's letter of 13 November 1927, addressed to the *Reichsarchiv.*
10 *This had been proposed by First Army's commander, General Kluck, in October 1914.* See *DW* V: 149, 171, 176.

at least as far as is humanly calculable—will be assured. We must guard against the French habit of bringing up one corps at a time to attack the enemy's position. All means should be employed toward striving for the element of surprise. The breakthrough must come as an unexpected blow and must succeed. The outcome of the campaign depends on it.

To the Commander of First Army, the conditions favouring such a breakthrough within the zone of First Army appeared to exist along First Army's left wing and Seventh Army's right wing. The study's recommendations were then put forward with the following premises. Four corps, two of which were already in place, were to cross the Aisne on a 20 kilometre front near Vailly and to the east of it and were to advance toward the Chassemy–Vauxcere Plateau. Four additional corps, as well as one cavalry corps, were to follow. These units would have to be quartered in far-flung sheltered areas between Ham and Montcornet in order to keep the enemy in the dark as to the point of attack. Their mission would be to enlarge the newly created gap by advancing against the enemy's rear forces in positions farther to the east, rolling these forces up, and eliminating them. The operation would then continue in the direction of Paris. Simultaneously with the beginning of the main offensive, a secondary attack was to be launched northwest of Soissons. For this purpose, only one additional division—to be furnished by the *OHL*—would be necessary.

The heavy artillery requirements of First Army's proposal were lower than those contained in Sixth Army's study. For the main offensive, 110 heavy batteries were thought necessary; for the secondary attack northwest of Soissons, twenty-seven were thought to be required. The ammunition estimates were, it followed, lower than those for First Army's proposed breakthrough on both sides of Arras. This proposal had all the hallmarks of success, at least as far as a tactical breakthrough was concerned, and the necessary forces could be made available. It would constitute a serious blow to the enemy. But how far would its strategic effects extend? And would this employment of forces be profitable if the campaign were to prove indecisive?

General von Kuhl was summoned to GHQ on 14 March for a personal interview on the subject. During the ensuing conference, he explained that as far as he was concerned a different operation—namely, an offensive in the Champagne—had more potential.[11] However, a rough estimate indicated that the forces required

---

11 On 18 March, Falkenhayn asked for the Third Army Commander's estimate regarding the prospects of and requirements for a breakthrough operation in the Champagne. The Third Army study, submitted in response to this request on 28 March, treated the breakthrough both as an independent main effort and as a secondary operation for demonstration purposes; this proposal, however, failed to leave any perceptible impression on Falkenhayn.

for such an undertaking were not available. This left the proposal for a break-through across the Aisne to the east of Soissons. That operation, however, was increasingly assuming the character of a local offensive, and thus lacked the potential to decide the broader war. This point was driven home when, on 15 March, Wild was asked for his opinion. He stated that First Army's suggestion that the proposed operation be continued in the direction of Paris was not feasible, given the forces proposed for the operation.

The two operational studies completed by Sixth and First Armies had been drawn up in expectation that the Battle of the Masurian Lakes would release considerable forces from the East for use in the West. Both studies had been requested in order to give the *OHL* a detailed estimate as to the requirements in troops and materiel (based on the experience gained to that point in the war) for launching such operations, and also to enable it to estimate the time required to make such preparations. Sixth Army's study had followed the proposed operation to its logical conclusion (i.e., the destruction of the British forces), though only in the form of an outline; whereas First Army's plan was content to dwell on the tactical features of the initial breakthrough. If after First Army's breakthrough the plan was to embark on a far-reaching offensive similar to the one proposed by Sixth Army, new forces would be necessary, and this would probably cause the total requirements for the offensive to reach the same level as those described in the Arras proposal.

Despite the enormous requirements in men and materiel that both proposals estimated would be necessary in order to effect a strategic breakthrough, Falkenhayn clung to his plan for an offensive in the Western Theatre with the means then at his disposal. On 16 March the commander of the newly organized Eleventh Army—the headquarters of which had been moved to Maubeuge—was given the following directive in writing:

> The *OHL* plans to break through the enemy front in the West after making an adequate number of troops available. To this end, strong reserves will be placed in readiness in rear of that front along the several railroad lines. The concentration of these reserves and their subsequent forward movement by rail to the point where the breakthrough is to be effected, will be regulated by the *OHL*. The time for placing the reserves in readiness and the place for the breakthrough operation proper have not yet been fixed. The Commander of the Eleventh Army will conduct the offensive in a zone of action that will be designated in due time. The Eleventh Army Commander's next task will consist of reconnoitring the terrain between La Bassée Canal[12] and the Avre near

---

12   According to the original document, this meant the canal leading from Béthune to La Bassée.

Roye for a breakthrough operation, with a view to piercing the hostile front north of the Somme on a width of from 25 to 30 kilometres and advancing thence to the sea. In the zones of action to be selected, it is planned to allot first of all, in addition to the troops already in position, as many infantry divisions (each of three infantry regiments) as will enable each division to occupy from two and a half to 3 kilometres of frontage. The necessary heavy artillery will be made available. With the aid of these forces the tactical break-through should be successful—including the piercing of the enemy's line. In rear of the rupture, the OHL intends to place as many additional forces in readiness as will be required to exploit the tactical breakthrough for strate-gic purposes. The reconnaissance must be initiated as early as possible ... [and] the result will be submitted to the OHL in the form of a report no later than the end of March.

Besides defining reconnaissance objectives, this order provided basic instruc-tions as to the number of troops to be engaged. It also differentiated sharply between the tactical actions involved in the breakthrough and its strategic exploita-tion. The OHL did not commit itself to staging the operation in the sector that was to be reconnoitred, but it must be assumed that the commander and staff of Eleventh Army were aware that Falkenhayn was inclined to launch an offensive to the north of the Somme. In mid-March he apparently regarded the execution of the task he had assigned as entirely feasible, at least as far as troop requirements were concerned. According to Falkenhayn's instructions, if ten divisions were employed on the front line (of which approximately four were already in the zone delineated for the breakthrough), then with the aid of the fourteen divisions that were being organized, it would be possible to place a second echelon of eight divi-sions in the rear of the forces designated to achieve the tactical breakthrough in order to complete the operations that would follow. Additional units that could be released from the stabilized front might then be used to reinforce this second echelon, or for other tasks such as diversionary attacks, or for guarding the remain-der of the front against possible enemy offensives. These calculations, of course, fell considerably below the requirements outlined in Sixth Army's study.

At this time, plans were in place to deploy the forces under the control of the OHL. According to a communication from the Operations Section of the OHL dated 19 March 1915 and addressed to the Chief of the Military Railways,[13] begin-ning on 23 March the following forces were to be gradually assembled: the Guard Corps in the region of Schlettstadt–Colmar; XXXXI Reserve Corps near

---

13 The original text gave the origin of this information in a footnote at the end of the previous sen-tence, but for purposes of clarity it has been inserted in the actual text at this point.

Aulnoye–Busogny–Hirson; Bavarian II Corps, including Bavarian 11th Infantry
Division, in the vicinity of Valenciennes–Douai–Cambrai; III Corps, including
111th Infantry Division, near Ath–Mons–Hal–Grammont; and XXXXII Corps,
which was to be organized from 119th and 121st Divisions. If it were possible, a
division of X Reserve Corps was also to be deployed in the region of Falken-
borg–Bensdorf–Bitsch. Second and Third Armies were thus to be reduced by one
infantry division each. As for the rest, it was merely a question of replacing the
older infantry divisions with the newly organized ones. The communication
continued:

> As a governing principle for the assembly of these corps, one thing is essen-
> tial: namely, it must be possible promptly to concentrate the several corps,
> either by rail or marching, in rear of the right wing of the field forces; at the
> same time, sufficient troops must remain available to provide adequate
> cover for the centre and left wing of our armies.

According to this plan, around the middle of April, sixteen infantry divisions,
of which seven were to be newly organized, would have to be in readiness behind
the Western Front, subject to the control of the *OHL*. Regarding cavalry divisions,
around the middle of March, four were still deployed on the Western Front.

Around the same time, preparations began for a strong GHQ artillery reserve
(*Heeresartillerie*). At the end of March these preparatory measures culminated in
a request to the War Ministry for the organization of forty old-type heavy batteries without teams, the crews for which were to be taken from replacement
units. To make it possible to release the more modern batteries from the front,
the new units were to be ready for service by the middle of April. According to
calculations which assumed that ten corps would go into action, 624 artillery
pieces—exclusive of the field batteries—would thus become available for a breakthrough attempt.

On 19 March a second study was presented to Falkenhayn that had been prepared at First Army Headquarters, dealing once again with the questions that had
been discussed at Mézières on 14 March. The study's preamble pointed out that
it would be necessary to take into account the number of available troops; if need
be, the offensive should become more localized. Regarding the offensive's direction, the army commander (Kluck) repeated his objection to a breakthrough near
Arras or Roye on the grounds that it would result in very large fronts and that even
if it did succeed in separating the British and French forces, the German Army
would then face two separate enemy groups. He considered it important that the
offensive be conducted in such a way that part of the German forces would make
their appearance in the vicinity of Paris relatively quickly. He also assumed that

the enemy would not try to defend the city in the manner of 1870–71,[14] or to defend it as a fortress as had happened at Antwerp and Maubeuge in 1914,[15] but that the enemy would make its main stand in strong defensive positions a considerable distance from the capital. The study argued that it was therefore important to advance rapidly on Paris in a direction along which such positions were less complete and their garrisons not easily made ready; there was no doubt that in such conditions the pressure on Paris would expedite the achievement of a military decision. Because the lack of necessary forces made it impracticable to stage an offensive in the Champagne, the study again recommended a breakthrough across the Aisne east of Soissons. Kluck believed that with seven additional corps he would be able to roll up the enemy positions toward the east for a considerable distance up to and including Reims. He also thought that he could envelop the enemy forces stationed along the Aisne and then march on Paris.

Falkenhayn's notes in the margins of this study indicate that he had an entirely different opinion than Kluck as to the potential impact of an offensive launched just north of the Somme. Opposite the sentence "after all, the British will still be at liberty to avoid destruction by retiring across the water," he wrote: "In that case, the French would be through with their ally." On the other hand, he concurred entirely with the study's following statement:

No matter where a breakthrough may be made, it must be supported in any event by a diversionary attack staged at some other point. This will best be accomplished by an attack which differs from the main offensive only in its limited objective and limited means, yet which requires a preparation just as careful, and likewise adequate artillery support.

Eleventh Army's commander had not been asked to submit proposals for such a diversionary attack; it would appear that Falkenhayn had reserved this for himself. On 17 March he directed Armee-Abteilung *Gaede*—on whose front an enemy

---

14 After the defeat at Sedan on 1 September 1870, the surviving French forces congregated in Paris, where the city was converted into a virtual fortress. The German armies surrounded the city on 15 September, but Moltke the Elder refused to assault the capital, instead opting to lay siege. The Siege of Paris lasted until 28 January 1871, when heavy artillery shelled the starving garrison and civilian population into submission. On the German General Staff's interpretation of the Franco-Prussian war, see Großer Generalstab, Kriegesgeschichtliche Abteilung, *Der deutsch-französische Krieg, 1870–7*, 8 vols. (Berlin: E.S. Mittler & Sohn, 1874–81).

15 Both Antwerp and Maubeuge (on the Franco-Belgian border) had proven to be significant points of resistance during the German sweep into France in the summer and early autumn of 1914. Maubeuge was taken in a thirteen-day siege, falling on 9 September; Antwerp did not surrender until the second week of October. See Erich von Tschischwitz, *Schlachten des Weltkrieges: In Einzeldarstellungen bearbeitet im Auftrages des Reichsarchiv Band 3: Antwerpen, 1914* (Berlin: Stalling, 1925).

offensive could not very well have any appreciable effect—to suspend its previously approved attack and to go over to the "defensive as planned." Falkenhayn had
little faith in Fourth Army's gas offensive, which had been under preparation since
the beginning of February and was still awaiting execution. It was evident that for
the purpose of luring away the enemy's reserves at the right time, the gas attack—
which depended on the weather and had never been tested—could not be relied
on because of the uncertain meteorological conditions. Even so, on 19 March he
asked Second Army's commander whether any plan had been prepared for a surprise attack from the direction of Fricourt–Mametz and from Dompierre in order
to pinch off the French positions at Maricourt. He wanted to know what additional
infantry and artillery forces, as well as time requirements, Bülow considered necessary in order to mount such an operation, and whether he believed it could be
profitable. Bülow estimated that the troop requirements would be high and that
the expected results would not be in fair proportion to the effort. On 29 March,
Seventh Army's commander was ordered to report the number of additional
forces he would require in order to clear the right bank of the Aisne from Berry-
au-Bac on downstream of the enemy, and on which day—after the receipt of such
an order—he would be able to carry out the operation. Heeringen stated that one
corps and thirty-three batteries, most of which would have to be heavy, together
with the necessary ammunition, would be adequate for the task.

Even before the results of the extended reconnoitring operations had been
submitted, the OHL issued two general directives toward the end of March to the
armies in the West. The first of these, dated 29 March, dealt with the security of
the current positions, which, after units were withdrawn, would have to be held
without incurring great losses. To this end, a number of precautionary measures
were recommended regarding the improvement of the wire; the construction of
bombproof shelters using reinforced concrete to accommodate front-line garrisons; and the construction of communication trenches, rear positions, and supporting points. Also, thorough preparations were to be made for the future
employment of artillery. In connection with these instructions, the OHL directed
all concerned to carry out a "careful reconnaissance in anticipation of launching
an attack." It instructed that this reconnaissance was to be

> carried out on the premise that, in the event that the OHL orders an attack,
> each division of three infantry regiments in the first line would be allotted
> a battle strip (*Gefechsstreifen*) of two and a half to 3 kilometres. These plans
> of attack are to concern themselves primarily with subduing the opposing
> enemy with the aid of all available technical means and artillery fire. In this
> respect, the plans are to be prepared with due diligence, paying attention to
> every detail.

These plans drove home the point that "both the defence and attack must be prepared so perfectly so as to guarantee success at any point."

A second directive, issued on 31 March, titled the "Training of the *OHL*'s Reserves," also provided general instructions. It emphasized that "the reserves stationed in rear of the front line under the control of the *OHL* are destined first and foremost for the offensive"[16] and that the training of these troops was to be conducted with this in mind while "careful instructions in the technical means of attack will be stressed." The directive did not contain any uniform instructions for attacks on fortified positions, but instead directed attention to "the best experiences of the units," which would have to be supplemented "by the study of the report prepared by First Army dealing with the attack on Soissons." To this end, training camps were to be established, "in which fortified positions arranged in several lines behind one another were to serve as objectives during the instruction." These exercises were to begin with problems involving small units and to extend progressively so as to encompass the division. Furthermore,

> divisional exercises should generally be governed by the principle that the first line is solely charged with the tactical breakthrough which is to be preceded by a strong artillery preparation. For the strategic exploitation of the breakthrough, the *OHL* will place in readiness strong additional forces made up of other units along second and third lines ... It is impracticable to prescribe the length of the preparatory period. The earlier that the units are ready for action, the better for all concerned. Not one day must be lost.

This directive proved to be inadequate. It required the respective commanders to base the reserves' training on the unit's own experiences and those of First Army in the fighting at Soissons. Almost nothing was said about artillery tasks, especially for heavy artillery, or about co-operation with the attacking infantry. Suffice it to say that these directives were altogether insufficient to serve as instructions for the purpose of training the Western Army for the exceedingly difficult and unfamiliar tasks involved in a large breakthrough operation directed against the British and French.

On 31 March the reports of Oberst von Seeckt, Eleventh Army's Chief of Staff,[17] and of Oberst Tappen arrived at GHQ. At this point, Tappen reverted to his former position as Chief of Staff of the Operations Section of the *OHL*.

---

16 In the original, Falkenhayn struck out the words "breakthrough and" before the word "offensive."

17 At this time, Eleventh Army was without a commander because Fabeck had assumed command of First Army in Kluck's absence (he had been wounded).

The study prepared by Eleventh Army examined the problem of finding the place between La Bassée Canal and the Avre at Roye where a breakthrough operation would offer the best strategic prospects. Based on the premises that the distance from Albert to the mouth of the Somme was the shortest route to the sea, that the left wing of the German offensive would be protected by the Somme, and that the trunk line Paris–Abbeville–Boulogne could be cut early on, it was decided that the line Arras–River Somme would be the most strategically favourable place for a breakthrough. After making a detailed estimate of the tactical considerations along the entire front, Seeckt recommended a breakthrough attempt along a 25 kilometre sector of the front between Arras and Albert, extending from a point slightly to the north of Ficheux down to Thiepval. Here, too, the difficulties were considerable. They arose not only from the strength of the enemy's front line, but also from the numerous towns in the area, which had unique features making them highly defensible. The report read:

> In this highly cultivated part of northern France, the country extending approximately to the latitude of Doullens (i.e., the zone that would be first affected) is more open than most of the other sectors on the Western Front that were taken into consideration. The proposed offensive avoids outstanding and strengthened points of defence such as Arras, Albert, Lihons, and avoids any natural obstacles that might be easily defended.

Nor did Eleventh Army's staff count on a speedy victory. The report maintained that an actual rupture in the enemy line (i.e., the actual separation of the enemy forces) would not be realized until the attack's centre had progressed well beyond Doullens. Thus a continuous renewal of the attacking troops' striking power would be necessary in order to keep the advance flowing—this would be essential for operation's success. Additional strong forces would have to follow the attack in the beginning. Forces echeloned to the left of the first line would have to carry the left wing of the breakthrough operation forward, approximately to the vicinity of Bonneville, with a view to furnishing cover against enemy action from Amiens and the line of the lower Somme as far as Condé Folie. Farther downstream, cavalry divisions would have to take over the provision of security in a southerly direction. The right flank of the breakthrough contingents would have to move northwestward on Warlus–Gouy-en-Artois. Troops that had been held in readiness until then would have to be inserted into the gap that would open between the right flank and the rest of the forces committed to the breakthrough. These forces would have orders to advance on Avesnes-le-Comte. In connection with the secondary attack that would be launched to the north of Arras, the question remained whether French forces should be surrounded in their positions.

The further course of the operation (i.e., the advance against the Franco-British forces to the north of the breakthrough point) seemed to depend mainly on the actions taken by the enemy. If their behaviour compelled the centre and left wings of the breakthrough forces to change direction northward, it would be necessary for the army following them to place itself on their left by moving westward while still in rear of the breakthrough troops. However, if the enemy failed to affect the situation in the manner described, the original breakthrough forces would be able to continue their march to the sea; the troops to their rear would be required to occupy the gap that opened to the west of Avesnes-le-Comte. The study did not deal with the decisive action that would have to be staged against the enemy, which at that point would be isolated to the north of the breakthrough zone.

Regarding the actual breakthrough battle, the study stated that one corps would have to be employed for each five kilometres of front. Counting the divisions that were already in position along the front, this represented a total of five corps for the breakthrough zone. The additional supporting corps, which were also to provide cover against Amiens and enter the line with a view to advancing on Avesnes-le-Comte, increased the requirements of the breakthrough forces to nine corps. It was estimated that five corps would be necessary for the reserve army that would follow them. This would bring the total requirements up to fourteen corps—not counting four cavalry divisions—of which one and a half corps were already in position.

As for artillery, the study provided for approximately 125 high-angle batteries—each assigned to soften up 200 metres of front—of which about two-thirds could be light field howitzer batteries. Thirty heavy batteries would also be required, as well as engineer and *Minenwerfer* units. For a battle that would last three days—which was thought to be sufficient to overcome the enemy's positions—about seventy-five ammunition trains of every description were considered necessary. One-quarter of this quantity of ammunition was to be made available at the front on a daily basis.

The second reconnaissance report submitted to the *OHL* on 31 March, that of Oberst Tappen, no longer exists. According to Tappen's statements (to the *Reichsarchiv*), his report essentially agreed with First Army's study of 13 March.[18] Furthermore, he was convinced that a breakthrough and subsequent operation would decide the war through an advance on Paris and that the forces required for such

---

18 According to the entries appearing in Seventh Army's war diary, at a conference at Seventh Army Headquarters, Oberst Tappen said that the proposals contained in First Army's attack plan were sound.

an undertaking might be made available. However, in a letter to the *Reichsarchiv* dated 3 June 1930,[19] he wrote that his report stated that he would be unable to work out a definite estimate in this respect until he returned to GHQ. In all other respects, Tappen preferred a breakthrough operation to the north of the Somme because he felt that such an operation afforded a better prospect of being exploited strategically. That said, Seeckt's investigation would determine whether the soldiers necessary would actually be available.

To WHAT EXTENT FALKENHAYN WAS TAKING THE AMMUNITION SITUATION INTO account in his deliberations cannot now be ascertained. True, the production of new ammunition during the first months of 1915 had made further progress, and it had been possible to largely refill the ammunition columns through a policy of careful expenditures. Yet the requirements of the Eastern Front, and the great expenditures occasioned by the defensive battle in the West, meant that the *OHL* was able to gather only a limited ammunition reserve. The stocks of field artillery ammunition were the most plentiful as the manufacture of this type of ammunition had increased during the month of February to 100 trainloads. For the time being, a further increase was prevented by the scarcity of powder. The difficulties producing heavy artillery ammunition had yet to be entirely overcome; however, the efforts at increasing production had begun to make themselves felt.[20] During February it had been possible to double the output of heavy field howitzer ammunition; in March and April it was predicted that it could be trebled; it was possible to promise the *OHL* that in May production would increase fourfold. The manufacture of new 10 cm shells and mortar rounds was expanding in similar proportion. It could be assumed that by May 1915 the powder shortage would be relieved; thus the *OHL* was justified in expecting that it would not be hampered in its decisions during the coming summer months by an inadequate ammunition supply, which had hitherto been the case. Notwithstanding all this, the available ammunition stocks were insufficient for the operation that was scheduled to begin on or about the beginning of May. While the stocks would be adequate for breaking through the enemy's front line, a risk so daring could hardly be defended. Because operations would be taking place out in the open and would have to be carried on for at least one month with all the force that could be gathered, the

---

19 *The fact that this information was taken from a letter by Tappen to the Reichsarchiv of 3 June 1930 was originally noted in a footnote at the end of this paragraph. However, this information has been inserted into the text for the sake of clarity.*
20 See *DW* VI: 429–30.

danger was great that the subsequent operation might stall while the situation was highly unfavourable.[21] Moreover, as already mentioned, it was expected that a large-scale German offensive in the West would in turn cause the Russians to launch their own attacks in order to relieve their allies, and that therefore the ammunition requirements in the East would simultaneously increase.

EVIDENTLY FALKENHAYN WAS INCLINED, AS EARLY AS MID-MARCH, TOWARD staging an offensive north of the Somme. He did not doubt that the requirements for this offensive would be high. His own attacks at Ypres,[22] as well as his own defences against enemy attacks, had shown him that considerable superiority at the breakthrough point (which could not be too narrow) and an attack launched in surprise were the prerequisites for success. Moreover, he had considered all of this in his planning, as indicated by his directive to Eleventh Army on 16 March. Eleventh Army's staff, it is true, had called for more than twelve new corps, thus arriving at requirements that did not lag far behind those set forth in Sixth Army's study. It was possible, of course, to reduce the requirements in many instances, but doing so would undoubtedly increase the risk still more. The First and Sixth Army studies had quite properly emphasized that operations could not be allowed to stall under any circumstances and that no illusions could prevail with respect to the number of troops that would have to be employed. This is sufficient proof that at that time, the higher German commanders and their chiefs of staff possessed a much clearer view of the tremendous difficulties involved in breakthrough operations than the leaders on the enemy's side.

The study submitted by First Army offered no way out of this difficulty. True, the requirements in men were to be satisfied from the available reserves, yet First Army had planned only for the initial tactical breakthrough and not at all for the larger operations that were to follow. The requirements for the latter—if the war was to be decided in this manner—would have to be fixed at least as high as for a breakthrough in the direction of the coast. Along the Aisne, then, there was a chance to administer a crushing blow to the enemy by conquering a considerable piece of territory; but whether a victory could be gained that would cause the French government to sue for peace was very doubtful to say the least, considering the existing balance of power.

---

21 Generalleutnant Sieger, the Director of Ammunition Supply, was kept in the dark regarding all these plans; otherwise he could have proved without difficulty that the ammunition situation in the spring of 1915 absolutely prohibited an offensive operation on a large scale in the west. This information is taken from a letter from General Sieger addressed to the *Reichsarchiv* on 31 May 1931.

22 *In October and November 1914.*

At any rate, planning an operation to decide the war in the West presupposed the most detailed and time consuming of preparations. If the *OHL* issued the necessary directives at the beginning of April, an operation could not be expected to begin before the middle of May. Then the operation itself—even if it took a favourable course—would take one to two months. Until then the forces on the Western Front could exert no serious influence on the events in other theatres of operations. Falkenhayn could afford to burden himself with such a responsibility only if he was firmly convinced that he would achieve, by straining every effort, a victory in the West that would decide the war and thus compensate for any unfavourable development on other fronts.

Oberst von Seeckt was again summoned to Mézières, this time on 6 April. There Falkenhayn announced to him that he concurred with his reconnaissance report and that the recommendations contained in it were to form the basis for "the great breakthrough operations in the West ... if they were to be executed."[23] During this interview, Seeckt expressed his opinion about the prospects of a breakthrough operation across the Aisne along the lines of the proposal submitted by Kluck's First Army. A second study, which Seeckt submitted on 11 April, contained the gist of his statements made during this conference. His plan, which differed somewhat from that of First Army in its details, required that in addition to the forces that were to effect the first breakthrough (six corps aside from the two already in the line), an army be provided for the subsequent operation. This latter army, the strength of which was not mentioned, was to advance southwest and in conjunction with Seventh Army administer a decisive blow to the enemy forces on the right bank of the Marne. In this connection the right flank would be most exposed to danger, for the enemy might be able to gather considerable forces in order to attack it. On the whole, the forces that Seeckt required for this operation were hardly less than those estimated for the offensive between Arras and Albert. "The great breakthrough (on the Aisne)," he stated in his estimate, "offers prospects for initiating a decisive operation under favourable conditions. From considerations of a different nature, however, it is believed that the breakthrough to the north of the Somme is nevertheless much more promising."

On 6 April, Falkenhayn commissioned Seeckt to study the military situation in the East, which might render necessary the employment of the reserves that were available in the West. Yet elements of these reserves had to be committed to action on the very next day, when hostile pressure against the positions of Armee-Abteilung *Strantz* reached the tipping point. On the evening of 12 April there were ten divisions—to which four more were added on 19 April—stationed in the rear

---

23 Memorandum from General Seeckt, addressed to the *Reichsarchiv* on 13 November 1927.

of the Western Front, ready for service and subject to the *OHL*'s control.[24] By withdrawing divisions from the front it might be possible to increase this number further. Accordingly, on 10 April, Falkenhayn had a talk with Fourth Army's Chief of Staff (Ilse) during which he discussed the practicality of withdrawing several divisions from that portion of the front. He soon discarded the idea. For the time being there was no possibility of removing any forces from the front lines such as were required for the attack proposed in the studies of Sixth and Eleventh Armies.

There is no doubt that Falkenhayn had intended to decide the war in the West ever since the reorganization of the Western forces had opened to him the prospect of obtaining and controlling strong reserves. On 16 March he indicated this intention in unmistakable terms in a directive issued to Eleventh Army. Yet ominous developments in the military situation in the East, inadequate forces in the West (given the requirements of a breakthrough), and above all the ever-growing tension of the political situation, caused him to doubt more and more whether it would be possible to execute any plan after all.

The Political Situation's Influence on Military Decision Making

To the Dardanelles Offensive

As early as January 1915, military decisions—especially Conrad's—had been made under the weight of the vacillating political attitudes of Italy and Rumania. In the months that followed, the international political situation came to influence the Central Powers' conduct of the war to an ever-growing extent. On 11 January 1915, in unambiguous language, the Italian Ambassador in Vienna demanded for the first time that Count von Berchtold agree to cede territory that formed part of the Dual Monarchy. At that time, however, no specific demands were made as to the parts of the empire that were to be involved. At the same time, disquieting news was received from Rumania confirming that relations between Rome and Bucharest were cordial. The Rumanian prime minister told the Austro-Hungarian ambassador quite plainly that his position would become untenable if the Russians were to occupy the province of Transylvania—in addition to Bukovina—as it would then become impossible to resist a "(march) into Transylvania in order to receive it from the Russians as a reward." Conrad, for his part, expected to be able to quickly eliminate the imminent danger of the international political situation through a

---

24 X Corps and X Reserve Corps.

victory on the Carpathian Front. Baron von Burian, who had replaced Count von Berchtold as Minister of Foreign Affairs on 13 January, agreed with Conrad and was determined to await the outcome of the impending operations.[25] For the time being the new foreign minister decided to reject Italy's demands as well as the Germans' suggestions regarding those demands. The exchange of ideas, both orally and in writing, that took place on this subject between the chiefs of staff of the two allied forces indicated a sharp contrast in opinion, the origins of which (for the most part) lay in their conflicting views as to the best way to conduct military operations. This was similar to what had happened over the Serbian question. Conrad maintained that it was indeed possible to defeat Russia, after which the political situation would automatically solve itself; Falkenhayn did not count on achieving a decision in the war in the East and therefore considered it necessary to exploit the neutrality of Italy and Rumania, which meant that the Dual Monarchy would have to make territorial concessions. In the end, the pressure exerted on Vienna from German political and military quarters had such a negative affect that Burian considered an oral discussion of the issue to be necessary. So he went to German GHQ on 24 January as a member of the entourage of the Austro-Hungarian Crown Prince. His attempt to make the Austro-Hungarian attitude toward territorial concessions prevail did not succeed and did nothing to bridge the differences in outlook between the two allies. Moreover, the fighting on the Carpathian Front did not bring the victory that the Central Powers had expected, which prompted Falkenhayn—who considered it his duty—to wire Chancellor Bethmann Hollweg on 6 February as to the offensive's doubtful future. He stated that "a general turn in the situation in favour of the Austro-Hungarian forces could no longer be expected, at least not within a foreseeable span of time."[26]

This unexpected information caused the Chancellor to take new steps with regard to the proposed territorial concessions before the stall in the Carpathian offensive became fully known to the neutrals. He asked Falkenhayn to assist him by pressuring Conrad. Accordingly, a communication from the German Chief of Staff containing an earnest admonition arrived at Teschen on 8 February. After dwelling on the unfavourable situation in the Carpathian Theatre, the letter continued as follows:

---

25 It was at the instigation of the Hungarian Prime Minister, Count Tisza, that Count von Berchtold was relieved by Baron von Burian as "Minister at the Royal Court."

26 For an overview of Rumanian strategy in 1914–1915 see Glenn E. Torrey, "Rumania and the Belligerents 1914–1916," Journal of Contemporary History 1, no. 3 (1966): 171–91. For the most comprehensive treatment of Rumanian involvement in the Great War, see Glenn E. Torrey, ed., Rumania and World War I (Iasi: Center for Rumanian Studies, 1998).

However, it will be necessary to solve the Italian–Rumanian issue in accordance with our position by about the middle of the month[27] or [the situation] will become unfavourable for us. Therefore time must not be lost, especially since I do not believe that any victory that may be gained in East Prussia will have any influence one way or another on this question for the simple reason that such a success can no longer make its influence felt in a timely fashion. It is for this reason that I take the liberty to return once more to the issue, and I beg your Excellency to accept my statements as they are written—namely in frank and open comradeship and true fraternal faith. By the possible desertion of Italy, and even to a greater extent Rumania, to the camp of our enemies, we shall be deprived of the certain expectation of terminating the war victoriously along the entire line. The consequences of a defeat, however, are self-evident: the position as a great power of Germany as well as that of the Dual Monarchy would be ended; indeed, one must fear that Panslavism, in conjunction with Italian and Rumanian irredentism, would disrupt the unity of the Monarchy. To avert such a calamity, no sacrifice is too great so long as it does not endanger the existence of our realms. Such a case, however, cannot be reached through the proposed peaceful understanding between Austria-Hungary and Italy with the co-operation of Germany. Such a settlement would, of course, have to take the form of a treaty with the objectives clearly defined with commitments that would not have to be carried out until after the conclusion of peace; it would mean, so to speak, a revival of the Triple Alliance. For the Italian government, which certainly is not interested in entering the war on the side of our enemies, such a tool would represent a suitable weapon whereby it would be able to sway public opinion in our favour. To us allies, the covenant would immediately bring—aside from allaying our most pressing military apprehensions—highly important economic advantages. Then too, there is the prospect that Italy, as well as Rumania—once these two powers have compromised themselves with respect to the Entente—will after all have to side with us in the end.

On receipt of this communication in Teschen, a confident atmosphere nevertheless prevailed at the *AOK*. There the military authorities did not consider the political situation to be at all critical, at least not after a conference on 5 February between Burian and Conrad. According to new instructions that the Italian Ambassador in Vienna had made known on 28 January, Italy would only consider compensation in the form of "territorial concessions from the possessions of the Dual Monarchy" as it "would not do to promise Italy territory of a belligerent state,

---

27 Owing to the assembly of the Italian Chamber of Deputies on 18 February.

because that would imply a breach of its neutrality. [Therefore] Austria-Hungary is at liberty to voluntarily surrender some of its own land." Time was pressing, and the authorities in Rome were anxious to have an affirmative answer in principle from Vienna before the Chamber of Deputies assembled on 18 February. In spite of all this, Baron von Burian hoped to be able to protract the negotiations through counter-proposals until the Central Powers' military situation had been improved by a victory on the Russian Front. After that, he reasoned, Italy would hardly join the Entente. Conrad shared these hopes and therefore rejected the suggestions made by Falkenhayn in a reply on 10 February. A subsequent verbal attempt to change Conrad's opinion through representations to the Austro-Hungarian liaison officer at German GHQ also failed. Conrad and Burian agreed that it was necessary to await the final result of the Carpathian campaign and of the new German offensive, which had just begun in East Prussia, before making any far-reaching and unfavourable political decisions.

Meanwhile, Falkenhayn did not remain idle. When on 15 February Italy—having become impatient because of the protracted negotiations—threateningly and formally objected in Vienna to any new operations on the Balkan Peninsula, he sounded another warning note on 18 February, pointing to the military situation in East Prussia (which was not as satisfactory as might have been desired) and again suggesting that concessions would have to be made to Italy. But it was impossible to have the German view accepted. During a conference in Teschen on 20 February, attended by the German Chancellor, the Austro-Hungarian Foreign Minister, and the two Chiefs of the General Staff, the expectation of a timely military success was still influencing the decision making of both Burian and Conrad, who continued their opposition to the German point of view.

To make it easier for Vienna to decide on the cession of territory, Chancellor Bethmann Hollweg offered a new proposal on 1 March. He stated that as compensation for the Trentino, which Austria-Hungary was to cede to Italy, Germany would be willing "upon a favourable conclusion of the war to assist Austria in obtaining the entire coal mining region of Sosnowiec."[28] In accordance with the Chancellor's desires, Falkenhayn supported this move in a statement regarding the military situation in the Eastern Theatre, which was, as it turned out, not very favourable. According to his statement, the absence of any decisive success on the Carpathian Front—even the fall of Przemysl—had to be assumed, with all the immeasurable consequences that would reflect on Austria-Hungary's prestige in the Balkan states. "The situation, to be sure, is not without hope," the statement

---

28 *Sosnowiec is an important city in the Upper Silesian coal-mining basin between the Oder and Vistula rivers. The coalfields lay at the crossroads of the German, Russian, and Austro-Hungarian Empires.*

concluded. "Nevertheless it is so grave that it would be a catastrophe if everything were not done in order to prevent new enemies from entering the war against us."

In the meantime, Vienna's negative attitude was beginning to antagonize Rome. Prompted by a grim report from Falkenhayn about the unfavourable military situation in Bukovina, on the evening of 6 March the German Chancellor was on the verge of travelling to Vienna to exert his personal influence on the Emperor and Baron von Burian. But just at that moment a report from Tschirschky (the German ambassador) arrived which stated that Austria-Hungary was ready to agree to the fundamental principles of the Italian negotiations in return for the coal mining region of Sosnowiec and additional German compensations. Specifically, Vienna considered it acceptable to cede the Italian-speaking part of the Tyrol—to take effect after the conclusion of peace—provided that the redrawing of the border favoured Austria. Italy, however, would have to agree to observe a benevolent neutrality and allow Austria-Hungary a free hand in the Balkans. It would seem that the Austro-Hungarian government was no longer shutting its eyes to the exigencies of the international and military situation.

Falkenhayn welcomed the prospect of a peaceful settlement with Italy with, as he put it in his telegram to Conrad of 10 March, "sincere satisfaction." He then asked Conrad to insist, in view of the political situation, that the negotiations be brought to a speedy conclusion "in order to enable us to derive full advantage from it both in the Balkans and Rumania." In a later communication to Conrad on 13 March, Falkenhayn considered it not at all impossible that "in the event that negotiations with Italy were concluded quickly … Rumania and perhaps in the end even Italy would enter the war on our side after all."

THE APPARENT RELAXATION OF THE POLITICAL TENSIONS BETWEEN THE DUAL Monarchy and Italy offered Falkenhayn an opportunity to devote his whole attention to the Serbian problem.

Owing to political and military developments on the Balkan Peninsula, the problem of establishing safe communications between the Central Powers and Turkey had become more and more acute in recent weeks. At the beginning of the year, Constantinople had estimated that its available ammunition stocks would last until mid-March at best, provided that expenditures were carefully economized. The news that Admiral von Usedom of the German Navy (who was in charge of coastal fortifications at the Dardanelles and the Bosporus) had voiced his doubts regarding the ability of the Dardanelles forts to resist repeated enemy naval attacks was bound to create misgivings—indeed, it had a profoundly depressing effect on the Turkish statesmen. To reassure them, a communication from Falkenhayn addressed to the Turkish Ambassador in Berlin and sent as early as 14 January stressed that as always, he adhered to the idea of mounting a campaign against Serbia and was hopeful that he would be able to deal with this issue in March. He sent a similar wire to Generalfeldmarschall Baron von der Goltz in Constantinople.

The results of the military operations in the Turkish Theatre were not of the kind to raise the low morale in Constantinople. Reports emanating from the Caucasus Front at the end of January left no doubt that the second offensive, launched in that theatre at the turn of the year, had ended with a serious reversal, early successes notwithstanding. The Turkish Third Army, led personally by Enver Pasha and numbering some 70,000 rifles, had advanced against Kars and Tblisi toward the end of December but had collapsed completely under Russian counterattacks in the snow and ice that prevailed in the mountains. In the middle of January the remnants of the Turkish forces found themselves again along their start line near and to the east of Erzurum. For the time being at least, the enemy was no longer pressing them. The Turks' failure gave the Russians the option of employing those forces that were no longer needed in the Caucasus against the Central Powers— if they chose to do so. The prospect that the Turks might incite rebellion in the Caucasus and on the Turko-Persian frontier districts by proclaiming *jihad* (holy war) had also begun to fade.

In mid-January the Turks opened an offensive in the direction of the Suez Canal.[29] This had been planned long before, and the German High Command had great hopes for its success. The Turkish Expeditionary Corps, numbering about 20,000 men, reached the canal in different places during the night of 2 and 3 February. Attempts at crossing it, however, were frustrated by British vigilance. Though their losses had been slight, the Turkish forces began to retire on 4 February, for now that the element of surprise had been lost, the prospects for success were seen as unfavourable. This demonstrated that it was impossible to seriously threaten Great Britain's interests in Egypt using so small a force.[30]

Soon after the withdrawal from the Suez Canal, the Entente fleets launched an offensive against the Dardanelles. It seems that the impetus for this undertaking originated in London, with a Russian call for assistance. The Russians desired relief with regard to the situation in the Caucasus, which at the turn of the year

---

29 See *DW* V:562.
30 *Elements of the Turkish Fourth Army left Beersheba on 14 January under the command of Dejmal Pasha and his German chief of staff, Kress von Kressenstein. On the Turkish campaign in the Middle East in 1915, see* Field Marshal Lord Carver, *The Turkish Front, 1914–1918* (London: Sidgwick and Jackson, 2003); Michael Hickey, *The First World War: The Mediterranean Front, 1914–1923* (Oxford: Osprey, 2002); and Ahmed Emin Yalman, *Turkey in the World War* (New Haven: Yale University Press, 1930).

was becoming quite difficult for them. In response to an urgent request from Grand Duke Nicholas, the Russian government asked for a "demonstration against Turkey."[31] St. Petersburg received an affirmative answer on 3 January, which des- ignated the Dardanelles as the most suitable point for the action. An existing operations plan, to which the British Committee of Imperial Defence had previ- ously given serious consideration, provided for an offensive against the Dard- anelles for the purpose of taking Constantinople and opening the passage to the Black Sea. The plan called for the co-operation of the army and navy, in conjunc- tion with the armies of Greece and Bulgaria, which the British hoped would join in the attack.[32] However, Chancellor of the Exchequer Lloyd George proposed to leave only a small British force in the Western Theatre in order to assist the French and to send the bulk of the British land forces to the Balkans with the aid of the navy. From the Balkans, in conjunction with the Serbian Army, he planned to attack the Austrians; the armies of the other Balkan states—and perhaps also of Italy—would then probably join. Simultaneously, about 100,000 men were to land on the Syrian coast in the region of Alexandretta with a view to cutting off those Turkish troops that were moving by rail in the direction of the Suez Canal. Although Lord Kitchener was not unfavourably disposed to the Balkan project, none of these plans were accepted owing to the emphatic objections of Sir John French, Commander-in-Chief of the British Forces in France, who strongly main- tained that a breakthrough along the Germans' Western Front remained entirely feasible. Thus only the operation along the Dardanelles by parts of the British and French fleets was planned. Instead of a mere demonstration, however, the Admiralty began to consider mounting a serious naval offensive using British and French naval forces in the middle of February against the Dardanelles fortifica- tions with the ultimate objective of capturing Constantinople. This was more in

---

31 On 2 January 1915 the Supreme Commander of the Russian forces, Grand Duke Nicholas, asked the British government to find a way to pressure the Turkish forces to relieve the situation in the Carpathians. The following day the War Cabinet determined that the only place where such a demonstration would have an effect would be the Dardanelles.

32 A plan to open the straits, mainly using Greek troops, had first been proposed in September 1914, before Turkey entered the war, by First Lord of the Admiralty Winston Churchill. This plan fell apart when Greece refused to join. The idea was revived in December by the Secretary of the War Council, Maurice Hankey, supported by Churchill and First Sea Lord John Fisher. Hankey favoured a peripheral campaign to strike the Central Powers at their weakest link. His plan called for the French to hold the Western Front while three new British corps, assisted by Bulgaria and Greece, aimed to knock the Ottoman Empire out of the war. Ultimately the plan was scaled back to the limited naval operation championed by Churchill. A good overview of the origins of the Gallipoli campaign is Martin Gilbert, "Churchill and Gallipoli," in Gallipoli: Making History, ed. Jenny Macleod (London: Frank Cass, 2004), 14–43. The most in-depth study is Geoffrey Miller, Straits: British Policy Towards the Ottoman Empire and the Origins of the Dardanelles Campaign (Hull: University of Hull Press, 1997).

step with the thinking of Grand Duke Nicholas. At the end of January the British War Council decided to expand these plans to include the co-operation of land forces later in the Dardanelles undertaking; this, however, was to be initiated by the fleets. One British and one French division were allotted for this task. Russia began to organize an expeditionary force of its own in Odessa,[33] in order to enable Russian troops to participate in the eventual capture of Constantinople.

Soon, however, Lloyd George's Balkan project again attracted attention. After the Russian victory on the Caucasus Front, Grand Duke Nicholas no longer attached any weight to the Dardanelles offensive, which had been designed to relieve the situation. Now he strongly advocated the Balkan undertaking, of which he had only recently become aware. Plans were being considered to land troops on Greek soil at Salonika in order to bring about a separate peace with Vienna. It was intended that from Salonika, the Serbian Army, reinforced by Russian, French, and British divisions, would advance against Austria-Hungary's Southern Front.[34]

Meanwhile, the British Admiralty had been tirelessly encouraging preparations for a naval attack on the Dardanelles. Initially the plan had been to attack with the combined parts of two fleets without attempting to land troops. On 19 February the Franco-British naval force, which had been on patrol in front of the straits ever since Turkey's entry into the war, began to bombard the four outer works protecting the channel's entrance. On 25 February the fleet continued the bombardment. The antiquated forts were soon put out of action; however, the principal centre of resistance, Fortress Chanak, remained intact. The military and political effects of this enterprise meant that the fighting in the Near East was bound to become a focal point in the war. The defences on the Bosporus and the Dardanelles were protecting the Turkish capital, and for the Turks, holding them was mainly a question of having enough ammunition. The rapid establishment of secure communications between Turkey and the Central Powers had become a problem that could no longer be ignored. In a telegram dated 1 March, Enver Pasha pointed out the danger posed by a breakthrough on the two straits. He noted that if such a breakthrough were to happen, the several Turkish corps stationed in Europe would be cut off from Asia:[35]

---

33 Formed from Caucasus troops; later it became V Caucasus Corps. *See* William A. Renzi, "Great Britain, Russia, and the Straits, 1914–1915," *Journal of Modern History* 42, no. 1 (1970): 1–20.
34 *For an overview of the origins of the Salonika campaign, see* Dutton, *The Politics of Diplomacy,* 17–48.
35 *The Turkish Second Army and elements of Fifth Army were stationed on the European side of the Sea of Marmara.*

In the event of strong enemy troop landings from both straits and participation with the enemy on the part of Balkan States, our position in Europe
will, in the end, become untenable unless we can count on Austro-German
pressure on the Balkan States in the near future. Because the distribution
of the Turkish forces is dependent on this contingency, a telegraphic answer
is required.

In addition, he asked for several large submarines to defend against the enemy's
breakthrough operation.[36]

At first, Falkenhayn tried to give hope to the Turkish generalissimo by promising in general terms that the requested "pressure on the Balkan States was being
prepared." Enver Pasha, however, urged that Serbia be defeated. "In the event that
Germany and Austria can spare troops from their home theatres of operations,"
he wired on 9 March,

> it will be highly important, both for the situation in the Balkans and con-
> nection between Turkey and its allied states, to defeat Serbia and thereby
> open the road for the army's necessities of which we have been in need
> these many months. With this action, those Balkan states that are still vac-
> illating will doubtless be brought into line to join the cause of the Central
> Powers. A speedy opening of this connection—and then keeping it open—
> is a matter of life for Turkey.

The seriousness of the situation was made clear in a telegram from Admiral von Usedom, which was given to Falkenhayn on 10 March. The admiral's
telegram read:

> Despite the relatively slight successes of the enemy, the destruction of all the
> works at the Dardanelles cannot be prevented for any length of time if the
> ammunition and mines that were ordered months ago do not arrive very soon,
> or unless the defence is assisted by means of submarines from the homeland.

Falkenhayn had already voiced his opinion regarding this matter the day before
to the representative of the Foreign Office attached to the *OHL,* who, pursuant to
instructions from the Chancellor, was urging that the planned campaign against
Serbia be executed as soon as possible. Falkenhayn believed that it would be necessary to hold on for the time being because

---

36 *On the naval campaign in the Dardanelles, see* Michael J. Mortlock, *The Landings at Suvla
    Bay, 1915: An Analysis of British Failure during the Gallipoli Campaign* (Jefferson, NC: McFar-
    land, 2007); Stephen Roskill, *Churchill and the Admirals* (New York: Morrow, 1978); Victor
    Rudenno, *Gallipoli: Attack from the Sea* (New Haven, CT: Yale University Press, 2008); and
    Michael Wilson, *Destination Dardanelles* (London: Cooper, 1988).

such an undertaking, however important it might be for the entire conduct of the war, would hardly have any effect on the Dardanelles issue itself; for it would be necessary first of all to solve the problem of ammunition supply before victory at Orsova[37] could be hoped for—even under the most favourable of conditions.

When Falkenhayn placed German troops at the disposal of Austria-Hungary for the offensive in the Carpathians—specifically, to relieve Przemysl—he had expected a speedy victory. Afterwards he had planned to turn around rapidly in order to carry the Austrians along in an attack on Serbia, as Conrad would never otherwise have consented to marching against Serbia from the north. Falkenhayn was well aware that Przemysl was of less importance for the course of the war than were the Balkans, but his efforts to convince the Austrians of this had been futile.

There remained one possible way of providing quick assistance to Turkey (which was now in an extremely precarious situation). Falkenhayn believed that greater pressure had to be placed on Rumania to open the transportation routes to Turkey, thus enabling the rapid shipment of ammunition stocks, which were now stored in considerable quantities along Rumania's frontiers. The prospects for accomplishing this task seemed rather promising. On 16 March, Falkenhayn sent the following message to Enver Pasha:

> Military Attaché Leipzig reports (from Constantinople) that the governor of the Dardanelles District requested that ammunition should be shipped to the front by way of Rumania without further delay lest the Dardanelles be lost. In answer to this request, we shall, of course, exert heavy pressure on Rumania. At the same time, I would beg your Excellency to exert your great influence upon the defenders at the Dardanelles so that they will not lose their heads. This much is certain: the Dardanelles cannot be conquered, even while only a limited ammunition supply is at hand, so long as they are being defended at all; and I am sure that there is no lack of brave men in the Ottoman forces. A winter campaign against Serbia was impracticable because of the unfavourable road and weather conditions. Even after these conditions improve, it will not be possible to execute the campaign fast enough so as to influence the present attack on the Dardanelles. Nevertheless, efforts will be made towards accelerating it with all the means at our disposal, in view of its importance for the general situation on the Balkan Peninsula.

---

37 Situated in the Negotin area.

Rumania's attitude in the weeks prior to this telegram had vacillated in concert with shifts in the military situation and in the progress of negotiations between the Dual Monarchy and Italy. The links between the negotiations with Italy and the situation in the Balkans were evident. The initial victories in the Carpathian offensive had warned Rumania to reconsider its position; so had the threat made by the German ambassador, Baron von dem Bussche, to the effect that the Rumanians would encounter German troops should they decide to invade Transylvania. In mid-February the German ambassador had been able to report that King Ferdinand, too, had admitted that a great improvement in the situation had taken place, although he was supposed to have added that matters had as yet not progressed to the point where Rumania could afford to commit itself to war.

In Bulgaria and Greece the general political atmosphere was as quiet as in Rumania. This, however, began to change in the second half of February, when the decisive victories anticipated by the Central Powers in the Eastern Theatre failed to materialize and the attacks of the Franco-British fleet on the Dardanelles began. The exaggerated reports of Entente victories generated an excitement in the Balkan states that was quite obvious, and one could not ignore the fact that Bulgaria, if it were to lose faith in the ultimate victory of the Central Powers, might endeavour to join the Entente so as to avoid being left out in the cold at the conclusion of peace. In Athens, too, political excitement was reaching the boiling point. Notwithstanding the King's efforts to maintain neutrality, it became increasingly probable that Greece would join the Entente camp.

In Rumania a crisis was at hand. As quickly as the situation had improved during the first half of February, it now deteriorated owing especially to the fact that Italy's attitude was becoming ever more menacing: as the month progressed, an Italian declaration of war on Austria-Hungary seemed imminent. The German Ambassador in Bucharest reported that the Rumanian prime minister was alleged to have said that if such a declaration were made, neither he nor the King would be able to restrain the country from fighting Austria.

Not until news was received that the Entente's successes at the Dardanelles were actually slight and that for the time being the tension between Vienna and Rome had relaxed did the situation return to calm. Bulgaria resumed its policy of strict neutrality; in Greece, with the resignation of Prime Minister Venizelos,[38] King Constantine's neutral attitude was able to prevail. In Bucharest especially,

---

38 Eleftherios Venizelos was the pro-Entente Prime Minister of Greece. In early 1915 he supported the British plan for a combined Greco-Entente attack on the Dardanelles. King Constantine, however, favoured a neutral and pro-German stance, which led to Venizelos's resignation on 21 February. He subsequently returned to power with a new mandate. On Venizelos's war leadership, see Michael Llewellyn Smith, "Venizelo's Diplomacy, 1910–23: From Balkan Alliance to

Rumania's very sober estimate of the situation meant that the threat of war was no longer immediate.

Thus hope prevailed that if Rumania was pressed hard enough, it would eventually allow the transit of ammunition through its territory to Turkey. If this transpired, the most serious danger to the Dardanelles would be averted. On 9 March, Falkenhayn addressed a request to the Minister of Foreign Affairs urging "that by taking advantage of the favourable developments in the Italian issue, that the utmost pressure be brought to bear on Rumania in order to induce her to permit the passage of ammunition without delay." Indeed, at this juncture Falkenhayn viewed the general situation as so favourable that he believed it justifiable to go even further. He questioned "whether it would not be advisable to ask Rumania to take part in the negotiations between the former Triple Alliance Powers from the start and thus to cause her, if at all possible, to enter the war."

The unfavourable military situation on the Carpathian Front, especially the impending fall of Przemysl, in mid-March caused Falkenhayn to ask Conrad again to promote "political negotiations between Austria-Hungary and Germany, on the one hand, and between Italy and Rumania on the other, in such a manner that the latter will join us, or at least compromise themselves in the eyes of the Entente Powers beyond hope of recovery." Yet Conrad did not expect much from this proposed move in Bucharest; now, as ever, he clung to the view that the Balkan issue could only be settled by defeating Russia. "Rumania's attitude and her entry into the war on our side as hoped for by your Excellency," he replied, "will depend chiefly on our situation and successes in East Galicia and Bukovina." Falkenhayn, however, declared that he was in no position at that time to make additional forces available for the Austro-Hungarian Front.

Notwithstanding Conrad's negative attitude, the diplomatic step that Falkenhayn had desired was taken in Bucharest on 19 March. However, the earnest representations of the German ambassador, Baron von dem Bussche, which were accompanied by veiled threats, failed to have the desired effect. The Rumanian prime minister held to the view that it was impossible, out of consideration for the Entente and public opinion, to comply with the wishes of the Central Powers. Bussche gained the impression that pressing the issue too hard would have the

---

Greek-Turkish Settlement," in *Eleftherios Venizelos: The Trials of Statesmanship*, ed. Paschalis M. Kitromilides (Edinburgh: Edinburgh University Press, 2006), 152–57. *On the position of Greece, see various essays in* Institute for Balkan Studies, *Greece and Great Britain during World War I: First Symposium* (Thessaloniki : Institute for Balkan Studies, 1985); and George B. Leontaritis, *Greece and the First World War: From Neutrality to Intervention, 1917–1918* (Boulder, CO: East European Monographs, 1990). *See also* Zisis Fotakis, *Greek Naval Strategy and Policy 1910–1919* (London: Routledge, 2005).

exact opposite effect as was hoped and might even drive Rumania into the arms of the Entente.

So a corridor for German ammunition shipments through Rumania to Turkey remained closed for the time being, which presented a serious problem for the defence of the Dardanelles. Also, considerable time was bound to pass before it would be possible to crush Serbia. Thus for the time being Turkey was left to its fate. It would have to try to master the ever-increasing difficulties by relying on its own resources.

To the Employment of the GHQ Reserve in the East

After the fall of Przemysl on 22 March, General N.Y. Ivanov's Russian forces swept past the city to push the Central Powers' armies back though the Carpathian passes toward the Hungarian Plain.[39] If they succeeded in getting through the mountains, there would be nothing standing between the Russian armies and the Hungarian capital of Budapest.[40] As the Dual Monarchy faced the Russian advance, the political situation in the Balkans grew worse. Russian successes in the Carpathians and at Przemysl were pushing Italy and Rumania into the arms of the Entente. As Robert Foley notes, this led Falkenhayn to place a new emphasis on the Eastern Front.[41] If the Russians could be handed a significant defeat, perhaps Italy and Rumania might be dissuaded from declaring war. If not, he feared that Austria-Hungary would seek a separate peace. As the crisis worsened, news arrived that the Entente had opened a front in the Dardanelles.[42]

ON 18 MARCH THE EXPECTED NEW BLOW WAS STRUCK AGAINST TURKEY ON THE Dardanelles.[43] However, by the evening of 19 March it was clear that the attack of the Anglo-French fleet had been repulsed; also, that the enemy's losses in ships had been considerable whereas the Turkish casualties and losses of materiel had only been slight. Yet excitement at this favourable outcome was dampened by anxiety

---

39 *DW* VII: 125–32.
40 Foley, *German Strategy and the Path to Verdun*, 131.
41 Stone, *The Eastern Front 1914–1917*, 127–29.
42 Falkenhayn, *General Headquarters and Its Critical Decisions*, 78ff.
43 *The naval bombardment of the forts.*

over what the next days would bring. For reasons of prestige, it seemed highly improbable that the Entente powers would abandon their Dardanelles venture because of the reverse that they had just suffered. It was expected, rather, that the enemy would risk everything in order to gain their objective. This estimate was soon confirmed by reliable information that a comprehensive land attack—in conjunction with a new naval attack—was being prepared for the Dardanelles. It was thought that this was being done in order to induce Greece, Bulgaria, and Rumania to join the Entente, with the ultimate goal pressuring the Central Powers to sue for peace. These serious developments strengthened Falkenhayn's resolve to push for the Serbian campaign with all the means at his disposal and, moreover, to begin the campaign before the great offensive he was planning in the West.

First he tried, with the aid of the Foreign Office, to make certain that Bulgaria would co-operate in the Serbian venture, or at least to induce the government in Sofia to permit Turkish troops to pass through Bulgarian territory for the attack against Serbia. Next, he made one more attempt to win over Conrad regarding the Serbian campaign, notwithstanding the latter's objections. In a communication dated 21 March, Falkenhayn proposed to Conrad that the Austro-Hungarians go over to a defensive stance both on the Carpathian Front and in Bukovina and that Conrad relieve the four German divisions of the Southern Army using Austrian units in order to employ them (reinforced by other German forces if possible) against Serbia. These proposals met with an unfavourable reception at the Austro-Hungarian General Headquarters in Teschen. They were made all the more unfavourable by the fall of Przemysl on 22 March and by the fact that the *AOK* now had to assume that the Russians would reinforce their Carpathian Front. Conrad thus declined Falkenhayn's proposals. The subsequent written exchanges between the two General Staff chiefs failed to lead to an agreement on the issue.

Meanwhile, the Turks had helped themselves as far as was possible. On 24 March, Enver Pasha organized Fifth Army from the five divisions stationed on the Dardanelles and an additional division brought up for that specific purpose; he then placed this army under the command of Generalfeldmarschall Liman von Sanders, Chief of the German Military Mission. Progress had also been made regarding ammunition. The Commander-in-Chief of the straits, Admiral von Usedom, had the modern ammunition originally earmarked for the Bosporus batteries transferred to the Dardanelles; at the same time, ammunition from naval stocks was being modified so that it would fit the calibres of the guns along the strait. Mines were brought up from the Trebizond and Smyrna, though they could hardly be spared there. In spite of all the difficulties, it was still possible to manufacture artillery ammunition, even for the heaviest calibres. Yet owing to the inadequacy of materials and trained personnel, it was impossible to obtain satisfactory results in a timely fashion. Nor was it possible to count on the appearance of German submarines for several more weeks. Without prospects for an early opening of communications with Central Europe, Turkey meanwhile was obliged, in her principal theatres of operations, to confine herself to the defensive. In a letter of 23 May addressed to Falkenhayn, Enver Pasha depicted in glowing terms what the Ottoman Empire would be able to accomplish if its armament was completed with the aid of the German war industry:

I should not like to see our alliance with Germany and Austria become a burden for these [two] powers, but I am merely endeavouring to assist our allies with all the means at my disposal. This could be accomplished much more effectively if Serbia were defeated; in consequence, Bulgaria's attitude would become more stable, Rumania more tractable, and the now absent communication link between us and Germany, as well as Austria, would be established. I expect, thereafter, to be able to make considerable additional forces available for the common cause. Turkey still has one-half million men in reserve all of whom have served with the colours and are subject to be called up as soon as arms can be obtained ... A resumption of the offensive against the Suez Canal and Caucasia might well be taken into consideration, should this more favourable contingency arise. Indeed, because as it may be assumed that Bulgaria and Rumania would also be induced to join our alliance under these circumstances, the basis for direct co-operation on our part with the Austro-German forces in Europe could be established. The direction that our offensive on European soil would take would no doubt have a decisive effect on Russia's persistence for it would hit the latter's weak left wing and lead into the provinces where Russia could be struck at her most vulnerable point.

These prospects served to confirm Falkenhayn in his intention to open the road to Constantinople. To do so, it would first be necessary to win over Bulgaria. But the chances of this happening were not very good, at least according to a report of the military attaché received on 26 March, which relayed the exorbitant demands that the government in Sofia was making and, moreover, the bad impression left by the fall of Przemysl. Apparently, King Ferdinand did not want to be prevailed on to abandon his stance of vigilant inaction, despite the alluring offers tendered by Falkenhayn—specifically, a plan calling for a joint campaign against Serbia. According to the proposal, two Austro-Hungarian divisions were to advance from Bosnia, ten German and Austro-Hungarian divisions from the north, and the Bulgarian forces from the east and southeast. As the total strength of the Serbian forces that might offer resistance in the north would amount to 100,000 men at best, and provided that Misch were threatened simultaneously, it was thought that the forces of the Central Powers and Bulgaria—taking into consideration the numbers and disposition described above—could succeed in bringing the enemy to terms in a very short time. Bulgaria would then enjoy complete freedom to acquire as much Macedonian territory as it thought proper.[44]

While passing through Sofia on his journey to the German GHQ in late March, Generalfeldmarschall von Goltz tried to convert the King to the Central Powers' cause but was unsuccessful; indeed, he was not even received. Goltz, who continued his journey via Bucharest, had to admit that the general attitude had also worsened considerably in Rumania, compared to the atmosphere that had prevailed during his visit in mid-December 1914. Yet on 29 March in Teschen he succeeded in convincing Conrad of the need to execute the Serbian campaign in short order. Moreover, he promised the services of two Turkish corps to assist him. After making known certain reservations and conditions, the Austrian Chief of the General Staff declared his willingness to embark on the operation against Serbia. Above all, however, he thought it would be necessary to induce Bulgaria to commit itself to participation in the campaign. This, though, meant that Turkey would have to cover the rear of the Bulgarian forces and even actively co-operate with them.[45] Conrad fleshed out his ideas further by informing Falkenhayn in writing that he considered a joint operation against Serbia feasible on the following premises:

Bulgaria is to mobilize and concentrate her principal forces for an advance via Misch with smaller forces moving by way of Zajecar. As soon as the Bulgarians start their offensive, but no sooner, we shall attack, assisted by approximately four German divisions which must, however, not be taken from the German forces now engaged against Russia; these German units should be present and available at [the beginning of the operation]. Turkey is to cover Bulgaria against Greece and Rumania, in case these countries should begin hostilities, and must cooperate as far as possible with the aid of about two corps that are to be placed at the disposal of the Bulgarian High Command. I have communicated these ideas to our Minister of Foreign Affairs.

---

44 On Bulgaria's entry into the war, see Wolfgang-Uwe Friedrich, *Bulgarien und die Mächte 1913–1915* (Stuttgart: Steiner, 1985); and Richard C. Hall, *Bulgaria's Road to the First World War* (Boulder, CO: East European Monographs, 1996).

45 *Bulgaria and Turkey had competing interests in the Balkans and had recently fought two bitter wars. The idea that the two powers could now co-operate would be difficult to realize. On the Balkan Wars, see Richard C. Hall, The Balkan Wars, 1912–1913: Prelude to the First World War* (London: Routledge, 2000).

Falkenhayn replied on 30 March that no definite decision had yet been made by Bulgaria and that in the meantime, preparations for the offensive would have to be made. He considered it vital that the question of equipment for the German troops be settled and that it be decided who was to exercise supreme command; he added that, owing to the German relations with Turkey and Bulgaria, a German general would be the logical man for the post. He generally concurred in the preliminary conditions that Conrad had advanced as a basis for the joint operation, adding that he had submitted similar proposals to Bulgaria some time ago. In his response, Conrad took a decided stand against the idea that a German general should exercise supreme command in the Balkans.

However, the agreement with Italy and the participation of Bulgaria were as yet not assured, and the conversations that followed on the subject of the Serbian campaign failed to yield any palpable results, despite Goltz's efforts during his sojourn at German GHQ in the early part of April. Goltz, in this regard, made the following entry in his diary:[46]

> I went to Falkenhayn at about 10:30 and had a long conversation about the situation. He professes to agree with me entirely. Many people, he said, had voiced to him a similar opinion before, but nobody had ever been able to tell him from where he was to take the necessary forces. The Austrians were barely able to hold the Carpathians without assistance. All forces were stalled, and in France likewise. An attack of the new British armies was now expected. Behind our armies six divisions had finally been gotten together after much toil and effort … These (Serbians) have a strength of 200,000 men. It will therefore be necessary, in order to have preponderance in numbers, to gather 250,000 troops, the equivalent of ten divisions. That he considers impossible … Falkenhayn states that he has been working on the convention [with Bulgaria] for the last six weeks … Yet Bulgaria seems to be disinclined. Everybody suggested taking action in Serbia's case, but no one seemed to be able to propose a new means that would allow it to be done. I then replied that I was not to blame, since I was bringing assistance in the shape of two strong, first-class Turkish corps. General von Falkenhayn recognized that, although without definitely committing himself to my proposal.

On his departure from GHQ on 3 April, Goltz took with him a letter from the Kaiser addressed to the Sultan as tangible proof of his work; in the letter it was promised that the Serbian campaign would be launched "in the near future." He was certain—and justly so—that Falkenhayn concurred in his estimate of the

---

46 Generalfeldmarschall Colmar Baron von der Goltz, *Denkwürdigkeiten* (Berlin: E.S. Mittler & Sohn, 1932), 400.

Balkan situation and that his estimate had fortified Falkenhayn's determination to translate the plan of campaign into action as soon as the general situation would permit. Within a few days of the Generalfeldmarschall's departure from GHQ, Falkenhayn was already in possession of a written promise, dated 12 April, from Enver Pasha to the effect that "he would place two corps at the disposal of the Bulgarian Army for a joint operation against Serbia." In a subsequent exchange of telegrams, Falkenhayn, after some hesitation, fixed the date for a possible campaign against Serbia for late May, provided that matters had clarified by then with respect to Bulgarian co-operation.

Yet only too soon were these plans to be relegated to the background by the change in the international political situation. The Central Powers' relations with Italy had again been aggravated, no doubt by the fall of Przemysl. On 20 March, Italy demanded "a concrete offer" from Austria, which was made on 27 March. In it, Austria offered the Southern Tyrol—including the Trentino—in exchange for Italy's benevolent neutrality. Sonnino, Italy's Minister of Foreign Affairs, however, declared the offer to be "very inadequate"; he then made further far-reaching demands along the coast. Conrad observed this development with ever-increasing apprehension. On 1 April he expressed his frustration in a telegram to Falkenhayn:

> In considering the negotiations regarding territorial concessions to Italy on the one hand, and the information received today regarding Italian troop movements to our frontier on the other, I am inclined to believe that Italy will conduct the negotiations in a more formal manner, with a view to breaking them off abruptly in order to realise thereafter her aspirations with respect to Austro-Hungarian territory by military means. These troop movements must be considered to represent the equivalent of a preparation for a general mobilization and concentration of Italy against us. As to the negotiations, we certainly have, in the interest of the common cause of Germany and Austria-Hungary, gone to the limit of what can possibly be done to meet the Italian demands. I have invited the attention of your Excellency repeatedly to the precariousness of our military situation if such a contingency arises [an Italian declaration of war] and beg to do so again. I would, therefore, request that your Excellency exert your influence, with all the means at your disposal, upon the German Ministry of Foreign Affairs so that they will bring pressure to bear upon the Italian government in order to force them to keep their demands within those bounds that will still render possible a mutual peaceful settlement. This action is necessary in view of the incalculable consequences that will result not only for us, but for the German Empire as well.

In his reply, Falkenhayn was forced to declare that German diplomacy was no longer able to do anything further to stave off the Italian threat but that nevertheless, efforts would be continued in Rome with the utmost energy. Yet he contended that the key to the entire issue rested in the hands of the Austrian Foreign Office. He also noted that the official announcement of Austria's willingness to agree to eventual territorial concessions had not been made, despite his urgent request, until several weeks after Emperor Franz Joseph had voiced his agreement. He suggested that it was necessary to take into account Sonnino's peculiar character. Procrastination, he believed, would merely incite the Italian foreign minister to take steps that might become dangerous for the Central Powers. If anything were to be accomplished at this late hour, it would be necessary to bring the negotiations between Vienna and Rome to a close without delay and in a most liberal manner. To be or not to be was the question ... a question in which matters of delimitation and similar issues should play no part. Falkenhayn went on to say that if Austro-Hungarian diplomacy succeeded in inducing Rome to agree to a settlement, Italy's entry into the war on the side of the Central Powers at some later time would be assured. "Your Excellency will not assume, I hope," Falkenhayn's telegram concluded,

> that I do not possess a complete and sympathetic understanding of the restraint which the procedure depicted above will impose upon anyone in Austria-Hungary that is called upon to give expression to my conviction, and therefore I would again beg your Excellency to exert your influence on the Viennese government along these lines most insistently.

Conrad immediately replied that as late as 1 April he had exerted pressure on the Austrian Ministry of Foreign Affairs by depicting the situation as clearly as was possible. "But considering Italy's perfidy," he continued,

> we will have to be prepared that Italy will also demand our coastal possessions, which would automatically put an end to our existence. In the last contingency [an Italian declaration of war], the only way out would be, in agreement with Germany, to come to terms with Russia in order to make peace so as to meet the Italian pretensions with the sword.

Falkenhayn immediately forwarded Conrad's statements—which mentioned peace with Russia for the first time—to the Chancellor. This communication was supplemented by a wire of 2 April from the German liaison officer attached to the AOK, General von Cramon,[47] which read:

---

47 Promoted to this grade 22 March 1915.

His Excellency, Conrad sent yesterday very grave notes, both in writing and by wire, to the Ministry of Foreign Affairs in Vienna regarding an instantaneous settlement with Italy. Possible wishes for Pola and the Adriatic coast will, however, not be conceded. Rather than submit to Italy's extravagant territorial demands, a settlement with Russia, in agreement with Germany, and cession of Galicia are being preferred.

Apprehension that if Austria-Hungary were attacked by Italy it might endeavour to make a separate peace with Russia caused Falkenhayn to call an oral meeting in Berlin on 4 April. The chief subject of the discussion was the threat of Italy's entry into the war and the grave situation on the Carpathian Front. Falkenhayn pointed out that, according to the impression he had received, Austria-Hungary seemed to be in no hurry to reach a settlement with Italy. Conrad denied this and placed the blame on Rome. At any rate, the two General Staff chiefs were still hoping for a peaceful compromise if the negotiations were pushed promptly to conclusion. Conrad stated that Austria-Hungary was in no position to conduct a war against a new enemy unless a separate peace was concluded with Russia. Falkenhayn maintained that a settlement with Russia was out of the question at that moment. He warned against placing too many forces in opposition to an Italian invasion of the Dual Monarchy, on the grounds that this would merely lead to dispersion.

Both General Staff chiefs viewed the situation in the Carpathians with great concern. Falkenhayn, however, was opposed to reinforcing that front with additional German troops, despite Conrad's repeated requests for such assistance. In explaining his position, the German Chief of Staff cited his inability at that time to definitely ascertain where it would be desirable to employ the newly organized units involved—in the West, in the East, or against Serbia. As for the Serbian campaign—which in Austria's view was contingent on Bulgarian cooperation—Conrad emphasized the need to postpone the operation in any event, for the high water in the Danube would not permit any large-scale crossings before the end of May. Bulgaria, too—so he contended—was deeply reserved in its attitude and was apparently determined to await a clarification of the still murky situation.

The conference in Berlin dissipated Falkenhayn's worries that Austria-Hungary might come to a separate agreement with Russia without first asking Germany to participate in the negotiations. On the important question as to what was to be done if Italy entered the war, the conference failed to achieve solidarity. Conrad endeavoured to reach such an agreement during the days that followed through an exchange of ideas in writing. Immediately on his return to Teschen he informed Falkenhayn that the signs had increased that Italy had finally resolved to enter the war: in Rome, the authorities were apparently no longer content with acquiring Italian-speaking territories and were clamouring for purely German soil extending up to Mount Brenner. Concessions of this nature, he declared, were out of the question. The Italian government was looking for a cause for conflict in all matters so as to be able to intensify the situation according to its needs. He pointed out that matters on the Carpathian Front were not satisfactory and that a serious reverse there would draw not just Italy but also Rumania into the war. In such an event, the enemy invasion would have to be opposed militarily. To this end, he needed ten divisions: seven to be used against Italy and three against Rumania. If these forces were taken from the Austro-Hungarian Front facing Russia, the latter front would be rendered unholdable. He therefore asked to be informed whether German units could replace these troops.

In his answer, Falkenhayn avoided the question that had so clearly been put to him; instead he renewed his demand that the Dual Monarchy abandon without a fight the territories coveted by Italy and that a final settlement of the issue be postponed. First, he said, the Central Powers would have "to get rid of one of its main opponents." Furthermore, whether the opponent to be defeated was in the West or in the East could not be determined before the required troops were actually available—a situation that had not yet arisen.

Conrad rejected Falkenhayn's point of view. He replied that he could not permit Italy to reach out for lands inhabited by Germans and Slavs without resisting; otherwise, the Dual Monarchy's position as a great power would be undermined. Moreover, one had to consider the possibility that Italy was planning to advance as far as Vienna. To allow such an advance without offering armed resistance would be unthinkable. So he again asked whether, in the event of a war with Italy, Germany would be willing to replace the comparatively few forces that would have to be withdrawn from the Eastern Front. Regarding the employment of German reserves, he could only point out (as he had done before) that their entry into action on the Eastern Front would hold much promise for the general situation.

Falkenhayn, in his reply of 8 April, again evaded the question put to him by Conrad. He once more warned against dispersing Austrian forces and maintained that it was now most important to impress on the diplomats that it was urgent for the negotiations between Vienna and Rome to be successfully concluded. Faced with these arguments, Conrad remained attached to his original point of view; now, even more insistently, he demanded an answer to his question of 5 April as to whether the German High Command would be willing to make German forces from the Carpathian Front available as replacements for Austro-Hungarian units that might have to be withdrawn in order to fight Italy. In his answer of 9 April, Falkenhayn refused the request but emphasized his readiness "to take advantage of any favourable opportunity that would appear in the East" as soon as the necessary forces became available. The next day he sent a telegram to the Chancellor with the following request:

> Exert utmost pressure in Vienna in order to effect acceptance of Italian demands even if excessive. At the same time, announce Germany's willingness to give greater military assistance in the East and if necessary to cede Prussian territory.

This telegram was followed on 11 April by a request to the Foreign Office that it influence the Austro–Italian negotiations so that "in case war with Italy proves to be unavoidable, sixteen days will remain for preparations, counting from the moment the decision is made."

General von Falkenhayn's attitude during his conversations with Conrad regarding actions to be taken in the event of an Italian declaration of war was the product of the difficulties inherent in the political and military situation confronting the German High Command. If promises were made to the Austrians, Vienna might well be unwilling to make substantial concessions in negotiations with Rome. If so, negotiations might be broken off and Italy would then make her appearance as a new enemy. Conversely, if no assistance were promised, the Viennese government might find itself compelled, by a Russian invasion of Hungary, to enter into separate negotiations with St. Petersburg.

It goes without saying that developments in April 1915 placed a great strain on the mind of the German Chief of Staff, who was shouldering the entire responsibility for the conduct of German operations on all fronts.[48] At the same time, the question as to which front should become the war's centre of gravity for the immediate future was becoming more pressing. Falkenhayn fervently hoped to execute the great offensive in the West, after a striking a sharp blow against Serbia. In the best analysis, his differences with the Austro-Hungarian High Command were rooted in this desire. Conrad strove to obtain the decision in the East; Falkenhayn wanted to achieve it in the West; each adhered to his conviction with great tenacity. The grave situation on the Carpathian Front, the developing crisis between Vienna and Rome, and the growing realization that available forces were inadequate led Falkenhayn to doubt more and more whether his objective in the West could be achieved. Ever since the conference in Berlin, he had been unable to close

---

48   *DW X contains a lengthy evaluation of Falkenhayn's leadership, which will be translated in Germany's Western Front, Vol. III. As his biographer notes, Falkenhayn was an elusive character who seemingly lacked a central purpose or direction. See* Holger Afflerbach, *Falkenhayn: Politisches Denken und Handeln im Kaiserreich* (Munich: R. Oldenbourg, 1994). *Foley's* German Strategy and the Path to Verdun *takes a more sympathetic view of Falkenhayn. See esp.* 131–33 *and* 140–47.

his eyes to the fact that immense dangers in the form of the expected Russian invasion of Hungary and Italy's seemingly imminent entry into the war were threatening the life of the Dual Monarchy and, at the same time, the common cause of the Central Powers. Consequently, during those days he was very seriously considering the advisability of shifting the war's centre of gravity to the East and abandoning the plans he had harboured thus far.

On 10 April the Italian Ambassador in Vienna demanded the immediate cession of the Southern Tyrol, including Bolzano, the Isonzo (including Gorizia), and Gradiska. In addition, Trieste was to become a free port and an independent state. Finally he demanded the islands near Lissa, recognition of Italian sovereignty over Valona, and Austrian assurances of her disinterest in Albania.

A straightforward acceptance of these exorbitant demands was impossible, but it was important to gain time. After an oral discussion at German GHQ, on 12 April, Chancellor Bethmann Hollweg sent the following instructions to the German diplomatic representatives in Vienna and Rome:

> According to General von Falkenhayn, the military situation, both in the West and the East, is very favourable. All French attacks have been repulsed, the new British armies are not causing any apprehension ... If Italy remains quiet, we confidently expect the war to end in our favour. Italy's entry must be averted without fail.

In this regard, Prince von Bülow in Rome was to try to induce the authorities "to desist from making exorbitant demands" and to counsel Ambassador Tschirschky in Vienna to yield to their demands as much as was possible. "However," the Chancellor continued, "in an extreme case, Austria must make up her mind to concede everything, which would still be less disastrous than the unavoidable collapse of the Monarchy."

Falkenhayn assisted in the efforts of the German Imperial Government by speaking to the Italian Military Attaché in Berlin, Lieutenant Colonel Bongiovanni. Bongiovanni reported to the Italian Chief of Staff on 13 April that he had "just returned from General Headquarters where the Chief of Staff discussed with me with great clearness, calm, and cordiality the situation that has developed as a result of the Austro-Italian negotiations; this was done in two long conversations." He conveyed that Falkenhayn had explained to him how the German government and the general himself had continuously strived to induce Vienna to come to an understanding with Rome and that even at that moment every effort was being made toward inducing Austria to accept the conditions proposed by Italy. Falkenhayn told the *Oberstleutnant* that Italy, however, must realize that in the event of war between Italy and Austria-Hungary, Germany would carry out her obligations under their alliance. It would be possible to delay the Italian forces for a long time in the regions of the Austro–Italian frontier, which lent themselves well to defence, and the Italians would certainly find themselves opposing German troops before reaching either Budapest or Vienna. Falkenhayn, he continued, then gave a brief estimate of the military situation, as a result of which Falkenhayn concluded that Germany would be able to bear the burdens of the war for a long time. That is, it could afford to permit events to take their course and to maintain its present excellent position without touching its reserves. An eventual Italian entry into the war would neither decide nor end the campaign. The general was convinced that Italy should instead strive for hegemony in the Mediterranean; yet it could never hope to attain that if the British and French were victorious. Falkenhayn used the occasion to emphasize that the offers of Austria and Germany to Italy and Rumania—offers that were intended to keep them out of the war—were positive because the territory concerned was at Austria's disposal, whereas the offers of the Entente Powers included nothing but the proverbial "bearskin."[49]

CLEARLY RECOGNIZING THE HOPELESSNESS OF THE MILITARY AND POLITICAL situation of the Dual Monarchy, Falkenhayn finally decided to employ the *OHL*'s reserves in the East in order to gain a decisive victory over the Russians on the Carpathian Front; if possible, he would deploy them before Italy entered the war. This decision meant postponing indefinitely the great offensive in the West, as well as the offensive against Serbia, for which large-scale preparations had already been initiated. This decision was made possible by Falkenhayn's faith in the German Western Front's powers of resistance, a faith based on the brilliant defence that front had put up against the French breakthrough offensive. This faith justified the risk entailed in substantially reducing GHQ's reserves in the West.

On 10 April the General Staff chief discussed the planned operation on the Eastern Front for the first time in the presence of the Kaiser. It was decided to stage the offensive in the Gorlice area and to employ a new army—Eleventh Army— which would have to be organized for that purpose. With this decision, the war's centre of gravity was definitively shifted to the Eastern Theatre. For the third time in only a few months, developments in the East had demonstrated quite impressively that without a complete defeat of the enemy on the Eastern Front, it would not be possible to decide the war in the West and thereby end the war on all fronts. Everything now depended on making sufficiently strong forces

---

49   *The proverb refers to a person selling a bearskin before the hunt.*

available for the campaign right from the start, so that its offensive power would not slacken after the initial successful blow but would steadily increase until it had a decisive effect.

That Falkenhayn only temporarily abandoned his plans for the West may be inferred from a conversation he had with Oberst von Seeckt on 16 April, according to which the general hoped, after striking the blow in the East, "that it would be possible after all to decide the war in the West."[50]

---

50 From a letter by General von Seeckt of 13 November 1927, addressed to the *Reichsarchiv*.

PART II

Spring and Summer

4

THE GENERAL SITUATION OF THE
CENTRAL POWERS IN MAY

GENERAL VON FALKENHAYN MAY HAVE BEEN A WESTERNER AT HEART, BUT HE *understood that the weight of operations had to be shifted to the East to support Germany's beleaguered ally as well as to influence the neutral powers' decision making. On 2 May, Mackensen's new Eleventh Army launched a large-scale attack into Galicia.[1] On the first day of the offensive the Germans captured 17,000 Russian prisoners and eight guns, precipitating a full-scale Russian retreat to the San.[2] A week later, Falkenhayn declared that the immediate threat to Germany's ally had been parried.[3] The General Staff Chief then called on Mackensen to continue the campaign with a drive first toward the Wislok and then on to Przemysl and the San. Falkenhayn's aim was to retake the city and permanently forestall an Austro-Hungarian collapse by establishing a new defensive line along the river, which his allies could then hold as he turned his attention elsewhere.[4] While the renewal of the Gorlice–Tarnow offensive on 19 May eventually brought great strategic successes,*

---

1 *DW* VII: 378–86.
2 *DW* VII: 389–401; Foley, *German Strategy and the Path to Verdun*, 139.
3 Stone, *The Eastern Front 1914–1917*, 135–41; see also Oskar Tile von Kalm, *Schlachten des Weltkrieges: In Einzeldarstellungen bearbeitet im Auftrages des Reichsarchiv Band 30: Gorlice* (Berlin: Stalling, 1930).
4 *DW* VIII: 139–42.

Przemysl was not retaken until 4 June. In the meantime, the arrival of Russian reinforcements in Galicia temporarily threatened the line on the San.⁵ In the Mediterranean, the Franco-British infantry landings on the Dardanelles on 25 April 1915 added to an overall gloomy picture, which grew darker still as Germany faced a new offensive in the West. With Serbia still undefeated and the Central Powers waging a war on four fronts, Italy prepared to finally enter the fray on the Entente's side.

The Intervention of Italy

When Falkenhayn decided to launch a major relief attack in Galicia on 13 April 1915, he was clearly aware of the Dual Monarchy's precarious situation, but he only temporarily considered forgoing his offensive plans in the West. The task of forcing the Russians to retreat from their front in western Galicia all the way to the Lupków Pass was assigned to Generaloberst Mackensen, who accomplished this when he reached the Wislok on 8 May. At that point, Falkenhayn faced the question of whether to be satisfied with the successes in the East or to resume his plans in Serbia and the West. As it happened, he agreed with Conrad's proposal to exploit the victory in the Galician Theatre by pursuing the Russians to the River San: "The opportunity must be exploited to strike the enemy a decisive blow from which he would be unable to recover."

This decision resulted in the temporary abandonment of offensive plans in the West. It could therefore be expected that the enemy would take advantage of the weakened German Western Front by mounting major attacks, the outcome of which remained, at best, in doubt because of the enemy's increasing numerical superiority.

In the beginning of May 1915 only ninety-seven German infantry divisions were deployed in the Franco-Belgian Theatre. It was estimated that the enemy had 110 to 112 divisions, which were, on average, considerably stronger than the German divisions. Behind the Western Front the OHL had reserves of approximately seven and a half infantry divisions; it also had a number of heavy batteries that, in the event of an enemy attack, would be sufficient to increase the artillery of an army to almost double strength within a few days.

In the Russian Theatre, 111 and a half German and Austro-Hungarian infantry divisions faced approximately 114 Russian divisions between the Baltic Sea and

---

5 Foley, 143.

Bukovina.[6] The Austro-Hungarian units deployed on the Serbian border amounted to 234,000 men; the Serbian Army was estimated at 210,000 men;[7] against Italy, 112 battalions[8] provided border protection. This level of encirclement taxed Austria-Hungary's strength to the extreme.

Between the middle of March and the middle of May, nine infantry divisions and two cavalry divisions were redeployed from the West to the Eastern Front. Falkenhayn wanted to withhold his decision about whether additional forces could be withdrawn from the West for the benefit of the East until after the expected enemy offensive. For him the decisive consideration was that a return of forces from the East to revitalize the situation in the Western Theatre had to be avoided if at all possible as long as the operations against Russia promised success.

Additionally, the developing political situation in Italy, Turkey, and the Balkans could strongly influence decisions in Galicia and on the Western Front. Thus the Central Powers paid particular attention to political considerations in May 1915.

The considerable tension was made especially clear during discussions between the two General Staff chiefs. On 30 April and 2 May, Falkenhayn sent two consecutive communications to Conrad urging him to acquiesce to the Italian government's demands.[9] On 4 May, Kaiser Wilhelm supported this approach in a similar request sent to his Imperial ally. On the same day, the Viennese Cabinet declared that it was prepared to make far-reaching concessions.[10] This coincided with Italy's notification to the Austro-Hungarian Empire on 4 May of her abrogation of the Triple Alliance. On 5 May the German ambassador, Count von Bülow, reported from Rome that the Italian Foreign Minister, having inspected the Viennese offers, had informed him that the Austro-Hungarian proposals would have settled everything had they had been made fourteen days earlier. Bülow then asked whether such a settlement was still possible; Baron Sonnino remained silent. The Italian Council of Ministers' response, which described Austria-Hungary's proposals as "not representing a sufficient basis for negotiations," was received on 6 May. On

6 Along the Rumanian border only about 9,600 men were deployed, consisting of Austro-Hungarian Constabulary Guards reinforced by *Landsturm* units.

7 The total strength of the Serbian Army was estimated at 232 battalions in addition to 36 squadrons, 536 field guns, and approximately 240 heavy guns. The Montenegrin army, which was divided into individual small detachments, numbered 53,000 men and 140 guns. *See* General Staff, War Office, *Armies of the Balkan States, 1914–1916* (London: HMSO/Battery, 1996).

8 Not including the garrison of the Austro-Hungarian border fortifications.

9 See *DW* VII: 343–44.

10 In addition to turning over the largest part of the Trentino, these concessions included a surrender of limited areas on the Isonzo, including Gradiska; the establishment of an Italian University in Trieste; and an expression by Austria-Hungary of disinterest in Albania, on condition that they be provided with "guarantees against the establishment of a third power."

the same day, Emperor Franz Joseph sent a telegram to Kaiser Wilhelm stating that these latest concessions represented "the ultimate limit of any conceivable accommodation."

The seriousness of the Italian crisis caused the Central Powers' leading statesmen and their General Staff chiefs to hold a conference on 7 May in Teschen, by which time the latest news from Rome sounded somewhat more hopeful. On 26 April, Italy had entered into an agreement with the Entente;[11] however, it had reserved a grace period of four weeks in which to decide whether this agreement would actually come into effect. At the time it seemed that there was still a faint hope that Italy could be kept out of the war.[12]

Up to this point in the war, Falkenhayn had responded evasively to Austro-Hungarian requests for military assistance in the event of an Italian entry into the war,[13] stating that such a decision could only be taken under "concrete circumstances." Aside from the military situation, and from the fact that any dilution of forces could only be viewed as unfavourable, Falkenhayn's position was based on the fact that attempts were ongoing to compel the Austro-Hungarian Empire to acquiesce to even the greatest concessions to Italy. But now the situation had changed. It was hoped that, owing to the great successes on the Eastern Front, more forces would soon be available. Also, Vienna had truly conceded as much as it could, perhaps even more. This explains why, in the discussions at Teschen, Falkenhayn was prepared to commit German forces to the Italian border if necessary, although the extent of such a commitment would have to depend on the general situation at the time of Italy's entry into the war.

On 8 May, Chancellor Bethman Hollweg wired Count von Bülow in Rome regarding the political result of this meeting and informed him that the Cabinet in Vienna was "in the final equation, willing to concede everything."[14]

Furthermore, remarks by former Italian Prime Minister Giolitti (who had previously favoured the Triple Alliance) regarding the seriousness of the situation finally caused the Austro-Hungarian and German Ambassadors in Rome to announce additional Austrian concessions to the Italian Foreign Minister on

---

11 *The Treaty of London committed Italy to enter the war on the side of the Entente Powers in exchange for territorial and economic concessions.*

12 In reality the Salandra Cabinet had already committed itself to war in the treaty of 26 April, which contained a clause stating that hostilities would be initiated in four weeks' time. On 6 May, General Cadorna, Chief of the Italian General Staff, explained that the army would be operational on 20 May at the earliest. See Antonio Salandra, *L'intervento 1915* (Milan: Garzanti, 1930), 174–76, 242.

13 See *DW* VII: 364.

14 On Bethmann Hollweg's role in the crisis, see Konrad H. Jarausch, *The Enigmatic Chancellor: Bethmann Hollweg and the Hubris of Imperial Germany* (New Haven, CT: Yale University Press, 1973), 239ff.

10 May without waiting for Vienna's consent. These concessions included the cession of all areas inhabited by Italians in the Tyrol and on the western banks of the Isonzo, including Gradiska; the declaration that Trieste would be made a free Imperial city and a free port, and that an Italian university would be established there; and, finally, a declaration of complete Austro-Hungarian disinterest in Albania. Germany advised the Italian government that it would be prepared to vouch for the implementation of these concessions.[15]

These concessions far exceeded the ones previously offered; indeed, they exceeded those which Italy had been demanding only a few months earlier. Nevertheless, the Austrian Foreign Minister, Baron von Burian, retroactively gave his permission to their announcement in Rome. The only question was whether the concessions had come too late, for Italy had already committed itself to the Entente. Everything now depended on the domestic political situation in Italy, which, at the last hour, seemed to be taking a turn in favour of the Central Powers because of the Italian Parliament's strong resistance to the war policy of Prime Minister Salandra, who tendered his resignation on 13 May. However, on the afternoon of 16 May, when King Victor Emmanuel III refused to accept Salandra's resignation, it became evident that a decision in favour of war had been made.

Although it appeared that the Central Powers' ever more impressive successes in Galicia would not change Italy's position, hope remained that the Italian position might positively affect the unstable situation in the Balkans. Above all, it was expected that Rumania's attitude toward the Central Powers would become friendlier. Hope also returned that Bulgaria could be won over. The Ottoman government's demand—that Serbia be defeated in order to create a secure connection from Germany to Turkey—became ever more pressing as a result of the major British and French landings at Gallipoli.[16] In order to finally gain Bulgaria's support against Serbia, both General Staff chiefs agreed in Pleß on 12 May to inform Sofia that, owing to the positive situation in Galicia and the favourable water levels in the Danube, they would immediately prepare a campaign against Serbia; however, this was made conditional on Bulgaria's agreement to co-operate militarily. Consequently, Germany's Foreign Minister Gottlieb von Jagow proposed that the Bulgarian government immediately dispatch an authorized officer to German

---

15 On Italy's territorial ambitions, see John Gooch, *Army, State, and Society in Italy, 1870–1915* (New York: St. Martin's, 1989), 165ff. On Austria-Hungary's last-minute concessions to Italy, see Rezni, *In the Shadow of the Sword:* 171–91.

16 See *DW* VII: 364–65. On 25 April 1915, British and French troops landed at Cape Helles, Ari Burnu (ANZAC Cove), and Kum Kale. The Turkish soldiers and German officers defending the peninsula managed to prevent any significant movement inland by the Entente forces. A further landing was made on 6 August 1915 at Suvla Bay, but again resulted in a significant loss of life without any tangible results.

GHQ, where official delegates from Austria-Hungary and Turkey would join him to conclude a military convention. However, because of the ominous developments in Rome, Bulgaria's response to this offer was a long time coming. Bulgaria intended to wait and base its decision on further developments in the general situation.[17]

In the meantime, in a memorandum dispatched to Pleß on 14 May, Conrad proposed that if Italy entered the war he would go over to the defensive in Galicia after reaching the Dniester–San line and then use the forces thereby freed up (which he estimated to be ten Austrian and ten German divisions) to attack Italy; he believed that a simultaneous campaign against Serbia could still be conducted using sufficient German and Bulgarian forces.

Considering the precarious situation in Turkey, Falkenhayn was only able to agree to the defensive proposal in Galicia because he believed that a military success in the Balkans was of primary importance. For that reason he planned to attack Serbia first, while at the same time remaining on the defensive against Italy.

On 16 May, Falkenhayn made the following counter-proposal: in Galicia, in addition to the German Eleventh Army, seventeen to eighteen Austro-Hungarian and seven German divisions, totalling approximately thirty-five divisions, would be made available for operations against Serbia and Italy. The attack against Serbia was to be planned immediately. Against Italy, Austria-Hungary was to assume responsibility in Carinthia, Carniola, and the coastal area with approximately sixteen divisions. In the Tyrol, Falkenhayn was prepared to give the same mission to German forces; the Austro-Hungarian fortifications and forces presently stationed there were to be placed under German command. A decision regarding the size of the German force to be deployed in the Tyrol could not be made at the time, but it would be sufficient to prevent an Italian advance into the Tyrolean lands.

In his response of the following day, Conrad reiterated that only twenty divisions could be taken out of the Galician Front; he intended to deploy all of them against the Italians in order to defeat their thirty divisions, which were probably advancing by way of Villach and Ljubljana in the general direction of the line Danube–Vienna–Budapest. However, he did not want to relinquish the defence of the Tyrol, which he wanted assigned to the Austro-Hungarian and possibly available German forces under Austro-Hungarian command. Defence against Serbia—and if necessary Rumania—was to be the responsibility of those Austro-Hungarian forces deployed in the Balkans.

---

17 *According to Richard C. Hall, by this point Bulgaria was already moving toward intervention on the side of the Entente.* See Richard C. Hall, "Bulgaria, Romania, and Greece," in *The Origins of World War I*, ed. Richard F. Hamilton and Holger H. Herwig (Cambridge: Cambridge University Press, 2003), 398.

In response, Falkenhayn repeated his operational proposal; however, he now assessed the forces to be freed up in Galicia as only twenty-nine divisions. In other words, he believed that the Central Powers would be able to field forty-nine divisions against Serbia and Italy, once the twenty divisions of Austria-Hungary's Balkan Army were added.[18] On 17 May he wrote:

I do not want to address the question of their deployment until I have received a response from Bulgaria, which will hopefully come tomorrow or the day after. In any case, I would venture to say that it should be possible to keep Serbia under control with nine divisions and to attack the Italians with forty divisions; or to possibly conduct a short, fierce attack against the Serbs with thirty-one and a half divisions, which has the potential of firmly binding Bulgaria to us, as well as Turkey and Rumania, and which will very drastically delay the Italian advance, at least until the Serbian matter has been settled.

An agreement over the most important issues was not reached. While Conrad maintained his position that they should "initially use all available forces exclusively against Italy," and while the Austro-Hungarian Chief of Staff viewed a campaign in the Balkans as "unfeasible for the time being,"[19] Falkenhayn reserved his response as to whether the attack should be launched first against Serbia or Italy.

Only after a personal conversation in Teschen on 18 May was a certain level of accommodation between the two opinions reached: five divisions of the Austro-Hungarian Fifth (Balkan) Army were to be transported immediately to the area west of Zagreb, where they could be assembled on 5 June. Only two divisions, in addition to border security and fortification garrisons, were to remain on the Serbian border. Their immediate reinforcement by three German divisions from Galicia was anticipated. Furthermore, the Austro-Hungarian VII Corps was to be transported to Klagenfurth, and one Austro-Hungarian and two German divisions were to be moved to Maribor–Ptuj. The latter three divisions, as well as five divisions of the Austro-Hungarian Fifth (Balkan) Army, were to constitute a

---

18 General von Falkenhayn's conclusion that Austria-Hungary had twenty divisions on the Serbian border is explained by Falkenhayn's interpretation of Conrad's remark that the Austro-Hungarian Balkan Army consisted of approximately 240,000 men. Falkenhayn converted these forces into twenty divisions. Conrad countered this assumption by stating that the majority of the forces stationed along the Serbian border consisted of *Landsturm* units. The fully operational combat units were only 80,000 rifles strong. As a matter of fact, the Austrian Official History of the War (II: 277, 348) also mentions that the Balkan forces were used as a "great reserve" for the Austro-Hungarian Northern Army at the beginning of 1915 and later served as a "Reserve Army for the establishment of a front against Italy."

19 Letter to the German Chief of the General Staff dated 18 May 1915.

reformed Fifth Army commanded by General von Boroevic. A new German unit was also to be activated, the *Alpenkorps*, which was to be commanded in the Tyrol by the National Defence Commander, General der Kavallerie Dankl. Command over the entire Italian Front was to be turned over to General der Kavallerie Archduke Eugen.

These decisions addressed only the most important issues; even so, Falkenhayn proposed to launch an attack, limited in both time and area, against Serbia. He wanted to use these forces later for the planned attack against Italy.

How greatly the attack against Serbia consumed Falkenhayn was evident in the fact that on 19 May he again tried to create favourable conditions for it. Through the Foreign Office's representative at GHQ, von Treutler, Falkenhayn demanded that additional diplomatic efforts be made in Sofia to finally receive a clear response to the query of 12 May regarding Bulgaria's co-operation. In a letter sent to Teschen on the same day he emphasized:

> I am certain that the Serbian matter can be dealt with prior to the beginning of the Italian offensive. According to all of my information, the Italians will not show up in full strength until the beginning of June and, according to Your Excellency's personal statements, will have to march and fight for at least four weeks prior to becoming truly menacing. Therefore, this will not come to pass until the beginning of July. Thus, in the meantime the Serbian question can surely be settled.

Events then took place that fundamentally altered the decisions of both General Staff chiefs: on the evening of 19 May it became known in Teschen that Bulgaria had declined to participate in a campaign against Serbia and the *AOK* in Vienna was informed that the Italian declaration of war could be expected within twenty-four hours. Conrad now wrote to Pleß that he was convinced that "we now must face the new enemy together with all of our might and that this operation cannot be hamstrung based on possible future intervention in our favour by a doubtful third party (Bulgaria) or against us by another third party (Rumania)."

However, on the same day, 19 May, GHQ received reports of extremely strong Russian attacks against Eleventh Army. Based on this, and on Bulgaria's refusal, Falkenhayn deemed it advisable to maintain the focus of the Eastern war on the Russian Front for the time being and to initially conduct defensive actions against Serbia and Italy.

To this end, on 20 May he sent urgent directions to Teschen stating that under no circumstances should any additional forces be moved against Italy, except for the five divisions of the Balkan Army, the Austro-Hungarian VII Corps, and the

German *Alpenkorps*; those still positioned in Poland and Galicia were needed in order to "finally relieve the Central Powers of the Russian peril for good." Until "the final defeat of Russian offensive ability in Galicia" was achieved, the withdrawal would have to wait.

Nevertheless, to achieve clarity for later decisions, Falkenhayn requested information as to exactly how the *AOK* intended to conduct its attack against Italy. At the same time, he mentioned that according to his estimate "the beginning of decisive battles was inconceivable within seven weeks," at which point they would be east of the line Graz–Maribor–Zagreb. From his immediately issued response, it was evident that Conrad expected the Italians to advance in two directions: via Ljubljana–Maribor against the line formed by the Danube between Budapest and Győr; and via Villach–Leoben against Vienna. He intended to surround, attack, and defeat the right Italian flank; meanwhile, the left Italian flank would be stopped in Carinthia by the troops garrisoning the border together with the forces assembled there. The attack was to be conducted by Fifth Army, which initially was to be deployed west of Zagreb with five divisions and in the vicinity of Maribor with three divisions. Conrad emphasized:

> I expect an invasion across the border by strong Italian forces immediately following the declaration of war and therefore probably on 23–24 May. Then I will have to assume an elapsed travel time of three, at most four, weeks for the 200 kilometre distance from the border to Maribor–Zagreb, which means the 14th of June, or the 20th of June at most. I am fully aware that eight divisions are not nearly sufficient for the attack and that everything must be done to ensure that additional forces follow instantaneously. The railroads must be fully exploited during the period until 20 June so that at least twenty divisions, which I consider to be the minimum for the decisive battle, can be assembled in the area Graz–Maribor and west of Zagreb.

However, Falkenhayn disagreed with these plans. Considering the situation in Galicia, it could not be expected with any certainty that the twenty divisions to be used for Conrad's planned attack against Italy would be available in the foreseeable future. In these circumstances, Falkenhayn pressed for the deployment of all available forces for defensive operations on the border. On 21 May he travelled to Teschen for a personal exchange of ideas. After long debate, an agreement was reached: both General Staff chiefs agreed to first conclude the operations in Galicia. Since at that time it could not be foreseen when those operations would be concluded, the plan to deploy three divisions to Maribor, as well as to the Serbian border, was temporarily out of the question. In the course of this debate it turned out that Falkenhayn saw the situation in these two theatres in a considerably more positive light than did the *AOK*. He did not believe that the Serbs would launch an offensive, and he did not rate the Italian offensive capabilities very highly; also, as already noted, he expected their arrival on the Maribor–Zagreb line considerably later than Conrad did. Since additional reinforcements could not be expected for the time being, he considered the presence on the border of five Austro-Hungarian divisions, which were being brought up from the Balkans, to be vital for stopping the Italians on the Isonzo in purely defensive operations. Despite emphatic objections and concerns, he managed to win Conrad over to this plan. Also, the slow progress of offensive operations in Galicia may have convinced Conrad that a release of those forces for an attack against Italy could no longer be allowed. With this in mind, the following telegram was sent to Pleß on 22 May:

> Due to the currently reduced forces against Italy, and after considering all the circumstances, I have decided to temporarily conduct defensive operations against Italy by deploying the majority of Fifth Army, ordered from the Galician theatre of war, as well as the forces on their way to Carinthia, as far forward as possible and therefore to first disembark the troops from the trains on the Isonzo and at Villach.

Although disagreement persisted for several days, with that the strategy for the coming battles with Italy was finally established. The issue of conducting the war on a number of fronts was also finally clarified on 21 May: the Central Powers would continue the offensive on the Galician Front and conduct defensive actions in all other theatres.

ON 23 MAY 1915 AT AROUND 3:15 IN THE AFTERNOON, ITALY DECLARED WAR ON Austria-Hungary, but not on Germany. The German government limited itself to the severance of diplomatic relations; even so, the Italian government could have no doubt that its forces would also face those of Germany during an invasion of the Austro-Hungarian Empire. In the middle of January 1915, Count von Bülow had advised Baron Sonnino, the Italian Foreign Minister, that in the event of war between Italy and Austria-Hungary, "Germany would stand with her whole strength" by its ally's side.[20] The reason why Germany initially limited itself to severing diplomatic relations with Italy could be found in its relationship with Rumania, and in Germany's desire to preserve shipments of raw materials across the Italian border if at all possible. Although the available information did not

---

20　Count Bülow's telegram dated the 18 January 1915 to the Foreign Ministry.

suggest that Rumania posed an immediate threat, on 21 May Prime Minister Bratianu told Baron von dem Bussche, the German Ambassador in Bucharest, that the preservation of Rumanian neutrality would be made easier if Italy, not Germany, issued the expected declaration of war. In response to a query from Falkenhayn on the same day, the German Chancellor informed the General Staff chief that King Ferdinand had assured the German ambassador that Rumania had not entered into any agreements with Italy and therefore "an Italian initiative would not result in Rumanian's intervention." Although increasing pressure from the Entente was creating a precarious situation, it seemed that the Italian King still hoped to maintain Rumanian neutrality. The Reich Chancellor continued:

> On the other hand, Bratianu seems to be conducting negotiations with Russia behind the King's back, although he denies it.[21] It is not known whether these negotiations led to any results. Rumania was very impressed by our victories in the Carpathians. Consequently, Rumania's entry into the war is unlikely at the present time; however, this possibility is not out of the question in the future. As long as no crisis takes place in the Bucharest government, Beldiman[22] considers an alliance with us to be out of the question. An operation against Serbia would provide further guarantee of Rumania's remaining quiet.

Thus for the time being, the situation in Rumania seemed to have calmed. Now the German Chief of the General Staff again attempted to open the way for ammunition transports to Turkey via Rumania. Again he was unsuccessful.

At this time, reassuring news arrived from Greece.

Despite a number of crises, the Turkish battles at Gallipoli did not warrant serious concern. Of the fifty-two divisions of the Turkish Army, eleven were deployed at the Dardanelles. The 65,000 French and British troops that had landed there were unable to advance against the Ottomans' tenacious defence. It had to be assumed that the final outcome of this battle would ultimately depend on unimpeded supplies of German war materiel. Nevertheless, based on reports from Constantinople received around the end of May, Falkenhayn gathered that for the time being, the Ottoman Empire would be able to hold the straits on its own. Therefore, he could justify postponing the offensive against the Serbs.

---

21 These negotiations did actually take place. Due to Bratianu's extreme demands, Sasanow became suspicious and believed that Rumania was purposely presenting excessive demands in order to avoid an agreement with Russia and to "evade a war." Basically, Russia had already recognized Rumania's right to occupy those areas of the Austro-Hungarian Empire that were inhabited by Rumanians in the fall of 1914.

22 The Rumanian Ambassador in Berlin.

Regarding a declaration of war on Italy, Turkey took the same position as Germany: a war had to be avoided, at least as long as the situation in the Balkans was not settled.

Overall, Italy's declaration of war did not strongly influence the military position of the Central Powers. At the same time, however, the economic consequences of Italy's decision *did* threaten to affect the Central Powers. In particular, the continued flow of supplies across the Italian border was now uncertain.

The Worsening of the Economic Situation and the Decision to Make Economic Warfare by Submarine

Up to this point in the war, Italy had played an important role in supplying foreign raw materials. Since Britain had declared the North Sea a war zone, a considerable amount of American cotton had to be imported via Genoa. The initial difficulties that Italy caused were subsequently eliminated through the actions of the United States. However, since declaring war on Austria-Hungary, Italy had cut off all exports to Germany. The German economy was now almost entirely dependent on its own production and reserves and on small quantities of vital imports from bordering neutral countries. The Army Administration was attempting to deal with this situation by taking previously arranged measures. Dr. Walter Rathenau had resigned as head of the Raw Materials Department of the Prussian Ministry of War (*Kriegsrohstoffabteilung,* hereafter the *KRA*) in February 1915. He had been succeeded by Major Koeth, and under his leadership the government's management of crucial raw materials would be developed in an organized manner for the duration of the war. Based on previous experience, the *KRA* made a clear distinction between the army's needs and those of the civilian population. The *KRA* attempted to limit the requirements of the civilian population more and more to areas of absolute need. Careful inventories were made of the reserves available in the domestic and occupied areas, and of presently available resources along with newly available ones, which were systematically developed. Raw material distribution was strictly controlled and prioritized in accordance with the ever-increasing demands of arming and equipping the army. Artificial materials often replaced natural raw ones; in this regard, German science and its inventive spirit earned substantial recognition.[23]

---

23 *In the original, a footnote pointed readers to the second volume of* "Kriegsrüstung und Kriegswirtschaft," *the German official history of the economic war. This second volume was never published. A more detailed examination of the German economy from the beginning of the war will be found in Volume I, Part II, of this series.*

Italy's entry into the war further restricted the diet of both the army and the home population. Italy's action ended imports of certain foods and animal feeds that could have replaced some of the scarce foodstuffs on the home front. The closing of the Italian border was felt all the more strongly because by the winter of 1914–15 it had become necessary to place the most important foodstuffs, such as grain products, under government control. These measures noticeably affected all levels of society and reminded the public of the seriousness of the situation.

The import blockade led to serious shortages in animal feed; as a consequence, considerable amounts of bread grains and potatoes were being used to feed livestock. When prohibitions against this proved insufficient, the government ordered an extensive butchering of pigs, which lasted until May. To prevent potato shortages in the summer, which would especially affect the poorest segments of the population, a specially formed government authority purchased all available potatoes. In addition to this, the shortage of oats was becoming critical, which meant that they had to be requisitioned solely for military use. When the oats shortage further deteriorated, even barley had to be requisitioned. Finally, the sugar shortage led to the distribution of unrefined sugar. Further interventions into the nation's free economic life had to be expected in order to secure adequate supplies for both the army and the German population. The agricultural areas so far occupied by German forces were helping sustain the army. The methodical cultivation of fields in enemy territory during the coming harvest promised to further aid the army, but such efforts could not relieve the homeland to any large degree.

In October 1914 the Austro-Hungarian Empire, too, began encountering difficulties in feeding its people. This began to impair its fighting abilities. Before the war, Austria and Hungary had formed a duty-free zone within which Hungary's agricultural surplus almost entirely covered Austria's shortages of key foods and animal feeds. When in early 1915 the war placed pressure on Hungary's economic situation, the Hungarian government responded by confiscating grains, flour, and corn. This compelled Austria to take measures similar to those in Germany, given that Galicia and Bukovina—Austria's most important agricultural areas—had become war zones and were thus unusable. In extensive negotiations, Austria attempted to arrange for continued foodstuff subsidies from Hungary both to relieve the Austrian economy and to supply their common army. Despite these efforts, Hungarian assistance grew ever sparser. The food situation in Austria, then, was a chronic and serious concern. Given all this, Italy's entry into the war was a serious blow to the Central Powers' entire economic situation, for one of the last available avenues for imports had been closed. This was exacerbated by the almost ten-month blockade of the North Sea and the resulting severe deterioration of the economic situation in Germany. The introduction of economic warfare by submarine was largely a result of the increasingly critical economic situation in Germany.

Immediately after the war's outbreak, in an attempt to get the warring parties to conduct the naval war in accordance with international law, the United States proposed that the warring parties commit themselves to the London Declaration of 26 February 1909 concerning the Laws of Naval War,[24] which the seafaring powers had accepted but not yet ratified. The German government immediately agreed to the American proposals; Germany's enemies, however, rejected them. The reason became abundantly clear in the months following the outbreak of war, when Britain and France initiated schemes aimed at starving and isolating Germany. Adopting means that best served their interests, and in contravention of the London Declaration and all previous customs of international law, the enemy nations arbitrarily manipulated the contraband rules of war by extending the right of search and seizure to include neutral vessels. These measures, intended to isolate Germany, were tightened even further on 2 November 1914 when the British Admiralty designated the entire North Sea as an exclusively military area. With that, neutral trade with Germany was largely paralyzed.

In consideration of the risks these developments posed to the Central Powers' entire war effort, on 7 November Admiral von Pohl, Chief of Staff of the German Admiralty, proposed to the German Chancellor that a blockade of the British Isles and the north and west coasts of France by submarine be established as a countermeasure. The thought of using U-boats to conduct economic warfare had never occurred to the leaders of the German Navy prior to the war. But after the first months of war and the first U-boat successes, the suggestion came from the submarine front that this weapon would be most effective if utilized against the enemy's trade. From the outset it was the prevailing opinion that U-boats would be unable to guard the shipping lanes using conventional cruiser tactics—that is, surface, stop ships, and investigate them for nationality and cargo. As a precondition of economic warfare by submarine, submerged U-boats would have to be allowed to sink enemy shipping with torpedoes and without warning. At first it was considered possible to accurately differentiate between neutral and hostile shipping; this, however, became an issue at the end of January 1915 when it was suggested that British merchantmen were flying neutral flags in order to deceive German U-boats. The German Admiralty wanted to deal with this difficulty by denying neutral commercial shipping access to the waters around England through unconditional German submarine warfare, which was planned mainly as a countermeasure to Great Britain's violation of the rules of contraband and blockade.

---

24 For the other occurrences in the war at sea in 1915, see *DW* IX.

The navy believed that the strongest impact of commercial warfare by submarine would be to deter shipping. The German Imperial Government voiced concern over the suggestion that commercial war be conducted in this manner; it feared confrontations with neutral powers, especially with the United States. Given these differences of opinion, the Chief of the General Staff was content to emphasize that the interests of the land war would be served by restricting enemy traffic in the English Channel. The exchange of opinions between the German Imperial Government and the navy about using U-boats in commercial warfare, with regard to both political considerations and international law, continued until the end of January 1915. Not until 1 February, at a conference also attended by Falkenhayn, did the Chancellor express his willingness to put his concerns aside and to defer to the Admiralty chief's demands. After a presentation by Admiral von Pohl on 4 February, the Emperor approved commercial warfare by submarine. The Chief of the Admiralty Staff announced that the waters around Great Britain were to be declared a war zone as a "countermeasure to the [British] activities that, in violation of international law, were preventing neutral sea trade with Germany." With twenty-two operational U-boats, the commercial war by submarine began.[25]

The protests of the neutral powers—in particular those made by the Scandinavian countries, the Netherlands, and especially the United States—against the Entente's blockade and Germany's countermeasures were initially unsuccessful. The U.S. government proposed on 21 February that both warring parties discontinue their new methods of commercial warfare; in other words, Germany would abandon its commercial war by submarine, and the enemy powers would permit trade in foodstuffs. Germany agreed to this proposal; Great Britain rejected it.

On 11 March 1915 the British government responded to the German declaration of commercial warfare by submarine by further tightening its blockade. In total disregard of the rights and interests of the neutral countries, Britain's new measures primarily targeted German trade through the neighbouring Nordic

---

25 See Marinearchiv, *Der Krieg zur See 1914–1918: Der Handelskrieg mit U-Booten Band 1—Vorgeschichte* (Berlin: E.S. Mittler & Sohn, 1932); Marinearchiv, *Der Krieg zur See 1914–1918: Der Handelskrieg mit U-Booten Band 2—Februar bis September 1915* (Berlin: E.S. Mittler & Sohn, 1933); and Marinearchiv, *Der Krieg zur See 1914–1918: Der Handelskrieg mit U-Booten Band 3—Oktober 1915 bis Januar 1917* (Berlin: E.S. Mittler & Sohn, 1934). *Good introductory English-language sources include* Holger Herwig, *German Naval Officer Corps: A Social and Political History, 1890–1918* (Oxford: Oxford University Press, 1973); idem, *"Luxury" Fleet: the Imperial German Navy, 1888–1918* (London: Ashfield, 1987); and Wolfgang Wegener, *The Naval Strategy of the World War* (Annapolis, MD: Naval Institute, 1989). For an overview of the postwar controversy, see Philip K. Lundeberg, "The German Naval Critique of the U-Boat Campaign, 1915–1918," *Military Affairs* 27, no. 3 (1963): 105–18.

countries and Holland. The British intention was to isolate Germany from the rest of the world as if it were a fortress under siege and thereby mortally wound not only its armed forces but also its population.

As a result, commercial warfare by submarine continued. The sinking of the British passenger vessel *Lusitania* on 7 May 1915, during which a number of American citizens perished, led to a serious diplomatic confrontation between Germany and the United States. The U.S. government lodged a serious protest and demanded that in future a vessel should only be sunk after it was first stopped and searched and only if all customary measures for the protection of passengers were observed. The German Admiralty did not feel that it could acquiesce to these demands without reducing the effectiveness of its submarines because of the ever-growing number of armed enemy vessels.

The German government tried to arrive at a compromise between political priorities and the conduct of the naval war by imposing restrictions on the sinking of enemy passenger vessels by submarine as well as by stipulating that only enemy merchantmen could be sunk without warning.

Falkenhayn agreed with this view, but told the Emperor on 31 May 1915 that the continuation of the commercial war by submarine had to be made conditional on the avoidance at all costs of the danger of war with the United States. Falkenhayn's point of view was also motivated by the fact that he still hoped Bulgaria would join the Central Powers, which would be more unlikely should the United States enter the war.

The Manpower and Ammunition Situation to the End of the Year

In accordance with Falkenhayn's demands that new combat reserves be activated, and as far as the status of the reserves and the armament industry permitted, the Army Administration continued its attempts to create new units.

Early in the summer of 1915, immediately after Italy's declaration of war on Austria-Hungary, a unit suitable for combat operations in the mountains was formed in accordance with the *OHL's* request. Formed using both Prussian and Bavarian troops and designated the *Alpenkorps*, it was comprised of a reinforced infantry division. Its two *Jäger* brigades consisted of the Royal Bavarian Infantry Lieb Regiment and three *Jäger* regiments, with the addition of several *Jäger* battalions and ski formations.

In the Western Army, in addition to the fourteen infantry divisions formed during the spring of 1915, over the course of the summer, 183rd, 185th, 187th, and 192nd (Saxon) Infantry Brigades were created, reinforced first by pioneer and signal units and later by a unit of light field howitzers. As a result of the critical supply situation, the expansion of these brigades into divisions and the formation of additional units for the Western Army had to be suspended for the time being. Since the existing units could not be brought to full operational strength because of the lack of supplies, it made no sense to plan for the creation of new formations. In the Eastern Army, 4th Guard Infantry Division was created at the beginning of May, mostly from elements of the Guard Reserve Corps. At the end of the month, 107th Infantry Division was formed following the same procedure as had been used to create the previously mentioned 101st, 103rd, and 105th Infantry Divisions. By utilizing existing command centres and units, as well as a few new formations, 108th and 109th Infantry Divisions were created in a similar way in October 1915.

The available *Ersatz* and *Landwehr* divisions continued to be upgraded, and new *Landwehr* divisions were formed from already existing or newly created units. By the end of 1915 the number of *Landwehr* divisions had increased to twenty. At the same time, a number of heretofore makeshift units—often named after their leaders—were reorganized and upgraded. The *Posen* Corps became 83rd and 84th Divisions; the *Zastrow* Corps became XVII Reserve Corps, with its Divisions *Wernitz* and *Breugel* becoming 86th Infantry and 85th Landwehr Divisions; the *Dickhuth* Corps became 87th Division; Division *Menges* became 88th Division; and Detachment *Westernhagen* became 89th Infantry Division.

By the end of 1915 the German Army consisted of a total of 159 divisions—compared to 92 divisions at the beginning of the war[26]—and contained eleven cavalry divisions, which did not increase in number. The army also contained various independent brigades.

Additionally, and often in connection with these new and reorganized formations, numerous smaller units were deployed or mobilized, including combat, rear echelon, and *Landsturm* units, column and supply units, and military authorities and agencies. These all served to complete and reinforce the larger organizations that had been inadequately equipped before, such as the numerous foot artillery units, air force units, and new technical formations, to name just a few.

Finally, the *Ersatz* and training units continued to grow in proportion to the increase in demand. The infantry *Ersatz* battalions had already doubled by February 1915; each was equipped with two recruiting depots. The *Ersatz* formations of the other service arms were also augmented or reinforced. Based on positive experience, the Army Administration continued to integrate field recruit depots with corps or independent divisions at the front. In this way, the recruits who

---

26 Including the reserves in the main fortifications and excluding the independent brigades.

had been transferred out of the *Ersatz* battalions at home could complete their training under the guidance of personnel with combat experience.[27]

The continuing expansion of the army placed a twofold strain on the supply situation: each newly formed unit dispatched to the active army used up spare supplies not only when it was being formed but also for its maintenance in the field. This problem was all the more pressing because the supply needs of the combat units were extraordinarily high owing to continuously high casualties. By the summer of 1915 an average of 300,000 replacements[28] were being dispatched to the field each month—250,000 to the infantry alone. Thus a single month's worth represented the strength of seven and a half corps at full strength—the equivalent of almost half the strength of Germany's peacetime army in 1913.

The replacement situation was further complicated by the ever-increasing number of deferments and exemptions being granted to those liable for military service, because of the needs of the wartime economy. Since other means to alleviate the growing labour shortage at home had failed, it had become the Army Administration's responsibility to meet the war industry's demands for personnel. These demands had to be met in order to satisfy the incredible growth in demand for armaments so that the army at the front could continue to fight. For that reason, the number of eligible personnel exempt from military service had grown to more than one million by the summer of 1915.

The army's supply of replacements was not yet in jeopardy, but the time was drawing ever closer when the flow of new replacements would slow, which would have serious consequences. This eventuality could only be postponed by ensuring that an intolerable load was not placed on the reserve situation through the creation of new formations. After only a few months the 1915 age class, including the first *Landsturm* contingent, had already been used up. Therefore the 1916 age class had to be called up much too early, in the fall of 1915. It had to be expected that this age group—which included recuperated soldiers and additional replacements generated by the conscription of deferred men and changes to the conscription rules—despite all attempts at frugality, would last half a year at most.[29] Therefore, beginning at the end of 1915, the 1917 age group was called up.

---

27 In this connection, for each corps or division, an infantry *Ersatz* unit was created at the Belgian military training grounds at Beverloo and in Warsaw in May and December 1915, respectively. For the training of officer candidates, numerous courses were conducted on domestic drill grounds and firing ranges.

28 Approximately one-sixth of this number was recovered soldiers.

29 A law enacted on 4 September 1915 authorized the additional draft of such personnel who had been declared unsuited to duty during the peacetime draft and who, according to previous legal provisions, were exempt from military service.

Given the inevitable worsening of the replacement situation, yet unperturbed by various demands from the front and in complete agreement with the War Minister—Generalleutnant Wild, who was at GHQ—Deputy War Minister von Wandel insisted on the strongest possible economization of the army's replacements. In September 1915, Wild reported to the Chief of the General Staff that the supply of replacements to the army could only be maintained at present levels for approximately one year. Therefore, the circumstances demanded "the greatest economy with the available human materiel [*Menschenmaterial*] ... especially considering the potential consequences if the supply of replacements runs out before all military tasks have been satisfactorily completed." The army and unit commanders were repeatedly reminded that requests for replacements were to be made solely to meet urgent needs and that demands for new formations were to be minimized.

With its unilateral control over replacements, the Army Administration, in close co-operation with the *OHL*, was able to prioritize needs. This meant that replacements could be held back for short or long periods from sufficiently supplied units or, eventually, along entire army fronts. These efforts were facilitated by the fact that since the summer of 1915, infantry units were not usually kept at full war strength: battalions were kept at a reduced strength of 800 men in the west and 900 men in the East.

The maintenance and growth of the army's fighting strength depended on satisfying the immense and constantly increasing need for materiel. Ammunition requirements remained one of the Army Administration's primary concerns; indeed, the need to ensure these were met had a decisive impact on the *OHL's* decisions. The major offensive in Galicia and the expected defensive battles on the Western Front—both vast theatres of war—would place an extreme demand on the expenditure of ammunition.

In accordance with Falkenhayn's requirements, the Army Administration was accelerating the manufacture of the more effective cast and pressed steel projectiles, while at the same time reducing mass production of the inferior grey cast-iron projectiles, which inhibited the artillery's effectiveness. At first this change presented considerable problems, since the manufacture of the new projectiles was more complicated than that of the simple grey cast-iron ammunition. Thanks to the War Ministry's advance planning and the proficiency of German industry, it was possible to overcome these difficulties quickly, which meant that the delivery of cast and pressed steel projectiles could be accelerated. However, the production of new ammunition—indeed, the manufacture of ammunition in general—pushed the limits in terms of supplies of powder and explosives. Because the Army Administration's timely plans to significantly expand powder-manufacturing facilities had slowly begun to show results since March, the manufacture of powder and the associated manufacture of explosives satisfied the necessary increases in production. The main difficulty was shortages of saltpetre and nitric acid. However, an immediate crisis had been averted by the manufacture of synthetic saltpetre, which by February 1915 was producing large and timely quantities of the chemical. Owing to these numerous obstacles, the new factories were only gradually able to increase their output.

The manufacture of ammunition was controlled by the situation at hand. Under the system that had been developed, allocations for the field artillery or foot artillery—or within the arms—could be increased or decreased, and the manufacture of one calibre could be reduced in favour of another. Because of the artillery's significant requirements, and because explosives were also required for close-combat weapons and for other uses (such as by the pioneers), infantry ammunition had to be sharply reduced.

Between May and July 1915 the monthly manufacture of powder increased according to plan from 2.6 to 3.4 million kilograms per month. However, over the following months, because of a shortage of nitric acid and owing to major disruptions caused by large explosions and fires in the powder factories, the powder supply was sometimes considerably short of anticipated increases, the result being that the monthly output at the end of the year amounted to 4.3 instead of 5 million kilograms. Based on the manufacture of powder, the following monthly ammunition supplies were sent to the front:

Figure I: Munitions Trains Sent to the Field Army—May to December 1915

	May	June	July	Aug.	Sept.	Oct.	Nov.	Dec.
Infantry munitions trains (per approximately 2.5 million cartridges)	42	45	42	42	42	42	45	43
Field artillery munitions trains[30]	101	150	157	142	142.25	171.25	151	135.5
Howitzer munitions trains (per 6,000 guns)	79.25	105	89.5	104.5	97	126	111	114.33
Heavy mortar munitions trains (per 2,000 guns)	27.5	32.5	35	42.75	37	43	47.5	53
10 cm gun munitions trains (per 10,000 guns)	9	10.75	12	11	13	12	14.5	14

30   One field artillery munitions train carried 26,880 rounds and a munitions train for one field howitzer carried 12,000 rounds.

In the summer months of 1915 these supplies compared to the munitions requirements of the Field Army were as follows:

Figure II: Munitions Trains Required by the Field Army—May to December 1915

	May	June	July	Aug.	Sept.	Average Consumption
Infantry munitions trains	47	43	41	32	47	42
Field artillery munitions trains	133	135	126	128	160	136
Howitzer munitions trains	83	93	109	95	111	98
Heavy mortar munitions	34	39	35	36	45	39
10 cm gun munitions trains	9	9.5	12	10.5	13	10

With that, the supply and demand of ammunition were approximately balanced during the months in which the major battles took place. Occasionally, higher requirements were met using the reserves of the Chief of the Field Munitions Department. Supply problems, which arose frequently, especially during pursuit operations in the East, were primarily the result of unfavourable supply ratios. Nevertheless, thanks to the performance of the manufacturing and procurement authorities at home, it was possible to satisfy the high demand for munitions in the major combat areas, albeit by aggressively reducing consumption in the quiet sectors.

The reduction in munitions requirements brought about by the decline of combat operations after the fall of 1915, as well as the continuing curtailment of activities in all non-crucial sectors, facilitated the accumulation of considerable reserves, which had reached sizable dimensions by year's end. The Army Administration was fully prepared to deal with expected further increases; it was anticipated that the manufacture of powder would reach a planned 6 million kilograms by the spring of 1916.

5

THE WESTERN FRONT FROM THE MIDDLE OF APRIL TO THE BEGINNING OF AUGUST

Operations to the Start of the Spring Battle at the Beginning of May

The OHL and the Western Army in April

During the early months of 1915 the German forces on the Western Front had been involved in heavy defensive engagements, which culminated in the winter battle in the Champagne. Despite the commitment of their strongest forces and the bitter month-long fighting, the French did not manage to break through the front lines of Third Army. The British attempt to overrun Sixth Army at Neuve Chapelle also failed, with heavy casualties, as did a French encircling attack against the St. Mihiel Salient. So with the soldiers encouraged by a sense of superiority and a regained confidence by virtue of the recently won defensive battles over the enemy's Western forces—despite their smaller numbers—in the middle of April the German Western Front stood firm. According to Falkenhayn, in the *OHL* the conviction was beginning to take hold "that in the foreseeable future the enemy in the west would not be able to force a decision even if newly formed German forces on the Western Front would have to be committed in the east in order to break the Russian offensive power."[1]

This realization encouraged the *OHL* to decide on 13 April to temporarily forgo the implementation of the offensive plans on the Western Front in favour of temporarily shifting the emphasis of the war effort to the Galician Theatre.

---

1 Falkenhayn, *Die Oberste Heeresleitung 1914–1916*, 56.

During the end of March and beginning of April the Intelligence Assessment Section of the *OHL* reported that it anticipated that the Allied forces in the West would increase during the summer months.

Regarding the disposition of British forces, it was expected that the first "Kitchener army" would appear at the front "during April at the earliest" and that the second and third of these armies would not appear "before summer." The commitment of at least four of the Kitchener armies, with six divisions each, was anticipated. With the addition of Canadian and Indian units, thirty-five or thirty-six British divisions were expected to be assembled in France over the course of the summer.

In the French army, the 1915 class had been engaged at the front since the middle of March. Those of the 1916 class, approximately 180,000 men, were to be called up at the beginning of April, while those of the 1917 class were to be drafted in April and May. At the same time, previously exempt or unfit members of a number of age groups were to report for further examinations. In a report dated 24 March the Intelligence Assessment Section of the *OHL* summarized its findings: "With these measures the French military administration ruthlessly presses even the last halfway able man into service with a weapon." The formation of three new army corps—XXXI to XXXIII—seemed to bear this out. A strengthening of the Belgian Army over the next months was not expected.

Major German offensive actions in the West had to be discontinued, but the *OHL* was not ready to give the enemy the upper hand by entirely limiting itself to defensive operations. Lively activity on the front lines combined with offensive raids "were intended to hide the troop transfers to Galicia."[2]

These offensive operations were contemplated in Flanders as well as by Armee Abteilungen *Strantz* and *Gaede*. Fourth Army was finally to execute the long-planned gas attack, the commencement of which especially interested the Chief of the General Staff, who wished to determine the effectiveness of this new weapon.

Fourth Army's Gas Attack at Ypres

Prior to the Great War, only the French had planned to utilize gas as a weapon. In their army, a 26 mm rifle grenade loaded with an ethyl bromo-acetone charge, which caused a suffocating effect, had been introduced as a weapon for attacking fortified positions.[3] At this time, Germany was not preparing to wage a war in which gas would be used as a weapon.

---

2 Ibid., 72.
3 *These grenades, weighing about half a pound and fired from a specially designed rifle, were known as "cartouches suffocantes" and were introduced during the first months of the war.*

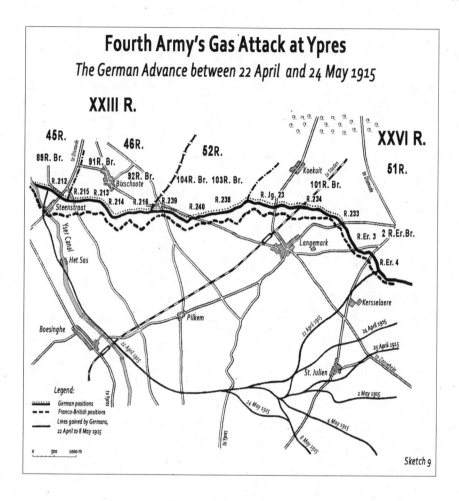

Fourth Army's Gas Attack at Ypres
The German Advance between 22 April and 24 May 1915

Sketch 9

At the beginning of the war, foreign newspapers repeatedly reported—incidentally without any reproach—the use of new and sinister French weapons, which were said to be fatal without any external symptoms.[4] The French chemist Turpin was named as their inventor, and in fact he did offer such a weapon to the French Ministry of War, but it was tried and found to be ineffective. Within the Prussian Ministry of War, similar proposals submitted at the outbreak of war were ignored.

Since the beginning of the static trench war in 1914, the proximity of the opposing trenches had often impeded the firing of high-explosive shells, since they

---

4   *Reports describing the use of a new chemical dubbed "turpinite" appeared in the British press in the autumn of 1914. Along with photographs of dead German soldiers who had supposedly succumbed to the effects of this new chemical weapon, the stories were reprinted in many newspapers in Allied countries.*

would place one's own soldiers at risk from shrapnel. In addition, the tactical situation meant that the explosives could not effectively be brought to bear against the deeply dug in enemy. At this point the search for more effective weapons began. At the beginning of 1915, French leaders requested all available rifle gas-grenades for the front lines. On 21 February the French Ministry of War issued an order to the armed forces regarding the utilization of rifle gas-grenades; in the meantime, it also introduced gas hand-grenades. The order stated: "The fumes generated by these projectiles are not fatal, at least if they are not inhaled in excess." Since the amount of the gas inhaled was hardly up to the individual soldier involved, the potential for a deadly effect was, without doubt, clear. By the end of February, numerous reports from the Western Front regarding the deployment of these weapons against German soldiers were being received.[5]

The German leaders had to consider the possible deployment of chemical weapons by the enemy and were not willing to be taken by surprise. Initially the objective was merely to use gas to drive the enemy from the protection of its trenches into the effective range of artillery fire.[6] By the end of 1914 the development of an artillery projectile (15 cm high-explosive shell 12T) had been completed. In addition to its considerable explosive capability, it also contained the gas ingredient xylyl bromide, which was similar in its effectiveness, albeit less lethal, than the French version. This so-called "T-Shell"[7] was first used on the Russian Front at the beginning of 1915; however, owing to the intense cold, the results were unsatisfactory.[8] A prerequisite for success was mass effectiveness. To achieve this with shells carrying gas was initially out of the question because of a lack of artillery pieces and suitable propellants. Therefore the alternative of releasing the gas where air currents would carry it toward enemy positions became the most viable option.

The existing conventions of international law—The Hague Land Warfare Conventions of 29 July 1899 and 18 October 1907 and The Hague Declaration of 29 July 1899—did not anticipate a war waged with gas.[9] The Hague declaration merely forbade the use of projectiles that had the exclusive purpose of broadcasting suffocating and poisonous gases. Based on the declaration's "all participation

---

5 War diary, Reserve Infantry Regiments 27 and 28, 28 February 1915, and other reports from the front.

6 *The German army used 3,000 converted howitzer shells, known as "Ni-shells," which contained the irritant "double salts of dianisidine," near Neuve Chapelle on 27 October 1914. This first German foray into chemical warfare went unnoticed by the Allies.*

7 *The "T-Shell" was named for Hans Tappen, a German chemist.*

8 *In January 1915, T-Shells were used by IX Army near Bolimow on the Eastern Front with little or no effect.*

9 *Article 23, however, banned the employment of poison or poisoned arms. An annex to the declaration of the same date read: "The Contracting Powers agree to abstain from the use of projectiles the object of which is the diffusion of asphyxiating or deleterious gases."*

clause," the question as to whether this declaration was still binding on all the belligerents after Turkey, as a non-signatory of the agreement, became a party to the war on 3 November 1914, remains debatable.[10] Even if one assumes that the declaration remained binding among the signatories, the utilization of projectiles like the German T-Shell, which combined fragmentation with gas, was in accordance with international law since the dissemination of the gases was not the "exclusive objective" of the weapon. In contrast, the French rifle grenade had the single objective of spreading poison gases. Therefore the French rifle gas-grenades represented the first violation of international law governing the waging of war with gas. The method for dispersing gas into the air[11] was an invention of the German war industry and did not contravene any existing conventions of international law. Nor did the introduction of a gas weapon violate humanitarian laws, since the percentage of casualties from fragmentation projectiles was, and remained, considerably higher than from the use of gas in combat operations. Soldiers affected by exposure to gas were almost always totally rehabilitated without any physically debilitating after-effects.[12]

Initially, chlorine gas was chosen for combat because its production in sufficient amounts was possible without impeding the munitions industry in the homeland. The dispersion of liquid chlorine from numerous steel cylinders in the front trenches promised to create a cloud that would inundate the enemy positions with sufficient density, despite the loss of some of the gas to the air. Additionally, chlorine gas had the right properties: it did not leave any appreciable residue, which meant that the German forces could mount immediate attacks; and it had less of an effect on the human body than ethyl bromo-acetone and chloracetone, which the French used. The creation of gas protection equipment was developed in parallel with the production of this offensive weapon. During 1915 a gas mask was developed for German soldiers to protect their faces and respiratory systems.

In January 1915 the tests had progressed to the point that Falkenhayn decided to provide Fourth Army with the 6,000 large chlorine gas cylinders that were ready for deployment; another 24,000 smaller versions were still in the manufacturing

---

10 Article 2 of the 1899 Convention reads: "The provisions ... are only binding on the Contracting Powers, in case of war between two or more of them. These provisions shall cease to be binding from the time when, in a war between Contracting Powers, a non-Contracting Power joins one of the belligerents." Article 2 of the 1907 convention contained a similar clause: "[The regulations] do not apply except between Contracting Powers, and then only if all the belligerents are parties to the Convention."

11 Here the term "into the air" is taken to mean the dispersal of gas without the use of a projectile.

12 These assertions about the legality of the use of gas were based on very literal readings of the conventions governing land warfare.

pipeline. The *OHL* ordered Fourth Army to deploy the new weapon during an operation on the Ypres Salient. It was calculated that on average, one large or two small cylinders would be required per running metre of frontage. The technical supervision was in the hands of the Privy Councillor, Professor Haber, who had been entrusted with the management of the newly formed chemical department of the Prussian Ministry of War. The execution was assigned to newly formed pioneer units with specially assigned meteorologists under the command of Oberst Peterson. Considerable difficulties, however, remained to be resolved, as commanding officers as well as rank-and-file soldiers viewed the untested weapon with distrust if not with complete disapproval. Even the *OHL* viewed the gas weapon less than enthusiastically; indeed, it refused to deploy it during the impending breakout offensive in the Galician Theatre, not wanting to depend on the timing of this apparently quite unreliable weapon. The operation on the Ypres Salient was therefore intended to test its combat effectiveness.

On the morning of 21 April, Falkenhayn held a conference in Thielt with the commanding officer of Fourth Army, Generaloberst Albrecht Duke of Württemberg. There he insisted on an early execution of the gas attack, where Fourth Army "should not aim for too wide an objective, but rather execute the attack at the first favourable opportunity." Based on the positive weather forecast, the operation was ordered to begin at 06:45 on the morning of 22 April.

Fourth Army tasked XXIII and XXVI Reserve Corps with the execution of the attack. The available gas cylinders were installed in their positions north of Ypres from Steenstraate to Poelcappelle. Except for units of 43rd Reserve Division, no larger forces were available for exploiting a potential advantage.[13] The XXIII Reserve Corps was assigned the difficult objective of fighting its way across the Yser Canal. The primary objectives of the attack were as follows: for XXIII Reserve Corps, a line from northwest of Steenstraate through Lizerne to southwest of Pilkem; and for XXVI Reserve Corps, the high ground along the Boesinghe–Pilkem–Langemark–Poelcappelle road. A further objective of the attack was "the capture of the Yser Canal, including Ypres."

---

13 General der Artillerie Ilse provided the *Reichsarchiv* with a report dated 16 November 1931 as follows: "Fourth Army Headquarters had requested that a division be made available to allow them to take advantage of the potential success of the gas attack with a strong follow-up attack in order to roll up the Ypres Salient. General Falkenhayn turned this request down because he did not have sufficient forces at his disposal in the spring of 1915 and also because he doubted that the attack would meet with success. Another factor that contributed to his refusal to provide a division was the concern that many weeks could pass before the gas attack would become a reality. Falkenhayn could not and would not release a division for that period of time." The files of the *Reichsarchiv* do not contain this information. It appears that the request and the refusal were verbal.

Due to a lack of favourable winds, on the morning of 22 April the attack had to be postponed until the late afternoon. This caused a severe problem, since all preparations had been made for an attack at dawn. The commanding general of XXIII Reserve Corps, General der Infanterie von Kathen, immediately expressed his concern about mounting an attack in full daylight, while the commanding general of XXVI Reserve Corps, General der Infanterie Baron von Hügel, emphasized that the success of his corps could only be expected if his flank was protected by a simultaneous attack by XXIII Reserve Corps. Fourth Army's Chief of Staff, Generalmajor Ilse, attempted to allay these concerns by telephone but issued the following unequivocal orders: "The commander-in-chief categorically expects XXIII Reserve Corps to advance with XXVI Reserve Corps to reach Hill 20 near Pilkem without fail."

At 18:00 the gas cylinders installed opposite French 87th Territorial and 45th Infantry Divisions were opened. The Belgian General Staff had warned the French High Command about the possibility of a German gas attack a few days before, but apparently the warning had been disregarded. The wind blew from the north at approximately two metres per second, and a solid white-yellow wall rolled toward the enemy trenches. Even before it reached them, in some areas the enemy was observed retreating after firing a few rounds. Simultaneously, the German trenches were hit with spirited enemy artillery fire. At 18:15, immediately following the gas cloud, the German infantry began its attack.

In the area of XXIII Reserve Corps, in front of Steenstraate, the release of the gas was not entirely successful. As a result, the left wing of 45th Reserve Division commanded by Generalleutnant Schöpflin was only able to advance slowly under strong enemy defensive fire. It was very late when the village of Steenstraate was taken with heavy casualties by units of 45th and 46th Reserve Divisions. A continuation of the attack in the direction of Lizerne was beyond the capabilities of the already exhausted units. The main body of 46th Reserve Division, commanded by Generalleutnant Hahn, quickly advanced to the canal near and north of Het Sas, traversed it, and took the western bank; across from Boesinghe, they were able to reach the canal in only a few places.

In front of XXVI Reserve Corps' right wing, the psychological impact was massive. The assault units of 52nd Reserve Division commanded by Generalleutnant Waldorf proceeded without resistance, reaching their objective on the hills near Pilkem at 18:40. There they halted, since the neighbouring divisions had fallen behind. The advance of 51st Reserve Division to the east was considerably more difficult. The gas in front of its lines near and east of Langemark was either not effective or the units did not attack immediately. Therefore the extreme right wing of the French and the Canadians adjacent to the east were able to offer stubborn resistance. It was not until 19:00 that the village of Langemark—the scene of heavy and bloody fighting in earlier battles—was in German hands. The commanding officer of 51st Reserve Division, Generalmajor Friedrich von Kleist, then received orders to take the bridges across the Haanebeek Creek south of Langemark as well as St. Julien on the same day if possible.

The 37th Landwehr Brigade, which was in immediate reserve, was made available by order of Corps Headquarters to the successful 52nd Reserve Division and was brought forward to Pilkem. Around 19:45 this division reported on its attack on the heights south of Pilkem. In front of its advance, the artillery and reserves of the enemy were apparently swept back in a panicky retreat. However, the enemy had moved reinforcements to St. Julien against 51st Reserve Division, thus impeding its advance. Aerial reconnaissance revealed movements by rail on the tracks between Hazebrouck and Poperinghe, which led to the assumption that the enemy was moving additional reinforcements into the zone of operations. Consequently, 102nd Reserve Infantry Brigade, which had been held back in the Houthulst Forest, was moved up to Koekuit at this late hour. Around 21:30, 51st Reserve Division reported taking both bridges across Haanebeek Creek southwest of Langemark; they were still fighting for the other bridge to the south. Both divisions were ordered to hold their positions and to continue the attack the next day, with 37th Landwehr Brigade ordered to establish a supporting position on the heights near Pilkem. The commander of the heavy artillery was instructed to advance and reposition his batteries during the night so as to be in a position to bring the enemy on the west side of the canal and in city of Ypres within range of the artillery.

In summary, on 22 April, XXIII Reserve Corps had thrown the enemy across the canal between Steenstraate and Het Sas and XXVI Reserve Corps had penetrated to a line from south of Pilkem to northwest of St. Julien. The captured enemy forces amounted to 1,800 unwounded French and 10 British soldiers; captured materiel consisted of 51 artillery pieces and approximately 70 machine guns.

By the evening of 22 April the enemy had suffered a wide breach between the canal and St. Julien. Only weak French forces remained southeast of Boesinghe and, mixed with Canadians, north of Kersselaere. The breach was only barely secured by British forces, and a cohesive line no longer existed. Movements of reinforcements and supplies were severely hampered by heavy German artillery fire aimed at the canal crossings near Ypres. Clearly, the enemy's position in the Ypres Salient had become seriously threatened.

Encouraged by the successes of the first day of combat, Fourth Army's commander believed he was justified in expanding the original objectives, which had extended only to the Yser Canal. Therefore he issued orders on the morning of

23 April to continue the attack in the "direction of Poperinghe." The XXIII Reserve Corps was given a line from Pypegaele–Gegend to southwest of Boesinghe as its next objective. The XXVI Reserve Corps was ordered to continue the advance in a southerly direction, with its right wing sweeping along the canal, in order to attack the enemy positions in front of XXVII Reserve Corps from the rear. To accomplish this mission the army reserve (elements of 43rd Reserve Division), commanded by Generalmajor von Runckel, was assigned to XXIII Reserve Corps. The 86th Reserve Brigade was immediately engaged and replaced a brigade from 45th Reserve Division, freeing that division for other combat missions. Additionally, two regiments of the Marine Corps were moved into the area of Staden–Houthulst.

During the night of 22 and 23 April, in XXIII Reserve Corps's sector, the left wing of 45th Reserve Division was repeatedly attacked at Lizerne. Although the German forces were able to repel these attacks, as a result of them they were unable to launch their assigned combat missions with any sustainable energy. Consequently, 45th Reserve Division was only able to reach the sector of Yperlée Creek west of Steenstraate on 23 April. The enemy had established defensive positions in front of 46th Reserve Division along the Lizerne–Boesinghe road by adding reinforcements. Therefore this division's attack met with limited success as well.

Initially on 23 April, XXVI Reserve Corps had only to deal with British counterattacks. In order to support the advance of 51st Reserve Division, at 08:45, Hügel ordered the commander of the gas units to install all available gas cylinders in this division's sector. The XXVI Reserve Corps' commander inferred from the attack order that had been issued at noon that Army Headquarters

> considered the operation against Poperinghe to be the main undertaking and the advance of XXVI Reserve Corps to be of secondary importance. Since sufficient forces for advancing on Poperinghe across the canal were not available, the success of this venture was in question from the outset. The advance of the corps on the right wing along the canal was also impossible, as long as the neighbouring corps had not taken Boesinghe and would be further advancing on Poperinghe. This was thought to be the only way to remove the strong enemy artillery unit on the opposite side of the canal.

According to reports received by XXVI Reserve Corps, the enemy had dug in approximately 500 metres in front of the German lines; as well, reinforcements had been brought in from Ypres. Around 18:30, Anglo-French forces launched a counterattack along both sides of the Ypres–Pilkem road, with French forces striking across the bridges near Boesinghe. Although this attack was repulsed, XXVI Reserve Corps' forward movement had been stopped. On 24 April, 52nd Reserve Division was ordered to hold the positions it had gained. Following a gas attack early on 24 April, 51st Reserve Division and 102nd Reserve Infantry Brigade were ordered to take the ridge north of Wieltje and Frezenberg.

In the meantime the *OHL* had intervened, informing Fourth Army Headquarters "that Poperinghe was not even considered an operational objective at this time, rather that at the present the closing of the Ypres salient could be the only concern."[14]

On the morning of 24 April, elements of 45th and 46th Reserve Divisions stormed the strongly contested village of Lizerne. After heavy fighting with heavy losses that lasted late into the night, 46th Reserve Division's left flank succeeded in taking the eastern bank of the canal opposite Boesinghe.

At 05:00, gas was released north of St. Julien in XXVI Reserve Corps' sector, and 101st and 102nd Reserve Infantry Brigades immediately attacked behind the thinly developing cloud. With heavy fighting their attack advanced slowly, at first west of Kersselaere and later to the east of it as well. The fate of this village, which was defended tenaciously by the enemy, was not decided until mid-day. South of Kersselaere, in the farms and hedgerows of St. Julien, the enemy continued to resist. In the afternoon, Fourth Army Headquarters assigned both regiments of the Marine Corps to XXVI Reserve Corps; at 14:45, Hügel again ordered the advance west of St. Julien. The regiments of 51st Reserve Division did not reach St. Julien until 19:00, and only then after heavy fighting. Again they had to vacate the village soon afterwards as a result of counterattacking British battalions. In the sector of neighbouring 52nd Reserve Division, the day generally passed quietly. For 25 April, Hügel planned a continuation of the ordered attack. The deployment was planned for 05:15. This time Oberst Peterson had been ordered to install gas cylinders in the sector of 52nd Reserve Division east from the Ypres–Pilkem Road to the forest west of St. Julien.

On 24 April, XXVI Reserve Corps and the right wing of XXVII Reserve Corps stepped into the attack. The following plan was agreed upon: at the beginning of the day a combined brigade[15] of 53rd (Saxon) Reserve Division commanded by Generalmajor von Schmieden deployed behind the left wing of 51st Reserve Division was to join the attack, execute a turn, and roll up the enemy from the

---

14   This was probably ordered by telephone on 23 April and afterwards confirmed in writing. In this regard General Ilse stated in his comments dated 16 November 1931 addressed to the *Reichsarchiv*: "This message was ... correctly received. However Army Headquarters was mistaken and has admitted this error because they did not establish Poperinghe as the operational objective but explicitly mentioned attacking in the direction of Poperinghe, the village located on the road running straight in a westerly direction from Ypres. As mentioned, this was meant to merely indicate the general direction of the attack by XXIII Reserve Corps."

15   *Subsequently referred to as Brigade Schmieden in the text.*

northwest in front of 38th Landwehr and 106th Reserve Infantry Brigades. While this attack was being executed, Brigade *Schmieden* would advance from Poelcappelle against a strong enemy; in other words it would have to mount a frontal assault. Not until this obstacle had been removed would it be possible to execute the turn to the southeast. On the evening of 24 April the brigade's right wing fought to a standstill on the hills northwest of Gravenstafel.

West of the canal on 25 April the artillery bombardment against XXIII Reserve Corps increased to the point that a successful continuation of the attack was out of the question.

On 25 April, XXVI Reserve Corps regained possession of St. Julien, which had been vacated by the enemy. The 51st Reserve Division had orders to reach the objective established on 24 April: the ridge north of Wieltje and Frezenberg. Neighbouring 52nd Reserve Division was to enter the battle in a supporting role. At 07:00, seven British battalions launched a surprise attack southwest of St. Julien against the German forces that had been deployed for the attack. The incredibly powerful enemy assault, which came in waves, could not be entirely repulsed until 08:00. With that, the combat capabilities of the German forces had deteriorated; only the regiments on 51st Reserve Division's left wing gained minimal ground through tenacious fighting east of St. Julien.

In the approaching darkness, on XXVII Reserve Corps' right wing, the Fortuin–Mosselmarkt road was reached and around 1,000 Canadians were taken prisoner. However, with the aid of reinforcements south of the road, the enemy, which had previously been driven back, continued its resistance.

The intentions of Fourth Army's commander became clear after he issued orders on the afternoon of 25 April following a conference with the commanding general of XXIII Reserve Corps. General von Kathen emphasized the need to continue the attack in order to take Boesinghe. However, Fourth Army's commander opposed this plan, arguing that

> the outcome of this attack is doubtful. It would result in great sacrifices while it would be difficult to hold that much ground on the western bank. The Corps should be satisfied with its present accomplishments ... Fourth Army's objective is primarily to close the salient east of Ypres with the attack by XXVI Reserve Corps. Only then could an advance past Boesinghe be considered.

On the afternoon of 26 April a number of strong French attacks were directed against the area of Steenstraate and Het Sas. They were conducted by territorial forces and elements of the recently activated 153rd Infantry Division supported by effective British and Belgian artillery fire. The 46th Reserve Division thus found itself in a precarious situation. The enemy took the position west of Het Sas, although the locks on the canal could be held. In the meantime, Lizerne was attacked at 18:00 from a northerly direction and taken by the enemy. The German forces occupied the old French trench, but owing to heavy enemy fire, a planned counterattack did not materialize.

Reports received by XXVI Reserve Corps during the course of the morning revealed that the enemy had assembled two fresh corps to the east of Ypres and was clearly planning a counterattack, which was initiated with aggressive artillery support. Shortly after noon, strong enemy forces—part of 28th British and 4th and 50th Territorial and Lahore Divisions—attacked from the canal to St. Julien, but every attempt failed due to the steadfastness of the German infantry.

As at St. Julien, on 26 April counterattacks in the area of Gravenstafel prevented a further advance by XXVII Reserve Corps.

Over the following days, the enemy's attempts to push 46th Reserve Division's badly mauled regiments (part of XXIII Reserve Corps) back to the eastern bank of the canal failed; again, the waves of these attacks broke against the German lines. The division was able, however, to hold the new positions on Yperlée Creek with the support of the 45th Reserve Division.

Between 27 April and 1 May, XXVI Reserve Corps ended its attack since the installed gas cylinders were considered to be too few in number. In light of the well-entrenched enemy and the weakness of the German artillery, an attack without the support of gas was considered almost hopeless. So a further advance by XXVII Reserve Corps' strong right wing to push through to Gravenstafel from the north was delayed.

In the meantime, the British Commander-in-Chief, Field Marshal Sir John French, grew concerned that the Germans would make further gains in the threatened Ypres Salient. On 27 April he had ordered the local commander to begin preparations for a relocation from east of Ypres to positions prepared in the rear. In response to emphatic protests by Foch, this plan was postponed despite the deteriorating military situation. A British signal was intercepted on the evening of 29 April, which read: "The situation of our forces, British as well as French, in Ypres is critical. We must be prepared for bad news." Fourth Army Headquarters saw this as confirmation that the enemy was finding it harder and harder to hold the salient east of Ypres and that, if pressure continued to be applied there, the enemy might soon evacuate itself to the rear.

On 2 May, combat units designated by Fourth Army and supported by gas attacked north of Ypres. Shortly after 18:00 both of XXVI Reserve Corps' divisions reported the opening of the gas cylinders installed between Pilkem and St. Julien. The effect on the enemy was lessened as the transmission of commands was badly hampered by destroyed telephone lines, which prevented a coordinated simultaneous release of gas. Also, the density of the gas cloud was diminished by gusting winds. The effect on an enemy equipped with simple protection devices was negligible. The attackers met insurmountable resistance.

On 3 May, 51st Division, which was to transfer the weight of the attack to the left wing, was reinforced by a marine infantry regiment. Aided by the terrain, which featured numerous individual farms, the enemy resisted tenaciously.

On 2 May, however, on the right wing of XXVII Reserve Corps, 38th Landwehr Brigade managed to gain some ground on the Fortuin–Mosselmarkt road. The 105th Reserve Infantry Brigade (*Schmieden*) adjoining in the east was stalled in front of a ferociously defended trench network in a forest north of Gravenstafel. Considering that these small and unimportant gains were resulting in high casualties, the commanding general, General der Artillerie von Schubert, proposed to Fourth Army that it abandon the costly preparations for an attack on Zonnebeke. Instead he suggested that the forces that were to be made available in the vicinity of Kersselaere (at least a division) be placed at the disposal of Fourth Army's commander in order to support a decisive attack by XXVI Reserve Corps on Ypres. Fourth Army did not accept this proposal. So on 3 May, 105th Reserve Infantry Brigade had to continue attacking the trench network occupied by the enemy. This attack was executed with determination and was crowned with complete success.

Under the pressure of these attacks, on the night of 3 and 4 May, the British forces evacuated their positions from Fortuin to southwest of Gheluvelt. The XXVI Reserve Corps Headquarters immediately ordered 51st Division to attack. The enemy's stubborn resistance ensured that despite continuous fighting, the attackers only reached a line stretching from Vanheule Farm to Haanebeek Creek.

On the left, in the southern part of the Ypres Salient, XXVII Reserve Corps and XV Corps did not initially meet any resistance. Schubert deployed the right wing of 53rd Reserve Division in the direction of Frezenberg and the left wing of 54th (Württemberg) in the direction of Eksterneft. The XV Corps reported that 39th Division's right wing was also now advancing on Eksterneft. By 16:00 the divisions were again facing strongly fortified enemy positions in the area northeast of Wieltje and Frezenberg and east of Hooge, which necessitated a carefully planned attack. This was ordered on the afternoon of 6 May.

Urgently desiring to push the enemy across the Yser as soon as possible, Fourth Army intended to continue the attack with an encircling movement from three sides. With this in mind, XXVI Reserve Corps was supposed to advance in a southerly direction in order to take the hills around Wieltje; XXVII was to attack the high ground facing it to the west; and XV Corps was to push the enemy back in a northwesterly direction between Bellewaarde Lake and Zillebeke Lake. The commencement of the artillery barrage was set for 08:00 on 8 May.

The main burden for the attacks was born by XXVII Reserve Corps. At 10:30 on 8 May, after a three-hour artillery preparation, the regiments advanced in favourable weather against the British 27th and 28th Infantry Divisions but found the forward trenches deserted. After coming under strong enemy artillery fire, the advance over open ground soon ground to a halt. As night fell, at least the commanding ridge west of Frezenberg and Eksterneft was in German hands.

Around 14:40 the next day, XXVIII Reserve Corps received the following message from Fourth Army headquarters:

> His Royal Majesty informs that according to an intercepted British order to retreat,[16] all indications are that the British have abandoned all resistance on the eastern bank of the Yser. At the present time Sixth Army is under attack by strong British forces.[17] All indications are that the British are assembling all available forces in front of Sixth Army.

In response, Schubert ordered a new artillery preparation from 15:30 to 17:00, which helped the attacking forces make small gains up to the line Verlorenhoek–Bellewaarde Lake. The objective "to push the enemy into his final position near Potijze" was not accomplished despite the sacrificial valour of the attacking regiments.

On 9 May parts of XXII Reserve Corps joined the battle, but with XXVI Reserve Corps and XV Corps' right wing were able to make only insignificant gains. Their attacks failed because of strong resistance in the enemy trenches

By 9 May the fighting around Ypres was generally over. The entire attack up until then had cost the Germans more than 35,000 lives. The British had lost 59,275 men between 22 April and 31 May. The French losses, according to their own calculations, were extremely high: on 22 April alone they lost 18,000 soldiers.

Despite the new gas weapon, the success of the action at Ypres did not extend past the initial gains. The objective of closing the Ypres Salient was not accomplished, mainly because on 22 April the element of surprise could not be sufficiently exploited owing to the approaching darkness. By early May the enemy had retreated to prepared positions between Wieltje and Little Zillebeke; there, despite heavy

---

16   As far as can be determined, no order to retreat had been issued. Instead, on 29 April and 1 May orders in the event of a retreat and evacuation of the positions east of Ypres were issued by the local commander, General Plumer. See *Military Operations: France and Belgium, 1915, Volume I*, 404–10.

17   See *DW* VIII: 48.

losses, it repeatedly attacked XXVI and XXVII Reserve Corps. The initial successes north of Ypres were mostly due to the employment of gas. This demonstrated to the commanders and rank and file its use as a new weapon, despite its
intrinsic shortcomings.[18]

The Offensive Battles of Armee-Abteilungen Strantz and Gaede

The heavy French attacks between the end of March and the middle of April
against both flanks of Armee-Abteilung *Strantz* failed, and the German defensive
front stood fast. Only on the Combres Heights did the situation become precarious. There, relief was to be provided through an attack by V Corps, under the command of General der Infanterie von Oven, which had at its disposal 9th and 111th
Infantry Divisions.

The attack was to advance the army's positions to the north on the Meuse
Heights along both sides of the Grande Tranchée de Calonne to the line Côte des
Hures–Les Taillis de Saulx. On 24 April, 111th and 9th Infantry Divisions began the
attack and were successful. The Germans took approximately 1,600 prisoners and
captured twenty guns. The attack against the Combres Heights the next day by 10th
Infantry Division was stopped by strong enemy resistance. In the other sectors
held by V Corps, the French resistance soon increased so that despite the deployment of 113th Infantry Division, the German attack gained scarcely any ground.
A part of the sector southwest of the Combres Heights was taken from the enemy.
Even though the objectives had been achieved only in part, the precarious situation on this front improved. By this time 2,500 prisoners of war and 30 machine
guns had been added to the previous count. On the evening of 3 May, General
Strantz ordered the continuation of the attack toward and east of Grande Tranchée
de Calonne. Despite performing with incredible valour, on 5 May the troops had
made only small gains in the area of the interposed 33rd Reserve Infantry Division in the centre of the attacking front. On 7 May the offensive activities came
to a preliminary conclusion.

Concurrent with these battles, on the southern front of the *Armee-Abteilung*,
strong French attacks developed on 22 April. On 5 May, elements of Bavarian III
Corps, with 80th Infantry Brigade attached, began a counterattack. In a determined

---

18 In his memorandum to the *Reichsarchiv* dated 30 August 1931, General von Schubert emphasized that the use of gas during the Ypres operation was only effective one time and that was
on 22 April north of Pilkem: "The flaw in the use of the gas was mostly caused by the differences in the terrain … consequently it was impossible to achieve uniform results on an
extended front. Additionally, the use of the gas was limited since the timing of the release could
never really be maintained."

The Offensive Battles of Armee-Abteilung Strantz

24 April to 7 May 1915

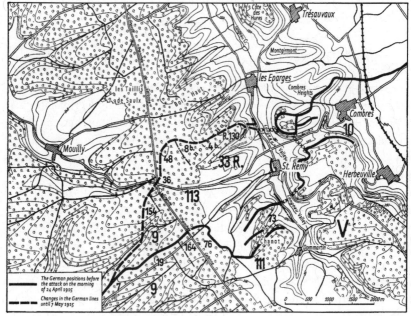

advance that often featured vicious hand-to-hand combat, the objective—the enemy's trenches in the Bois de Ailly—was taken, and 2,000 prisoners of war fell into German hands.

In the sector of Armee-Abteilung *Gaede*, the French managed to take the Vieil Armand in early April; from there they were able to place the Colmar–Mulhouse railway line under direct artillery fire. On 25 April, after a first failed attempt, the hill was successfully retaken, but the summit was again lost on the following day. In the meantime the Bavarian Reserve Division was involved in serious battles southwest of Munster, which forced a withdrawal on the left wing on 17 May.

During April, besides the greater part of Division *Fuchs*, 42nd Cavalry Brigade of 7th Cavalry Division (which had been provided by Armee-Abteilung *Falkenhausen*) had left Upper Alsace, while fifteen battalions arrived as reinforcements, among them Bavarian 1st Territorial Brigade (which had formerly been released to Antwerp), two rifle battalions, and ten batteries. Some parts of these forces were integrated into existing *Landwehr* divisions; others contributed to the new

12th Landwehr Brigade. Thus, by early May, Armee-Abteilung *Gaede* consisted of one reserve division and four *Landwehr* divisions.

The Actions of the French and British Commanders to the Beginning of May

During the heavy winter battles of 1914–15, the French Supreme Command was unable to realize its major offensive objective—namely, a concentric attack in the Champagne and the Artois, which was intended to cut off the German salient in between. The failure of the planned attack in the Artois was primarily due to Field Marshal French's refusal to order the immediate replacement of IX and XX Corps—which were slated to take part in the offensive—with British forces. In the meantime, the French Tenth Army's preparations in the Artois had continued during the spring of 1915. Since the French General Staff were convinced that the *OHL* was about to shift the war's emphasis to the East because of the situation in the Russian Theatre, the early opening of an offensive appeared to show promise. The reasoning was that the Entente's superiority in numbers had to be exploited in order to relieve the Russian Front.

To that end, Field Marshal Foch, commander of Provisional Army Group *North*, presented Joffre with detailed proposals. His memorandum of 19 March stated that only an attack could force a decision. Considering the present state of trench warfare, he wrote, an attack would succeed only if it was a large-scale *action générale* and only if it was an *action décisive* conducted in a tactically advantageous location. Regarding the first consideration, all the armies staged between the sea and Verdun would have to launch attacks in order to at least hold the enemy under the threat of an offensive. The main thrust, and with it the decisive action, was to be executed by Tenth Army north of Arras. The operations would be supported by a British diversionary attack south of Armentières toward Warneton–Messines and simultaneously at La Bassée. Foch believed that an attack by the Belgians on both sides of Dixmude would also be desirable. Joffre approved these recommendations, and on 24 March he requested British participation. In speaking to Sir John French he emphasized that as a prerequisite, British elements would have to first relieve IX and XX Corps, whose participation in Tenth Army's attack would be essential.

A meeting was held on 29 March at French GQG in Chantilly, attended by the French Minister of War, Millerand, Joffre, the British Secretary of War Lord Kitchener, and Field Marshal French. There, the beginning of the joint offensive was set for 1 May. To provide assistance in relation to the relief of both French corps, Lord Kitchener promised the British Supreme Commander the timely deployment of two new divisions by 20 April.

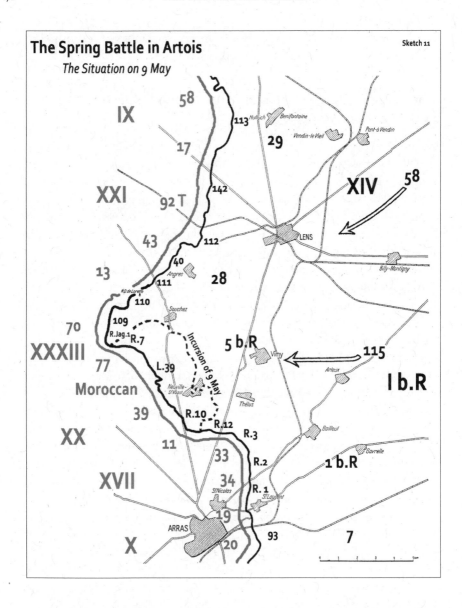

The Spring Battle in Artois   Sketch 11

The Situation on 9 May

On 24 March, Foch had presented his plan of attack for Tenth Army to the Supreme Commander. The main thrust was to be conducted out of the area of Carency–Roclincourt toward the heights southwest of Vimy; secondary attacks would be mounted on the slopes of the Lorette Spur and toward the high ground west of Bailleul. The artillery preparation, with an increased use of heavy guns, would take place over several days. All of this would require the reinforcement of Tenth Army with three fresh corps and approximately seventy-two heavy guns. Approximately 91,000 rounds for the heavy guns and 600,000 rounds for the field artillery would have to be made available. It was anticipated that the main and southern attacks would last ten days, while the thrust on the Lorette Spur would take six. The Supreme Commander agreed to these proposals and on 6 April informed Foch that he could now count on the commitment of IX and XX Corps for the execution of the offensive after each had been reinforced to the strength of three divisions. The deployment of an additional division was also planned.

On 9 April, Field Marshal French informed Foch that ten infantry divisions and five cavalry divisions (in reserve), as well as 500 field and 100 heavy guns, would participate in the attack. The main thrust of the British offensive was to be mounted from the line Neuve Chapelle–Festubert with the objective of reaching the Fournes–La Bassée road after breaking through the German front. Simultaneously, an attack on the area of Fromelles was planned. The offensive was to be launched on the same day as the attack by the French Army.

Reports received by GQG at the end of April reinforced the High Command's view that considerable German forces had been pulled from the front. For instance, by the middle of April significant elements of the Prussian Guard Corps had been identified in Alsace as reserves. On 20 April the Supreme Commander informed the headquarters of Fourth, Fifth, and Sixth Armies that the number of battalions and batteries on the German front between Arras and the Meuse had been considerably reduced. Whether these units had been taken out in order to be redeployed to another place or to form additional reserves was unknown. In any case, the French Supreme Command was of the opinion that the German defensive posture on the Franco-Belgian Front would not change for the time being. By 21 April the leaders of the French Army had been informed that thirteen new German divisions were being created from already existing units, which it seemed were to be placed at the disposal of the *OHL*.

In the meantime, Tenth Army (the command of which had been assumed by General d'Urbal on 2 April) was forming up the elements designated for the attack. Having been relieved by the British, IX and XX Corps arrived to the rear of Tenth Army between 9 and 16 April. The recently transferred 152nd Division joined IX Corps, and 153rd Division joined XX Corps. On 25 April the Moroccan Division that had been made available to Foch was scheduled to detrain at St. Pol; subsequently it joined XXXIII Corps.

Then an event took place at the last hour that threatened to thwart the forming up of the assault elements. Fourth Army's gas attack in the Ypres Salient had taken the Entente completely by surprise. It was only with the utmost effort that the units involved in this fighting had been able to avert the danger. In order to prevent a breakthrough, French IX Corps Headquarters as well as 18th, 152nd, and 153rd Infantry Divisions had had to be brought up without delay from Tenth Army. As compensation, the Supreme Commander ordered the transfer of XVII Corps and 53rd Infantry Division from Second to Tenth Army on 27 April. The XVII Corps took charge of the sector north of Arras, which had been designated for IX Corps; there it was joined by 17th Infantry Division, which had remained in that sector. On 4 May the Supreme Commander was finally able to order the return of IX Corps and 18th Infantry Division to Tenth Army after the military situation at Ypres had eased. Consequently, having placed 17th Infantry Division in the army's reserve, d'Urbal replaced this division with 18th Division and inserted IX Corps, which was to consist of 17th and 58th Divisions, on the army's left flank south of La Bassée.

On 30 April, d'Urbal reported to the Supreme Commander that Tenth Army would be ready for combat on 7 May. On 3 May, Sir John French reported that in his area the attack could commence on May 8. So Joffre ordered Tenth Army to begin its offensive on 7 May and expressed his approval for the date chosen by the British. Owing to inclement weather, the attack had to be postponed until the 9th.

To support Tenth Army's attack, and to divert the enemy's efforts in accordance with Foch's proposals, the French High Command directed the armies in the centre and on the right flank to conduct secondary attacks with limited objectives. On 5 May, King Albert of Belgium was asked to increase combat activities around Dixmude during the crucial days that were to follow.

In the sector between Loos and Arras, the French leadership correctly assumed that the Germans had deployed four infantry divisions; it was also expected that three and a half German divisions would be brought up soon after the offensive began. On the eve of the attack the French Tenth Army consisted of eighteen divisions and one cavalry corps. Of these, two and a half infantry divisions and one cavalry corps were initially in reserve and one territorial division was split up and tasked with excavating works. The British First Army consisted of nine infantry divisions, including one in reserve and two that were not involved in the attack. Additionally, the Supreme Commander had one more infantry division and two cavalry corps ready for action. The Tenth Army had 780 light and 310 heavy artillery pieces while British First Army had 516 light and 121 heavy artillery pieces. On 9 May, shortly before the opening of the offensive, Joffre ordered the immediate addition of two more divisions and simultaneously directed Second Army's High Command to place I Cavalry Corps, staged northwest of Amiens, at his disposal. Finally, Seventh Army was

ordered to transfer 6th Cavalry Division—which was presently under its command—into the army reserve around Hesdin–Anvin.

In the operational orders, the objective of the offensive was described as breaking through the German front. All attacking units were to advance with all their
might from the opening of the offensive and were to prevent the retreating enemy
from stabilizing the front by immediately commencing the pursuit.

The Beginning of the Spring Offensive in the Artois

General von Falkenhayn had always expected that when the war's centre of gravity was shifted from West to East—especially when this was combined with the
transfer of considerable forces to Galicia—the Entente would use the decrease
in strength in the West to mount a major relief offensive. After nine infantry divisions were transferred to the East at the beginning of May, the total strength on
the German Western Front had been reduced to about ninety-seven infantry
divisions. These divisions faced approximately 110 to 112 enemy divisions that
were superior in strength to the German units; this meant an enemy superiority of thirteen to fifteen divisions. Of the Western Army's ninety-seven divisions, the *OHL* directly controlled seven and a half divisions as a GHQ reserve.
Of these, 58th and 115th Infantry Divisions were staged in Sixth Army's sector,
one reinforced infantry brigade stood behind each of Second and Seventh
Armies, and 117th Infantry Division was deployed in Third Army's sector. The
VIII Corps was staged to the rear of Armee-Abteilung *Strantz*, while X Reserve
Corps was in reserve in the sector of Armee-Abteilung *Falkenhausen*. At this
time the combat units on the Western Front possessed about 4,000 modern
field artillery pieces—guns and light howitzers—in addition to 350 old field
guns. They also possessed heavy artillery pieces consisting of 615 high-trajectory
and 210 modern low-trajectory guns, as well as 190 old or captured high-trajectory guns, 320 low-trajectory guns, and more than 10 of the heaviest high-trajectory guns. Additionally, a reserve of foot artillery consisting of 128 heavy field
howitzers, 68 mortars, and 80 heavy low-trajectory guns was being assembled
by the *OHL*.

In order to compensate for the Entente's superiority in numbers, and as protection against enemy attacks, it was important to upgrade the defensive positions as much as was possible, for such improvements would result in an increase
in defensive capability on the Western Front. Before leaving for the Eastern Theatre on 4 May, Falkenhayn again reminded those armies that were most threatened
between the Oise and the sea—as well as those in the Champagne—to construct
and upgrade their rear positions in order to create increased security. Besides

The Spring Battle in Artois
The Initial Objectives of the Enemy's Attacks

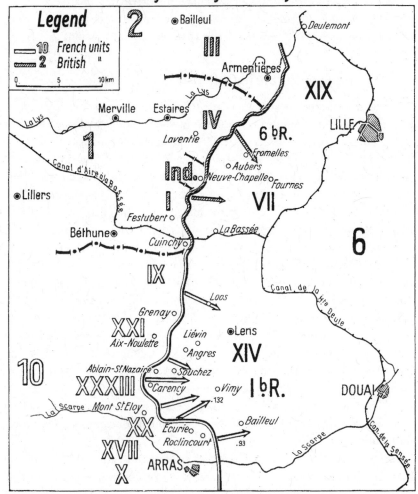

Sketch 12

improving the distribution in depth of the front-line trenches, he ordered the construction of positions at least 2 kilometres to the rear. Admittedly, the armies had very limited means with which to execute these directives. Except for the weak reserves, combat units were being ordered to hold the front lines *and* upgrade their positions because very few labour units were available. By insisting on the creation of rearward positions, the Chief of the General Staff did not by any means aspire to a strong secondary defensive system in the rear of the Western Armies, as had been suggested by General Wild in his memorandum of December 1914. Rather, the principle of holding the front lines during enemy attacks—and if they were lost, of quickly regaining them—was to be rigorously observed. On this point Falkenhayn found himself in complete agreement with the commanders of the Western Armies.

At this time there were no clear indications as to the time or place of a major Entente offensive; only in front of the German Sixth Army did the enemy's behaviour suggest an intention to attack.

Sixth Army's Operations, 9–14 May

Sixth Army,[19] under the command of Generaloberst Rupprecht, Crown Prince of Bavaria, held a sector of the front of approximately 90 kilometres west of the Menin–Cambrai line with thirteen infantry divisions; behind it, 58th and 115th Infantry Divisions were staged as reserves of the *OHL*. The artillery available to Sixth Army consisted of 520 field guns, 140 light field howitzers and 150 heavy guns; additionally, 58th and 115th Infantry Divisions had at their disposal 60 field guns and 12 each of light and heavy field howitzers. The German front-line trenches were generally located where Sixth Army's attacking strength had flagged in the fall of 1914. Consequently, its positions generally did not reflect the requirements of a favourable defensive line. West of Lille, the German front extended to La Bassée Canal and for the time being was located in the broken territory of the Flanders lowlands. There the groundwater rose close to the surface. South of La Bassée the ground was crossed by a multitude of waterways, which presented major difficulties when it came to constructing and holding positions. To the south, the flat and densely populated area around the coalmining country of Lens was dotted with sizable geographic prominences. In the vast open area south of the city, the German lines arched in a westerly direction and consequently covered the heights at Vimy. This ridge dominated the Douai Plain and, as a result, was of extraordinary significance. At the low-lying village of Souchez, the towering Lorette Spur extended wedge-shaped from the west into Sixth Army's front lines. Farther south, the German lines surrounded the outskirts of Arras on both sides of the Scarpe in a half circle and then ran

---

19 On 8 May, Sixth Army was deployed as follows from north to south: Bavarian II Corps, XIX Corps, Bavarian 6th Reserve Division, VII Corps, XIV Corps, Bavarian I Reserve Corps, IV Corps. The 58th Division was in reserve at Lille, and 115th Division was in reserve at Douai.

The Spring Battle in Artois
The British Attack on 9 May

Sketch 13

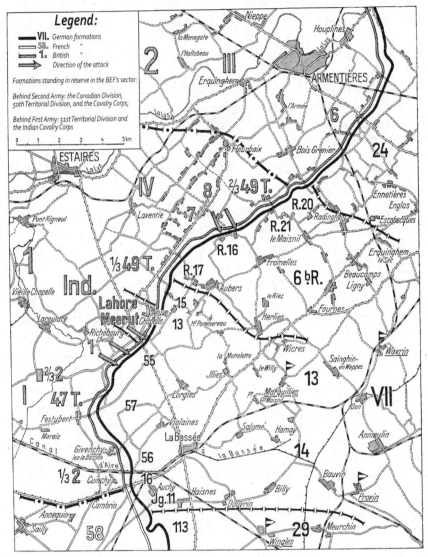

Legend:

VII.	German formations	
58.	French	"
1.	British	"
	Direction of the attack	

Formations standing in reserve in the BEF's sector:

Behind Second Army: the Canadian Division,
50th Territorial Division, and the Cavalry Corps;

Behind First Army: 51st Territorial Division and
the Indian Cavalry Corps

0   1   2   3   4   5 km

ESTAIRES

Nieppe
Houplines
la Menegate
l'Hallobeau
ARMENTIÈRES
Erquinghem
2
III
l'Armée
6
Fleurbaix
Bois Grenier
24
IV
8
2/3 49 T.
R.20
Ennetières
Englos
Laventie
7
R.21
Radinghem
Escobecques
Pont Rigneul
le Maisnil
R.16
Erquinghem-
le Sec
1/3 49 T.
R.17
Fromelles
6 bR.
Beaucamps
Ligny
Ind.
Aubers
le Riez
Vieille Chapelle
Lahore
Neuve
15
Herlies
Fournes
Lacouture
Meerut
Chapelle
13
H! Pommereau
Richebourg
l'Avoué
Wicres
Wavrin
55
la Mottelette
Sainghin-
en Weppes
1/2 32
Illies
le Willy
13
47 T.
Lorgies
Marquillies
VII
Festubert
57
Violaines
6 Maisnil
Don
Marais
Salome
Hamay
Annœulin
Canal
La Bassée
la Bassée
14
Givenchy-
lez la Bassée
56
Bauvin
d'Aire
1/3 2
Cuinchy
16
Auchy
Haisnes
Billy
Provin
Cambrin
Jg.11
Douvrin
Annequin
Sailly
58
113
Wingles
29
Meurchin

out on a flat ridge beginning at Tilloy. In the southern half of Sixth Army's sector, a clay layer of varying thickness covered the soil, which consisted of lime and chalk. During wet weather the clay impeded any movement; the excavated white lime was visible from a long distance and betrayed fortified positions to reconnaissance from both ground and air. There the army had only one favourable front-line position; the second line consisted of strongpoints only, as connecting trenches were still absent.

Except for the failed British attack at Neuve Chapelle in March, the enemy had not mounted any major attacks since the December offensive in the Artois. The rainy months had passed with continuous trench skirmishes, which had not resulted in any territorial gains to speak of by either side. Not until the end of April did a variety of preparations, as well as reports about newly formed units, suggest the possibility of a major and imminent enemy offensive aimed at breaking through north of Arras.

Since the beginning of May the enemy's artillery activity had intensified day after day. The mostly unsettled weather during this period made German aerial reconnaissance very difficult. During favourable weather the enemy's strong air superiority—especially regarding fighter aircraft—often neutralized any such activities. The front-line troops judged the situation in different ways. This was mostly because they still lacked sufficient experience in recognizing the enemy's preparations for an attack. Several divisions considered an imminent enemy attack as rather unlikely, mainly because the forward French trenches were more than 200 metres away and any advance that traversed such open territory under strong defensive fire seemed to offer little chance of success.

Suddenly on 8 May, units of French 43rd Infantry Division mounted an attack west of Liévin, which failed in bitter fighting. During the night of 8 and 9 May, enemy artillery fire, which was noticeably conducted by new heavy trench mortars, covered the German trenches in waves. On the morning of 9 May it abated. Only isolated artillery rounds disturbed the Sunday quiet, and the clear and beautiful weather favoured visibility.

At 06:00, however, gradual but constantly intensifying artillery fire began abruptly, especially in the sectors of VII Corps, XIV Corps, and Bavarian I Reserve Corps. Between 09:00 and 10:30 this fire increased to *Trommelfeuer*. Several brief breaks in the firing lured the German defenders out from their cover in expectation of an enemy attack; then each renewed barrage inflicted casualties. The impact of the German artillery, which was numerically inferior to that of the enemy, was necessarily minimal, and a black-yellow cloud of smoke and dust covered the German positions. The enemy had formed up for the attack so inventively that its preparations were nowhere visible. Therefore, the enemy assault that was launched

following numerous mine detonations caught the German forces and their commanders somewhat by surprise.

North of La Bassée Canal, British forces participated in the battle in a relatively
feeble way. They merely directed increased artillery fire against Bavarian II and XIX
(Saxon) Corps. By 06:00, however, they had launched an attack on the sector of
Bavarian 6th Reserve Division and against VII Corps' centre. North of Fromelles,
elements of IV Corps managed to break into the positions of Bavarian 6th Reserve
Division. Fierce hand-to-hand combat ensued within these positions. By evening
the attacking British soldiers had been either killed or captured. The I Corps and
the Indian Corps mounted repeated attacks at Richebourg l'Avoué; in places they
reached VII Corps' trenches, but there the enemy attack broke down.

The bulk of the attacking force was French. Around 1100 hours its main thrust
was directed at the left flank of XIV Corps and Bavarian I Reserve Corps between
Lens and Arras. A secondary attack by IX French Corps was launched at Loos in
XIV Corps' centre (29th Infantry Division). The enemy broke through on both
sides of the Béthune–Lens road; however, it was repelled by a vigorous counterattack. A Baden regiment deployed on the Lorette Spur was pushed back into the
rearward trenches with heavy losses. The same evening a Saxon *Jägerbatallion* was
sent as reinforcements. By order of the divisional commander, Generalmajor von
Trotta (also known as Treyden), this battalion was to retake the lost positions
together with the Baden regiment. South of the Lorette Spur the fiercely contested villages of Ablain, St. Nazaire, and Carency continued to hold.

Whereas XIV Corps was essentially able to maintain its positions (except for
the trenches at the Lorette Chapel), Bavarian 5th Reserve Division (commanded
by General der Infantrie Baron Kreß von Kressenstein) was pushed out of its positions south of Carency in I Reserve Corps' sector (under the command of General der Infantrie Ritter von Fasbender). Despite determined resistance, it was
pushed back to the general line Cabaret Rouge–Neuville-St. Vaast and southward.
The Bavarian 5th Reserve Division, which was deployed in the centre of the main
attack area, had been seriously weakened as a result of sending drafts to newly
activated units; these elements had been replaced by a Prussian *Landwehr* regiment
and dismounted cavalry units. Along its front, elements of the Moroccan Division
advanced as far as the German artillery positions at and south of Givenchy-en-
Gohelle. Reserves were quickly brought up and arrived just in time around noon
to prevent the enemy from advancing any farther. The Bavarian 1st Reserve Division neighbouring to the south, commanded by Generalleutnant Göringer, managed to repel the attack, although in some places fierce hand-to-hand fighting
was reported. The right wing of this division successfully interdicted the enemy,
which had broken through at La Targette.

In the early morning, enemy aircraft bombed Sixth Army Headquarters, La Madeleine en Lille, and the train stations around Lille itself without causing significant disruptions. Subsequent reports convinced Crown Prince Rupprecht that a major offensive was under way. Consequently, he implored Falkenhayn to release 115th and 58th Infantry Divisions from the *OHL*'s reserve behind the front line. This request was granted, and 115th Infantry Division was placed at the disposal of Bavarian I Reserve Corps, where it was quickly deployed to the rear of Bavarian 5th Reserve Division. The 58th (Saxon-Württemberg) Infantry Division was assigned to the army reserve and transported to the area east of Lens. Also, the army received a number of heavy batteries from the GHQ Artillery Reserve. On the afternoon of 9 May the extent of the French breakthrough became clear. The XIV Corps' left flank hung in the air, especially at Carency. Using the remnants of Bavarian 5th Reserve Division for a counterattack, the Commander-in-Chief of Sixth Army intended to regain as much ground as possible that same day. The entire 115th Infantry Division was also to be deployed for this purpose.

However, this plan could not be implemented. As a result of heavy losses, Bavarian 5th Reserve Division was unable to mount an attack. When 115th Infantry Division, commanded by Generalmajor von Kleist, arrived on the battlefield after dark, elements were immediately deployed as reinforcements on Bavarian I Reserve Corps' right flank. After some initial progress, a German counterattack from Souchez stalled in the face of heavy enemy fire at 20:00 hours.

In the evening it became clear to Army Headquarters that the enemy had inserted at least three and a half fresh corps above and beyond the units that had already been deployed in the position. In total, roughly twelve reinforced French divisions had attacked four German divisions. Despite this numerical superiority, the commander of Sixth Army was of the opinion "that the enemy's attack of today had weakened and that it would be possible to throw him back." Preparing for all eventualities, the *OHL* transferred 117th Infantry Division from the area of Rethel to Douai, but for the time being it was to remain under the *OHL*'s orders.

Crown Prince Rupprecht was well aware that it would be extremely difficult to create the conditions necessary for the important counterattack at Souchez to go forward. So he assigned two infantry regiments and one field artillery regiment of 58th Infantry Division to Bavarian I Reserve Corps and ordered that "the attack was to be conducted under the personal direction of the commanding general and that concentrated strength was to be kept tightly in his hands."[20] He then ordered that the new German artillery be deployed to the rear, east of the sharply

---

20 A letter dated 18 August 1931 from General von Fasbender to the *Reichsarchiv* regarding the extremely difficult terrain and combat conditions reads as follows: "The steep and wall-like eastern scarp of the Vimy Heights fell seventy meters between Givenchy and Farbus,

sloping heights at Vimy. Given the intense enemy fire, however, the attack could not be mounted until evening.

In the meantime, on the night of 9 and 10 May, the enemy had again captured the trenches on both sides of the Béthune–Lens road. The general in command, Generalleutnant von Haenisch, assigned the corps' last reserve battalion to Generalleutnant Isbert, commander of 29th Infantry Division. In the morning the German trenches were cleared of the enemy. Southwest of Souchez, however, in the early hours of the night, Turcos had taken the connecting trench between Carency and Souchez that had served as a combat position. With that, the village of Carency was almost cut off. In agreement with Haenisch, Army Headquarters saw only one way to alleviate the danger to XIV Corps' left flank: a vigorous counterattack originating from the line Souchez–Neuville-St. Vaast. This attack was necessary as, given tactical concerns and in consideration of the troops' morale, it was impossible to voluntarily evacuate the threatened sections of the line. Crown Prince Rupprecht thus ordered Bavarian I Reserve Corps to attack in concert with 58th and 115th Infantry Divisions. This meant that 28th Infantry Division's left flank would be supported by a single regiment of 58th Infantry Division, which had been brought up into the area of Souchez. Then, at around 16:00, after a fierce artillery bombardment, the enemy attacked with strong forces on the Lorette Spur. Again the attack waves surged against the German front but failed to make any major gains. During the afternoon, French 70th Infantry Division also repeatedly attacked Carency from the southwest and east. Through tenacious resistance, the German units were able to hold their positions.

At 19:00, 58th Infantry Division, commanded by Generalleutnant von Gersdorff, began the counterattack with two infantry regiments, joined in the south by elements of 115th Infantry Division, which had been deployed on Bavarian I Reserve Corps' right flank. The attack initially made good progress, but faced by vastly superior enemy forces, it also soon stalled. Given this situation and the fact that the enemy was marshalling considerable forces at Carency, 28th Infantry

---

dividing the entire terrain into two clearly defined combat sectors. In the east we had pushed the French back far enough over the crest of the ridge to create sufficient room behind the western slope to establish a defence in depth which included artillery positions. With the breakthrough, three quarters of our previously gained terrain had been retaken and this had accordingly pushed a major portion of our rear echelons into the eastern field of battle where they now faced a high wall. On the French side, the battle conditions had not changed. Whereas we had to pull all our batteries back into the eastern field of battle—thus forcing our guns to cease fire—even the forward French lines remained under the protection of their artillery and without repositioning any of their batteries they were still able to threaten us far into our rear areas."

Division expressed concern as to whether the Ablain–Carency line could hold out much longer.

On 10 May, Bavarian 1st Reserve Division held its positions through a bitter defensive struggle during which the focal point of the battle remained the area of Neuville-St. Vaast on the division's right flank. Over the following days the Bavarians attempted to restore the situation by mounting costly and futile counterattacks, supported by elements of IV Corps and 115th Infantry Division (which had been brought up for this purpose). Only small parts of the village of Neuville-St. Vaast were retaken by assault.

On 11 May, Bavarian I Reserve Corps Headquarters concluded that the general situation had deteriorated and that it was now uncertain whether Ablain and Carency could be held. On that basis, Army Headquarters reported to the *OHL* that "under the circumstances, prior to an evacuation of the front line, forces must be made available to protect the lines to the rear." Falkenhayn thus made 117th Infantry Division available and advised that VIII Corps Headquarters, together with 16th Infantry Division, were to be moved to into the *OHL*'s reserve at Douai. The 117th Infantry Division, commanded by General der Infanterie Kuntze, was moved up into the area southeast of Lens.

While these preparations for a possible evacuation were being made, the Sixth Army Commander spared no effort in trying to avoid the loss of Ablain and Carency as in all probability their evacuation would ultimately result in the abandonment of the commanding Lorette Spur. With this in mind, at 08:00 Crown Prince Rupprecht, accompanied by his Chief of Staff, Generalmajor Krafft, travelled to Hénin-Liétard for a meeting with the commanding generals of XIV Corps and Bavarian I Reserve Corps. The result of the meeting was "an order to hold this part of our line." The fact that there were no new attacks on the morning of 11 May helped the Commander-in-Chief make the decision. Indeed, the attacks did not begin until the afternoon and even then they were uncoordinated, peculiarly timed, and irregularly spaced. Ultimately they were repelled with considerable losses to the enemy.

However, an order taken from a French officer captured near Loos revealed that the enemy intended to break through at any cost.[21] Since XIV Corps no longer had any reserves at its disposal, in the evening a regiment of 117th Infantry Division was assigned to be deployed "only in the event of an extreme emergency." At the same time, 28th Infantry Division urgently requested the relief of its worn-out and shaken forces on the Lorette Spur, where elements of French XXI Corps had firmly

---

21   In fact, it was from General d'Urbal, the Commander-in-Chief of French Tenth Army, ordering a crucial general attack for 11 May. See *French Official History,* III: 48.

established themselves. In response, this threatened sector of the front was initially supported by elements of 58th Infantry Division.

By noon on 11 May, Sixth Army's Commander-in-Chief had received the following telegram from the *OHL*:

> At the very least, his Majesty expects the army to hold its present line under any circumstances. Whether this objective is accomplished defensively or with secondary attacks must be judged locally. In any case, with reasoned deployments and firmly coordinated leadership, the available infantry and heavy artillery ought to be strong enough to prevent a continued enemy advance. His Majesty acknowledges the outstanding bravery displayed in the recent battles with appreciation.

Crown Prince Rupprecht's response was as follows: "His Majesty the Kaiser may rest assured that Sixth Army will do everything in its power to stop the enemy offensive. This commitment has been maintained from the inception. We will not voluntarily relinquish any ground to the enemy. At this time a major counterattack does not hold any promise, but we continue to reserve this option."

On 12 May the heavy fighting continued. The night before, General von Fasbender had reported that there was an impending breakthrough at Neuville-St. Vaast that would endanger the artillery lines. Consequently, the staff of 117th Infantry Division and two infantry regiments were placed at his disposal. Army Headquarters requested and received permission from the *OHL* to take over the elements arriving from VIII Corps, which were detrained at a forward railhead in the area of Hénin-Liétard. The *OHL* also ordered the transfer of a reinforced brigade of 15th Infantry Division into GHQ Reserve at Douai. Falkenhayn further suggested that command over the forces tasked with retaking the lost ground be turned over "to a general familiar with the local environment who believes in success and is committed to the task, e.g. the commanding general of VII Corps [General der Infanterie von Claer]."

In the morning, Crown Prince Rupprecht again ordered XIV Corps to hold the fiercely contested village of Carency come what may. The commanding general, Generalleutnant von Haenisch, relayed this order to 28th Infantry Division and, in an effort to guard against any reversals, simultaneously ordered that pioneer companies be quickly brought up to dig a fall-back trench to the rear of his endangered left flank. Meanwhile, the situation on the Lorette Spur appeared to have improved. There, 28th Infantry Division reported that a Saxon regiment from 58th Infantry Division had apparently retaken the old line on the northern slope. On the other hand, the military situation in the encircled village of Carency remained perilous. The Bavarian I Reserve Corps was unable to mount a relief attack. Above all else its objective was to hold its own threatened line of Souchez–Neuville-St. Vaast–St. Laurent. Around 16:00 the French launched strong—albeit unsuccessful—attacks.

Pursuant to the *OHL*'s suggestion that a unified force at the battle's focal point be created, Army Headquarters on the evening of 12 May ordered the formation of Armee-Gruppe *Fasbender*,[22] to consist of all units deployed in the sectors of XIV Corps and Bavarian I Reserve Corps. An army order stated that Armee-Gruppe *Fasbender*'s primary mission was "to hold on to the present positions at all costs and to create a continuous and—in the long run—defensible line of resistance between Carency and Neuville-St. Vaast" as soon as possible. To further this order, a German attack was mounted on the evening of 12 May at the cemetery south of Souchez, but it failed. The support that had been expected from Carency did not materialize because at dusk, French XXXIII Corps had attacked and despite heroic resistance had seized the almost completely surrounded village.

After the loss of Carency, Haenisch, commanding XIV Corps, viewed the situation as perilous. So that night he visited Generalmajor von Trotta (commanding 28th Infantry Division) at Lens in order to decide with him jointly and quickly on measures to be taken. He ordered that trenches be dug in a general line extending from the Lorette Spur to the Church at Ablain to Souchez. The artillery was directed to immediately bring Carency, which was occupied by the enemy, under howitzer fire. Based on a report—which later turned out to have been incorrect— stating that coloured French forces had also broken through north of Ablain, a battalion from 117th Infantry Division was assigned to 28th Infantry Division. Pursuant to Corps Headquarters' request, a regiment from 16th Infantry Division was moved to Lens as its replacement.

The precariousness of the combat situation became clear on the morning of 13 May. On 28th Infantry Division's right flank, the Baden units held on to their original trenches while the Saxons firmly held their original positions on the northern slope of the Lorette Spur. French forces were occupying the former German trenches on both sides of the Lorette Chapel between the Muddy Hollow (*Schlammulde*) and the path leading to Ablain. Adjoining this break in the line, grenadiers from Baden clung desperately to a ravine. Farther south, most of Ablain had to be evacuated under heavy pressure from the French, but the attackers had not advanced beyond the village. After bitter and bloody fighting, the enemy's strength had also been sapped; except for a local foray at Neuville-St. Vaast, the

---

22 *An* Armee-Gruppe *is approximately equivalent to an* Armee-Abteilung *in that it is smaller than an army but larger than a corps. However, unlike the latter, the* Armee-Gruppe *is a temporary formation usually brought together for a specific purpose and dependent on a larger army.*

French mounted no serious attack on 13 May. But there could be no doubt that this was only a temporary lull. Sixth Army Headquarters possessed statements from prisoners of war which suggested that III French Corps would soon join the battle.[23]

At the same time, Sixth Army was being stretched to the limit. The Army Commander assessed the combat capability of his fighting units as follows: the overextended 29th Infantry Division was worn out in the extreme; 28th Infantry Division was almost at the end of its usefulness; and Bavarian 5th Reserve Division was totally spent. The Bavarian 1st Reserve Division and 58th and 115th Infantry Divisions had suffered severely. By now the total losses to these units— which had carried the brunt of the fighting between 9 and 13 May—amounted to about 20,000 men. So on 13 May, Crown Prince Rupprecht requested the immediate transfer of two mixed infantry brigades, one to Pont à Vendin and the other to Vitry en Artois; he further requested the assignment of the reinforced brigade from 15th Infantry Division. To deal with the impending attacks, he intended to replace worn-out units with fresh ones. To meet all contingencies, he suggested that the OHL provide an additional corps. Falkenhayn agreed to his request, and that afternoon, Fourth Army's 85th Reserve Infantry Brigade (which was assigned to XIV Corps) detrained at Pont à Vendin while Second Army's combined 52nd Reserve Infantry Brigade[24] arrived for Bavarian I Reserve Corps; at the same time, X Reserve Corps' 2nd Guard Reserve Division arrived at Douai from Alsace. In addition, the OHL assigned General der Infanterie von Lochow of III Corps to "lead the Armee-Gruppe that will be formed using units now amassed in the sectors of XIV Corps and Bavarian I Reserve Corps."[25]

On the night of 13 and 14 May, regiments of 117th Infantry Division began to relieve 28th Division. The Bavarian 5th Reserve Division, reduced by two-thirds of its original strength, was gradually withdrawn over the following day; VIII Corps (16th, 58th, 115th, and half of 15th Infantry Divisions), commanded by General der Infanterie Riemann, was to replace it in the Souchez–Neuville-St. Vaast sector.

The OHL had acceded to the demands of Sixth Army Headquarters and assigned new combat-ready units, thus providing Sixth Army with ample reinforcements. In the process, GHQ Reserve had been deployed almost in its entirety, which exposed other parts of the fronts to danger. No additional forces were

---

23 In fact, French III Corps, minus 5th Infantry Division, had arrived at Avesnes le Comte on 10 May; some of its units were already deployed to XXI Corps starting from 13 May.

24 99th Reserve Infantry Regiment with parts of 12th, 16th, and Bavarian 20th Infantry Regiments, plus artillery.

25 *In other words, General Lochow was to assume command of* Armee-Gruppe Fasbender.

available. In response to the demand for at least one additional division, Falkenhayn wired Sixth Army's Commander-in-Chief on the 14th:

> In the beginning of the offensive north of Arras, Sixth Army was in a consid-
> erably more advantageous position with respect to the number of rifles per
> metre of front than, for example, Third Army in the Champagne or Armee-
> Abteilung *Strantz* between the Meuse and Moselle, which were both facing
> similar circumstances. What is more, to my knowledge, the enemy you are fac-
> ing is neither superior in number nor in quality.[26] In spite of this, Sixth Army
> has received both entirely fresh units of all arms as well as heavy artillery and
> munitions considerably faster and more abundantly than was the case in the
> aforementioned examples. Not less than nine and a half divisions are presently
> available for a front of barely twenty kilometres. Even though several of them
> have suffered badly for reasons that need not be discussed, according to all
> previous experiences we must expect that this force ought to be able to hold
> such a front for a reasonable period of time against any attack. During this
> endeavour it will perhaps suffer heavy casualties. That cannot be helped.
> Therefore it is out of the question to deploy the entire GHQ Reserve in order
> to supply relief to a sector of the front that is already well endowed because
> at any moment a much more pressing need may develop at another place. As
> a matter of fact, X Reserve Corps's division in Douai represents the last com-
> bat ready reserve available to the *OHL*. Considering these circumstances, I
> would ask that the request before me be reconsidered and that I be informed
> of the outcome. General von Lochow's opinion will be valued.

Crown Prince Rupprecht responded to the *OHL*'s wire as follows:

> The request for X Corps' division was not only submitted in consideration of
> Armee-Gruppe *Fasbender*'s situation (General von Lochow has not yet taken
> command) but also in support of the entire army where additional British
> attacks (and therefore along a 50 kilometre front) are expected. At the same
> time, immediate resumption of these attacks is expected. Since the enemy
> has not mounted any major attacks since last night it must be concluded that
> he is marshalling new forces. That he has already abandoned this operation,
> or that he is going to attempt it elsewhere, is improbable. Army headquarters
> does not intend to deploy the last reserve on the Western Front unnecessar-
> ily, but it must be pointed out that only weak reserves are staged north of La
> Bassée Canal, which would hardly be able to restore the situation in the event
> of another successful breakthrough attempt. In the expectation that forces

---

26 The available documentation in the *Reichsarchiv* cannot confirm the correctness of Falken-
    hayn's calculation.

might still be made available for relief of Armee-Gruppe *Lochow* in addition to the requested 2nd Guard Reserve Division, I had yesterday requested at least a combined infantry brigade in the area south of Lille. I am aware that General von Lochow deems it necessary to relieve all of the units that have participated in the heavy fighting. This cannot be sufficiently accomplished with the forces available at present.

Falkenhayn's wires of 12 and 14 May caused Crown Prince Rupprecht to file a grievance with the Kaiser on 16 May. The Kaiser decided in favour of Sixth Army Headquarters on all essential points, prompting Falkenhayn to direct a letter "regretting the misunderstandings" to the Army Commander:[27]

> According to the established principles of leadership, the commander responsible for an overall operation is not only justified but duty bound to interject himself into the chain of command at the threatened front when he recognizes impending danger. Therefore it is the task of the leader to accommodate and support the commanders responsible at the front whose intellectual, moral, and physical capacities are already severely tried by lightening their responsibilities. In this case, Falkenhayn's intervention did not sufficiently consider these principles; in this tenor it was apt to insult the commanders at the front who had without exception proven themselves up to the task, despite the extremely difficult situation.

General Lochow's Assumption of Command on the Main Battle Front and Operations to the Middle of June

Lochow, who under the orders of the *OHL* was to assume command of Armee-Gruppe *Fasbender*, arrived at Sixth Army on 13 May and, along with his newly formed staff, moved into his new headquarters in Douai on the following day.[28] Based on inquiries made on 14 and 15 May, he developed the following overall picture of the main battle front: north of the Lorette Spur and in Bavarian 1st Reserve Division's sector, most of the old trenches, although damaged, remained in German hands. In the middle of the front but north of Carency Creek, XIV Corps was still holding on to segments of its original line in the Muddy Hollow, in Barricade Way (*Barrikadenweg*), and in the eastern part of Ablain. Here the enemy had not yet been cleared from the positions it had gained during the breakthrough at the Lorette Chapel. South of Carency Creek, the trenches were barely

---

27   Rupprecht, Crown Prince of Bavaria, *My War Diary*, Vol. I (Berlin: Deutscher National, 1929), 352.
28   His Chief of Staff was Generalmajor von Bergmann.

The Spring Battle in Artois
The German Positions between Angres and St. Laurent on 12 May

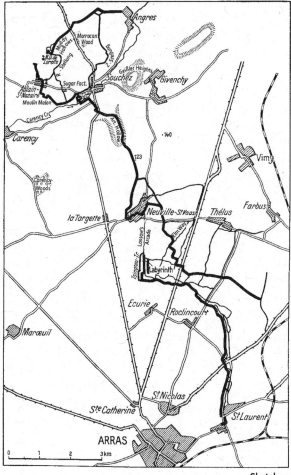

Sketch 14

defensible, held by the intermingled 58th and 115th Infantry Divisions, the remains of Bavarian 5th Reserve Division, and one regiment of 52nd Reserve Infantry Brigade. Behind the front, 16th Infantry Division, under Generalleutnant Fuchs, was about to move into the Souchez–Hill 123 sector (2 kilometres southeast of Souchez), while elements of 15th Infantry Division and the newly activated 1st Trench Mortar Battalion had arrived in the army's sector.

At this precarious time in the battle, Lochow assumed command on the night of 15 and 16 May.[29] He considered his first task to be the reorganization of the intermingled units and the creation of combat-ready reserves, a process that had already been initiated by General von Fasbender. The remaining units of Bavarian 5th Reserve Division were taken out of the line. The 58th Infantry Division was to be sent to the area of Douai, replaced by 16th Infantry Division. The battle front was then divided into three corps sectors: stationed on the right flank up to Carency Creek were XIV Corps with 117th Infantry Division and 85th Reserve Infantry Brigade; VIII Corps, with 115th Infantry Division and, for the time being, 58th Infantry Division, was stationed from Carency Creek to the Arras–Lens road; Bavarian I Reserve Corps (1st Bavarian Reserve Division and 52nd Infantry Brigade) was stationed from this road to the Scarpe.

Owing to the movement of the various infantry units, the artillery's chain of command was in disarray. It was thus reorganized so that sufficient field and heavy artillery batteries were available to each sector. Also, each area of the front was placed under unified command for barrage firing and for counter-battery work and to ensure that flanking support was secured for any other sector.

Lochow agreed with Sixth Army Headquarters that the Lorette Spur, which very much dominated the field of battle, had to be restored to German hands. Accordingly, XIV Corps was directed to launch an assault in order to close the gap in the line. The resulting attempts launched between the nights of 15 and 17 May failed. These daily battles wore out the regiments of 117th Infantry Division, which had to be temporarily relieved on the night of 18 and 19 May.

At the same time, aerial reconnaissance observed the deployment of massive enemy artillery. Since troop detrainings were also reported at Doulles west of Arras, a renewed attack between the Lorette Spur and Arras appeared to be imminent. Thoughts necessarily turned to thwarting the enemy's plans. There was no doubt that taking the elevated village of Ecurie would seriously disrupt the French artillery deployment; however, the forces necessary to take this position were insufficient, given the nature of the terrain and the prepared defensive installations. An attack on the Lorette Spur was also certain to fail, since it could be met by flanking fire from well-camouflaged enemy artillery. Also, conditions for a German attack to the immediate south of Souchez were disadvantageous because there was a lack of protected staging areas. On the other hand, the houses and basements of Neuville-St. Vaast provided good forming-up areas for attacking troops. Therefore Lochow decided to deploy his assault units there.

---

29 For the composition of Group *Lochow,* see Sketch 15.

The 15th Division (commanded by Generalmajor Vollbrecht and deployed at Neuville) was assigned the attack; it was to be supported by 115th Infantry Division. At 20:30 on 22 May the assault was launched. However, the artillery preparation had been only partly successful. Because observation conditions were poor, the assigned trench mortar battalion had been unable to soften up the southern part of Neuville-St. Vaast held by the enemy. Consequently—and despite support from light flame-throwers—the infantry were unable to penetrate the fortified village.

Meanwhile, the focus of the enemy attacks had extended northwards. After terminating their offensive North of La Bassée Canal on 10 May, the British attacked south of Neuve Chapelle in two places during the night of 15 and 16 May. This operation was motivated by strong demands by the French Supreme Commander, who during his visit to British Headquarters on 12 May had expressed disappointment regarding the results of British First Army's offensive up to that point and who had demanded that it immediately continue its attacks or take over additional sectors of the French front south of La Bassée Canal. General Field Marshal Sir John French decided to continue the offensive. Consequently, First Army again launched an attack against VII Corps between Richebourg-l'Avoué and Festubert, initially using three infantry divisions, which were later replaced by fresh forces. In the course of these tenacious and shifting battles, the British succeeding in pushing the German lines back to a depth of more than 3 kilometres. At that time, Bavarian and Saxon battalions were quickly brought up from the regiments deployed to the north (next to the Westphalians). They joined the battle, along with Fourth Army's mixed 38th Landwehr Brigade. As a result, the danger that temporarily threatened this sector was averted. On 20 and 21 May, British elements again attacked the German front on the Estaires–La Bassée road. All of their attacks collapsed owing to the defenders' indefatigable stand.

The fighting, which had continued almost uninterrupted since 9 May, had seriously reduced Sixth Army's combat effectiveness. The *OHL* repeatedly needed to bring up new units to the beleaguered Artois front. The X Reserve Corps' 2nd Reserve Guard Division, whose arrival had already been announced, was placed at VII Corps' disposal and on 18 May was inserted into the front between 13th and 14th Infantry Divisions. Since 19th Reserve Division (which formed part of X Reserve Corps) had already been brought up to Armee-Abteilung *Gaede*, on 15 May, at the latter's request, Falkenhayn directed Armee-Abteilung *Strantz* to free up 111th Infantry Division and 80th Infantry Brigade (from VIII Corps), which had recently been involved in heavy combat in the St. Mihiel Salient. Even if the *OHL*'s combat reserves were not yet fully operational, 111th Infantry Division was to be assembled at Douai while 80th Infantry Brigade was to return to VIII Corps, which was already deployed with Sixth Army. Furthermore, Falkenhayn did not

The Spring Battle in Artois
The Situation of Sixth Army on 15 May

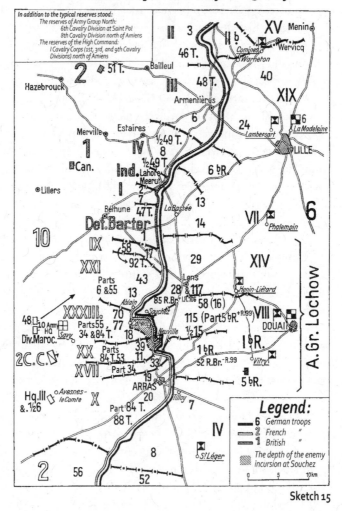

Sketch 15

continue to pursue his previous strategy of moving the infantry units of 103rd Infantry Division (which were then being assembled in Posen) to the Western Front via numerous transport routes so as to create the impression that the Germans were inserting major forces. Instead, on 17 May, Seventh Army was directed to pull 123rd (Saxon) Infantry Division out of the front lines, from whence it was immediately moved to Lille. With that, two divisions were again staged behind the front in the Artois, ready for combat. However, the remainder of the Western Front had been largely stripped of reserves. Except for 111th and 123rd Infantry Divisions, the OHL now only had Bavarian 8th Reserve Division (recently brought up from the Vosges), as well as units that were in the process of being made available as reserves.

Sixth Army had also received considerable artillery reinforcements since the beginning of the defensive battle. By 22 May the heavy artillery had grown from 100 high- and 74 low-trajectory guns to 209 high- and 98 low-trajectory guns. The number of heavy rapid-fire guns had thus doubled, and the OHL could now meet their ammunition requirements. Between 9 and 19 May, Sixth Army expended 508,000 field artillery and 105,000 heavy artillery shells.

On 19 May, Oberst Baron von der Wenge, Earl of Lambsdorff, previously X Corps' Chief of Staff, was appointed Chief of Staff to Sixth Army. The previous Chief of Staff, Generalleutnant von Krafft, was given command of the newly formed *Alpenkorps*, which was being deployed against the Italian forces; Sixth Army also had to contribute four *Jäger* battalions to the new *Alpenkorps*.

MAJOR ENEMY ATTACKS BEGAN AGAIN NORTH OF ARRAS ON 23 MAY FOLLOWING minor skirmishes over the previous days. At noon on Pentecost Sunday, fierce enemy artillery bombardments opened up on the centre of Armee-Gruppe *Lochow* from the Lorette Spur southward almost all the way to the Scarpe. Foch, Commander-in-Chief of French Army Group *North*, had ordered these bombardments so as to create a new jumping-off position. The primary objectives of the main attack were Souchez, the surrounding heights, Neuville-St. Vaast, and the maze of trenches known as the Labyrinth, which protruded from the main line between Neuville-St. Vaast and Ecurie. At 16:00, waves of French infantry rolled against the German front. At Ecurie and farther south the enemy assault units were spotted as they were forming up and were brought under artillery fire; as a result, the attacks against this part of the front collapsed. Farther north the French attacked in dense lines and succeeding in gaining a foothold in several sections of the German trenches. Not until nightfall—and only then after fierce hand-to-hand fighting—was the enemy ejected with considerable losses.

On witnessing the severe losses, Lochow requested fresh units from the OHL. He was assigned IV Corps—located to the south—in exchange for two worn-out divisions, which were to be sent to a quiet sector south of the Scarpe. So that these reorganizations would not negatively affect the defensive battle, on 24 May the OHL also assigned Sixth Army's 111th Infantry Division, which was staged at Douai. Armee-Gruppe *Lochow* assigned these replacements as follows: 111th Infantry

Division took over 8th Division's sector; 115th Infantry Division, having suffered badly at Neuville-St. Vaast, was replaced by 58th Infantry Division; Bavarian 5th Reserve Division remained in GHQ Reserve at Biache for the time being and later—at the beginning of June—replaced 7th Infantry Division. The VI Corps, commanded by General der Infanterie Sixt, was deployed in the second line west of Douai, where it would be called upon to attack when the time was right.

On 25 and 26 May, renewed French attacks were directed with full force primarily against the Liévin–Souchez sector; they were mounted at noon on 25 May and then on the following day at 16:00. Ignoring their own losses, the massed infantry of French IX and XXI Corps attacked repeatedly. At times the German trenches at Liévin and on the Lorette Spur were lost but were eventually retaken in counterattacks mounted by units gathered from 85th Reserve Infantry Brigade, as well as from 28th and 117th Infantry Divisions. Hand-to-hand combat with coloured French soldiers was especially fierce. On 27 May, French 70th Infantry Division took the Ablain cemetery and the trench sections connecting to the south. Because heavy enemy fire would make it extremely difficult to retake the line, and since the part of Ablain that remained in German hands was in danger of being enveloped, on 28 May Generalleutnant von Haenisch (with General von Lochow's agreement) ordered that the fiercely contested village be evacuated and that the troops retire to an entrenched fall-back line on both sides of the sugar factory west of Souchez.

The fighting continued into the last days of May. On the morning of 29 May, 85th Reserve Infantry Brigade repelled a French attack on the Aix–Noulette–Souchez road. That morning, strong enemy infantry columns were observed marching on both roads leading from Béthune in the direction of Lens and Souchez. News spread among the local population—apparently through agents—that on 30 May Lens was going to be the target of a heavy artillery bombardment in order to facilitate a French breakthrough planned for this direction. Lochow, however, only momentarily considered reinforcing his right flank, having recognized this ploy as a deception. Indeed, on 30 May only a few rounds fell on Lens, just as it was relatively quiet on XIV Corps' front. On the other hand, in the early morning the entire sector of Bavarian 1st Reserve Division came under heavy artillery bombardment, which gradually extended northward to VIII Corps' sector. Around 17:00 a strong attack was launched between Souchez and Roclincourt; it was repelled in hand-to-hand combat. According to information from prisoners of war, French 19th, 20th, and 53rd Divisions had been involved in the attack. To their rear, III Corps was staged and ready to complete the breakthrough. There was no doubt that renewed heavy fighting lay ahead.

On the evening of 31 May, elements of French XXXIII Corps attacked between Angres and Carency Creek and took the German trenches on both sides of the sugar factory west of Souchez. In fierce fighting that continued throughout the entire night and into the next day, XIV Corps units from Baden succeeded in retaking the trenches north of the factory by direct assault. However, the factory itself and the trenches to the south of it remained in French hands.

On the evening of 1 June the enemy renewed the attacks on Neuville-St. Vaast and Tsingtau Trench to the south. In Neuville a Saxon Regiment of 58th Infantry Division counterattacked and pushed back the French,[30] who had initially been successful. However, Tsingtau Trench remained firmly in the enemy's hands. In order to centralize control of the battle in the Labyrinth, Lochow charged General von Fasbender (commanding Bavarian I Reserve Corps) with the defence of the confused maze of trenches and gave him the composite 58th Infantry Division[31] for the purpose. The 58th Infantry Division's former sector at Neuville-St. Vaast was assigned to 15th Infantry Division. With that, VIII Corps was reunited.

Renewed British attacks southwest of Lille also demanded constant attention. As before, however, within the framework of the overall operations, these attacks maintained the character of diversionary ventures. In the first half of June, west of La Bassée, several successively deployed regiments of VII and XIX Corps had to fight off heavy attacks, but the Westphalian and Saxon units managed to hold their positions despite heavy losses. The village of Givenchy-lez-la-Bassée, which was located in a commanding position, was hotly contested in costly fighting and represented the focus of those battles.

During June, the battle's centre of gravity remained with Armee-Gruppe *Lochow*. From then on, hardly a day passed without fierce fighting in the Labyrinth.[32] Each foot of ground was contested, and the continuous fighting severely tried the valiant defenders, who often had to go without food or water. Time and again the enemy mounted attacks, attempting to force a breakthrough along the dwindling German lines. On 4 and 5 June, Neuville-St. Vaast was fiercely assaulted again. The fighting there lasted throughout the night of 5 and 6 June. On 6 June, Foch ordered that the French offensive be strengthened, and the battles flared again on 8 June. Decimated by overwhelming trench mortar fire, the companies of a Rhineland regiment evacuated the eastern section of Neuville-St. Vaast and moved to a trench east of the village. The remaining regiments of 15th Infantry Division also suffered badly in the intense fighting on 8 June.

---

30 The newly deployed French 5th Infantry Division of III Corps.
31 It was composed of an infantry regiment of 8th, 58th, and 115th Infantry Divisions.
32 In three days' fighting beginning on the 30 May, French 53rd Infantry Division used no less than 24,000 hand grenades. See *French Official History*, III: 70.

French attacks on the Lorette Spur were closely linked to the forays against Neuville-St. Vaast and the Labyrinth. There, the continuous fighting had exhausted the forces attached to XIV Corps Headquarters to the point that relief became an urgent necessity. Thus Army Headquarters was forced to replace them with forces from IV Corps. As a consequence, the planned use of this corps for an attack had to be abandoned. The 117th Infantry Division and 85th Reserve Infantry Brigade were transferred to General Sixt, commanding IV Corps, upon the takeover of the sector. The 115th Infantry Division replaced Bavarian 5th Reserve Division deployed south of the Scarpe and was designated as part of the *OHL*'s reserve.

On the evening of 7 June, Falkenhayn arrived in Douai from the Eastern Theatre for a personal briefing on the situation by his combat commanders. He realized that Sixth Army's energy was exhausted as a result of the almost uninterrupted defensive battles and that fresh units needed to be brought up in order to prepare for new battles; it could be expected that the great offensive in the Artois would continue, if only because the Entente possessed vastly superior forces (by approximately 600 battalions). Lochow personally guaranteed the Chief of the General Staff that his Armee-Gruppe's positions would be held even against greatly superior enemy forces, but only if the worn-out troops were relieved before they were entirely exhausted, redeployed to calmer areas, and replaced by rested units. Consequently, on 9 June, Falkenhayn ordered the exchange of First Army's 5th Infantry Division for 115th Infantry Division and the exchange of 123rd (Saxon) Infantry Division, stationed at Lille, for 117th Infantry Division. Additionally—as already mentioned—XIV Corps was to change positions with IV Corps (which was located to the army's rear) and was to again later replace VI Corps, which for the time being was to remain at the *OHL*'s disposal. By 11 June, 5th Prussian Infantry Division was already deployed at Neuville-St. Vaast from the GHQ reserve to relieve the totally exhausted 15th Infantry Division.

Operations of the Remaining Armies on the Western Front from the Middle of May to the End of July

The commanders of the Entente wanted to support the major offensive in the Artois by staging attacks, or by threatening to attack, on other fronts. As a result, almost every German army on the Western Front was subjected to increased combat activities.

On Fourth Army's front (commanded by Generaloberst Albrecht Duke of Württemberg), the Germans still had the initiative. Although the attacks mounted on 22 April had largely been concluded by 9 May, Fourth Army still intended "to push the enemy back into his bridgehead—using gas cylinders in the event of

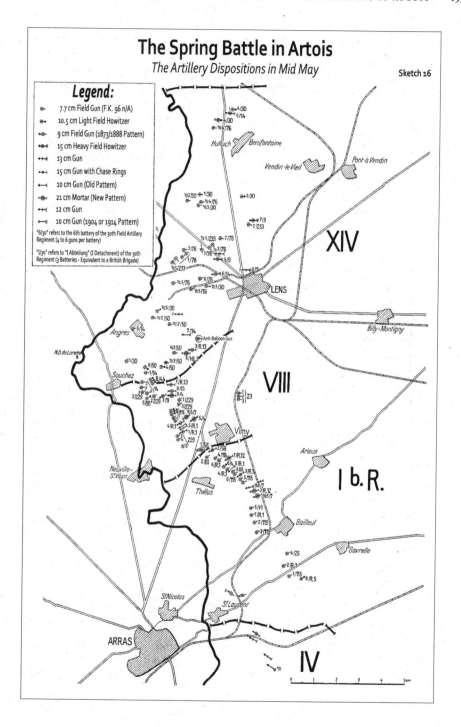

The Spring Battle in Artois
The Artillery Dispositions in Mid May

Sketch 16

Legend:

⊨━	7.7 cm Field Gun (F.K. 96 n/A)
⊨━	10.5 cm Light Field Howitzer
⊨━	9 cm Field Gun (1873/1888 Pattern)
⊷━	15 cm Heavy Field Howitzer
⊢━	13 cm Gun
⊷━	15 cm Gun with Chase Rings
⊢━	10 cm Gun (Old Pattern)
⊷━	21 cm Mortar (New Pattern)
⊢━	12 cm Gun
⊢━	10 cm Gun (1904 or 1914 Pattern)

"6/30" refers to the 6th battery of the 30th Field Artillery
Regiment (4 to 6 guns per battery)

"I/30" refers to "I Abteilung" (I Detachment) of the 30th
Regiment (3 Batteries - Equivalent to a British brigade)

favourable winds, but otherwise without them" in order to acquire the line Yser Canal–Ypres–St. Eloi. Another assault by XXVI and XXVII Reserve Corps in the direction of Ypres between the Pilkem–Ypres road and Hooge was planned.

Accordingly, both corps launched their attacks on the morning of 13 May, although they were unable to use gas owing to the unfavourable weather. It soon became apparent that success was out of reach because of the enemy's steadfast performance. Generally, the *OHL* rejected Fourth Army's further offensive operations, wiring on the following day: "The attacks in the direction of Ypres are so costly in terms of blood and ammunition that their continuation can only be supported if the success desired can be guaranteed, or if substantial enemy units can be prevented from intervening in the battles north of Arras as a result." Despite this directive, Fourth Army Headquarters continued planning attacks in the hope of achieving small-scale successes. However, before anything came of this, the enemy launched an attack north of Ypres. After repeated strong French attacks against the area between Steenstraate and Het Sas on 15 and 16 May, the German positions on the canal's western bank had to be abandoned. The enemy cautiously pursued German forces as far as the canal.

The last major German attack was launched east of Ypres on 24 May. Although 54th (Württemberg) Reserve Division (commanded by General von Schaefer) initially gained considerable ground with a forceful thrust, British resistance soon stiffened, stalling the German attack north of Hooge. On the same day, the *OHL* sent a wire to all armies in the West that the Western Army was to maintain a defensive posture in consideration of the need to reach a decision in other theatres of war. Consequently, Fourth Army shifted to the defence and on 1 June, with an eye to operational priorities, offered XXII Reserve Corps[33] to Falkenhayn for deployment on other fronts. Falkenhayn immediately accepted the offer in "sincere appreciation," and despite the heavy battles that continued on the Western Front decided to transfer the corps together with Bavarian 8th Reserve Division to the Eastern Theatre as reinforcements. This decision was all the more audacious given that the removal of these two and a half divisions came at a time when the Artois Front was being subjected to the most severe attacks. There, only 123rd Infantry Division and 187th Infantry Brigade remained in the *OHL*'s immediate reserve.

After the heavy fighting of April and May, a certain quiet descended on the Ypres Salient.[34] Not until July did fighting flare up again, in the area of Hooge. Widespread flooding on Fourth Army's northern flank precluded major combat operations.

---

33 Without 85th Reserve Infantry Brigade, which since 13 May had been on the strength of XIV Corps in the Artois battle.

34 After the relief of the French, only British troops remained in the Ypres Salient.

Relative quiet reigned north of the Artois Front in June and July. Meanwhile, to the south in the sector of XIV Reserve Corps of Second Army, elements of French XI and XIV Corps mounted an attack at 05:00 on 7 June against the left flank of Generalleutnant Karl von Borries's 52nd Infantry Division in the area of Hébuterne. In the dense morning fog, the numerically superior enemy succeeded in penetrating the German positions. However, in a seven-day battle, it was possible to limit the enemy's gains to the forward positions jutting out west of the Serre with the help of rapidly deployed support.[35] German losses as a result of the stubborn fighting from 7 to 15 June amounted to roughly 4,000 men; the French lost 10,350. On 10 and 19 July, 28th Reserve Division was able to repel further weak French attacks, which were assisted by explosions that churned up the heights southwest of Fricourt.

The enemy also went on the offensive against neighbouring First Army.[36] On 6 June, elements of the reinforced French XXXV Corps attacked at Moulin-sous-Touvent, 10 kilometres west of Nouvron, and took several segments of trench. Fighting surged back and forth on 6 and 7 June, during which time 18th Infantry Division, which had been at the centre of the attack, lost 43 officers and 1,720 enlisted men.[37] Even though the fighting extended to the middle of the month, there could be no doubt that these attacks were diversionary in nature and that they were not the precursors to a major offensive. Still, given the precarious situation, First Army Headquarters decided to deploy its final reserve, an infantry regiment of 123rd Infantry Division, which had just been deployed. This decision led Falkenhayn to transfer the newly formed 183rd Infantry Brigade to First Army.

In Seventh Army's[38] sector, the months of May, June, and July passed without notable incident. The only exceptions included a Saxon grenadier regiment's successful foray on 10 May near La-Ville-aux-Bois, 2 kilometres northeast of Pontavert, and several failed counterattacks by French 5th Infantry Division.

On Third Army's front[39] the months following the winter offensive in the Champagne were characterized by relatively uneventful trench warfare, although

---

35 Parts of 26th and 28th Reserve Division and 185th Infantry Brigade.
36 On 8 May, First Army was deployed as follows from north to south: IX Reserve Corps (plus 15th Landwehr Division), IX Corps, IV Reserve Corps, and III Corps.
37 Between 7 and 16 June the enemy had lost 7,905 men.
38 On 8 May, Seventh Army was deployed as follows from west to east: VII Reserve Corps, and XII Corps (reinforced by 123rd Infantry Division); in reserve at Laons: a composite infantry brigade.
39 On 8 May, Third Army was deployed as follows from west to east: VI Corps, XII Reserve Corps, and VIII Reserve Corps (reinforced by 50th and 54th Infantry Divisions); 117th Infantry Division was in reserve near Rethel.

minor skirmishes above and below ground continued. Third Army considered major enemy attacks to be unlikely, as did the neighbouring Fifth Army.[40]

On the front of Fifth Army the initiative was decidedly on the German side. On the morning of 20 June, after an extensive artillery and *Minenwerfer* preparation, units on the left flank of XVIII Reserve Corps (9th Landwehr Division) and the right flank of XVI Corps (27th Württemberg Infantry Division) mounted an assault on the Argonne's western edge, capturing a section of enemy trenches with the aid of flame-throwers. After three days' fighting (which began on 30 June), XVI Corps (commanded by General von Mudra), took French 42nd Infantry Division's well developed positions north of La Harazée. After intensive preparations, on 13 July, 33rd Infantry Division launched a powerful assault and seized the strongly fortified heights west of Boureuilles, which had been occupied by elements of French V Corps. At the same time, 34th Infantry Division launched a secondary operation north of Le Four de Paris, capturing additional sections of the enemy's trenches. Since 20 June, 6,663 prisoners of war and 117 machine guns and trench mortars had been captured. All French counterattacks were repulsed.

As in the hotly contested areas of the Argonne Forest, lively fighting continued in the St. Mihiel salient. On the afternoon of 20 June, following intense artillery preparations, elements of French II and VI Corps attacked V Corps on Armee-Abteilung *Strantz's*[41] northern flank on both sides of the Grande Tranchée de Calonne. Although 9th Infantry Division repulsed four repeated attacks, the enemy's fifth attack succeeded, breaking through to the second line east of the main road. In fighting that surged back and forth over the following days—even spreading into 10th Infantry Division's sector—the reinforced V Corps mainly held its ground. In an effort to take the pressure off those units fighting on the Tranchée, the Headquarters staff decided to seize the commanding hill southwest of Les Eparges. On 26 June a regiment of 10th Infantry Division took most of the Bergnase,[42] thereby gaining excellent observation positions over the French positions on the Combres Heights. Strong enemy counterattacks, especially on 3 and 6 July, were repulsed in a tenacious and bloody defence. Heavy fighting persisted in the centre of the army front, especially south of St. Mihiel. After repelling French

---

40 On 8 May, Fifth Army was deployed as follows from west to east: XVIII Reserve Corps, XVI Corps (reinforced by 27th Infantry Division), VI Reserve Corps (reinforced by 2nd Landwehr Division), and V Reserve Corps.

41 On 8 May, Armee-Abteilung *Strantz* was deployed as follows from north to south: 5th Landwehr Division, V Corps (reinforced by 111th and 113th Infantry Divisions and 33rd Reserve Division), and Bavarian III Corps (reinforced by 80th Infantry Brigade and Bavarian Ersatz Division); and from west to east Guard Ersatz Division, 10th Ersatz Division, 8th Ersatz Division, and 121st Division. VIII Corps (minus 80th Infantry Brigade) was deployed to the rear.

42 *Les Éparges Hill; translated as 'mountain in the shape of a nose.'*

forays on 8 May and 19 June, on 7 July, Bavarian III Corps (commanded by General Baron von Gebsattel) mounted a counterattack that breached the enemy line west of Apremont along a wide front. French attempts to regain their former trenches lasted until 12 July, but ultimately ended in failure and heavy casualties. On the southern part of the front, 121st Infantry Division had to defend itself against numerous enemy attacks in the Bois le Prêtre; in the second half of May and on 8 June, the French succeeded in establishing themselves in the western part of the woods. Then, on 4 July, the reinforced 121st Infantry Division, commanded by Generalleutnant Wagner, mounted a counterattack. The enemy was pushed back on a 1,500 metre front, and 1,000 prisoners of war were captured as well as several trench mortars and three artillery pieces. Vigorous French counterattacks were again repulsed.

In Armee-Abteilung *Falkenhausen*'s sector,[43] the fighting rose in intensity during the second half of June. On 21 and 22 June the enemy managed to take a section of the German advance positions at Gondrexon in the sector of Bavarian 1st Landwehr and 19th Ersatz Divisions. On 22 June, XV Reserve Corps' 30th Reserve Division took the hill at Ban-de-Sapt but lost it as a result of overpowering enemy counterattacks on 8 and 24 July.

In Alsace the French had been attacking since April up the Fecht Valley in Armee-Abteilung *Gaede*'s sector.[44] Following intense artillery bombardments, on 5 and 7 May the enemy's 47th and 66th Infantry Divisions attacked the hilly positions west of Metzeral. The enemy initially broke through under the cover of smoke, but was repelled in bloody hand-to-hand fighting by infantry of Bavarian 8th Reserve Division.[45] On 14 June, 19th Reserve Division, which had taken over Bavarian 8th Reserve Division's positions,[46] was violently attacked. Despite determined resistance, the heights west of Metzeral and at Sondernach—as well as the

---

43 On 8 May, Armee-Abteilung *Falkenhausen* was deployed as follows from north to south: 61st Reserve Brigade, Bavarian 1st Landwehr Division (reinforced by 60th Landwehr Brigade), 19th Ersatz Division (reinforced by Bavarian 5th Landwehr Brigade), and XV Reserve Corps (reinforced by 84th Landwehr Division and 52nd Landwehr Brigade). Seventh Cavalry Division was deployed behind the front at Saarburg; X Reserve Corps was deployed near Strasbourg.

44 On 8 May, Armee-Abteilung *Gaede* was deployed as follows from north to south: Bavarian 6th Landwehr Division, Bavarian 8th Reserve Division, 12th Landwehr Division, 7th Landwehr Division, and 8th Landwehr Division.

45 As the situation developed, on 2 June, 187th Infantry Brigade was moved into the *OHL*'s reserve from Laon into the area of Schlettstadt. Between 17 and 20 June, two regiments of this brigade were temporarily put at the disposal of Sixth Army.

46 Bavarian 8th Reserve Division had temporarily been placed at the disposal of the *OHL* and on 2 June had been transported to the east. On 12 June, X Reserve Corps Headquarters was moved from the Straßburg area to southern Hungary. See *DW* VIII: 199, 242.

summit of the Hilsenfirst—were lost. Over the following days, the village of Metzeral also fell into enemy hands. On the night of 22 June the west bank of the
Fecht was evacuated without interference from the enemy. A new line of defence
was established extending from Mühlbach across the heights east of Metzeral to
the Hilsenfirst. At this line the French advance was stopped. The 19th Reserve
Division and the units attached to it[47] lost 111 officers and 3,565 enlisted men. The
enemy suffered even greater losses—according to French figures, in excess of 6,000
men, with 580 prisoners taken.

On 20 July the enemy resumed its attacks in Upper Alsace, this time farther
north and in the direction of Munster. After an hour-long artillery barrage, French
129th and 47th Infantry Divisions attacked Bavarian 4th Landwehr Division's sector on the Barrenkopf as well as Bavarian 8th Reserve Division's positions[48] on the
Reichsackerkopf. The heights were held throughout heavy fighting that lasted
until 22 July. Despite valiant resistance, the dominating position of Lingekopf, 5
kilometres north of Munster, fell into enemy hands on 27 July. The situation
threatened to take a serious turn, but then the Bavarians (reinforced by elements
of 19th Reserve Division and 187th Infantry Brigade) mounted strong counterattacks and managed to largely push back the enemy's gains on the Barrenkopf and
to the north.

On 31 July, French Seventh Army decided to abandon its attack in the Vosges.
Only French 129th Infantry Division continued to try to seize the German positions on the Barrenkopf.

The Renewal of the Major Offensive in the Artois: Operations from 16–18 June to the End of the Spring Offensive

After failing to break through in the Artois in May 1915, the French Supreme Command could not have doubted that given the precarious situation of their Russian allies, the offensive would have to be resumed as soon as possible. Moreover,
the Entente enjoyed clear numerical superiority. On 12 June the French General
Staff estimated the total strength of the German Western Armies to be 1,128 battalions, facing 1,764 Franco-British-Belgian battalions. This estimate closely approx-
imated the actual figures.

The French Supreme Command could count on the co-operation of British
forces for the continuation of the offensive. In responding to related queries, Field

---

47   Principally units deployed from 187th Infantry Brigade.
48   In the early days of July, Bavarian 8th Reserve Division had returned to Upper Alsace from
     the east.

The Spring Battle in Artois
The Situation on 16 June

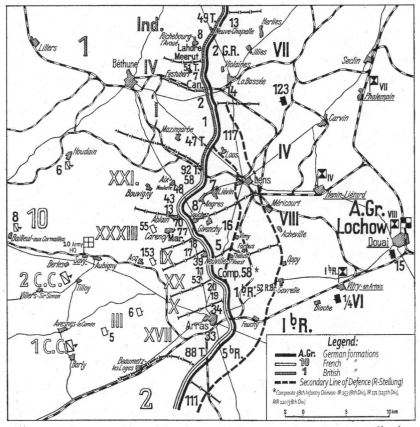

Sketch 17

Marshal Sir John French initially agreed to attack simultaneously with three divisions north of La Bassée Canal and possibly farther south with two more divisions, while at Ypres a raid was to be executed using one division. The serious shortage of heavy artillery ammunition, however, soon forced him to limit what had originally been planned as a broad-based attack to an assault by one corps (IV Corps). On French Army's front, secondary combat operations were to be conducted in the areas of Second, Sixth, and Seventh Armies, in conjunction with the main offensive, which was again to be executed by Tenth Army. Diversionary raids and increased artillery activity were planned in the areas of Fifth and Fourth Armies as well as in the area of XXXVI Corps. The Belgians had likewise committed to increased activities in their sector.

Based on his experiences in previous battles, Joffre paid particular attention to simplifying the command structure along the entire front and to reinforcing Tenth Army. On 13 June provisional Army Groups *North* and *East* (which had by then been created) were given permanent status and a new Army Group *Centre* (commanded by General de Curières de Castelnau) was formed. From that point, army group commanders were to independently execute the operations ordered by the Supreme Commander, assign sectors and forces to the armies under their control, and form their own army group reserves. Additionally, Foch was tasked with closely liaising with the British and Belgians to ensure uniform allied operations. By the middle of June, Tenth Army had been considerably reinforced in anticipation of the new offensive, which brought it to a total of twenty-three infantry and three cavalry divisions compared to the eighteen infantry and three cavalry divisions it had at the beginning of the first Artois offensive. First Colonial Corps, which was scheduled to arrive at Doullens beginning on 15 June, as well as five cavalry divisions, were added to Foch's army group reserve. The High Command also had at its disposal 152nd Infantry Division (stationed to the rear of XXXVI Corps southwest of Hondschoote), 51st Infantry Division (deployed to the rear of Second Army's northern flank southeast of Doullens), and XII Corps, which as of 16 June was located at Amiens.

Previous battle experience was to be taken into consideration when executing these new combat operations. This time the Supreme Commander placed special emphasis on the positioning of reserves close behind the front line, on the simultaneous advance of the assaulting units, on the complete silencing of German machine-gun nests, and on the thorough destruction of obstacles prior to the infantry's advance. The new offensive was supposed to be launched on 31 May. However, the absolute necessity to reorganize some units and to prepare the ground properly forced repeated postponements. Joffre insisted that the attack not begin until all preparations had been completed; as a consequence, the assault was delayed until 16 June. The French leaders specified that the objective of this attack was to break through the German lines. According to the Supreme Commander's secret directive to Foch, Tenth Army's assault was to commence on 14 June at 10:40 and was to proceed with a maximum effort, employing all measures to ensure that decisive successes were achieved and exploited. However, should the desired results remain unachieved after a few days, the attack was to be discontinued immediately so as to allow for its resumption on a broader basis at a later date.

On the German side of Sixth Army's front, General der Infanterie Sixt's IV Corps assumed command of XIV Corps' sector on 14 June. Relative quiet prevailed north of the Béthune–Lens road; thus 117th Infantry Division was moved to this sector after it had been deployed on the Lorette Spur for many weeks. Farther south, however, trenches in the sectors of 7th and 8th Infantry Divisions remained embattled, especially at Liévin and Angres, where many of the positions were in a barely defendable condition. During the short, bright nights, frequent enemy harassment fire—aided by spotlights—made it extremely difficult to repair these trenches, and the work resulted in heavy casualties. South of the Aix–Noulette–Souchez road, the so-called "Muddy Hollow Position" was not seriously affected by enemy fire. Because of the incessant enemy attacks, however, this valley had become a field of corpses, and owing to the constant fighting it had been impossible to bury the fallen. The permeating odour of putrefaction made eating difficult; indeed, it bothered the defenders more than enemy fire. Despite repeated attempts, the infantry was unable to close a 300 metre gap to the switch trench, which ran in a passable condition toward the much contested sugar factory and from there—in barely defensible condition—along the road running from the sugar factory to Souchez. On the marshy chateau grounds, two damaged trenches had been laboriously repaired using sandbags; the village of Souchez itself had been heavily fortified. Because there had been no major attacks since the week following Pentecost, in VIII Corps' sector 16th Infantry Division's trenches had been repaired between Souchez and Hill 123; on the other hand, the trenches of the newly deployed 5th Infantry Division were in a deplorable state. On the front of Bavarian I Reserve Corps, the composite 58th Infantry Division had defended the Labyrinth with unwavering courage despite considerable casualties. Neighbouring to the south, Bavarian 1st Reserve Division and the completely exhausted 52nd Reserve Infantry Brigade had been deployed without relief since the beginning of the spring offensives. Despite severe damage to the trenches, all French attacks had been repelled there as well.

As before, the artillery was still arranged in divisional groups, and their co-operation was frequently evaluated and improved. A number of batteries south of the Scarpe had been combined in order to keep the French artillery deployed north of the Scarpe under flanking fire.

In accordance with Lochow's orders, a second line was created extending from Loos to Lens to Vimy and Thélus, and a third was planned from east of Lens to Oppy and Feuchy. The latter was located so far to the rear that, in the event of an enemy attack, the heights at Vimy would become useless for artillery support.

Since 12 June, indications had been clear that major new attacks were looming. On 14 June at noon, enemy reconnaissance platoons advanced along the entire front from Angres to Neuville-St. Vaast, but German defensive fire kept them from reaching their objectives. The French artillery barrage raged with steadily growing intensity. In Souchez, Givenchy, Thélus, and Farbus the largest-calibre shells were used; these even broke through concrete shelters and basements. A large number of command posts and staging areas for the reserves were in this way put out of action.

When day broke clear and sunny on 16 June, the wire and trenches in the German front lines had been severely damaged. The infantry had already suffered severe casualties from the furious enemy artillery barrage, and at noon infantry attacks were mounted in depth along the entire front between Liévin and the Scarpe. Since the German artillery had also been severely affected, the defensive barrage was ineffective. The presence of French observation aircraft, coupled with the lack of German combat aircraft, was especially debilitating. Wave after wave of infantry surged against the German front. Supported by reserves, these continuous enemy attacks eventually succeeded in breaching the German lines at several locations. At the end of the day, the situation was as follows. At Liévin and Angres, French XXI Corps was established in the trenches formerly held by 7th Infantry Division. Communication with the Muddy Hollow was severed. On the Lorette Spur, 8th Infantry Division had to abandon the switch trench. The enemy had also taken a newly excavated trench about 300 metres to the rear. The attack by French XXXIII Corps had penetrated the edge of the village of Souchez, where bitter fighting raged in the streets. In the sector of 16th Infantry Division, besides a number of lesser penetrations, south of Souchez the Moroccan Division had broken through to a rearward line on a front of more than 1 kilometre and had there established itself. The Moroccans' combat patrols had also reached the German batteries, and additional defensive lines were unavailable. French IX Corps had vigorously attacked 5th Infantry Division (from Brandenburg, commanded by Generalmajor von Gabain); several of the French companies lost almost three-quarters of their strength, at which point the attacks collapsed. Elements of French XX, X, and XVII Corps had broken through in the sector of the composite 58th Infantry Division and into the Labyrinth as well as in numerous locations farther south along the front of Bavarian 1st Reserve Division; hand-to-hand fighting raged everywhere. The situation was becoming extremely precarious.

In a heroic and unswerving defence, the German front held. That night, elements of Armee-Gruppe *Lochow* mounted a successful counterattack. The 7th Infantry Division, commanded by Generalleutnant Riedel, cleared the trenches west of Liévin and Angres; however, attempts to retake the positions southwest of Angres were unsuccessful. The regiment deployed in the Muddy Hollow also repelled all attacks, while the forces of 8th Infantry Division, commanded by Generalmajor Baron von Hanstein, cleared the enemy from the second Lorette switch

line. The 16th Infantry Division only managed to clear the less significant sections of the line penetrated by the Moroccans, and this enemy unit continued to
hold the wedge south of Souchez. Owing to the intense French fire, attempts to
dig a switch line were only partially successful. To prevent a deeper enemy advance,
heavy German batteries targeted the breakthrough location in a continuous barrage (*Dauerfeuer*), which prevented further French attacks; only the churchyard
at Souchez fell into enemy hands. By daybreak the Labyrinth and Bavarian 1st
Reserve Division's trenches had been cleared of the enemy. This hand-to-hand
fighting resulted in the capture of about 700 French prisoners of war.

The enemy's breakthrough attempts, which had been executed with maximum force and without regard for heavy losses, again failed before the heroic
German front-line forces and their tenacious resistance.

Nevertheless, Sixth Army's situation remained grave. Based on the army's staff
report regarding these massive enemy attacks, the *OHL* placed VI Corps (which
was arriving from Third Army) at its disposal. The first elements of 22nd Infantry
Brigade were standing at the ready at the railway stations of Vitry and Biache and
were placed at the disposal of Armee-Gruppe *Lochow*. On 16 June these elements
were offered to VIII Corps in case 16th Infantry Division was unable to hold its
position. For the time being, however, the commanding general, Riemann, did
not consider this assistance to be necessary.

On the same day that the heavy French attacks were launched (16 June), a
message from Falkenhayn regarding the seriousness of the situation was transmitted to all armies on the Western Front:

> According to reliable information, the French and the British are going to con-
> tinue their offensive at Arras while attacking our front at other locations.
> [At Arras] we must expect serious breakthrough attempts as well as diversion-
> ary operations in other locations with the objective of diverting our forces.
> His Majesty expects the armies to frustrate the breakthrough attempts and
> to hold their positions with their typical heroism and tenacity. In general, the
> armies cannot count on receiving reinforcements from the *OHL*'s weak GHQ
> Reserve. These must be saved for extreme emergencies. I would appreciate
> consideration of this circumstance when filing requests with the *OHL*. Addi-
> tionally, the general situation urgently demands that all armies return the
> reserves which the *OHL* provided to them. If forces were transferred from the
> East in order to reinforce the Western Army, the positive progress of the
> offensive there would be inhibited. Thus, each soldier on the Western Front
> must be made aware that through his tenacious resistance, he is playing a
> crucial role in the victories in the East and that without his help these vic-
> tories could not be achieved.

On 17 June the French renewed their attacks against Armee-Gruppe *Lochow*. This time they managed to penetrate 5th Infantry Division's cratered trenches. There, as well as against 7th Infantry Division and Bavarian I Reserve Corps, the enemy was thrown back after meeting with initial success. In 8th Infantry Division's sector, French XXI Corps was able to advance along the Aix–Noulette–Souchez road and with that it became impossible to hold the Muddy Hollow any longer. It was thus evacuated during the night.

The strength of the defenders was sapped by the battle, which had raged almost uninterrupted. According to a report filed by Bavarian I Reserve Corps Headquarters, the combined 58th Infantry Division was no longer capable of fighting. However, Lochow considered the withdrawal of 16th Infantry Division to be even more urgent, and he consequently ordered its relief by 11th Infantry Division of VI Corps.

Considering the situation, the *OHL* also attempted to provide Sixth Army with additional forces. In response to a request from Lochow, on 17 June the *OHL* assigned 15th Infantry Division—which had been relieved only a few days earlier—"just in case" and authorized Sixth Army Headquarters to make use of 123rd Infantry Division "in the event of an extreme emergency." Expediting the transportation of VI Corps' 12th Infantry Division turned out to be impossible because its last units would not arrive at Sixth Army before the evening of 19 June. So on 17 June the staff of Fifth Army and Armee-Abteilung *Falkenhausen* agreed to immediately move 187th Infantry Brigade[49] and Armee-Abteilung *Strantz*'s 5th Ersatz Brigade to Sixth Army. As directed by the *OHL*, Fourth Army also made 53rd Reserve Division available, thus freeing up Bavarian 3rd Infantry Division on Sixth Army's northern flank, which in turn relieved 58th Infantry Division.[50] In addition to these forces, thirteen heavy batteries were transferred; they were to arrive at Sixth Army beginning on 19 June.

Since General der Infanterie von Pritzelwitz, commanding VI Corps, had more seniority than Lochow, on the evening of 17 June the *OHL* ordered that Armee-Gruppe *Lochow* be deactivated after VI Corps was deployed. However, Sixth Army Headquarters insisted that the reinforcements it had requested be deployed and that the planned reliefs be completed before this happened. For this reason, VI Corps was not yet deployed, but remained at the disposal of Sixth Army Headquarters.

At this point, Lochow began to restructure his forces according to the following plan: IV Corps Headquarters was to continue to command the northern sector, with 117th Infantry Division and 123rd (Saxon) Infantry Division deployed

---

49 Minus one infantry regiment, which remained with Army Detachment *Gaede*.
50 58th Infantry Division was then transferred to Fourth Army.

on the right flank; the southern portion of the sector was to be held by 7th and 8th Infantry Divisions, with the corps' reserve consisting of 3rd Ersatz Brigade.

In the centre, 11th and 5th Infantry Divisions initially remained assigned to VIII Corps Headquarters, which was familiar with the area. Since future fighting would require the consolidation of IV Corps (which had already been considerably weakened), the plan was to insert 12th Infantry Division north of the 11th so as to allow for the quick deployment of VI Corps. The III Corps' 6th Infantry Division (which was expected to arrive soon) was to be held in army reserve at Douai. In the southern sector, General der Infanterie von Fasbender commanded three Bavarian infantry divisions outside the gates of Arras (3rd, 1st, and 5th Reserve). The VIII Corps' 15th and 16th Infantry Divisions were to be withdrawn into the area of Douai and transferred to First Army.

On 18 June the enemy attacks weakened, leading the *OHL* to believe that pressure in the Artois was winding down and that for the time being the enemy's offensive strength had been broken. To make the reserves as strong as possible for the events that lay ahead, on 21 June the Chief of the General Staff of the Field Army directed Sixth Army Headquarters to pull forces out of the front:

> Since Sixth Army's tenacious resistance has broken the month-long attempts of the French and British to break through, it cannot be ruled out that the army's front may soon become quiet and that the enemy will shift his forces in order to attack elsewhere. Reinforcing Sixth Army stripped the rest of the Western Front of all its reserves. The *OHL* must be able to deploy new reserves to meet any eventuality. This can only be accomplished by withdrawing elements from Sixth Army in order to replace them with rested units from other armies. In preparation I therefore request ... that at least two infantry divisions—aside from VIII Corps and the 123rd Infantry Division—be withdrawn from the front and assembled in the rear at suitable railheads as soon as the situation permits. The wartime establishment of these units is to be restored. Concurrently, I am initiating the withdrawal of strong (draft-horse) units from the GHQ Artillery Reserve.

On the same day, Falkenhayn ordered 187th Infantry Brigade from Sixth Army to return to Armee-Abteilung *Falkenhausen* because the fighting in Alsace had made the relief of Armee-Abteilung *Gaede*'s 19th Reserve Infantry Division an urgent necessity.

Crown Prince Rupprecht and Lochow, however, did not concur with the *OHL*'s supposition that the combat situation in the Artois was easing. On 22 June, Lochow submitted an assessment of the situation, stressing his opinion that the enemy's attacks were not over at all and could be expected to resume with renewed vigour. He added that if the *OHL* were unable to make fresh units available continuously, then given the heavy wastage of forces, the possibility must be considered of occupying a newly constructed line to the rear. On 24 June his staff relayed this report to the OHL with a note stating: "There are no indications that the French offensives are at an end and there can be no other decision but to hold the present position, but to this effect additional relief forces and artillery are required."

In this disagreement between the OHL and the local commanders, Falkenhayn's opinion proved to be correct. On Sixth Army's front, major enemy attacks did not recur.

ON 18 JUNE, AFTER CONSIDERING THE MINIMAL RESULTS THAT HAD BEEN attained in the most recent attacks, Foch decided to discontinue the Artois offensive for the time being. He made his decision in consultation with the corps commanders and with the agreement of Tenth Army's Commander-in-Chief, General d'Urbal. Foch then ordered Tenth Army to hold and expand the conquered positions and reported to Joffre that the corps involved in the battle urgently required a few days of rest. Following that, the three northern corps (XXI, XXXIII, and IX) were systematically to advance on Souchez and Hill 140 to the southeast of the town with the aim of securing that sector of the front as a jumping-off point for a new offensive. Once this had been accomplished the three southern corps (XX, X, XVII) would resume their attacks. In this way, Tenth Army could still be expected to reach its initial objectives.

French losses were extraordinarily high: since 9 May they had amounted to roughly 100,000. British losses totalled 32,000. German losses came to 1,560 officers and 71,512 enlisted men.

Until the end of June, German Sixth Army continued efforts to clear its positions of intruding enemy forces. However, IV Corps' attempts to remove the French emplacements on both sides of the Aix–Noulette–Souchez road were unsuccessful. The troops of 8th Infantry Division had already suffered too much as a result of the previous battles on the Lorette Spur. Starting on 19 June the French concentrated their artillery fire against the positions between Angres and Souchez. In order to increase the strength of this threatened sector, Lochow now decided to insert 12th Infantry Division (commanded by Generalleutnant Chales de Beaulieu) into the front at Souchez. On 25 June another strong assault was mounted there, but after initial success, the French were everywhere repulsed by the Silesian regiments. The enemy attempted another attack north of Souchez, but that one failed as well in the late evening of 27 June. Since 18 June, 11th Infantry Division (commanded by Generalleutnant von Webern) had taken over the sector of 16th Infantry Division. After costly fighting in the trenches, on 16 June the French troops that had penetrated the position south of Souchez were repulsed.

The Labyrinth remained embattled until 24 June, when the fighting abated there as well. This enabled Bavarian 3rd Infantry Division (commanded by Generalleutnant Ritter von Wenninger) to retake all of the trenches and to restore them to a reasonably sound defensive condition. With the *OHL*'s consent, the hopelessly exhausted 52nd Reserve Infantry Brigade was exchanged with Second Army's 185th Infantry Brigade on 25 June; it was then deployed at the front to the north alongside Bavarian 3rd Infantry Division. In this manner, well structured and organized command structures were established. On 28 June all necessary preparations for the formation of VI Corps Headquarters were finalized. Pritzelwitz assumed command the following day; at the same time, Armee-Gruppe *Lochow* was disbanded.

Even though the prevailing impression at the *OHL* was that the battles in the Artois were subsiding, the area north of Arras still had to be considered the most important combat area on the Western Front. For the moment, Falkenhayn believed that the possibility of French attacks simultaneously employing strong British forces was serious enough to warrant the return of elements of the Eastern Army to the French Theatre. On 26 June he advised Sixth Army Headquarters that XXXXI Reserve Corps and 56th Infantry Division would be staged to the rear of the army's front line. Bavarian 8th Reserve Division, which had only recently been transferred to the Eastern Theatre, was to be returned to the Imperial Lands.[51] Sixth Army Headquarters believed that this action would imperil the progress achieved in the offensive in Galicia. It advised the *OHL* that even in the event of renewed enemy attacks—which until then agents had reported as being imminent—the army would be able to hold its positions without reinforcements from the East. So Falkenhayn amended his orders on 27 June, leaving XXXXI Corps on the Eastern Front. Only 56th Infantry and Bavarian 8th Reserve Divisions were returned to the West.

In July, only local raids were reported against elements of IV and VI Corps. These attacks focused on Souchez and mainly affected the forces of VI Corps.

Reflections on the Spring Offensive in the Artois

The enemy attacks in the Artois that had begun in early May had stopped by the end of June. The objective of these attacks had been to break through the German front, and the conditions for this major Franco-British offensive had by no means been unfavourable. Sixth Army received no reinforcements before 9 May; only

---

51 *Alsace and Lorraine.*

The Spring Battle in Artois

The Composition of Armee-Gruppe Lochow
at its Dissolution on 29 June 1915

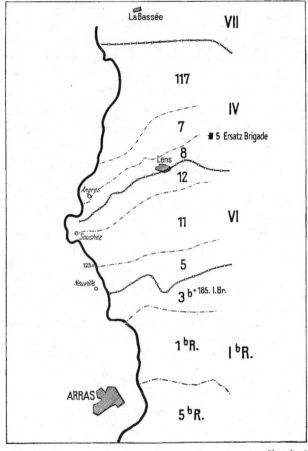

Sketch 18

two of the seven and a half GHQ Reserve divisions were staged in its sector at the beginning of the spring battles. The German salient north of Arras, as well as the excellent observation conditions, invited a comprehensive enemy attack from both sides. The arrival of British reinforcements had freed up French divisions for the attack, which further facilitated secondary British assaults. Both the terrain and the rail lines favoured the inconspicuous staging of major enemy forces.

However, the Entente powers were unable to bring their considerable superiority in infantry numbers entirely to bear during the first and second attacks in the Artois. Between 9 May and 18 June, twenty German infantry divisions[52] deployed at the front had faced and halted thirty-three infantry divisions of British First Army and French Tenth Army.[53] The enemy's forces were in no position to conduct a simultaneous offensive in the Champagne, as had been planned at the beginning of the winter offensives; had this been mounted in the middle of June, in all probability it would have placed the German Western Army in an extremely precarious position. Despite incredible sacrifices, the enemy armies fighting in France and Belgium had not been able to provide any tangible relief to the hard-pressed Russians.

These meagre results were all the more surprising given that the Entente commanded a militarily valuable numerical superiority of roughly 600 battalions over the German Army. The explanation for this failure can be found in two factors. First, the enemy High Command was uncompromising in its refusal to weaken its secondary fronts in favour of the main offensive front. Also, despite all the experience gained during the winter offensive in the Champagne, the French leadership apparently still had no clear perception of the incredible difficulties inherent in mounting a breakthrough attempt on the Western Front. By March the Germans had made strategic calculations as to the requirements for forces and materiel and had arrived at higher numbers than those available to the French Tenth Army in the spring of 1915. A comparison of Foch's plan of attack for French Tenth Army to the breakthrough proposals presented to Falkenhayn by several German Chiefs of Staff (especially those of Generals von Kuhl and von Krafft and Oberst von Seeckt) demonstrates that Falkenhayn received far better advice than Foch. The amounts of personnel and materiel that the German commanders considered necessary for a war-deciding operation far exceeded those that Foch requested and, it follows, those that Joffre supplied to Tenth Army.

---

52 Bavarian 6th Reserve Division; 13th, 14th, 29th, and 28th Infantry Divisions; 1st and Bavarian 5th Reserve Divisions; parts of Bavarian II and XIX Corps; 58th, 115th, 117th, 15th, and 16th Infantry Divisions; 52nd and 85th Reserve Infantry Brigades; 38th Landwehr Infantry Brigade; 2nd Guard Reserve Division; 5th, 123rd, 11th, 7th, and 8th Infantry Divisions.

53 Of the British First Army: 49th Territorial Division; 8th and 7th Infantry Divisions; the Lahore and Meerut Divisions; 1st Infantry Division; 47th Territorial Division; 2nd Infantry Division; 51st Territorial Infantry Division; and the Canadian Division. Of the French Tenth Army: 58th and 17th Infantry Divisions; 92nd Territorial Division; 43rd, 13th, 70th, and 77th Infantry Divisions; the Moroccan Division; 84th Territorial Division; 39th, 11th, 33rd, 34th, 19th, and 20th Infantry Divisions; 88th Territorial Division; 18th, 53rd, 5th, 6th, 55th, 48th, and 153rd Infantry Divisions.

The French leadership attributed the failure of the attacks mainly to the effectiveness of German artillery and to the machine guns that often remained in operation up to the time of the assault. Based on these battles, the French gained the impression that in trench warfare, a breakthrough was feasible only at the very beginning of an offensive. It had to be expected that with every day that an attack continued, the strength of the enemy's resistance would only increase. French Tenth Army's extraordinarily severe losses,[54] and its immense expenditure of artillery ammunition,[55] combined with the fact that a similar consumption of force had taken place with the British, had forced the temporary cessation of the attacks.

Despite all this, the French and British High Commands continued to believe it possible to achieve a breakthrough along the Western Front. They were aware, however, that the Germans were improving their defensive system and that they held superiority in machine guns and especially in heavy artillery. It followed that a breakthrough would depend on meticulous preparation and the commitment of considerably larger numbers of attacking forces and materiel. Joffre had already considered all of this in the middle of June prior to the opening of the second offensive in the event that it became necessary to abort an unsuccessful battle.

The brunt of the successful defence was borne by the infantry of the German front-line divisions, who, despite being reduced by enemy fire, managed again and again through unwavering and incredible valour to halt the attacks of an enemy that was vastly superior in numbers. In the course of the ongoing offensive, the energetic and thoughtful German leadership averted the danger of a breakthrough by restoring the balance of forces through the quick introduction of reinforcements brought up from elsewhere on the Western Front.

German artillery, especially heavy artillery, played an important role in defending against these enemy attacks. The existing peacetime equipment of the German forces—and in some instances the fortresses—in terms of modern materiel, coupled with the availability of serviceable supplies of older equipment and appropriate ammunition, meant that it was possible to supply the Artois Front with sufficient heavy artillery throughout the defensive battles.

At the beginning of the offensive the artillery ratio had been roughly one German gun for every two enemy guns; by the end of May it had been possible to improve this ratio to roughly two to three. By then, with regard to 10 cm and

---

54 French losses for the period 9 May to 18 June amounted to 102,500 men.
55 The overall consumption of artillery ammunition for the French Tenth Army alone between 3 May and 18 June amounted to 1,813,490 field artillery shells and 342,372 heavy artillery shells. In about the same time span around 1,903,000 shells for the field and 272,000 for the heavy artillery were supplied to the battlefront of German Sixth Army.

higher calibre guns, it seemed that the Germans had achieved superiority, especially in terms of the quality of materiel (i.e., rapid-fire guns). The supply of ammunition proved to be sufficient, and in the course of the battles the German heavy artillery's improvement with respect to tactical and technical firing (*Schiesstechnisch*) had again proven its considerable combat effectiveness.

Also, the rail system supported the defence to great effect. The Chief of the Field Railway System implemented improvements to the rail network in the winter of 1914–15 with a view to equalizing the inferiority in numbers in the Western Theatre by improving operational mobility. This would facilitate the quick reinforcement of units on threatened fronts. Improvements to the most important transportation lines increased efficiency, while the ever tighter organization of operations and an increase in running speeds led to substantial improvements in the efficient movement of troops as well as their punctuality. The reliable management of troop transports increased the High Command's confidence in the railways' performance; accordingly, at times it was able to largely strip the Western Front of reserves for the benefit of the Eastern Front.

The German Western Forces could take pride in the successes they had achieved, successes that had been made possible by their tenacious defence. Without their sacrifices, the great victories in the Eastern Theatre would never have been possible. Indirectly, these brave fighters, especially those in the Artois, played an outstanding part in the glorious victories in the East.

The Reorganization of the Western Army at the Beginning of August

Given that it was necessary to continue the offensive in the East, the German Western Army had to remain in a strategically defensive posture full of privations for an extended period. Thus the strength and defensive capability of the trench system required special attention. On 3 July the *OHL* informed Army Headquarters in the West that the Supreme Warlord had designated General der Infanterie von Claer, formerly Commanding General of VII Corps,[56] as the general responsible for the Engineer and Pioneer Corps at GHQ. He was tasked with carrying out on-the-spot inspections and with making the arrangements necessary with each Army Headquarters "in order to ensure that the positions on the Western Front were uniformly upgraded, and to encourage the practical application of the most recent experiences in this area." Claer would later

---

56 Replacing General von Claer at the head of VII Corps was General von François, who had been commanding general of XXXXI Reserve Corps.

report his impressions to the Supreme Warlord. General der Artillerie von Lauter, commanding the foot artillery at GHQ, was directed to amend the existing regulations for the utilization of artillery in trench warfare and to evaluate its effect on the fighting units.

Besides upgrading the entire trench system, the Germans immediately began reorganizing the units of their Western Army, which had been torn apart during the defensive battles. Once the battles in the Artois had ended, the *OHL* returned the units that had been brought up as reinforcements from various sectors of the front to their original armies. The Guard Cavalry Division, which had been staged to the rear of Fourth Army in the General Government of Belgium, departed for the Eastern Theatre on 6 July, leaving only 7th Cavalry Division in the West.

At the same time, Falkenhayn began to place a number of larger combat-ready units at his disposal to the rear of the Western Front. The execution of these orders continued into the beginning of August.

These changes served to consolidate and reorganize the German Western Army. In mid-July it became noticeably apparent that the military situation was relaxing. Up until 15 July the *OHL*'s Intelligence Department had received only isolated indications that the French forces deployed in front of Sixth Army in the area of Arras were weakening. At this time it was assumed that the French intended to mount a major new offensive north of Arras—or between Arras and Albert—and that the units that had been decimated during the battles in the Artois had been replenished and were again operational. From 15 July until the end of the month, however, numerous reports arrived from the front—especially from Second and First Armies—pointing to enemy movements to the south across the Somme. Based on the results of both aerial reconnaissance[57] and agent reports,[58] Crown Prince Rupprecht became convinced that the enemy had extracted major forces from the combat area in the Artois. On 24 July he expressed his opinion about this to the *OHL*: "the battle at La Bassée and Arras" was over for the time being. Two days later, Falkenhayn replied:

> The observations of the army combined with reports received here, confirm the *OHL*'s opinion that the renewal of the offensive against Sixth Army's left flank is not expected for the time being. Trench system development should now be completed to the point that the army ought to be able to put appreciable forces at the disposal of the *OHL*. The probability

---

57 After the deployment of German combat aircraft the enemy's air superiority was no longer so noticeable.

58 In particular, the message that French XX Corps was detraining behind the front in Nancy.

of an enemy offensive in another location increases. Preparations for this eventuality must, therefore, be made. Therefore I ask that in the near future you consider extracting III Corps, less the 185th Infantry Brigade.[59]

Because the battles in the Artois had ceased, Falkenhayn did not hesitate to take advantage of the changed situation by relieving units and staging stronger forces in GHQ Reserve. Except for 185th Infantry Brigade, the following units were to be made available to the *OHL:* Sixth Army's 123rd Infantry Division, with a number of horse-drawn heavy field howitzer or mortar batteries, as well as 183rd Infantry Brigade. The 54th and 58th Infantry Divisions, as well as 1st Minenwerfer Battalion, were transferred to the Eastern Theatre beginning on 20 July.

Falkenhayn called the Chiefs of Staff of the Western Armies to Metz for a conference on 29 July.[60] He opened the meeting with a warm expression of appreciation for the Western Army and expressed gratitude in the name of the Supreme Warlord: "The achievements of the Western Army in these difficult times stand with dignity alongside those of the Eastern Army; a justly written history of the war will one day elevate and acknowledge these achievements as even being superior."[61] Reviewing the situation in the Eastern Theatre, he referred to the tenacity of the Russians, who, by exploiting natural obstacles and their almost inexhaustible manpower, had precluded an assessment regarding the conclusion of operations. No new offensive by the Eastern Army was being planned that would occupy its forces into the winter; even so, the Western Army would have to remain on the defensive for an extended period. The "Iron Wall in the West" against whose defences all enemy attacks had been smashed would have to continue to stand firm.

At that time, nothing was known about the Entente's intentions. The British seemed to want to deploy strong forces and a large amount of ammunition to the Dardanelles;[62] the French offensive force near Arras had been disbanded. At this point it was not clear whether new units had replaced the worn-out corps or whether a new enemy breakthrough attempt was to be undertaken at another place along the Western Front. Nor were there indications that the enemy was

59 On 26 May, 185th Infantry Brigade (of three regiments) was placed at the disposal of Second Army Headquarters. At the end of June the *OHL* explained that two regiments of the brigade had been supplied in lieu of the return of the composite 52nd Reserve Infantry Brigade of Sixth Army.
60 Also present at this meeting were Quartermaster General Freytag-Loringhoven, Intendant General von Schöler, and the Chief of the Field Aviation Service Major Thomsen. The Chief of the Operations Section, General Tappen, was held up in Pleß by operations in the East.
61 From the diary entry of Oberstleutnant von Mertz of 29 July 1915.
62 Ibid.

planning a major offensive in Alsace or Lorraine, the execution of which would be difficult in any event.[63] It was difficult to understand why the Entente would stand as a passive witness to Russia's defeat.[64] In the end, Falkenhayn agreed with the conclusions reached by all the Chiefs of Staff of the Western Armies: significant Entente attacks could not be expected in the coming weeks.

Falkenhayn concluded the conference in Metz by highlighting the need to repeatedly undertake small offensive forays in order to gather information about the enemy, especially the British, whose strength was now estimated at twenty-seven divisions.[65] More important, reserves needed to be staged behind the Western Front; these would be at the disposal of the OHL.

That Falkenhayn viewed the situation on the Western Front positively at this time is reflected in a diary entry made by General Tappen on 30 July: "There (in the West), morale is very good. Additional reserves can be made available."

In the meantime, the reorganization of the German Western Army had been completed. As a result the following reserves were staged at the OHL's disposal behind the front: 54th Reserve Division at Roulers; 123rd Infantry Division around Roubaix; III Corps, with one division at Valenciennes and one at Cambrai–Le Cateau; 85th Reserve Infantry Brigade with 15th Reserve *Jäger* battalion at Carignan; and 56th Infantry Division at Saarburg.

As well, the following units were now being assembled: 115th Infantry Division at Mézières; 113th Infantry Division at Metz; 183rd Infantry Brigade at Morhange; and 185th Infantry Brigade at Mulhouse.

Thus by the beginning of August, Falkenhayn had almost nine infantry divisions at his disposal in GHQ Reserve on the Western Front, which he planned to further reinforce during August. The OHL's foot artillery reserve consisted of twenty-one heavy field howitzer batteries, nineteen mortar batteries, and nine heavy low-trajectory batteries. At this point it seemed that elements of the GHQ Reserve deployed in the West were temporarily available to take on tasks in other theatres of war without unnecessarily endangering the Western Front.

---

63 A letter from General von Kuhl to the *Reichsarchiv* dated 9 February 1931 states specifically that Falkenhayn said "a large offensive in Alsace or Lorraine is not probable."

64 From the diary entry of Oberstleutnant von Mertz of 29 July 1915.

65 The Intelligence Section of the OHL calculated that as of 27 July 1915, of these twenty-seven divisions, fifteen British divisions were at the front. The Belgian Army was estimated as having six infantry and two cavalry divisions at the front.

6

Overview of the Multi-Front War during the Summer

Italy's entry into the war had dominated much of the strategic debate during the first half of the year. However, Italy proved to be a less formidable adversary than either Falkenhayn or Conrad feared. Operations on the Italian Front began soon after Italy's declaration of war with the first of twelve Italian offensives across the Isonzo, a river surrounded by mountains just inside the Austrian border. After several initial Italian forays that resulted in the capture of Caporetto but failure at Gorizia and Tolmino, on 23 June 1915, 250,000 Italian troops tried to cross the Isonzo along the Kras Plateau. Although the Italians faced only 115,000 Austrian troops, they lost 15,000 men as masses of infantry tried to cross the river to the enemy's high ground beyond. The Austrian casualties were only 10,000. The First Battle of the Isonzo ended in failure on 7 July, but a new offensive across the same ground was launched on the 18th. This time 260 Italian battalions faced 129 Austro-Hungarian, and again the Italians suffered horrendous casualties of 46,000 men. The second Isonzo offensive also failed to secure the river crossings and petered out by 3 August. The successes of the Central Powers on the Italian Front, against the Russian army, which was now retreating beyond the San, and against the French and British at the Dardanelles now made a campaign against Serbia more realistic. More important, Bulgaria and Rumania were dissuaded from joining Italy and the Entente. It again seemed possible that one or both powers might be induced to co-operate in a campaign against their Balkan rival.[1]

The General Situation to the Beginning of August

On 21 May the German and Austro-Hungarian General Staff Chiefs agreed to continue to make their primary effort in the Galician Theatre and to maintain defensive positions on the other fronts. Falkenhayn was determined to adhere to this decision over the following months despite Italy's entry into the war and the sometimes precarious situations at the Dardanelles and on the Western Front.

With increased success in the Eastern Theatre, the operational goals had continuously broadened. While the initial goal in the Galician Theatre had been limited to relieving Russian pressure on Austria-Hungary's Carpathian Front, on reaching the Wislok the pursuit had continued to the San in order "to deal the enemy a blow from which he would not be able to recover." Afterwards, operations against the enemy were to continue east of the San "until a decision commensurate with our goals" (i.e., the final defeat of Russian offensive strength in Galicia) had been achieved. Finally, it was intended that by coordinating the Austro-Hungarian and German Eastern Fronts, the main enemy forces in Poland would be defeated and thus "a decision in the campaign" against Russia would be reached. Given these circumstances, it was clear that all available forces from the other theatres of war were needed in the East. With the increasing military requirements of the Eastern Front, the two General Staff chiefs did not hesitate to stretch the German Western Army, as well as the German Army on the Serbian Front, to their limits by withdrawing units from those sectors. From the middle of April until the first half of August these transfers amounted to no fewer than fourteen and a half infantry and reserve divisions from the West, plus three German divisions from the Serbian Front, for a total of seventeen and a half divisions. By 14 April, eight divisions had been transferred to the East. The transfer from West to East of one division on 3 May, two and a half divisions on 2 June, two on 19 July, and one on 8 August followed. Of these divisions, only two would be returned to the Western Front. Because the objectives on the Russian Front expanded only gradually, the deployment of these forces did not take place all at once but rather little by little. Thus a "campaign-deciding" result had not been achieved.

---

1 *DW* VIII: 25–33.

Because of the growing need for forces in the East, all demands in the other theatres of war that exceeded minimum requirements had to be deferred for the time being. The planned offensive against Serbia, which was necessary because of the precarious situation of the Ottoman Empire, had to be postponed a number of times. As a consequence, the way to the Orient and the supply route to Turkey, which was involved in heavy fighting on the Gallipoli Peninsula, remained blocked.

Yet even after Italy entered the war, diplomatic efforts to achieve a lasting solution to the highly complicated Balkan problem—which affected the entire conduct of the war—continued with growing importance. The danger was that the neutral Balkan states might follow Italy into the enemy's camp. Notwithstanding all of the successes in the Galician Theatre, the Balkan states had just watched the last major European power join the Entente; they had also noted the precarious situation at the Dardanelles as well as the tensions between the United States and Germany that had followed the sinking of the *Lusitania*. This posed a considerable problem for the Central Powers. The sharp differences of opinion brought on by excessive Bulgarian demands during recent negotiations between Bulgaria and Turkey also seemed to indicate unfavourable developments, as did the Rumanian government's growing resistance to remaining neutral. Suspicions grew that Rumania was bound by diplomatic agreement to follow Italy's example.

Instability in the Balkans was the impetus for a conference attended by the leading statesmen and the General Staff chiefs, held on 25 May at German GHQ in Pleß. There, Rumania's position was debated thoroughly. Falkenhayn maintained that efforts had to focus on winning over Rumania by offering military and economic guarantees. Everyone agreed that the differences between Bulgaria and Turkey had to be bridged.[2] Recent reports indicated that the court of the Ottoman Emperor was willing to surrender Bulgarian territory up to the Maritz Line in return for an alliance, so the possibility of an agreement between these two states seemed possible. The successful conclusion of such an agreement was the first condition for the creation of a "Balkan Alliance," which Falkenhayn again encouraged over the course of the conference. As a further prerequisite he insisted on a rapprochement between Austria-Hungary and Serbia.

Alarming news from the Dardanelles soon aggravated the political instability further. On 9 June, Baron von Wangenheim, the German ambassador, reported from Constantinople that the recent attacks by the combined Anglo-French forces

---

2 *Bulgaria and Turkey had fought two wars in 1912 and 1913. See* Richard C. Hall, *The Balkan Wars, 1912–1913.*

on Gallipoli had badly shaken Turkish resistance.[3] The enemy artillery had gained considerable dominance, and Turkish ammunition production was unable to keep up with requirements. "Unless an agreement with Rumania can be reached very quickly that will allow the transportation of ammunition [through its territory to Turkey], the fall of the Dardanelles must be contemplated … In my estimation the Dardanelles cannot hold out for longer than one month."

Immediately afterwards—in the middle of June—success in the Galician Theatre began to affect the mood in the Balkans to the point that the transfer of most of the German units stationed in southern Hungary to the Galician Theatre seemed possible.[4] The Entente's failure to win Rumania and Bulgaria over to its side was largely a result of the improved situation. But even though a Rumanian move to the enemy camp had been prevented, the Rumanian government remained firm in its refusal to grant passage to Turkey for urgently needed ammunition transports. The situation was aggravated by the fact that the crisis on the Dardanelles had apparently reached its apex toward the end of June. According to the Army Commander there, Generalfeldmarschall Liman von Sanders, on 30 June the German ambassador had described the situation in the darkest of tones. While the Turkish troops' stand on the Dardanelles was beyond reproach,

the enemy consistently brings additional heavy guns to bear covering us with a barrage of heavy shells day and night. Although our complement of guns is entirely sufficient, the shortage of ammunition has grown so critical that the moment can now be predicted when our artillery will be unable to withstand the enemy attack … It seems unavoidable that the Turkish resistance will be broken in the very near future … According to Admiral Usedom, the fortress will be able to hold out for just three days once the land army is defeated. Therefore Generalfeldmarschall Sanders[5] requests that the highest authorities be informed that the Dardanelles will be lost, unless a sufficient supply of ammunition is procured immediately.

In light of this report, it is clear why the demand for an attack on Serbia in order to rescue Turkey was urgently renewed. In his report of 2 July, Major Friedrich Baron von der Goltz, the German Military Attaché in Sofia, stated that there could be no doubt that Bulgaria, despite her apparently amiable negotiations with

---

3 *Following a sustained bombardment, on 4 June British troops made a final attempt to gain the original objectives of the 25 April landings. Though the Third Battle of Krithia was more successful than earlier attempts, it ultimately failed to achieve significant gains.*

4 General von Falkenhayn also expressed the same thoughts in his letter to General Enver Pasha.

5 Sanders's later comments regarding this telegram indicate that the military authorities did not judge the situation as seriously as the ambassador described.

Germany, was basically unwilling to support Germany on the issue of supplying Turkey with war materiel. This would only change, he contended, if there was a break between Bulgaria and Russia, and there was only one way to make that happen: attack Serbia.

A telegram from Bethmann Hollweg on 4 July contained the same conclusion. He requested that Falkenhayn comment on the query from the German Ambassador in Constantinople regarding the measures that would need to be taken if the enemy succeeded in breaking through on the Dardanelles. A decision would have to be made whether, after the Dardanelles fell, Turkey should continue fighting in Thrace, or retreat to Asia Minor, or sue for peace. The German Chancellor added that from a political perspective, it was the prevailing opinion that Germany would probably be able to convince Turkey to hold out in Thrace, keep Rumania quiet, and persuade Bulgaria to join the Central Powers even after the Entente occupied the Dardanelles. Also, it would be vital to attack Serbia as soon as the military situation permitted.

The German Imperial Government stressed the urgent need for Serbia's quick subjugation (*Niederwerfung*) in order to provide Germany's threatened ally with the necessary aid. However, Falkenhayn maintained that at this point it was necessary to thoroughly exploit the victories against Russia. On 6 July he replied to the German Chancellor that "if Turkey can hold the strait for another five to six weeks, the defeat of Russia will in all probability be abundantly clear and at that point we can surely expect a position from the Balkan States that will be more favourable for our purposes."

With these comments, Falkenhayn was indicating that he had begun to agree with Conrad that after a decisive result against Russia, a Balkan campaign designed to secure a connection with Turkey would no longer be necessary. At this point the *OHL* was anticipating the military defeat of Russia—and thereby a decision in the Balkans—through a continuing offensive in southern Poland in combination with a simultaneous attack by Army Group *Gallwitz* on the Narew River. This is indicated in two documents: Generaloberst Pleßen's diary entry of 19 July, which characterized the campaign in the East as already having been decided; and one of Falkenhayn's situation reports, intended for certain parliamentarians, which the Chief of the General Staff transmitted to the German Chancellor on 22 July. In this report Falkenhayn emphasized that the Serbian campaign would surely become redundant when, as he hoped, Russian power had finally been vanquished, after which "Rumania and Bulgaria would cause trouble no further."

The political leadership, however, did not believe that military victories solely could achieve such far-reaching results. In his detailed reply to Falkenhayn's

communiqué on 6 July, Gottlieb von Jagow, the German Secretary of State, contended that Russia would not be ready for peace until it was sure the Entente
would fail to take the Dardanelles. In order to hold the strait, Serbia's subjugation
would be necessary. Jagow then added that Falkenhayn apparently expected a
winding up of the Russian operations in five to six weeks, at which point it would
be possible to muster the 250,000 men that would be required to attack Serbia. By
then, he pointed out, the Dardanelles might already have fallen. His communiqué
concluded that even under such unfavourable circumstances, Serbia's defeat would
be necessary in order to win over Bulgaria, to help the Turks who were besieged
in Thrace, and, if possible, to liberate Constantinople.

Before the military and political leadership could reach a consensus on the
various military and political alternatives, the German Ambassador in Constantinople made a more positive assessment of the ammunition supplies and, with
that, the entire military situation on the Dardanelles. On 5 July he reported that
the situation at Gallipoli had improved for the time being now that ammunition
had been transferred from the abandoned positions at Tschataldscha[6] to the Dardanelles; it was also not out of the question that the principal threat might be
eliminated by the end of the month through successful ammunition production.[7]
A letter from Goltz on 8 July provided further reassurances. In it he emphasized
that the shortage of ammunition continued and that

> everything consistent with the general interests of the allies must be done
> to provide supplies .... However, if I am asked if it is necessary to accede to
> especially aggrieving conditions imposed by the Balkan States or to forgo
> other decisive operations just to save Turkey, i.e. in order to bolster her
> resistance, then I must decidedly respond in the negative ... If it depends
> here only on us, then we'll get through this even without help from others.

These reports encouraged GHQ in the opinion that the Dardanelles situation
could be relieved by strengthening the Russian offensive.

The defeat of Russia would bring an end to the Balkan problem and at the
same time end the danger on the Italian Front. If Tsarist Russia withdrew from
the Entente in a timely manner, a conclusion to the multi-front war could be
reached.

---

6 *A line of fortifications west of Constantinople, where the Bulgarian offensive during the Balkan
   War of 1912 and 1913 came to a halt.*
7 Command of ammunition production was given to a German naval officer, Captain Pieper.

The *OHL*'s Peace Efforts

Falkenhayn understood the significance of a peace accord with Russia for the outcome of the war, so in the spring and summer of 1915 he spared no effort to achieve one by taking advantage of the advantageous military situation in the Eastern Theatre. When Przemysl fell on 3 June, resulting in the capture of the San Line, he appealed to the German Chancellor via the Foreign Office's representative at GHQ, the envoy von Treutler, "to take advantage of the presently favourable circumstances in the Russian Campaign in order to make a serious effort to reach a cessation of the hostilities between us and Russia." To accomplish this, he suggested making the following proposal to the Tsar through a neutral power:

> Przemysl is in our hands, and the forces that this makes available will advance on Lemberg which will be taken in the near future. A new army will shortly be deployed to the Eastern Front.[8] In view of our successes, the possible but not probable entry of Bulgaria[9] and Rumania into the war will have no effect on the military situation, as did Italy's … Therefore we propose that the hostilities between Russia and ourselves be terminated. We are not demanding a breach of faith in the event that Russia feels obligated to her allies. Peace does not have to commence until our other enemies enter into peace negotiations or if the agreement of 4 September[10] becomes null and void due to the withdrawal of one of your allies.

With this communication, the Chief of the General Staff of the Field Army had renewed peace endeavours, which had been active for months but had temporarily faltered. Since September 1914, neutral European states had been making offers to mediate in peace negotiations—offers that had been rejected in London and Paris. In January 1915, U.S. President Woodrow Wilson had ordered Colonel House to contact the German and British governments for the purpose of discussing possible peace proposals. He had hoped that both parties would at least be willing to debate. However, it was considered non-negotiable that Germany would have to leave Belgium and consent to mutual disarmament. House arrived in Berlin at the end of March and consulted with the German Chancellor and Foreign Secretary. At

---

8 Here Falkenhayn was probably thinking about the new deployment of four and a half divisions in Galicia, on which he had finally decided on 2 June.

9 In the course of the Turko-Bulgarian negotiations, on a number of occasions the situation had become sufficiently critical "that it was not at all safe to assume that the Bulgarians would not attack Turkey today or tomorrow." From a report of Baron von Wangenheim, the German Ambassador attached to the Foreign Office, 16 June 1915.

10 The Governments of Great Britain, France, and Russia had mutually committed themselves not to enter into a separate peace during the course of the war and to accept proposals for peace only with the consent of the allies. See *DW* VI: 405.

this time, however, only matters of direct interest to the United States were touched on, such as American ammunition supplies to the Entente and England's blockade of Germany. The Belgian question was not discussed. The German Chancellor told House that in principle, the German government would be prepared to join a new convention for the security of the oceans. At that point the consultations were temporarily broken off as a result of the sinking of the *Lusitania* by a German U-boat.

In addition to House's overtures, in the early months of 1915 a neutral European state attempted to facilitate contact between the warring sides for the purpose of achieving peace. Influential British circles did not seem to oppose this idea; in Russia as well, the idea initially appeared to be positively received. The Tsar rejected the notion of a separate peace but was not opposed to beginning peace negotiations with Germany through neutral mediation. During April, prospects for this consultation grew more and more unfavourable now that Italy was expected to join the Entente. From England, news arrived that raised doubts about the possibility of peace; concurrently, Russia assumed a negative posture.

Because of the impending termination of Vienna's relationship with Rome, and the various differences between Italy and Serbia regarding the coastal areas of the Adriatic, in May the time was right for a rapprochement between the Dual Monarchy and Serbia. Germany suggested that the Austro-Hungarian government negotiate a separate peace with Serbia on the basis that the Negotin District would be ceded to Austria-Hungary, thus securing a direct connection to Bulgaria; in return, Serbia was to be given northern Albania and granted the merger it desired with Montenegro. The Austro-Hungarian Secretary of State, Baron von Burian, was not opposed to these efforts; however, he thought it appropriate that this suggestion originate with the Serbian government. According to a communication to Conrad from the Austro-Hungarian Foreign Ministry on 30 May, this was deemed to be unachievable: "Burian wants to build golden bridges[11] for them—the Serbs— but they are not coming." Over the following weeks Germany[12] pursued the idea of a rapprochement between Austria-Hungary and Serbia.[13]

---

11 *This is a proverbial German expression meaning that Burian wanted to present Serbia with a way out of the war that would still leave the country's dignity intact.*

12 A quote from the notes of Minister of War Wild dated 16 June 1915 reads: "I advocate ... peace with Serbia ... Serbia: Little door to the Adriatic, Bulgaria, Macedonia, Greece, Epirus, Rumania, Bessarabia, and Bukowina." Even though these plans apparently did not develop beyond contemplation, they still indicate how much the creation of a Balkan Alliance that would be allied with the Central Powers was desired by the military side in order to bring about a peace.

13 Regarding the later efforts of the Central Powers to reach a peace with Serbia, the Serbian General Staff's Official History reads: "On 21 June, Bulgaria announced her availability for consultations with the Federation of Four under the condition that the previously demanded part of Serbia-Macedonia be ceded to her immediately and not after the war. Serbia, which was familiar with the Bulgarian mentality, was extremely disturbed by Sofia's demands. Germany

Such was the situation when Falkenhayn's peace proposal reached the German Chancellor on 3 June. The same day, Bethmann Hollweg responded by pointing to the failure of his own peace efforts to date. By his experience, it was most probable that the Tsar would firmly reject the planned proposal for the cessation of hostilities. And even if, contrary to all expectations, the Tsar were to accept Falkenhayn's proposal, he would make his acceptance conditional on a cessation of hostilities with all of Germany's enemies or a commitment from Germany not to use its forces presently deployed in Russia in any other theatre of war. So the Chancellor believed. Furthermore, the Tsar would respond to a clearly formulated proposal only after consulting with his allies. Bethmann Hollweg emphasized that

> any proposal from us has to be made with the precondition that we are willing to conclude a peace agreement with all of our enemies based on the present status of the war. I doubt that our enemies would be [accepting of such an agreement] following Italy's attack. Under the best of circumstances, a peace could be achieved on the basis of the *status quo ante*, in any case. Whether this would be the way to go is exclusively subject to the military's evaluation.

Finally, in evaluating the entire situation, the Chancellor suggested that Germany would hardly be in a position to offer the Russians substantially more than the Tsar would expect to gain from staying with the Entente. Furthermore, Germany's peace proposals to Russia might be seen as an indication of weakness by Rumania and Bulgaria; this would heighten the danger of those two states joining the enemy camp, driven there out of concern that they might be short-changed during the distribution of the spoils of war.

In spite of this response by the leader responsible for the German political situation, Falkenhayn did not miss any opportunity to resolve the matter of making peace. A new occasion was presented by a communication from Conrad to the Foreign Ministry in Vienna, which, paraphrased, stated: The present positive state of the war can be expected to result in the taking of Lublin, Cholm, Ivangorod,

---

and Austria-Hungary used this factor for a peace proposal ... Because the Austro-Hungarian motivations were all too transparent, the Serbian Government rejected this proposal with disdain. It was their objective that Bulgaria would be influenced to take the side of the Central Powers; if not, they would enter into an agreement with Serbia and Bulgaria would lose Macedonia." See the *Serbian Official History*, VIII: 171). According to archival investigations made by the German Foreign Office, Serbia was never presented with a real peace proposal; however, with the help of a neutral state the Central Powers directed inquiries to the Serbian government under which conditions Serbia would be interested in concluding a peace agreement with the Central Powers.

and possibly even Warsaw, and it must be used to break the enemy coalition and to eliminate Rumania and Bulgaria by reaching an agreement with Russia. We must build golden bridges for Russia to agree to a separate peace.

Falkenhayn passed a copy of this communication to Bethmann Hollweg, adding that he agreed with Conrad and emphasizing that the right time to approach Russia should not be missed.

In his response of 30 July the Chancellor pointed out that he had been pondering for months whether Russia would be disposed to a separate peace with Germany and that so far, the Russian government had consistently responded in the negative. Although a change of mood in Germany's favour had been detected, there was no discernable inclination in Russia for a separate peace; on the contrary, the understanding prevailed that Russia was bound by the word of its Tsar and could only make peace in concert with its allies. In St. Petersburg, his response continued, the serious defeats in Poland and Courland were not viewed as critical to the outcome of the war; these were seen merely as temporary setbacks, and with the deployment of the British troops currently in training, a major offensive by the Entente would begin in the fall. Based on this, Bethmann Hollweg believed that Falkenhayn's hopes were unjustified, because even given the unmistakable change of mood in Russia and a highly favourable continuation of German operations in Poland, Russia would not decide in favour of a separate peace. The Chancellor stated that such an opportunity would only present itself, if it ever did, when Russia finally had to abandon its hope for the fall of the Dardanelles[14] and Bulgaria's subjugation. His response continued:

> As Your Excellency is aware, it is here that I see the deciding situation. St. Petersburg has been informed that we would be satisfied with negligible conditions in consideration of a separate peace. I also call to their attention that the establishment of a longer lasting Austro-German administration in Congress Poland is liable to strengthen the Polish Freedom and Independence movements, so that Poland must be seen as lost to Russia in one way or another.

The Chancellor closed with the suggestion that the Entente would see an Austro-German peace proposal, in spite of the victories in Poland, as a sign of

---

14 When the German Chancellor associated Russia's readiness for peace with the success of the Gallipoli campaign in this manner, it should be pointed out that Russia was not interested in allowing its allies to conquer the straights alone. Under certain circumstances, the Tsar was even prepared to reach a separate peace with Turkey in order to deploy all his forces against the Central Powers.

weakness and deal with it accordingly as long as there was still hope of defeating Turkey, of making a favourable alliance with the Balkan states, and of breaking through in the West. He concluded: "Only when these expectations have been
eliminated, will we appear sufficiently strong to propose peace even if the enemy
does not make the first move."

FALKENHAYN'S PURSUIT OF AN EARLY PEACE IN THE MIDDLE OF JULY ALSO
explains his already mentioned plan to clean up Upper Alsace. Military considerations could hardly have been the driving force for this. In a letter of 14 May to
Falkenhayn, Conrad had expressed similar views when he declared that the minimum objective of the campaign in the East should be to "reclaim Austro-Hungarian territory and Russian-Polish territory on the left bank of the Vistula to be
ceded [to the Dual Monarchy] in compensation for the transfers of territory to
Italy." Conrad had been close to this objective in the middle of June when the
capture of Galicia's capital was at hand. It hardly seems a coincidence that the
German Chief of the General Staff aspired to recapture the last territories occupied by the enemy in Upper Alsace so that in the event of possible peace negotiations, the enemy would not be left holding a bargaining chip.

How much Falkenhayn was thinking of the possibility of peace, especially at
this time, is evident in the fact that in early June he forwarded a report regarding
"France's Economic and Military Status," prepared by the *OHL*, to the German
Chancellor as well as to the Foreign Office. It concluded that

> France's sacrifices in this war are so gigantic that the government cannot help
> but be held responsible for them before the people, and one day before his-
> tory, and will soon have to decide whether the future of the nation is not
> better served by the cessation of resistance than the continuation of the
> war which, despite all foreign support, is hopeless for France.

If this report's conclusions were correct, the willingness of the Entente to submit
itself to another winter of war had to be in doubt.

These circumstances probably explain Falkenhayn's secret verbal orders to
Generalmajor of the Pioneers von Mertens at Tenth Army Headquarters to
explore "military positions" in the Western Theatre roughly parallel to the Belgian border on the general line Nieuport–Lille–Douai–Hirson–Stenay–Metz.
This represented the shortest possible line behind the Western Front securing
Belgium and access to the sea. It also marked the possible starting line for a
major new offensive against the Entente. According to a remark by Mertens,

this seemed to represent a "Line of Demarcation,"[15] one that could be occupied in the event of an armistice and resulting peace negotiations.

Shifting the War's Centre of Gravity

Bethmann Hollweg in his 30 July response to Falkenhayn had correctly pointed to the great significance that winning Bulgaria over to the side of the Central Powers would exert on the initiation of peace negotiations with Russia. On this point, Falkenhayn was in complete agreement. Accordingly, over the previous weeks both men had left no stone unturned in their efforts to restart the stalled negotiations with Bulgaria. In the second half of July, braced by the universally apparent successes of the Central Powers, their efforts finally seemed to bear fruit. King Ferdinand and his prime minister, Radoslavov, declared their country's willingness to dispatch an officer to German GHQ with the authority to coordinate Bulgaria's participation in the campaign.

Falkenhayn received the news on 24 July, at a time when he was still hoping for an overwhelming military success. He briefly believed that if he achieved one, the Serbian campaign would no longer be necessary: with the defeat of Russia the Balkan problem would finally be resolved. Even though he had tried hard for it before, at this point the Bulgarian offer to participate in the campaign against Serbia did not seem especially urgent.[16] A few days later, however, at the beginning of August, reports from the battlefield were indicating an organized Russian retreat along the entire Polish Front, and he began to doubt the possibility of a great operational conclusion. So he welcomed the prospect of reaching such a conclusion with Bulgarian assistance. Conrad viewed this plan—which from its inception had been a German plan—with skepticism and was not entirely unjustified in his concerns regarding the damage it might inflict on the Dual Monarchy's image in the Balkans. He would have preferred to direct all of his efforts toward the defeat of Russia; having achieved that, he could then force Serbia into the Austro-Hungarian camp, thereby giving his forces a free hand for an offensive

---

15 Crown Prince Rupprecht of Bavaria wrote: "Around Noon I spoke with General of the Pioneer Corps who was travelling on the Western Front by order of the Commander in Chief in order to explore where to establish a Line of Demarcation in case of an armistice." See Kronprinz Rupprecht von Bayern, *Mein Kriegstagebuch* (Berlin: Deutscher National, 1929), 368). In contrast to this, the former Administrative Officer of the Operations Department of GHQ Major Dr. Mewes reports that Falkenhayn had not mentioned that the position was meant to be a potential Line of Demarcation to the Operations Department (from a letter to the *Reichsarchiv* dated 15 August 1931).

16 This is according to a telegram from Treutler to the Foreign Office of 27 July (from the Political Archive of the Foreign Office).

against Italy. But at the same time, he realized that the situation on the Russian Front provided little hope that his far-reaching plans could be realized and that any forces the German plans added to the war effort would certainly be welcomed by the Central Powers. So he agreed that negotiations for Bulgaria's participation in the campaign against Serbia should begin.

These negotiations began on 3 August at GHQ in Pleß, with the participation of Oberstleutnant Gantschew, the "empowered" Bulgarian officer. The progress of the negotiations, however, was severely hindered by the critical situation at the Dardanelles[17] and especially by the sinking of the U.S. steamship *Arabic* by a German submarine on 19 August. This incident seriously exacerbated the political differences between Germany and the United States, which was not without effect on the Bulgarians' position. It was only after tensions eased that the negotiations could be completed. Germany, Austria-Hungary, and Bulgaria concluded a military alliance on 5 September. It cannot be ruled out that concerns about a separate peace between Serbia and the Central Powers decisively influenced Bulgaria's final decision. On 15 September, Turkey also joined the military alliance.

The Central Powers' achievement of an alliance with Bulgaria was highly significant politically and militarily and could be expected to generate a response from the other Balkan states. If Serbia was defeated—and there could be no doubt about that—then the danger of a threat to Austria-Hungary's flanks would be averted and the crisis at the Dardanelles would be overcome. Also, the creation of a secure conduit to the Orient would open new alternatives for Turkey to wage war in Asia. It would firmly unite the Ottoman Empire with the Central Powers in a committed war alliance; and most important, it would deny Russia the shortest supply route to the other Entente powers.

Now that the Bulgarian question had been solved, the achievement of a separate peace with Russia began to assume great significance in the military situation in the Eastern Theatre.

It is true that the *OHL*'s hopes of defeating the main Russian forces in July did not prove to be entirely justified. As previously mentioned, at the beginning of August the possibility had to be considered that the Russians would succeed in escaping the Central Powers' flanking attempt in the area between the Bug, Vistula, and Narew Rivers with a skillful fighting retreat. In the opinion of *OberOst*, the final opportunity to achieve decisive success with a new offensive presented itself at the end of July and the beginning of August. On his return to Pleß from

---

17 This is according to a report to the *Reichsarchiv* of 25 January 1932 by the former German Military Attaché, Generalleutnant von Lossow.

the conference at Metz, Falkenhayn learned of the proposal to shift the war's centre of gravity from the Narew to the Nemen. According to Generalfeldmarschall von Hindenburg, no time could be wasted if the offensive proposed by *OberOst* in Posen on 2 July was to have any prospect of success. Falkenhayn's agreement to this plan would mean not only a discontinuation of pursuit operations in Poland— which, although not operationally decisive, might well succeed—but also the deployment of all available reinforcements, including available elements of the GHQ Reserve on the Western Front, to the left flank of the Eastern Front. It might even mean the postponement of the Serbian campaign until far into the future. Based on past experience, the Chief of the General Staff no longer saw this as a means to achieve a decisive decision in the campaign. At the same time, he was concerned that the forces necessary for this campaign would be unavailable for other fronts for the foreseeable future. He viewed the speedy execution of the Serbian campaign as even more important for the larger strategic situation than further significant but minor successes on the Eastern Front. Therefore he believed it necessary to limit the objectives in the East. He considered "a decisive victory appropriate to the objectives of the *OHL*" to be sufficient. He hoped to achieve this by forcefully continuing operations that were intended to weaken the enemy's will to fight as much as possible.

FALKENHAYN'S DECISION TO GO AHEAD WITH THE SERBIAN CAMPAIGN WAS MADE easier by the successful negotiations with Bulgaria and also by the apparently secure situation on the Italian and Western Fronts.

The Italians' second Isonzo offensive had ended with complete failure in the beginning of August, once again demonstrating the clear superiority of the Austro-Hungarian forces. It was thus hoped that in the future, Germany's allies would be able to deal with this threat on their own.

The conference at Metz had strengthened Falkenhayn's conviction that the German Western Front stood like an "iron wall" and that, despite the enemy's numerical superiority, it was equal to all challenges. The successful defence against the enemy's heavy attacks had instilled confidence along the entire German line. Thus the situation on the Western Front seemed to support the launching of operations in other theatres.

Eight and a half divisions were available as a GHQ Reserve behind the Western Front. At the end of July, Falkenhayn considered deploying the reserves to Upper Alsace in order to clear the enemy from German soil—a thought that had occupied him, albeit fleetingly, in June. Accordingly, during the conference at Metz, Generalleutnant von Knobelsdorf, Fifth Army's Chief of Staff, was ordered to initiate the necessary reconnaissance activities in Upper Alsace. Falkenhayn deemed the deployment of six divisions to be sufficient for this task.

On 28 August, in Berlin, Falkenhayn and Knobelsdorf discussed the outcome of this investigation. Two days later, on 30 August, Knobelsdorf presented his findings to the Supreme Warlord. Generaloberst Pleßen's diary for that day contains the following entry: "The *OHL* is contemplating a thrust into Upper Alsace in order to throw the enemy out of the remaining part of Germany." At the same time, the evaluations of the Intelligence Assessment Section of the *OHL* revealed that the Entente had deployed almost fifty infantry divisions behind its front. This increased the probability that the enemy would launch a renewed offensive while German forces were tied up in the East. Given these circumstances, the German Chief of the General Staff thought it advisable to extract more forces from the Eastern Front, not just for the Serbian campaign but also to protect the Western Front, which now required increased attention as well.

On 27 August, the day before his meeting with Knobelsdorf, Falkenhayn ordered Army Groups *Prinz Leopold* and *Mackensen* to occupy permanent positions on the Eastern Front. These measures were not immediately implemented; nevertheless, they marked the conclusion of operations in the East.

Now that Bulgaria had been persuaded to participate in the Serbian campaign, all other campaign planning took second place. The war's centre of gravity was beginning to shift from the Eastern Front to the Southeastern Theatre.[18]

---

18 *Meaning to the Balkans and the Serbian front.*

PART III

Summer and Autumn

7

Overview of the Military Situation
to the Middle of September

The first year of war failed to produce a military decision anywhere. None of the enemies surrounding the Central Powers had been defeated. Turkey's entry into the war on the side of the Central Powers in the fall of 1914, as well as Bulgaria's alignment in the late summer of 1915, represented political achievements to be sure, but these developments were offset by Italy's defection to the Entente, which was a serious setback. At the same time, the positions of Rumania and Greece remained uncertain and wavering.

The enemy blockade was affecting the economic situation of the Central Powers ever more seriously. Commercial warfare by submarine never became entirely effective because pressure from the neutral states—especially the United States— meant it was employed only intermittently. Also, serious diplomatic altercations between Germany and the United States over submarine incidents made it ever more doubtful that the United States would remain neutral.

Furthermore, despite the *OHL*'s ongoing efforts, there was no possibility of opening peace negotiations. Thus military operations had to continue.

Notwithstanding his original plans, at the beginning of 1915 General von Falkenhayn was forced to transfer the offensive emphasis to the East—a development that he hoped would be only temporary. By the middle of April he had decided to keep the war's focus on the Russian Front because of the precarious situation for Germany's allies in the Carpathians and Italy's threat to enter the war on the side of the Entente. Thus the army on the Western Front continued to protect the Eastern Army's back. This remained the case even though the Chief of the General Staff pursued only limited operational objectives on the Eastern Front until the summer. At the suggestion of Mackensen's staff and General Conrad, these operational objectives were temporarily expanded. In the middle of July Falkenhayn hoped to bring about a decision in the East by defeating the main Russian forces in Poland through a combined offensive on the German and Austro-Hungarian portions of the front. By month's end, however, he had abandoned hope of "totally defeating Russia." Once again, he limited the objectives in the East, even though a decisive campaign against Russia seemed especially favourable, given *OberOst*'s proposal to move the centre of gravity from the Narew to the Njemen so as to attack the enemy's northern flank as well as its rearward support system.

Falkenhayn was concerned that the considerable forces necessary for such a broad offensive would render impossible deployments to other fronts, thereby threatening plans to launch the Serbian campaign. Above all, however, he doubted that the operation would be a resounding success. So he withheld his approval of *OberOst*'s plan. The need to begin the campaign against Serbia in order to establish a link with Turkey appeared all the more urgent when, at the beginning of August, renewed British and French landings on the Gallipoli Peninsula again threatened the Ottoman Empire. Accordingly, Falkenhayn pressed for a conclusion to the diplomatic negotiations with Bulgaria as well as for a conclusion to the offensive against Russia.

In the meantime, operations on the Eastern Front were no longer resulting in decisive successes. On the Eastern Army's left flank, *OberOst*'s long-sought offensive against the Russian Army's northern flank finally began at the beginning of September—albeit belatedly and with insufficient forces. By the middle of the month it was blatantly obvious that the attack across the Wilna had failed to meet expectations. The enemy had been able to intercept the deep flanking attack and had evaded the blow through a timely retreat. Army Groups *Prinz Leopold* and *Mackensen*, positioned in the centre of the Eastern Front, pressed after the retreating Russian Army in a frontal pursuit through Poland, but on reaching the western edge of the extensive Rokitno Marshes, they finally discontinued their advance and established permanent positions. On the Eastern Army's right flank, the *AOK*'s attempt to liberate Eastern Galicia and to decisively defeat the Russians on their Southwest Front failed, as the attack stalled quickly in the face of Russian counterattacks.

Thus, by the middle of September the Central Powers' main combined offensive had perhaps dealt a severe blow to the Russian forces' combat effectiveness, but it had not brought about their total defeat.

DESPITE THEIR INFERIOR NUMBERS, GERMANY'S WESTERN FRONT HAD FRUS-
trated the enemy's breakthrough efforts in the Champagne and the Artois through
a successful defence. It seemed that the enemy had become exhausted, and the
situation in this theatre of war slackened accordingly after the middle of July. A
meeting with the Western Armies' General Staff chiefs in Metz at the end of July
confirmed Falkenhayn in his opinion that the Western Front stood unshaken and
able to repel all assaults. At this point it was even possible to stage almost nine divisions as a GHQ reserve behind the front lines.

It seems that at this point Falkenhayn was still hoping to achieve a decision on
the Western Front in 1915 by terminating offensive operations in Russia as quickly
as possible and accelerating the attack on Serbia.[1] It can be assumed that he based
his plans for the Western Front on an operational breakthrough north of the
Somme—an area defended predominantly by the British—an operation that he
had considered promising the previous spring. Now he considered mounting a
major diversionary operation before launching the main attack. For that purpose, Upper Alsace seemed a good choice, for the enemy forces deployed there
would not have enough time to participate decisively in a battle at another location if they were forced to repel a German attack. Admittedly, the obvious argument remained that considerable German forces would be required to tie up a large
proportion of the French reserves, and that those forces would later be missed at
the decisive moment; their absence would be especially critical given the Entente's
well-understood numerical superiority. So Falkenhayn considered it especially
important that the enemy be surprised by the proposed attack in Upper Alsace.

Very soon, however, the progress of the offensive in the East and the delay in
beginning the Serbian campaign—both of which had failed to meet expectations—
left no doubt in Falkenhayn's mind that the transfer of expendable forces from
East to West would take too much time and that a decisive offensive in France in
1915 was out of the question.[2] After considering the relative strength of the opposing forces, it became clear that even with the deployment of all available units from
the Russian Front as well as all combat reserves from the homeland, the forces necessary to mount a major offensive operation would not be available to Germany.
After all, the *OHL*'s Intelligence Assessment Division estimated that almost fifty
reserve infantry divisions were staged behind the Entente's front lines.

Despite the enemy's significant numerical superiority, and even though the situation in the French Theatre was growing increasingly serious (after having seemed
totally harmless through the month of July), Falkenhayn did not believe that the

---

1 Report to the *Reichsarchiv* by Generalleutnant Tappen, dated 30 September 1932. See also a
diary entry by Generalmajor Groener of 31 July 1915.
2 From a note to the *Reichsarchiv* from Generalleutnant Tappen, dated 30 September 1932.

enemy would mount a major offensive until the end of August. The German Chief of the General Staff contended that France and Great Britain had made no attempt to relieve the Russian Army in recent months—a time when it was suffering progressively severe setbacks—because both powers had recognized that they were unable to force a decision against the German Army in the West given the strength of their present and expected forces. He therefore contended that they had decided instead to wage a war of attrition.

Not until the beginning of September did Falkenhayn's opinion change. As a result of reports he received primarily from Third and Sixth Armies, he began to sense that attacks by the Entente might be imminent in a number of locations, although he still did not rate highly either their strength or their sustainability.

In the middle of September the Central Powers had around 293 infantry divisions in all theatres, which faced 349 enemy infantry divisions. In the West, 100 German divisions faced 150 British, French, and Belgian divisions; in the East, 103 divisions of the Central Powers—59 German and 44 Austro-Hungarian—faced 126 Russian divisions; against Serbia, Austro-Hungarian security forces of approximately 6 divisions, plus 10 German and 2 Austro-Hungarian divisions, faced 11 and a half Serbian divisions;[3] in the Italian Theatre, approximately 22 Austro-Hungarian divisions and the German *Alpenkorps* faced 38 and a half Italian divisions. In the Turkish Theatres, 9 Turkish divisions were stationed at Constantinople; on the Dardanelles Front, 17 Turkish divisions faced 13 Franco-British divisions; on the Caucasian Front, 11 Turkish divisions faced 6 Russian divisions; and in Syria, Arabia, and Iraq, 12 Turkish divisions faced 4 British divisions.

Obviously, given the enemy's numerical superiority, the Central Powers' situation was extremely tenuous. Strong German forces were tied down in all theatres, with the Eastern Front in particular still claiming a considerable proportion despite the victorious course of the major offensive. Without those forces from the East, there was no prospect of mounting decisive offensive operations in the West.

The moment for defeating Serbia seemed to have been chosen auspiciously, in that the Russian and Italian flanks were both completely secured, the latter owing to successful defensive engagements on the Isonzo. The necessary forces for the campaign were to be detached partly from the Eastern Army and partly from the West.[4] However, developments on the Western Front soon threatened to call everything into question.

---

3 Not including the units posted along the Bulgarian and Macedonian borders.
4 One and a half divisions were detached from the West and eight and a half divisions from the Eastern Front.

8

The Western Front from Mid-August to the Beginning of the Autumn Offensive

The Enemy's Situation and Plans in the Summer

Operations in the spring of 1915 had convinced Joffre that, even with sufficient forces and materiel, a breakthrough of the German lines could only succeed if the initial attack itself was successful. Since these conditions had not been met, the French Supreme Commander terminated the attack launched by Tenth Army (with some British support) north of Arras on 16 June.

The question now turned to how operations should continue. At the end of June 1915 the French Supreme Command maintained that, considering the Allies' general situation, moving over to a purely passive and defensive posture was out of the question. In the Eastern Theatre the situation of the Russian allies was still deteriorating: Lemberg had fallen on 22 June, and in Galicia the Russians were continuing to retreat along a wide front; Warsaw now appeared to be threatened as well. In the southeast, the Italians' offensive had not achieved any notable success, nor had the Italians provided any tangible relief for their allies. Despite all the demands that they attack, the newly organized Serbian Army insisted on waiting. At the Dardanelles, the British and French forces that had landed at Gallipoli had not made any headway. To that point, every attempt to draw the remaining neutral Balkan states into the conflict on the side of the Entente had failed. A large, quick victory in the West was of the utmost importance in order to relieve the hard-pressed Russian Army, to motivate the Serbs and Italians to take aggressive action, and to convince the vacillating Balkan states to enter the conflict as allies.

The political situation on the home front demanded a victory as well. The results of the recent battles had disappointed the French population and were instilling a pessimistic and critical attitude, which was being expressed in the press and in private conversations, as well as in the Senate and Chamber of Deputies in the form of questions and arguments. President Poincaré recognized that this was a serious problem, leading him to visit Joffre's headquarters in Chantilly on 23 June. At that meeting he referred to often repeated accusations that the Supreme Commander was issuing orders without consulting his subordinate commanders. In future, he suggested, Joffre should exchange experiences, hear recommendations, and discuss future operations with the three army group commanders, who had also been invited to the meeting. The generalissimo agreed, but only reluctantly, for he regarded this as an attempt to limit his authority. He did so only with the proviso that, as the commander in charge of and responsible for operations, future decisions would be made by himself, on his own and independently.

The government's concern about the military situation was later demonstrated in a written query from the Minister of War, which had been written at the president's instigation. Several members of the Cabinet joined Millerand in expressing their concern. The Minister's query sought to determine whether everything was being done at the front to provide security to the country and to ensure that the army stood ready to repel a German attack, or to initiate its own offensive any time and at any place. The government placed particular emphasis on obtaining the Supreme Commander's reassurances that all measures for defensive operations had been taken and that the present positions could be considered "impenetrable." In his response, Joffre stressed that the measures which enabled an effective defence were the subject of his constant personal attention and that since November 1914 he had issued numerous orders and directions specifically regarding this issue while at the same time ensuring that they were being carried out. (Actually, the first and second lines had only recently been reinforced with concrete structures.) While no segment of the front was considered to be impenetrable, in his opinion French forces would be able to successfully repel enemy attacks any time and at any place.

Attacks against the Supreme Commander from members of the armed forces had to be a more serious concern to Joffre than the attitude of the government. On 2 July, in the Army Commission of the Senate, Representative Charles Humbert read aloud an anonymous letter, purportedly authored by a corps commander, that was sharply critical of Supreme Headquarters.[1]

---

1   Raymond Poincaré, *Au Service de la France*, Vol. VI (Paris: Plon, 1928), 303.

The Supreme Commander found that Millerand, the Minister of War, who had always warmly interceded on his behalf, was an important supporter. However, loud complaints about mismanagement in various departments of the military administration were heard in the Senate and Chamber as well. The complaints centred on the fact that it had been impossible to satisfy the high demand for gun barrels to replace those damaged by defective ammunition. Also, the number of field batteries was insufficient to arm any new formations. Despite the appointment of an Undersecretary of State for munitions and the increased demands placed on private industry, it had not been possible to satisfy military requirements in general and those of the heavy artillery in particular. The medical service and the *intendance militaire* were also targeted for complaints.[2]

However, the force ratio still appeared to favour the Entente forces in the West, as Germany did not seem to have enjoyed a notable increase in forces. The French ascertained that between 12 June and the beginning of July the Germans had added only eight new infantry battalions. Thus it would be desirable to mount a pre-emptive attack on the enemy before additional forces could be withdrawn from the East. For the time being, however, France could not count on the availability of additional forces of its own. The 1915 age group had been called up in April but was not yet active; the next age group was now being trained and would not be ready for action in the autumn. Also, major reinforcements from Africa could not be expected any time soon.

The situation in Great Britain was different. There, sufficient combat forces were available. In addition to the twenty-two infantry divisions already deployed on French soil (not counting the territorial divisions), twenty-six new (Kitchener) divisions and one Canadian division were being trained and were almost combat ready. The British Supreme Commander, Field Marshal Sir John French, supported the idea of launching a major offensive with the French, but only if these reinforcements—or at least a large part of them—were made available. Like Joffre, he thought it would be a mistake to commit large forces in another theatre, believing that the war would be decided entirely in France. Yet after repeated requests, he had received neither reinforcements (except for three new Kitchener divisions and a few territorial units) nor a promise for their deployment in the foreseeable future.

This restraint was due to the fact that the British Army's leadership did not have a clear vision for the future conduct of the war. The results of the spring offensives in the Artois had been understandably disappointing, and it seemed doubtful that a breakthrough along the Germans' Western Front was even possible.

---

2 *The* intendance militaire *was a supply arm of the military that corresponded generally in its duties to the departments of the Quartermaster General and Finance within the British War Office.*

Meanwhile, prominent people were using all their influence to have major forces deployed to the Dardanelles with the objective of quickly conquering Constantinople.[3] Lord Kitchener, the prime minister's primary counsellor in military matters, was not inclined to deploy the last of his home reserves to France; for the time being he wanted to keep them under his own control. The extremely unfavourable state of munitions production only reinforced his preference. Though a special Ministry of Munitions had been established, headed by David Lloyd George, it had not yet been possible to increase the manufacture of ammunition to the point where even the expeditionary force's minimal requirements were being satisfied. Until something changed, the forces staged in France could not be supplied with enough ammunition for a major offensive, nor could the newly activated units at home be supplied with sufficient ammunition on their transfer to the continent. During a meeting between the French and British representatives responsible for ammunition supply in Boulogne on 19 and 20 June, the British representatives stated that the ammunition required for a major offensive in the West could not be delivered before the spring of 1916 as orders for artillery ammunition placed in the United States had not produced satisfactory results.[4] Therefore, it was desirable to limit ammunition expenditure. This meant adopting a purely defensive posture in the West, with the sole objective of holding the presently occupied positions at all costs.

French plans were seriously jeopardized by the British position. Joffre understood that the willingness that had been expressed repeatedly by the British Supreme Commander to co-operate in the next offensive could only be acted upon when the conditions that allowed for sufficient reinforcement from home were met. At the end of June he repeatedly tried to obtain a commitment through the French government's diplomatic channels. It must remain speculation whether these attempts to influence the British Cabinet would have succeeded, for just then extremely negative reports were received from the Russian Front that engendered very serious concerns for the fate of their Eastern ally. As expressed during a meeting of the French and British prime ministers in Calais on 6 July, these reports caused a total reversal in their assessment of the general situation. At this point, the British government declared its willingness to deploy all the newly formed units to France and the transportation of these units was scheduled to begin on 7 July. The following units were designated to embark for France: from 7 July until 2 August the Second Kitchener Army,[5] on 31 July a second Canadian

---

3 Winston Churchill, *The World Crisis 1915* (New York: Scribner, 1928), 385.
4 Twenty-six million rounds were ordered by the end of May 1915, but only 800,000 had been delivered.
5 Each Kitchener Army consisted of six divisions.

division, from 31 August until the end of September the Third Kitchener Army, the Fourth Kitchener Army from 31 October until the end of November, and the Fifth Kitchener Army at the end of the year. All of these would be followed by additional units in the spring of 1916.

Now that British participation was assured, all that remained was to secure the co-operation of France's remaining allies. The lack of a coordinated command structure was having a negative impact on the course of the war. The French Supreme Commander had exerted a decisive influence on operations on the Western Front by virtue of French numerical superiority and Joffre's personal reputation; however, the remaining allies (Russia, Serbia, Italy) had been conducting the war mostly according to their own designs. In a letter of 24 June to the Minister of War, the French Supreme Commander pointed out that this state of affairs was disadvantageous and suggested that it was a concern not only to him but also to Tsar Nicolas, the Italian government, and the Belgian prime minister. He suggested that the French government submit joint guidelines for any future operations to France's allies as well as through GQG. On 29 June, Joffre followed up his request with a recommendation that a conference be convened, to be attended by authorized delegates from all Allied countries as soon as was practicable.[6] This meeting took place in Chantilly on 7 July but did not bring any real results, because despite all of their courtesy, the representatives of the eastern allies and Italy were unable to provide specific assurances of their co-operation. Consequently, the French Supreme Commander could only count on the BEF and the weak Belgian Army for the new offensive he was planning.

JOFFRE HAD DECIDED THAT THE SECTOR OF ATTACK WOULD AGAIN BE THE AREA around Arras. It was hoped that in the event of a successful breakthrough there, the rear lines of supply and communications for the entire left flank of the German Army would be placed in serious jeopardy. Because past experience favoured the possibility of widening the field of attack in order to make it difficult for the Germans to quickly redeploy strong reserves from neighbouring sectors, this time the French and British were to attack with the aim of breaking through to the north and south of Arras. The attack was to be made under the overall direction of Army Group *North* and conducted by Tenth and Second Armies, together with elements of the BEF.[7] After the failure of Tenth Army's second attack in the middle of June, and considering the defensive measures taken by the Germans, both

---

6 According to the Italians, the conference was based on a suggestion by General Cordona.
7 At that time the French Second Army was deployed on both sides of the Somme.

senior officers and the rank and file doubted whether a third attempt in the same area could be expected to succeed. Consequently, GQG began to contemplate shifting the main attack to another sector. Eventually, the area held by Army Group *Centre* was settled upon; furthermore, the attack would be executed with complete surprise. For the Arras area, a secondary attack, with the objective of pinning down the enemy, was planned in co-operation with British forces. Joffre finalized his decision on 11 July, designating the Champagne as the primary area for the attack, even though Generals Foch, de Curières de Castelnau, and Pétain voiced their misgivings about mounting another breakthrough attempt.

The initial intention was to begin this new offensive as soon as possible. However, the combat readiness of the soldiers depended on several conditions that had not yet been met. The exhausted units of Tenth Army urgently needed rest. At the same time, manufacturing delays prolonged the time necessary to acquire the proper artillery ammunition, especially for the heavy artillery. The British Commander-in-Chief had promised that his First Army would be combat ready by the middle of July; however, this remained contingent on the arrival of reinforcements from Britain.[8] Since these conditions had not been met, on 20 June Joffre and Field Marshal French agreed at a meeting in Chantilly that the joint offensive would begin in five to six weeks, around the end of July or beginning of August. But even this time frame could not be met. When the Munitions Board was informed of the results of the conference, and when First Army's commander Sir Douglas Haig lodged serious misgivings regarding the date and sector of attack, and especially when it turned out that the British Third Army (which was slated to relieve the French units north of the Somme) would be unable to move into this sector before 8 August, both commanders decided to delay the beginning of the offensive until the end of August. This agreement was reached at a meeting between the two Supreme Commanders at British GHQ in St. Omer on 11 July. The offensive had to be postponed again to 15 September when the French Second Army could not complete its preparations any earlier.

Immediately after the cessation of the spring offensive in the Artois, Joffre had energetically begun to prepare the French Army for a new offensive. As was mentioned previously, given the resources available on the home front, no significant additional forces could be expected; thus the offensive had to be conducted with those forces already deployed, with priority given to the strongest units. To make the most of the available forces, in the sectors not involved in the offensive, territorial divisions would replace more experienced units. Furthermore, a number

---

8   According to French information, these assurances were based on Tenth Army's failure to break through.

of units that had not yet been assigned to a division were combined to form new divisions; at the same time, the combat strength of an infantry company was reduced from 220 to 200 men and the reserve regiments of corps were replaced with territorial units. By the middle of July it had become possible to free up forty infantry divisions for the Supreme Command to designate as "Army Group Reserves" behind the lines. The field artillery for these new formations was procured from existing corps or by deactivating individual territorial divisions. Since not enough modern 75 mm guns were available, planning had to include the use of antiquated 90 mm tubes. To remedy the shortage of heavy artillery, older heavy guns were taken from fortifications in the interior and coastal areas and distributed to the armies to free up modern and more mobile batteries. Using this equipment, the commanding general created a mobile heavy artillery reserve behind the front lines. With the War Ministry's approval, a special combat unit was created that the Supreme Command could deploy if necessary from the few long-range heavy batteries that were available; these units were augmented by their own dedicated aircraft. The trench artillery was reinforced by a number of 58 mm cannons and a few other modern artillery pieces. To accumulate sufficient ammunition, the entire front was ordered to limit its expenditure.

The French Supreme Command was especially interested in the gas weapon that the Germans had so successfully put to use. Since acquiring the steel canisters necessary to release the gas was problematic, plans for utilizing this weapon had to be abandoned for the time being.[9] However, both gas and incendiary projectiles were made available in large amounts.

Since the beginning of June the air force had seen a considerable increase in the number of bombers. In part, these were to be utilized against the elusive German long-range artillery that had appeared opposite Dunkirk, Verdun, and Dannemarie.

Fortifications underwent drastic changes as well. As per a presidential order of 6 August, fortifications along the front came under the command of Joffre. These were quickly divided into three *regions fortifies*—Dunkirk, Verdun, and Belfort—where from now on only the front-line fortifications were to be manned and ready for combat. All other garrison units were changed into mobile field units to be deployed to the front where needed. The fortresses of Toul and Epinal, located behind the front lines, were to be considered merely strong points and depots in the second and third lines.

Offensive planning did not prevent defensive measures. Existing rearward positions were improved and new ones constructed with the help of territorial units

---

9 On the other hand, the British commanders intended to use gas clouds.

and civilian workers contributed by the Ministry of War; the British also co-oper-
ated in this work.

While preparations for the offensive were progressing as planned on the French
side, the British Supreme Command grew more concerned about the intended
nature of their role. On 27 July, Field Marshal French declared the area south of
La Bassée Canal unsuitable for an attack and requested that he be allowed to
choose the sector for his offensive. In response, Foch reminded him of the importance of a joint attack on Tenth Army's northern wing and the disablement of the
German batteries near Loos and Hulluch, which would otherwise flank the French
attack from the north. However, the British Supreme Commander remained
unconvinced. In a letter to Joffre dated 29 July, he admitted that although he had
earlier agreed to make an attack south of the canal, at that time he had been
unaware of the considerable difficulties presented by an attack on Loos and Lens.
He now believed that an advance against the heights at Wytschaete–Messines and
Aubers, which would secure important observation points, would be more effective. If it succeeded, he wrote, the troops would occupy the most favourable winter positions; at the same time, these positions would represent a suitable starting
point for a spring offensive that, it was hoped, would drive the enemy from French
and Belgian soil.

Sir John's remarks led Joffre to believe that the British Field Marshal considered the attacks planned for the autumn to be merely preparatory to a decisive
offensive to be launched the following spring. He responded on 5 August that he
could not find a more favourable area of attack in front of the British sector than
between La Bassée Canal and the line Loos–Hulluch. Any offensive undertaken in
another place could only be a minor operation and limited in scope because it
would come under German artillery fire from both flanks. Since half of all the
French forces were to be employed for the agreed-upon double offensive in the
Artois and the Champagne, British participation with all available forces and
assets would be vital.

On 10 August, Field Marshal French declared that although he stood by his concerns, he would accede to Joffre's wishes since he was the "generalissimo"; he
would reinforce his First Army and make all preparations for the attack south of
the canal. Here he considered the main objective to be suppressing enemy artillery
and pinning down the German infantry. With this in mind, on 7 August French
instructed Haig to make the attack between Loos and Hulluch, mostly with artillery
and initially without the deployment of major infantry forces.

This certainly did not coincide with Joffre's wishes. On 14 August, the French
commander emphasized that the promised British assistance could only be effective if it came in the form of a strong, sufficiently broad attack, made with all

available forces, and carried forward by the will to achieve victory. Sir John was evasive, pointing out that although he was completely aware of the operational imperatives, his co-operation depended on the amount of ammunition allocated to him. At about the same time, Joffre learned from a French liaison officer at British GHQ that the Field Marshal was displaying a marked reluctance to comply with French wishes regarding the offensive. He reported that in order to create the appearance of compliance with the French demands, Sir John was planning three smaller independent attacks for Loos and the area to the north—each to be made with only one infantry division—while he prepared for a larger attack with an estimated six infantry divisions farther north near Violaines.

The differences of opinion between the two Entente commanders had grown sufficiently large to jeopardize successful co-operation in the impending offensive. In the circumstances, direct negotiations did not hold much promise. However, Lord Kitchener's visit to the French Front on 16 to 19 August opened the possibility of resolving the situation in another way. Deeply affected by the grim news from the Russian Theatre, Lord Kitchener, the British Secretary of War, recognized the need for a certain level of unified operational command in the Western Theatre and declared his willingness to present a proposal from Joffre to his government for approval:

> While British operations are primarily conducted on French soil and are contributing to the liberation of this said soil, the initiative for the combined activities of the French and British forces—especially concerning the deployment of assets, the determination of objectives, and the timing for each operation—will be exercised by the French Supreme Commander. It is understood that the Supreme Commander of the British Forces retains total freedom of choice over the means of execution.[10]

It can be assumed that Lord Kitchener conveyed this message to Sir John during his visit to British headquarters immediately afterwards. On his return to London on 21 August, Lord Kitchener directed the British Supreme Commander in the name of the government to energetically assume the offensive. On 26 August the French Minister of War was able to inform Joffre that the British government had accepted Lord Kitchener's proposal. With that, an important step toward the unification of Supreme Command on the Western Front had been taken. From this point on the French Supreme Commander could count on the co-operation of the BEF for the implementation of operations he considered necessary.

---

10 See James Edmonds and G.C. Wynne, *Military Operations: France and Belgium, 1915, Volume 1* (London: Macmillan, 1927).

During a visit to Chantilly on 22 August, Field Marshal French gave his assurances that the British First Army would attack south of the canal concurrently and in direct support of Tenth Army. He reaffirmed this commitment on 6 September by stating that for the offensive, First Army had six infantry divisions and 900 guns—270 heavy guns among them—at its disposal. In order to deceive the enemy, First Army's remaining six divisions would concurrently execute three local forays north of the canal in three different locations; farther north, Second Army (with a total strength of ten divisions) would attack with two divisions in the area east of Ypres. Third Army would hold its recently acquired sector between Boisleux and Lihons with six divisions. The Supreme Command would also stage three newly arrived Kitchener divisions and five cavalry divisions in GHQ Reserve in the operational sector of First Army.

Joffre had already turned to Belgian General Headquarters to ask the Belgian Army to co-operate in containing the enemy by attacking during the impending offensive. Because of local difficulties and their own weakness, the Belgians were only able to promise minor forays and increased artillery activity. However, with Foch's intervention, the French Supreme Commander managed to obtain a commitment from the British Naval Commander that the British Navy would bring the German-occupied Channel Coast under naval gunfire at the beginning of the offensive. In connection with this, Joffre directed the units of XXXVI Corps stationed at Nieuport to bring the German coastal batteries under fire at the same time.

To establish a link with the Italian Army, the Supreme Commander travelled to the Italian Front on 4 and 5 September and received General Cadorna's commitment to conduct a renewed and speedy attack on the Isonzo; this was planned for the end of September.[11]

Thus the French Supreme Commander had made extensive arrangements not just to commit the maximum French forces and assets to the often-postponed double offensive—which was now set for 25 September and was to be launched in the Artois and the Champagne—but also to ensure the maximum support of his allies. The upcoming events were awaited with optimism.

The Situation at the *OHL* to 22 September

At the time of Falkenhayn's conference with the Western Armies' Chiefs of the General Staff in Metz on 29 July 1915, the situation on this front seemed to be quiet and stable enough that an additional division could be detached from the

---

11　See *DW* IX: 327.

Western Army and redeployed to the East.[12] A few days later, on 8 August, 115th Infantry Division—which was in the *OHL*'s reserve south of Mézières—was also to be transferred. Because of these troop movements, the German Crown Prince voiced his concerns about further decreasing the strength of the Western Front; in his opinion this was no longer advisable "for reasons of security in the event of an enemy attack, and to have the ability to relieve the exhausted troops in the frontlines." He was advised that—except for 85th Reserve Infantry Brigade, which was to be reunited with XXII Reserve Corps—further troop transfers from the Western Front to the East were not being contemplated. With that the size of the forces deployed in the West reached their lowest level to date.

On the same day that Falkenhayn ordered 115th Infantry Division's transfer, he informed the Belgian General Government that six divisions would be arriving from the Russian Theatre in three to four weeks for approximately fourteen days of rest and that at the beginning of September the strength of the Western Army would again have to be increased, even if the campaign against Serbia necessitated the detachment of one or two well-rested divisions.

At the meeting in Metz, Falkenhayn had also directed Generalleutnant von Knobelsdorf, Fifth Army's Chief of Staff, to provide an opinion based on his personal inquiries concerning the feasibility of an operation intended to clear Upper Alsace of the enemy.

Apparently in order to ensure that preparations for these intended operations on the left flank of the Western Army were being properly coordinated, on 1 August Falkenhayn ordered that Armee-Abteilungen *Falkenhausen* and *Gaede* be placed under Fifth Army Headquarters, to which Armee-Abteilung *Strantz* had already been subordinated for some time. This formed a new German army group under the command of the German Crown Prince and with it a separate army group staff, as had been the case during the existence of the same command in the winter of 1914–15.

In his report of 13 August, Knobelsdorf argued that it would be difficult to drive the French from occupied German territory in the southern Vosges and that such an operation would not achieve a militarily significant result. On the other hand, an attack through the Sundgau against Belfort could lead to the capture of that important fortress. His report contended that it would not be necessary to use more infantry for such an attack than the eight additional infantry divisions necessary for the operation to liberate German territory in the southern Vosges. He added that although more assets should be accorded to the heavy artillery, the

---

12   At various times he intended to transfer all of III Corps to the East. See the diary of General-major Groener, 31 July 1915.

massive fortifications could be engaged from a great distance. Although General-major Tappen, Chief of the *OHL*'s Operations Division, pointed to the advantages of an attack on Belfort, in a note written in the report's margins Falkenhayn said that it would "divert attention from a later attack in another location." The General Staff chief did not immediately respond to this proposal. Rather, he requested Knobelsdorf's opinion as to whether "the intended result would not be achieved faster and more effectively by an advance in a southerly direction via St. Dié." Knobelsdorf's reply of the 19 August rejected this operational choice, pointing out that negotiating the many deep valleys that ran in a westerly direction would be extremely difficult and that such an operation would require an additional eight corps instead of four.

Not until 24 August did Falkenhayn respond with a telegram to Fifth Army Headquarters, which read:

> The recommendations contained in the reports of the 13th and 17th of August are approved and the necessary preparations ... are requested to begin immediately. Presently, the time for its execution has not been firmly determined ... The prerequisite for success is the utmost secrecy of all the preparatory measures.

Although an initial order had thus been given, it must remain open whether at that point Falkenhayn had truly decided to launch the attack on Belfort. At any rate, at that time he could not determine when—and to what extent—it would be possible to concentrate large forces on the Western Front.[13]

In the meantime the situation in the West had worsened. Sixth Army still could not afford to release strong reserves, even though it was three infantry divisions, one *Landwehr* brigade, and a number of heavy batteries stronger than it had been at the beginning of the spring battles at Arras, and despite a report dated 14 August suggesting that the enemy was not preparing to attack. On 24 August, Falkenhayn was forced to make available 123rd Infantry Division (staged behind the army).

Since the end of June, Third Army had been reporting that enemy sappers were at work on its front. This was initially interpreted as a purely defensive measure. As late as the end of July, Third Army Headquarters was reporting that immediate indications of an attack could not be observed anywhere and that while major attacks were entirely improbable, smaller attacks on both sides of Suippes could not be discounted. Since the beginning of August a more ominous tone had crept into the army's dispatches to the *OHL*. Even so, as late as the middle of

---

13 On 25 August—only one day later—the initial orders were issued for the detachment and transfer of the divisions from the Eastern Army for the campaign against Serbia.

the month, Third Army Headquarters still sensed that the enemy was in the process of reinforcing its defensive installations, although "the possibility that these preparations concern an attack against the left flank of the army is nevertheless being kept in sight."

On 16 August the *OHL* felt that Army Headquarters should be advised of intelligence reports mentioning an impending Entente offensive, even though the authenticity of the reports could not be confirmed. Over the following days and toward the end of the month, Third Army's reports to the *OHL* increasingly contained mounting indications of an impending attack.

The first orders for the transfer of forces from the Eastern Front to the West were issued on 28 August. They concerned the Guard Corps, which had been detached from Army Group *Mackensen* with orders to march from Brest-Litovsk to the area around Warsaw—a march that took almost fourteen days. Additional forces consisting of X Corps and three-quarters of XXII Reserve Corps were to follow; however, orders for their transfer were not issued until the beginning of September.[14] On 11 September the first elements of the Guard Corps began to entrain for their temporary transfer from the Russian Front to Belgium, followed on 12 August by X Corps; but by 24 September only three divisions had arrived in the Belgian rest areas assigned to them. On 30 August additional orders for the transfer of twenty-six heavy batteries from East to West were issued; on their arrival a number of modern and fully equipped batteries were to be transferred from the Western Army to Army Group *Mackensen*. The transport of the troops from Russia took from 11 to 20 September; afterwards they were allotted time for rest and for the maintenance of their equipment.

On 24 August the *OHL*'s Intelligence Division estimated the number of French infantry divisions available in continental France at 110 and a half, including fourteen territorial divisions of lesser value. Of this total, thirty-seven—fully one-third—were supposedly staged farther to the rear as reserves. Compared to Germany, the French commander had considerably more freedom to act and was thus able to consolidate his available forces more effectively. Of the thirty British divisions, twenty-eight were deployed in their entirety, including two of battalion strength. Not quite half (fourteen) were to be deployed at the front, with at least the same number staged behind. With this abundance of force, it was no wonder the British had taken over French XI Corps' sector, placing their right flank on the Somme.

Further increases to the French forces—less by increasing the number of men at arms than by creating new divisions out of existing units—were thought to be

---

14 The 85th Reserve Infantry Brigade was deployed with Third Army.

impossible, whereas significant growth in the BEF was expected. The six divisions of Third Kitchener Army were expected to arrive on the continent in the near future, while the combat readiness of Fourth and Fifth Kitchener Armies' additional twelve divisions seemed to be considerably delayed owing to difficulties with equipping and training the attached artillery. It was also known that in addition to these Kitchener divisions, the British High Command had begun to turn a number of territorial divisions of the second order (allegedly fourteen) into combat divisions; however, their appearance in France was not expected before 1916. Consequently the full development of the British Army was only anticipated for the following summer.

In the meantime, agents' reports received from the middle to the end of August regarding an impending Anglo-French offensive had deviated strongly from one another on specific details such as location and timing, and thus were not deemed credible enough sources on which to base firm conclusions. However, new reports (especially those from Third Army) that carefully weighed every possibility were more and more inclined to consider the possibility of a major enemy offensive. This brought about a change in view at the *OHL*. On 5 September, after receiving a strongly substantiated request for reinforcements from Third Army Headquarters, General Tappen noted in his diary: "We must seriously expect a major Franco-British attack in a number of locations."[15] The previous day, the armies in the West had been asked whether sufficient preparations had been made to repulse enemy advances—especially with regard to the ammunition supplies for firing positions—and whether such attempts could be pre-empted or at least interrupted by an increase in the expenditure of ammunition. Most of the armies responded to the first question in the affirmative while expressing doubt as to whether an increased expenditure of ammunition would succeed in the long term against an enemy advance. As a result, Falkenhayn recommended that ammunition be used for firing at identified batteries only.

On 7 September, Falkenhayn transferred 5th Infantry Division from the area of Valenciennes into the Champagne in order to have a reserve available to him in the event that it was needed behind Third Army. In contrast, no directives were issued to move the almost three divisions deployed as a GHQ reserve behind the Western Army's left flank, where they were being used from time to time to relieve exhausted elements of Armee-Abteilungen *Falkenhausen* and *Gaede*, to the centre and right flanks of the Western Army.

---

15 *It would appear that "strongly substantiated" is meant to suggest that the request was substantiated by evidence that an attack was highly likely on the front of Third Army.*

While the situation on the Western Front was intensifying, on the Serbian Front most of the promised Austro-Hungarian forces failed to arrive. Falkenhayn was thus required to considerably reinforce the German forces intended for that front lest the entire Serbian campaign be jeopardized; however, he found it impossible to do so without using forces from the Western Front. So after ordering the transfer of 85th Reserve Infantry Brigade on 18 August—over numerous protests from Third Army—he ordered the speedy transfer of III Corps a day later. Sixth Infantry Division and Corps Headquarters were to be the first to go, followed by 5th Infantry Division starting on the evening of 24 August. The first elements of XXII Reserve Corps, which had just begun the journey to Belgium by rail, were diverted to southern Hungary, where they were to participate in the Serbian campaign.[16] Third Army Headquarters' request that another brigade be allocated instead of 85th Reserve Infantry Brigade was only partly accommodated by transferring 183rd Infantry Brigade with nine battalions and three batteries from Lorraine to Third Army's rear, where it arrived on 21 and 22 September.[17] This brigade was to be made available to Third Army in the "event of an enemy attack."

On the evening of 22 September the following reserves were thus available to the *OHL* on the Western Front: 53rd Reserve Division at Roulers; 8th Infantry Division at Douai (although it reported that it would not be combat ready until 1 October, on 6 September it had been promised to Sixth Army Headquarters in the event of an enemy attack); 192nd Infantry Brigade, with eight battalions and three batteries, at Laon (the formation of this new unit was completed by the end of August); 5th Infantry Division at Attigny, which was expected to be transferred to the Serbian Theatre on 24 September; 113th Infantry Division west of Metz, which at this time had given its three infantry regiments to Armee-Abteilung *Strantz* in return for two regiments requiring rest and recuperation (the missing third regiment was to be ready for entraining twenty-four hours after the receipt of the appropriate order); 56th Infantry Division at Saarburg in Lorraine and in the Breusch Valley; 19th Reserve Division at Colmar; and 185th Infantry Brigade, with nine battalions and three batteries, at Mulhouse in Alsace (its infantry regiments were deployed to the front and had been replaced by other elements, most of them *Landwehr* that were in need of rest).

Additionally the following units had arrived in Belgium at almost full strength: the Guard Corps, X Corps Headquarters, and 20th Infantry Division (the advance transports of 19th Infantry Division did not cross Russia's western border until 21 September). Both corps, however, were supposed to receive a number of weeks

---

16 There 85th Reserve Infantry Brigade was reunited with its corps.
17 The artillery remained in Lorraine until mid-October.

of rest and replenishment. In terms of artillery, the *OHL* had at its disposal thirteen modern batteries that had arrived from the East and that were again fully operational, and more than eleven dismounted batteries, which would replace modern equipment in sectors not under threat.

With that the strength of the Western Army had increased compared to the beginning of August. Nevertheless, the Entente found the conditions favourable for their offensive. A contributing factor was that the Central Powers had found it necessary to launch the attack against Serbia immediately after the Russian campaign and that stronger German forces than anticipated had had to be committed to that campaign because of the unsatisfactory results of Austro-Hungarian operations in Volhynia.[18] Additionally, offensive operations on the Russian Front in the area of Vilna had yet to be concluded. The entire strength of the German Army thus had to be devoted to attacking simultaneously on the Northern and Southeastern Fronts even while protecting against dangerous reverses in the West. Only through Falkenhayn's audacity was this precarious situation overcome. However, he had left the Western Army dangerously weakened, and the distribution of the sparse forces available to the *OHL* did not correspond to the threat that was clearly discernible in the Artois and the Champagne.[19] When Falkenhayn departed Pleß on the evening of 21 September, the time would have been ripe to congregate the reserves behind Third and Sixth Armies, but this was not done.

This error was caused primarily by the *OHL*'s faulty evaluation of the Entente's intentions. Reports about threatened attacks in the Artois and the Champagne—especially the report from Third Army Headquarters of 5 September—had been sufficiently conclusive to remove any doubts about the enemy's extensive preparations in those sectors. However, Falkenhayn judged the moral fibre—especially of the French—to be insufficient to carry forward another attack with the utmost vehemence. The closing remark of his memorandum of 1 June 1915, titled "France's Interior Situation in May 1915," may be indicative:

> France's sacrifices in this war are so gigantic that the government cannot help but be held responsible for them before the people, and one day before

---

18 *By the middle of July the Central Powers' two earlier offensives towards the San and in Eastern Prussia had created a huge salient in Russian Poland. On 13 July the German and Austro-Hungarian troops advanced along a continuous line and the Russians fell back in a general retreat. By 24 August the Central Powers had reached Brest-Litovsk. Just over six weeks later, on 7 October, a combined German, Austro-Hungarian, and Bulgarian offensive struck Serbia simultaneously from the north and west. See Stone,* The Eastern Front 1914–1917, *165–94.*

19 A memorandum to the *Reichsarchiv* of 20 October 1932 from Generalleutnant Tappen points out that Falkenhayn may well have had definite intentions for this distribution, though anything tangible can no longer be determined.

history, and will soon have to decide whether the future of the nation is not better served by the cessation of resistance than the continuation of the war which, despite all foreign support, is hopeless for France.

Falkenhayn's view as reflected here seemed to be supported by the passivity of both Western enemies in the summer of 1915. He continued to express this judgment until just before the beginning of the enemy assault. Thus Einem's serious warnings against deploying the army reserves until after the enemy attacked went unheeded.

Events on the Western Front to 22 September

In the Artois

In the northern half of the Artois sector up to and including Bully Grenay, German Sixth Army was facing British First Army, which was commanded by General Sir Douglas Haig. In the southern half it faced French Tenth Army under General d'Urbal; the latter formed part of Army Group *North*, which was made up of French forces and controlled an area from the Channel Coast to Nouvron. The objective of the French attack was the heights between Liévin–Souchez and Bailleul; this was to be followed by a breakthrough and pursuit toward Douai. Even though the details had been decided early on, the British had on numerous occasions changed their opinion regarding the choice of sector and the timing of the operation.

From the inception of the plan, the commander of First Army had voiced serious concerns that the main sector for his attack was to be between La Bassée Canal and Loos. That area contained numerous points of resistance in and behind the German lines: it was densely populated and the villages had been upgraded into virtual fortresses. He believed that because of the shortage of heavy artillery and ammunition there were few prospects for a successful breakthrough in this area. Field Marshal French had initially considered supporting the French solely with artillery. Only on 21 August—when Lord Kitchener ordered that the French offensive be supported with all British resources, and when First Army Headquarters learned that a considerable amount of gas would be available for this attack—were all concerns set aside.[20] Based on previous tests, it was expected that the gas would provide considerable support to the attacking infantry.

---

20 The British gas was similar to the German chlorine gas and was dispersed through steel cylinders. Approved by the British Ministry of War in May, it was initially tested at home together with new smoke shells and, for effect, afterwards on a military training ground near St. Omer, where it was presented to the troop commanders on 22 August. Approximately 5,500 cylinders with 150 tons of gas were available for the beginning of the attack.

On the French side, as ordered by the Supreme Commander and Army Group *North*, Tenth Army Headquarters promptly began its preparations for this new offensive. Because the forces involved were made up essentially of those that had been in this area during the spring battles, the battlefield was familiar; thus preparations were aimed mainly at reorganizing and refreshing the exhausted troops.

TURNING TO THE GERMAN SIDE, SIXTH ARMY ON 16 AUGUST RECEIVED A MESsage from the *OHL* stating that "according to intelligence which cannot be verified, a general offensive on the Western Front is deemed to be possible in the near future." Sixth Army's commander, Generaloberst Rupprecht, Crown Prince of Bavaria, at first did not believe that this report should be given particular credence. Also, Sixth Army reconnaissance provided no specific verification of agent reports received on 22 August, which "spoke consistently of an imminent French attack against Alsace and in the area of Arras."

On the evening of 18 August a regiment from French XXI Corps attacked north of Souchez, penetrating the German lines in some places. By 20 August the exhausted regiments of 8th Infantry Division had ended the battle by retaking their positions. This division had to be replaced by 123rd (Saxon) Infantry Division on 25 August; it was subsequently quartered in Douai, where it was placed at the *OHL*'s disposal.

Enemy activity had been steadily intensifying since the end of August.[21] Nevertheless, Sixth Army Headquarters at first did not foresee any imminent new attacks even though Ritter von Fasbender, Commanding General of Bavarian I Reserve Corps, emphasized in a report dated 2 September that "the enemy was planning an attack." A few days later General der Infanterie Sixt, commanding IV Corps, reported that he "considered an attack on his frontlines [to be] possible." After these reports, Crown Prince Rupprecht reported to the *OHL* that he now considered the situation, especially south of the Scarpe, to be sufficiently tense to warrant the allotment of artillery support. In response to the *OHL*'s 2 September survey of all the armies in the West as to what preparations had been made in contingency for a joint enemy attack along the entire front, Sixth Army's commander responded on 6 September that, in such a case (although it was not then expected), Sixth Army Headquarters would request one division from the army reserve. Additional munitions would be required in order to sufficiently equip the batteries for defensive purposes. Soon after the dispatch of this report, aerial

---

21   The enemy's preparations were—at least as far as they appeared to the German side—similar to those described in the Champagne. In the Artois, however, they were not as clearly recognizable.

reconnaissance reported that the villages west of Arras had been occupied with a noticeable density of enemy troops and that there were numerous empty trains in the railway stations at Doullens, St. Pol, and Abbeville. Nevertheless, the war diary of Sixth Army Headquarters stated that the "possibility existed that the British were still extending farther northwards in front of the 11th Infantry Division and that the reported gatherings [of troops] were actually replacements." In order to secure speedy ammunition replacements, the OHL reinforced the munitions reserves in the rear of Sixth Army. Based on the OHL's suggestion, the General of the Foot Artillery at the OHL, General der Artillerie von Lauter, investigated the artillery measures that were to be adopted in the event of a defensive battle. Having found an inventory of 1,021 guns—including 265 heavy guns—he reported that the transfer of two heavy low-trajectory batteries was urgently required.

Since 12 September, VI Corps and Bavarian I Reserve Corps had been reporting that the enemy opposite them was systematically ranging in its guns. Because of this, and because Sixth Army Headquarters initially considered Bavarian I Reserve Corps to be in the most imminent danger, elements of the combined Saxon Brigade *Hammer* (from the army's reserve) were deployed on 5th Bavarian Reserve Division's left flank. On 18 September, Generalmajor Sontag, commanding 111th Infantry Division, reported that because the enemy's behaviour indicated "that an attack was probable, infantry and artillery reinforcements were needed." Consequently, he was given a battalion from Brigade *Hammer*. Based on reports received on 19 September, both Corps Headquarters changed their opinion and concluded that the enemy's activities "merely involved a feint in the area south of [the] Scarpe in order to then mount a more serious operation in the sector of Souchez–Neuville."[22] The air elements available to Sixth Army—nine reconnaissance squadrons with eight assigned single-seat combat aircraft and two artillery aircraft squadrons, which were not deployed until the end of September—had noticed signs that an offensive was imminent only in front of VI Corps and I Bavarian Reserve Corps. Photographs showed a gradual advancement of the enemy's trenches, a steadily increasing occupation of villages, and the accumulation of rolling stock in the yards at St. Pol and Doullens on tracks that ran toward Arras. Around the middle of September the number of enemy aircraft increased. An estimated ten British and eighteen French squadrons with a total of 264 aircraft in the first half of September represented three times the German forces, which totalled seventy machines, including only twenty-four armed C-Aircraft.[23] The situation in front of IV Corps became further unsettled as pilots, in their antiquated and unarmed aircraft, were

---

22 War Diary of Sixth Army Headquarters, 19 September 1915.
23 *Twin-seated biplanes with a light machine gun.*

only sporadically able to penetrate to the west. Here the enemy's system of positions did not indicate any specific preparations for an attack.

Despite the tense situation, on 20 September the *OHL* ordered that III Corps Headquarters and 6th Infantry Division—which at that time were staged in the rear of Sixth Army—be moved to the Serbian Theatre. Sixth Army's request that it be allowed to retain the three heavy batteries belonging to III Corps was denied. This further reduced the artillery's defensive potential, in that major elements of it had been detached after the spring battles had ended and moved to Sixth Army's rear, where they formed part of the heavy artillery that was to be placed at the disposal of the *OHL* for the Serbian campaign. The batteries that had arrived at the same time from the East as replacements were in urgent need of rest and were unaccustomed to the defensive battles on the Western Front.

On the morning of 21 September the prevailing opinion at Sixth Army Headquarters was "that a major French attempt at a breakthrough seemed to be imminent." During the previous night, German positions on each side of Arras had been subjected to intense fire while at Neuville-St. Vaast the enemy mounted a probe. The losses, especially for VI Corps, were considerable. The French artillery was described as greatly superior; VI Corps reported a fourfold superiority. Pritzelwitz and Fasbender had the impression that the enemy intended to methodically grind their positions into the ground; however, the attack did not seem to be forthcoming. Nevertheless, as a precaution, Crown Prince Rupprecht moved his solitary army reserve—which had been formed out of elements of 2nd Guard Reserve Division—behind his front's most threatened sector at Douai.[24] Two horse-drawn and two unhorsed heavy howitzer batteries and one mortar battery from the *OHL*, three horse-drawn howitzer batteries and one 13 cm gun battery from neighbouring armies, and four horse-drawn howitzer batteries from the army's northern flank were brought up to IV and VI Corps, Bavarian I Reserve Corps, and 111th Infantry Division. On 21 September, Sixth Army had 795 field guns, 172 high-angle guns and eighty-two heavy low-trajectory guns as well as one super-heavy low-trajectory gun. At 14:00 the enemy fire began to increase, while aerial reconnaissance reported numerous enemy columns advancing in a westerly direction toward Arras and the area north of the city.

After directing lively activity solely against the left flank of VII Corps in the morning, in the afternoon the British brought the entire front between Lille and Lens under heavy fire as well; it was not clear whether this meant that preparations for an attack were under way in that area also.

---

24 Consisting of the staff of the 26th Reserve Infantry Brigade with Reserve Infantry Regiments 15 and 91.

So, as of 21 September it was not yet possible to determine whether the enemy's planned attack had been widened. Based on reports received at Army Headquarters, Sixth Army concluded that while attacks "between Souchez and Maison Blanche and at Beaurains" were to be expected, farther south they would be merely "demonstrations." Indian soldiers who had defected to 13th Infantry Division reported that the British intended to attack on 22 September following a bombardment that was to commence at 09:00.

In the Champagne

On the French side, the Commander of Army Group *Centre*, General de Curières de Castelnau, was responsible for making preparations for the attack in the Champagne. In accordance with his instructions, in the attack's main sector between Moronvilliers and the Aisne the necessary arrangements were made by General de Langle de Cary, Fourth Army's Supreme Commander. Fourth Army was already deployed in its attack sector; the staff of Second Army—under General Pétain— would not arrive in Châlons-sur-Marne until 10 August, when it was to assume the eastern half of the battle front to just west of Perthes-lès-Hurlus. Until 20 September it was known as Group *Pétain* for reasons of secrecy.

The attack sector had few villages and lacked a communication network or watering holes, so a great deal of work was required to provide billets, build roads, and drill wells. To move supplies, at the end of July a railway track was begun along the route Cuperly–Auve–Ste-Ménehould. By the beginning of the attack the railway had been completed and was ready for operation, while at Châlons-sur-Marne two new bridges had been built across the river. In accordance with the Army Group's wishes, digging in both armies' front lines was to begin as close to the attack as possible.

ON THE GERMAN SIDE OF THE CHAMPAGNE FRONT, THIRD ARMY'S GENERAL- oberst von Einem (a.k.a. Rothmaler) and his Chief of Staff Generalleutnant Ritter von Hoehn held a line of approximately 70 kilometres with about eight infantry divisions. Toward the end of July, both on their front and on Fifth Army's right flank, the routine of quiet positional warfare began to change. Enemy planes flew over the German positions, observing them and apparently ranging batteries. Behind the French lines, major troop movements on the roads and railways were discernable. The German commanders could still not decide whether this meant that replacements were being brought up or whether new attack preparations were under way. Third Army Headquarters tended to believe the former.

At the beginning of August, south of Moronvilliers on the French railway lines Châlons-sur-Marne–Mourmelon-le-Petit and Châlons–Suippes, 23rd Reserve Division observed especially heavy rail traffic passing at ten-minute intervals. Aerial reconnaissance photos showed extensive new construction at the railway stations along these routes as well as the appearance of numerous branch lines with narrow-gauge tracks. Also, a number of airfields and extensive camps were being built around Châlons, Suippes, and Mourmelon. Reports came in of heavy traffic in men and wagon columns on the roads leading from Châlons to Third Army's front and to Fifth Army's right flank. The aerial photos clearly showed the beginnings of "honeycomb" trenches (*Wabengräben*), which the enemy used to stage its assault units.

This increase in combat activity made repair work on the German positions necessary, but progress was hindered by the proximity of the enemy—in some places the French and German sapheads were only a few metres apart—and by the almost continuous fire. Hand grenades and *Minenwerfer* soon became the main weapons of trench warfare. In contrast to the German ammunition shortage, the French seemed to have abundant trench mortar ammunition, which they expended generously. Owing to the close proximity of the opposing lines, the heavy artillery could only engage the enemy's trench mortars where it would not endanger the German infantry. In August this intensification of positional warfare, which was accompanied by increased subterranean mine warfare, caused heavy casualties among the divisions stationed at the focal point of the battle.

The chalk earth of the Champagne, which was only sparsely covered by topsoil, made all digging operations widely visible. In the rain, the soil changed to a slimy substance that made any movement inside and outside the trenches extremely difficult. In addition to repairing the front-line trenches, the combat units had to upgrade the rear positions as well. In an area as sparsely populated as the Champagne, it was necessary to undertake extensive new construction projects, which included the building of camps, roads, railways, wells, and a variety of rest stations.

On 20 August a deserter was delivered to VIII Reserve Corps. He announced that a major attack by French colonial regiments (which had already been staged at Somme-Suippe) was planned for the middle of September. Another French soldier who deserted at Aubérive on 31 August also reported that over the previous three weeks, reinforcements and war materiel had constantly been arriving at the front and that the intention was to begin an offensive in about two weeks. After the end of August the enemy's attack preparations in the Champagne visibly increased from one day to the next. On 5 September, Generaloberst von Einem reported to the *OHL*:

It is impossible to misinterpret the excellent aerial reports that show the enemy is systematically expanding his attack positions in front of the Army's left flank, exactly in accordance with Joffre's instruction of 15 April.[25] Remarkably good progress has been made on this work which, covered by strong artillery and trench mortar fire, continues without regard for casualties. Adding the troop and transport movements observed since July from the direction of Châlons to Suippes and Mourmelon, as well as the reports of prisoners and deserters and information found on the dead, everything points to replacements and reinforcements being moved forward. Although our intelligence does not paint a clear picture of the opposing forces, one must now reach the conclusion that it is no longer possible but rather probable that a carefully and long-planned attack is imminent. As a result, this attack will be both intense and sustained.

Every possible organizational and physical preparation has been made for the defence. Considering the expected force of the attack, however, we have insufficient forces. Additional artillery and infantry are needed to shorten the regimental sectors, thus creating an indispensable and important backbone. It would be too late to deploy these forces after the attacks have started as initial, localized enemy successes might be possible. These would bring counterproductive political consequences that could only be corrected at the cost of heavy casualties. An orderly distribution and deployment of infantry reinforcements would then no longer be possible and we would have to live from hand to mouth. Therefore the Army Staff considers a further commitment of forces as important, namely:

a) The 85th Reserve Infantry Brigade—which has already been assigned— must be staged in the front line. Since we are now without an army reserve, a replacement is desired.

b) The heavy artillery must be further reinforced to the extent that three modern heavy field howitzer batteries, one mortar battery, and one heavy low-trajectory battery be positioned in each of the five threatened divisional sectors; in addition to the already allocated equipment, nine heavy field howitzer batteries, three mortar batteries, and three 10 cm cannon batteries should also be assigned ...

Should the attack really come to pass, in accordance with the experiences gained during the winter battles, the regular replacement of the most seriously affected troops is vital. Based on the breadth of the attack, this could necessitate the commitment of additional troops.

---

25 This captured French order suggested that the French would use the experiences of the winter battles in the Champagne in planning future attacks.

In response to this report, Falkenhayn sent a telegram:

> It is not possible to equally equip those divisions with artillery as requested where an enemy attack is only thought to be probable. Only three mortar batteries and three heavy field howitzer batteries can be transferred, and the latter are available only until 12 September. I agree with the deployment of the 85th Reserve Infantry Brigade to the front line, however, for the time being a replacement is unavailable.

On 7 September, III Corps' 5th Infantry Division was transferred from Sixth Army into GHQ Reserve at Attigny.

On 9 September, Third Army reported:

> In the area of Beauséjour—on a front extending from a point approximately two kilometres to the east of the village as far as Prunay—combat continues throughout the day and night, the intensity of which declines from east to west. Further west, only occasional artillery fire is being directed against Berru. However, the actual intention to attack (that is, advance sapping, the upgrading of assembly points and connections to the rear, methodical but unobtrusive artillery ranging, and very strong aerial activity) is only being observed in the area two kilometres east of Beauséjour up to Aubérive inclusively and towards Point 181 (three and a half kilometres southwest of Vaudesincourt). Here the enemy is making advances, however our coordinated artillery and trench mortar fire seems to have slowed him down.

The following day, at a conference at GHQ that included the general in charge of the foot artillery, Third Army's commander requested six howitzer, two mortar, and three modern heavy low-trajectory batteries to reinforce his heavy artillery. The *OHL* replied that batteries were expected from the East, but not until 15 September. By 10 September the commanders of Fifth and Third Armies had both made arrangements with respect to providing mutual artillery support on their armies' boundaries.

The weak aerial reconnaissance assets available to the German side did not permit the routine, methodical spotting of newly identified enemy batteries, nor could the limited number of single-seater fighter aircraft prevent enemy aerial reconnaissance. Thus after the beginning of September the French enjoyed uncontested air supremacy in favourable weather, for Third Army had at its disposal only four reconnaissance squadrons, each comprising six reconnaissance aircraft, one giant aeroplane, and three Fokker fighter aircraft. Between 10 and 22 September the Army had also acquired six aircraft from Carrier Pigeon Detachment Ostende.[26] The number

---

26 *"Carrier Pigeon" was a euphemism for aerial bombers.*

of German anti-aircraft guns was also insufficient. For instance, until 29 September, XII Reserve Corps had only one stationary platoon and one or two mobile guns mounted on trucks. Therefore enemy aircraft were able to reconnoitre and spot throughout the day; at times as many as twelve of them were flying almost unimpeded above one divisional sector alone. Photos and maps recovered later proved that these aircraft had gathered extensive and detailed information about the German positions. They observed traffic in the German lines and rear areas, where they identified troop assembly points and supply routes, sometimes even at night from occasional flares of light. Still farther to the rear they landed soldiers who were familiar with the ground or local inhabitants with carrier pigeons to carry espionage and sabotage orders. Shortly before the beginning of the offensive, strong French bomber squadrons attacked distant railway stations, depots, and villages. On the night of 20 and 21 September a dirigible flew from the direction of Reims and bombed the railway hub at Amagne.

Nevertheless, the Germans' efforts with their severely outnumbered aircraft enabled them to assess the enemy's attack preparations, as well as the improvements the enemy was making to its railway stations, tent encampments, and airfields. Several air service squadrons and bomber attacks were launched against these newly constructed facilities. The Germans' repeated attempts to reconnoitre and range their artillery were supplemented as much as possible by a number of captive balloons.

Over the course of September, across from Third Army's centre and left flank and Fifth Army's right flank, the enemy drove its trenches to within 100 metres of the German lines. The French positions remained farther away only at Aubérive, Souain, and northwest of Massiges. Usually the new positions had been created by advancing numerous saps and then connecting the sapheads. The enemy trenches, which had at one time been far away, were advanced across no man's land under cover of darkness or camouflage nets; they were then consolidated (especially in the sector held by XII Reserve Corps). The French access trenches had been extended up to 5 kilometres to the rear and were positioned close together, roughly 1 kilometre apart. Completed honeycomb trenches and passages over rear positions became more numerous and clearly defined on aerial photographs. In the rear areas, the enemy extended and covered assembly points, apparently for the cavalry. Ramps led down to especially deep and widely excavated approach routes, allowing mounted troops to advance under protection close up to the front lines.

After the end of August the enemy artillery grew from one day to the next, as evidenced by the identification of numerous additional batteries despite attempts at camouflage. At the start of the infantry attacks it seemed as if more than one battery was identified for every known battery and observation post. Not until the heavy barrage began on 22 September did a clear picture of the French artillery develop.[27] The almost non-stop searching and sweeping fire seriously disrupted communications and thus command and control. The heaviest low- and high-trajectory guns began firing only immediately prior to the infantry attack.

The weak, hard-pressed, and besieged German artillery was of little help to the infantry. Accordingly the German front-line divisions suffered badly from the enemy artillery preparation, which lasted for weeks; only occasionally were they able to defend themselves against the enemy's attack preparations. Even so, small artillery operations were conducted in almost every divisional sector by combining all available batteries and trench mortars. There is no doubt that they were at least somewhat successful, for by the time the enemy began its offensive, its assault positions had not been entirely finished, which resulted in casualties. A few long-range German guns attempted to interrupt the French deployments and supply routes but were soon silenced by hostile fire. Owing to the artillery's numerical weakness relative to the length of the front, the German defensive fire was ineffective. Inadequate coordination between the infantry and the artillery was common, especially because the flares used by the trench garrisons to request artillery support could not climb to a sufficient altitude and often could not be seen through the dust and smoke created by the enemy's fire.

Requests from the German front-line divisions for artillery, ammunition, airplanes, and anti-aircraft guns grew ever more urgent. But those requests could not be adequately satisfied. Army and Corps Headquarters were in no position to develop significant artillery reserves.

The week-long preparatory fire and daily mine explosions caused considerable damage to the German fire trenches. Ultimately it took all available resources to make provisional repairs. In some places between Aubérive and Massiges (except for a portion of the line on Hill 196 north of Le Mesnil) the German front-line positions were pocked with mine craters and, being located on a frontal slope, became exposed to ground observation and enemy fire without protection. These positions included a number of parallel lines, one running approximately 75 metres behind the other. Protruding corners in a line were secured by switch trenches. The tendency of many subordinate commanders was to garrison the forward trenches—where the company sectors had an average frontage of 400 metres—with too many soldiers and machine guns at the expense of the standby and reserve troops.

---

27 For a comparison of both artillery deployments, refer to Appendix 2. The considerably higher field artillery deployment can be explained by the larger number of divisions employed.

Secondary lines of defence (*R-Stellung*)[28] were located 3 to 4 kilometres behind the forward trenches so that in the event of a breakthrough the enemy would have to redeploy its artillery in order to renew the advance. *R-Stellungen* were usually sited on reverse slopes and were therefore protected from direct observation. They had been readied for occupation by the reserves of the higher commands and recruiting depots; their artillery defences had also been prepared. *R-Stellungen* contained numerous ancillary observation points and decoy infantry and artillery positions; these were intended to disperse hostile fire.

Information was communicated in a well-planned manner using all means available. In addition to separate infantry and artillery networks, special cable trenches for the most important command posts had been dug. Most of the regimental, brigade, and divisional command posts were also staffed with flash signalling sections. These supplemented the heroic runners and horseback riders, who were employed even during the most intense fire. In these situations they were the only reliable means of communication and almost never failed.

The road network behind the army front was greatly improved by the recent completion of roads from St. Clément à Arnes to St. Souplet and from Gratreuil to Ripont. Immediately behind the front lines were numerous parks, depots, and small supply dumps (including ones for ammunition, close-combat materiel, pioneer equipment, construction material, and provisions) as well as medical facilities.

Over the vehement objections of Third Army's commander, 85th Reserve Infantry Brigade—which was deployed in one of the most threatened sectors north of Souain—was taken out of the front lines on the night of 20 and 21 September on orders from the *OHL*. This brigade was transferred to Army Group *Mackensen*. As a replacement, the *OHL* placed 183rd (Saxon) Infantry Brigade in GHQ Reserve north of Rethel in rear of Third Army. Initially three battalions of XIV Corps and two composite cavalry battalions of Cavalry Group *Lippe* were deployed in place of 85th Reserve Infantry Brigade.[29] In an assessment of the

---

28 *The abbreviated term* R-Stellung *was used to denote a continuous rearward defensive position, or a secondary line of defence. In some places these positions were echeloned one behind the other and designated as successive fallback positions and were thus termed R2, R3, etc. The R-Stellung was sometimes located several kilometres behind the front lines in order to force an attacker to pause and renew its advance with a fresh artillery deployment.*

29 The divisional cavalry regiments of Third Army were at the disposal of the supreme commander under the orders of Oberst Count zur Lippe and concentrated south of Rethel.

situation sent to the *OHL* on 21 September, Generaloberst von Einem wrote that the circumstances had "yet to be clarified" and that the enemy's "cavalier employment of infantry in labour, his increasingly intense artillery and trench mortar fire, and his increasing aerial activity—all of which seem purposeful and systematic—at the very least suggest that he is threatening to attack." On 22 September he reported: "This morning heavy barrages on the greater part of XII and VIII Reserve Corps. Reinforcement of heavy artillery is now imperative ... Additionally request permission to commit the entire 183rd Infantry Brigade in the event of an emergency." Based on prisoner reports and supplemental information, his headquarters was able to report to the *OHL* that a French attack under the command of General de Castelnau was "underway" against the German front from Aubérive to Massiges. The report stated that assault units had been staged along the approximate line Aubérive–Ville sur Tourbe. These consisted of XXXII, XXXV, VII, XIV, XI, and XX Corps. The report concluded that behind these corps, "further units are surely staged, probably IV, XVI, and I Colonial Corps, a Moroccan Brigade, numerous GHQ cavalry units, and possibly also XVIII Corps."

Facing these forces massed on the front lines were five German divisions: 24th (Saxon) Reserve Division, the loosely formed Division *Liebert*, 50th Infantry Division, Division *Ditfurth*, and Fifth Army's 21st Reserve Division.

On the Remainder of the Western Front

In the middle of September the commander of Fourth Army, Generaloberst Albrecht (Chief of Staff Generalleutnant Ilse) reported that preparations for an attack were being made at Ypres.[30] Behind Fourth Army's front, 53rd Reserve Division was in GHQ reserve at Roulers.

During August and September, lively firefights occurred in Second Army's sector, commanded by General der Infanterie Fritz von Below (Chief of Staff Generalleutnant von Hoeppner).[31] On both sides of the main Roye–Amiens road, the French prepared for an attack by driving their trenches to assaulting distance.

---

30 Fourth Army, headquartered in Thielt, consisted of eleven divisions including, from approximately north to south, the Marine Corps, Division Basedow, 4th Ersatz Division, XXIII Reserve Corps, XXVI Reserve Corps, XXVII Reserve Corps (without the 53rd Reserve Division), and XV Corps; the 53rd Reserve Division was in GHQ Reserve east of Roulers.

31 Second Army, which was headquartered in St. Quentin, consisted of eleven divisions including, from approximately north to south, XIV Reserve Corps (strengthened by 52nd Division), I Bavarian Corps (strengthened by 10th Bavarian Division), XVIII Corps, and IX Reserve Corps (strengthened by 15th Landwehr Division).

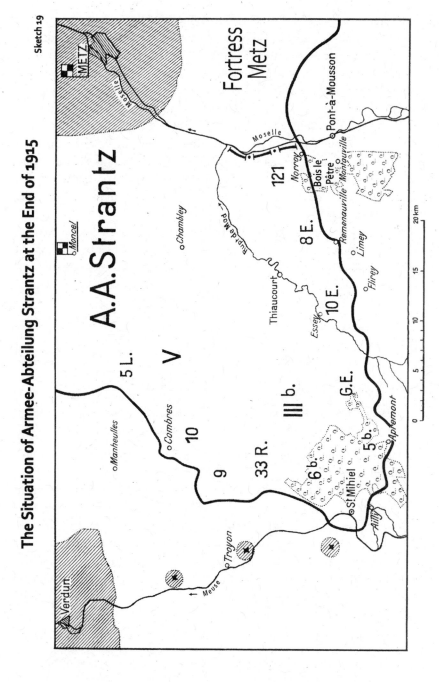

Sketch 19

The Situation of Armee-Abteilung Strantz at the End of 1915

Since the middle of July, increased railway and road traffic had been observed on the French side of First Army's sector, commanded by General der Infanterie von Fabeck (Chief of Staff Generalleutnant von Kuhl), especially around dawn.[32] South of Nampcel, combat activity had increased after the end of August while the enemy extended its trenches up to IX Reserve Corps' right flank. Initially it was unclear whether this signalled an intention to attack or was merely a feint. At the beginning of September, IV Reserve Corps Headquarters was designated for another assignment. Both its divisions were attached to the adjacent IX and VIII Corps. On 17 September, First Army was dissolved. The IX Reserve Corps was transferred to Second Army, and IX and VIII Corps were sent to Seventh Army. With First Army's previous headquarters becoming Twelfth Army Headquarters, Fabeck took over command of that army on the Eastern Front from General der Artillerie von Gallwitz.

Since early September, heavy rail traffic had been observed in front of Seventh Army,[33] commanded by Generaloberst von Heeringen (Chief of Staff Oberst Rudolph von Borries). Lively firefights had been taking place since early September. On 14 September, Seventh Army reported to the *OHL* that the enemy intended to attack:

> The enemy's advance—although delayed by our fire—against XII Corps and the left division of VII Reserve Corps is continuing in various locations ... Assuming that the main focus of the enemy's assault can be expected at another location—perhaps against Third Army—the advance against this army's left part may be seen as a preparation for a side attack or as an attempt to deceive. Nothing speaks to an actual enemy advance on Seventh Army's front; everything seems to be quiet in front of First Army.

Since the middle of September, enemy aircraft had been attacking Seventh Army's rear installations.

In Fifth Army's sector in the Argonne, under the command of Generalleutnant Wilhelm, the German Crown Prince (Chief of Staff Generalleutnant von Knobelsdorf), the lively combat activities of XVI Corps, under the command of General der Infanterie von Mudra, had on 11 August resulted in the seizure of the so-called Martin Works north of the Servon–Montblainville road, which was held by French 15th Colonial Division; on 8 September these activities resulted in the

---

32 First Army was composed of IX Reserve Corps, 15th Landwehr Division, IX Corps, IV Reserve Corps, and VIII Corps.

33 Seventh Army, which was headquartered in Laon, was composed of ten infantry divisions including, approximately northwest to southeast, IX Corps (strengthened by the 22nd Reserve Division), VIII Corps (strengthened by the 7th Reserve Division), VII Reserve Corps, and XII Corps; the 192nd Brigade was in GHQ Reserve east of Laon.

capture of the enemy's positions on both sides of Charmes Creek northeast of La Harazée to a width of almost 2 kilometres.[34] The Germans captured more than 2,000 prisoners, 48 machine guns, and 54 trench mortars.[35] Additionally, at the beginning of September the French artillery and trench mortar fire that had been directed primarily against XVIII Reserve Corps' 21st Reserve Division grew in intensity. An enemy attack against this division seemed probable.

The enemy artillery and trench mortar fire, which to that point had been minimal, increased toward the end of August in the sector of Armee-Abteilung *Strantz*, commanded by General der Infanterie von Strantz (Chief of Staff Oberstleutnant Fischer). However, Strantz's headquarters concluded from an appraisal of the enemy's behaviour that its efforts were aimed less at mounting an attack than at hiding troop movements and keeping the German command in the dark about its intentions. [36]

The situation of Armee-Abteilung *Falkenhausen*, under the command of Generaloberst von Falkenhausen (Chief of Staff Oberst Weidner), remained generally unchanged.[37] But from the beginning of September onwards, the heretofore weak French artillery fire strengthened.

At the beginning of August in the sector of Armee-Abteilung *Gaede*, commanded by General der Infanterie Gaede (Chief of Staff Oberst Hesse), French Seventh Army continued its offensive in the area of Munster that it had begun on 20 July.[38] On 1 August, after an extensive artillery preparation, French 129th Infantry Division

---

34 Fifth Army, headquartered in Stenay, was composed of eleven and a half infantry divisions including, approximately from west to east, XVIII Reserve Corps (without the 25th Reserve Division but strengthened by 9th Landwehr Division), XVI Corps (strengthened by 27th Infantry Division, 1st Reserve Ersatz Brigade, and the 13th Landwehr Brigade), 2nd Landwehr Division, VI Reserve Corps, V Reserve Corps (strengthened by the 77th Brigade). The strength of the artillery was 642 guns, including 234 heavy pieces.

35 The opposing X French Corps lost 4,272 men. See *French Official History,* III:323.

36 Armee-Abteilung *Strantz*, which was headquartered in Chamblay, was composed of eleven infantry divisions including, approximately north to south, V Corps (strengthened by 5th Landwehr Division), 33rd Reserve Division, III Bavarian Corps (strengthened by Ersatz Bavarian Division), Guard Ersatz Division, 10th Ersatz Division, 8th Ersatz Division, 121 Infantry Division. The 113th Infantry Division was in GHQ reserve west of Metz.

37 Armee-Abteilung *Falkenhausen*, which had its headquarters in Strasbourg, consisted of six infantry divisions including, from approximately north to south, 13th Landwehr Division, 1st Bavarian Landwehr Division, 19th Ersatz Division, XV Reserve Corps (strengthened by 61st Landwehr Brigade and 81st Landwehr Brigade). In army reserve the 7th Infantry Division was at Bensdorf and Finstigen and in the GHQ reserve the 56th Infantry Division was at Saarburg and Schirmeck.

38 Armee-Abteilung *Gaede*, headquartered in Homburg, was composed of five and a half infantry divisions including, approximately north to south, 6th Bavarian Landwehr Division, 8th Bavarian Reserve Division (strengthened by 187th Brigade), 12th Landwehr Division, 7th Landwehr Division, and 8th Landwehr Division. In GHQ's reserve, 19th Reserve Division was at Colmar and 185th Brigade was at Mulhausen.

The Autumn Battle in Artois
The Situation on 25 September 1915

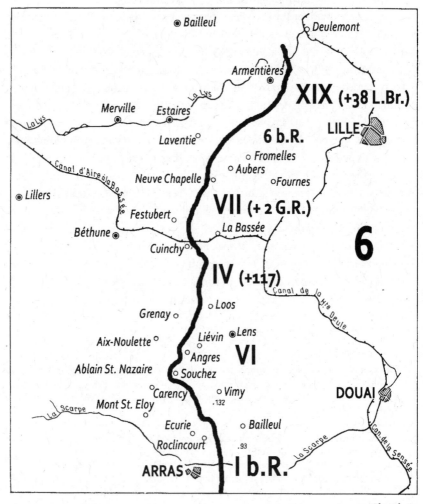

Sketch 20

attacked the positions of Bavarian 6th Landwehr Division on the line Lingekopf–
Schratzmaennele–Barrenkopf but only achieved minimal gains. Bavarian 6th
Landwehr Division had meanwhile been reinforced by elements of 19th Reserve
Division under the command of General der Kavallerie Ritter von Schmidt. In a
counterattack on 4 August, Bavarian 6th Landwehr Division regained the
Lingekopf—which had been lost on 26 July—except for a trench on the southwest

slope of the mountain. Repeated German attacks on 5 and 7 August did not succeed in throwing the enemy off the Schratzmaennele.

After 17 August a number of very strong French attacks were launched against Bavarian 6th Landwehr Division's positions as well as those of Bavarian 8th Reserve Division (commanded by Generalleutnant Baron von Stein) at Sondernach. The Lingekopf, which had again been lost temporarily on 18 August, was recaptured by Bavarian 6th Landwehr Division the next day. After a renewed artillery preparation from 22 to 24 August, the enemy's further attempts to retake the Lingekopf–Barrenkopf position were repulsed. As a result of a 9 September attack by 12th Landwehr Division, commanded by Generalmajor Mengelbier, the peak of the Vieil Armand fell into German hands. Subsequent enemy counterattacks were repulsed.

According to captured enemy orders, the objective of the French offensive— which had been conducted in July and August at Munster using strong forces and on which the enemy placed particular emphasis—had been the Rhine lowlands at Colmar; however, this operation did not result in any French successes worth mentioning. At the end of the battle, even though the enemy fire had been directed mostly at rear supply lines and villages and remained relatively intense until the inception of the autumn battles in the Artois and the Champagne, Bavarian 6th Landwehr Division remained in secure possession of the forward defensive positions at Lingekopf–Barrenkopf. The losses reflected the duration and bitterness of the fighting at Munster. From 20 July to 15 September, both divisions that had been engaged in combat (Bavarian 6th Landwehr Division and Bavarian 8th Reserve Division) and the attached units—especially both brigades of 9th Reserve Division—had lost almost 10,000 men, while the French counted their losses between 20 July and 9 September at 10,578 men.[39]

---

39 *See French Official History,* III: 353–54.

9

THE AUTUMN OFFENSIVE IN THE ARTOIS AND CHAMPAGNE

Preparations for the Battle, 22–24 September 1915

In the Artois

The enemy began actively preparing for the attack in early August. In Tenth Army's sector the main thrust was centred on the area of Angres–Roclincourt, where the objective was the ridge back and to the west of Vimy, a mere 800 to 1,200 metres from the front line. At the same time, Foch assigned special significance to the secondary attack against the German positions between Beaurains and Ficheux. This attack was designed to prevent the German batteries located south of the Scarpe from taking a hand in the battle north of Arras by putting the attack sector under flanking fire. Pursuant to the orders of the Supreme Commander, IX Corps[1] was to reinforce Tenth Army. It arrived on 25 August to take charge of the sector from Agny to the army's right flank. Owing to the attachment of 81st Territorial Division from Dunkirk, d'Urbal was able to replace 58th Infantry Division on the north flank of the army and hold it in reserve. Because of this increase in forces, Tenth Army Headquarters was able to commit fourteen infantry divisions to the initial attack, holding three infantry divisions in reserve.[2] Two additional territorial divisions were assigned to hold the sectors at Liévin, Arras, and Ransart, which were not immediately involved in the attack. To create an army group reserve, Foch positioned I Cavalry Corps

---

1 The 17th, 18th, and 152nd Infantry Divisions.
2 The 130th, 58th, and 154th Infantry Divisions.

south of Aubigny and a *spahi*[3] brigade to the north of the town. Tenth Army's artillery was reinforced by a number of heavy batteries. On 22 August, Joffre had made his heavy artillery reserves—consisting entirely of modern mobile units—available to Army Group *North*, which in turn allocated them to Tenth Army. Prior to the attack d'Urbal thus had 420 heavy guns in addition to the field artillery of the units under his command, and his "trench artillery"[4] had also been substantially reinforced. Although the French commanders refrained from using gas released from cylinders, gas and incendiary shells were made available in large numbers.

In the combat area, infantry and artillery positions were upgraded with great care: suitable shelters were created for the reserves, and secure land-line communications were installed. Special provisions were made for the cavalry pursuit that was to follow up a successful attack.

In the area controlled by the BEF, the line La Bassée Canal–Loos had been chosen as the primary front for First Army's assault. Secondary attacks were also planned at Aubers and Bois Grenier as well as in Second Army's sector east of Ypres. As preparations continued, complications arose with the plan to release gas. On the one hand it was only possible to disperse the gas when wind conditions were favourable. On the other, it was the express wish of the French High Command that the British attack be launched simultaneously with the French attacks. General Sir Douglas Haig thus had to issue orders for both contingencies. In the event of favourable wind conditions, gas clouds were to be released along the entire front between Givenchy-lez-la-Bassée and Loos. These clouds were to be immediately followed by strong infantry forces. If the weather prohibited the use of gas, however, the method of attack was to be slightly different, initially involving the employment of less significant forces. In both eventualities, the attack was to be preceded by several days of carefully executed artillery bombardments. For this task the Supreme Command had allocated to First Army three groups from the heavy artillery reserve even though the ammunition shortage demanded that certain constraints be placed on expenditures.

The main assault was to be launched by I and IV Corps with three divisions each. The III Corps was tasked with the operation at Bois Grenier; the operation at Aubers was assigned to the Indian Corps. In addition, elements of Second Army were ordered to launch a local attack at Ypres. First Army Headquarters' reserve was limited to 3rd Cavalry Division, which was staged southwest of Béthune. As

---

3 *An Algerian cavalry brigade.*
4 *The original text uses "Grabenartillerie"—literally trench artillery—as an irregular translation from French, which is then parenthetically equated to the German word "Minenwerfer."*

a GHQ Reserve, Field Marshal Sir John French had deployed the newly formed XI Corps with three divisions west of Béthune, the British Cavalry Corps in the area northwest of Lillers, and the Indian Cavalry Corps in the area of Doullens. Second Army was directed to place its 23rd Infantry Division on call. The deployment of artillery was executed on time and without incident, whereas the transportation and installation of the gas canisters did not take place until shortly before the attack, when they were installed under the strictest secrecy. The remaining preparations for the attack were camouflaged where possible.

As of 18 September the French and British artillery was in position. After the careful ranging in of the guns, Tenth Army began the artillery preparation between 18 and 20 September, followed by First Army on 21 September. Despite intermittent rain, seemingly satisfactory results were observed. Both armies were absolutely determined to force a breakthrough on the German front that would decide the war.

Since the middle of September the defensive positions and battery emplacements of German Sixth Army between Liévin and Blaireville had been subjected to heavy French artillery bombardments, which diminished only at night. The enemy used guns of all sizes all the way up to and including guns of the heaviest calibre. As a result, the German trenches were almost totally levelled in some places, and the wire obstacles, despite their width, had been pounded into the ground in many locations, even south of the Scarpe; in the built-up areas, even concrete cellars and those dug into the rock had been penetrated. Additionally, the enemy was using phosphorus shells that ignited everything flammable and covered the vicinity in smoke. The British artillery was not so heavy and focused on the sector of 117th Infantry Division north of Lens. Shelling also interrupted the German rail line between Meurchin and Pont à Vendin, which was vital for both supplies and troop movements.

On the morning of 22 September a strong increase in enemy fire was reported south of La Bassée on Sixth Army's front. Sixth Army Headquarters requested additional reinforcements of heavy artillery as well as the assignment of 8th Infantry Division, located near Douai. In response the OHL sent Sixth Army two additional dismounted howitzer batteries from Koblenz, which supplemented the two identical batteries that had been assigned from Metz the previous day, as well as the two horse-drawn howitzer batteries and one mortar battery, which had been staged to the army's rear. As to 8th Infantry Division, the OHL advised that Sixth Army could count on its deployment in the event of a strong enemy attack. Fourth Army also made available a 13 cm gun battery and committed itself to providing flanking support by using other long-range batteries.

On the evening of 22 September the following evaluations of the situation were recorded: General der Infanterie von François (VII Corps) did not expect an assault; General der Infanterie Sixt von Arnim (IV Corps) expected an assault south of the canal at La Bassée; General der Infanterie von Pritzelwitz (VI Corps) expected enemy assaults against 11th Infantry Division; General der Infanterie von Fasbender (Bavarian I Reserve Corps) expected attacks against his right flank and at Beaurains. Crown Prince Rupprecht "did not believe that a British assault was forthcoming on IV and VII Corps because the English had not advanced saps anywhere [along the line]." An assault by the French, however, "seem[ed] possible."[5]

On 23 September, Pritzelwitz visited Sixth Army Headquarters in Lille and described the difficult situation in his sector. He specifically emphasized the tremendous superiority of enemy artillery, which he estimated at 120 batteries, and he requested infantry reinforcements in order to rebuild the destroyed trenches. Only one mortar battery and two battalions from the army reserve (26th Reserve Infantry Brigade) could be made available to him; an additional battalion was dispatched to Bavarian I Reserve Corps. No consideration could be given to VII Corps and Bavarian 6th Reserve Division, both of which had also requested artillery reinforcement. At this point, the reserves available to Sixth Army's commander consisted of only three battalions and three heavy batteries.

On 23 September the fire strengthened along the army's entire front, although the war diarist at Sixth Army Headquarters recorded that "it could only be considered a harbinger of an attack in the area of La Bassée and to the south."[6] A number of enemy bomber squadrons bombed the vital railway stations at Douai, Somain,[7] Wallers, and Cambrai—all used to transport troops—causing considerable damage. Simultaneously the railway station at Pont à Vendin was destroyed by artillery fire. As a result of the enemy's bombing attacks, requests were made for an increase in the *OHL*'s allotment of combat aircraft. In addition to a few quickly allocated C-Aircraft, the *OHL* held out the prospect of sending a squadron from Carrier Pigeon Detachment Metz.[8] With their help, and without being able to prevent enemy attacks against the most important railway stations in the rear area, Army Headquarters' Air Force Detachment assumed the task of systematically protecting the relief and reinforcement units that were detraining and were about to be brought up.

---

5 War Diary of Sixth Army Headquarters, 23 September.
6 *The authorship of these comments was originally noted in a footnote but has been inserted into the text here for clarity.* War Diary of Sixth Army Headquarters of 23 and 24 September.
7 On the line between Douai and Valenciennes.
8 *The bomber detachment consisted of six squadrons with six aircraft each.*

On 24 September, fierce artillery fire—which at times rose to the level of intense bombardment—covered Sixth Army's entire sector south of La Bassée Canal. Aggressive reconnaissance forays by British units were repulsed at Hulluch and Loos, as were those launched by the French at Souchez, Neuville-St. Vaast, and Ecurie. The fiercest bombardment seemed to be directed against VI Corps' sector, where a "standing wall of thrown up pieces of clay" prevented any glimpse of German positions from the rear.[9] At least at this point there could be no doubt about an organized French attack on the line Angres–Ficheux. Whether the British would follow suit south of La Bassée Canal was questionable to Sixth Army Headquarters, for the enemy's front trenches were quite some distance away. The 117th Infantry Division, which was deployed there, only expected secondary forays against its right flank and on both sides of the Lens–Béthune road. North of La Bassée an organized British attack seemed improbable. On 24 September a French soldier who had deserted at Neuville-St. Vaast claimed that "a major assault would take place" the next day at 05:00, with the main assault "coming south of Arras." Sixth Army Headquarters considered this information to be credible and ordered a state of maximum defensive readiness. In case of an "extreme emergency" the OHL made available 8th Infantry Division, whose field artillery (except for one detachment) was already in action. The OHL also moved up two mortar batteries.

In the Champagne

In the Champagne the French armies also began their attack preparations at an early date. The units that were being brought up as reinforcements from other areas of the front did not arrive until later, so the troops already deployed completed the necessary entrenchments. The trenches across the entire attack sector were moved as close as possible to the German lines, and special provisions were made for the staging of the reserves in sheltered areas. The hilly, wooded terrain was the perfect place to house command posts. To facilitate the advance of strong cavalry units, which were to follow up a successful breakthrough, suitable access trenches and passages across the field fortifications had to be created. The High Command also dispatched the necessary heavy artillery well before the attack so that by 7 August, Fourth Army had seventy-seven heavy batteries and Second Army (Group *Pétain*) seventy-four with a total of 604 guns. As per General de Castelnau's orders, the field artillery and the high-trajectory guns needed to destroy wire obstacles were allocated to the assault divisions; the corps staffs would control the batteries required to counter the German artillery. The army staffs had

---

9   War Diary of Sixth Army Headquarters, dated 23 and 24 September.

Sketch 21

The Autumn Battle in Champagne
The Situation on 25 September 1915

The German line on 25 September at the
beginning of the French attack

0   5   10   15   20 km

direct control only over a special unit formed from a combination of long-range guns and a few mobile reserve gun batteries. For "trench artillery" Fourth and Second Armies collectively possessed around 370 58 mm guns and twenty-four guns of heavier calibre. An ample amount of ammunition had been made available. It was also planned to use incendiary shells and shells containing suffocating and tear gases.[10]

In Fourth Army's sector, nine infantry divisions stood side by side, prepared to launch the initial assault up to the heights south of the Py. Once the high ground had been taken, the forces in the second wave were to advance to the northern bank of the Py. In total the army had fourteen divisions and a few territorial units at its disposal; of these, four and a half divisions and II Cavalry Corps were being held in reserve immediately behind the front.

For the assault, the staff of French Second Army had staged nine infantry divisions on the front line. Of the divisions in the second wave, one was under the command of I Colonial Corps and three were controlled by the army itself. Another division (16th Colonial Division) was scheduled to arrive at Ste. Ménehould on 25 September; III Cavalry Corps was also at the army's disposal. The 2nd Cavalry Division at Dampierre le Château represented the Army Group's only reserve. As an initial objective the assaulting troops were to reach the line Arbre Hill (southeast of Somme Py)–Butte de Tahure–Fontaine en Dormois–Cernay en Dormois.

Except for the Moroccan Division (which did not arrive until 16 September), the elements designated for the initial assault were deployed in their sectors in Fourth Army's area by 20 August and in the area of Second Army ten days later. The second-wave formations were in place by 21 September, but the cavalry was not brought up from the rear until 23 and 24 September. The total strength of the assault forces thus amounted to twenty-seven infantry and seven cavalry divisions, which presented great difficulties when it came to providing food and shelter.

Third Army had initially been tasked with launching a major attack east of the Aisne, but constant German assaults in the Argonne placed serious demands on the troops, stymying those plans. Given the circumstances, Castelnau cancelled the preparation for these attacks and directed Third Army to remain in a defensive posture. At the insistence of the newly appointed Army Commander,[11] Castelnau finally permitted 128th Infantry Division—reinforced by elements of V and X Corps and supported by twenty-three heavy batteries—to launch a secondary attack between Servon and the western edge of the Argonne to eliminate the German batteries that were stationed there.

---

10 Lachrymatory gases.
11 General Humbert assumed command of Third Army on 22 July, replacing General Sarrail, who had been relieved.

After taking time to carefully range in their guns, the French artillery took advantage of the clear weather and began firing for effect on the centre and left flanks of German Third Army and the right flank of Fifth Army. The bombardment lasted for three days and three nights with only minor interruptions. It seemed to yield positive results. Twelve captive balloons and numerous aircraft directed the fire, which eventually spread out into the neighbouring sectors. The German first- and second-line trenches and the forward approach routes were subjected to the most intense bombardments. Despite their deep construction, the favourable ground, and constant repairs, the German defensive positions were steadily levelled; by the end they had become a series of indentations in the ground. Over the course of the bombardment the wire was almost totally destroyed. Although the shelters that had been constructed by miners withstood even direct hits, their entrances were often buried, trapping personnel inside.

The French artillery fired for effect on the German batteries, but this expended considerable ammunition and was truly effective only when direct observation was possible. When it was, it often rendered such batteries useless by direct hits or burials. At the same time, long-range artillery fire was concentrated on military encampments, railway installations, and access roads as well as on the crossings over the Py and Dormoise. This interrupted traffic and supply and put the important Bazancourt–Challerange railway line out of service.

During the heavy barrage the French infantry's patrolling activities had been minimal. However, in a number of locations they attempted to remove the surviving German wire obstacles immediately prior to the assault. In the meantime, the French emergency wire (*Schnellhindernisse*) had been removed to allow troops to cross the ground more quickly. It was not until the morning of 24 September that reinforced patrols advanced against the German positions. These aggressive reconnaissance operations extended along the front from Aubérive to the Aisne. Owing to heavy German defensive fire, they were forced to return to their jumping-off trenches. Once back in their own lines, they apparently directed intense fire on every location that had shown any signs of life.

On 24 September, Castelnau ordered all assault forces to commence their attack on the morning of 25 September at 09:15 (10:15 German time).

On 22 September, pursuant to Generaloberst von Einem's request, the *OHL* had made 183rd (Saxon) Infantry Brigade (staged north of Rethel) available in the event of an enemy attack. On the same day, German Third Army Headquarters intended to send an infantry regiment of this brigade to VIII Reserve Corps for the purpose of relieving the three battalions of XIV Corps that were deployed south of Somme Py. These three battalions were supposed to be billeted as reserves in the area of St. Etienne à Arnes; however, this movement was only partly completed. On 23 September the Army Commander assigned 183rd Infantry Brigade's staff—and the next day its entire complement of infantry except for two battalions held in army reserve at St. Etienne à Arnes along with XIV Corps' recently relieved battalion—to what he considered to be the most threatened formation: VIII Reserve Corps.[12] In return he requested the transfer of an entire infantry division from the *OHL*. Third Army reported that in a number of places the enemy had begun to cut paths through its wire obstacles, adding that an infantry assault appeared to be imminent. At noon on 24 September the *OHL* assigned 5th Infantry Division, which had been quartered at Attigny, to Third Army, thus cancelling its transfer to the Serbian Theatre. This division's three infantry regiments were brought up to Pauvres, Leffincourt, and Vouziers. Between 22 and 24 September the *OHL* had also assigned twenty-three batteries to Third Army.

The Situation at the *OHL* until Noon on 25 September

On the evening of 21 September, General von Falkenhayn left Pleß with the Emperor's entourage while Generalmajor Tappen, his key adviser, stayed behind to make preparations for the Serbian campaign.[13] Reports received on 22 September during his journey indicated that the situation of Sixth and Third Armies had already become more serious. In both these sectors of the front, fire increased on the morning of 22 September. Third Army described it as a heavy barrage along its entire front; Sixth Army reported *Trommelfeuer* only in isolated locations. The increase in the employment of enemy airplanes also suggested a major expenditure of force.

Despite clear indications that a major offensive was imminent, General von Falkenhayn remained firm in his opinion that these actions were merely meant to threaten an attack—a position that was not supported by the reports of the Western Armies. The Chief of the General Staff remained deeply reluctant to approve the allocation of reinforcements, and on 22 September these were limited to a number of heavy batteries. Even the final deployment of 8th Infantry Division and 183rd Infantry Brigade, which were staged to the rear and had been allocated to Third and Sixth Armies, had not been finally approved.

---

12 On 23 September, 183rd Infantry Brigade was subordinated to Third Army without restrictions. This was probably approved through verbal orders as written documents are absent in this regard.

13 Since 5 May, when the *OHL* had been transferred to Pleß, Colonel von Loßberg, the *OHL*'s liaison officer in Mézières, had been tasked with communicating reports from the Western Armies to Pleß and even directly to General von Falkenhayn, if necessary.

The Supreme Warlord, Kaiser Wilhelm, accompanied by Falkenhayn, travelled to Colmar and Strasbourg on 23 September and to Metz on 24 September.
Both days were taken up with inspections of all kinds and with discussions at the
three army groups on the army's left flank.[14] Continuing reports from the most
endangered armies confirmed that powerful enemy bombardments were continuing against parts of the Artois and Champagne Fronts. As of 23 September the
enemy had not launched an infantry attack; minor assaults on 24 September were
easily repelled. Falkenhayn again transferred a number of heavy batteries to Third
Army, although their deployment would take some time.[15] He accepted that in
response to the effects of the enemy's bombardment, it was necessary to quickly
and strongly reinforce the available artillery. However, he continued to maintain
that the enemy did not have the strength to fight its way through the German
positions in hand-to-hand combat. In the course of a telephone conversation
with Generaloberst von Einem on 24 September, Falkenhayn remarked that the
French "did not have the willpower." Nevertheless, he was prepared to leave 5th
Infantry Division—which was stationed to Third Army's rear awaiting an imminent transfer to the Serbian Front—on the French part of the front in order to
be available as a reinforcement for Third Army, on the condition that it be deployed
only in dire emergency. On the evening of the same day, Sixth Army Headquarters received a similar response when it sent the following inquiry: "Attack seems
to be imminent. In the event, may we have the 8th Infantry Division at our disposal?" Here, too, permission was granted with the proviso: "Deployment must
only be made in an extreme emergency." Otherwise, the distribution of the reserves
was unchanged.

When the General Staff chief arrived in Montmédy on the morning of 25 September, the reports awaiting him did not seem to require any new decisions.
British forces in Flanders had attacked some limited Fourth Army positions in
the early morning, and naval vessels had again appeared near Zeebrugge to bombard the city at long range, but the army had apparently been able to repel these
forays without approaching the *OHL* for assistance. On Sixth Army's front, the
French infantry had remained relatively quiet while the British had launched
assaults following the complete failure of those which they had attempted on the
evening of 24 September. According to reports from Sixth Army Headquarters, an
incursion aided by gas had taken place against Bavarian 6th Reserve Division that
morning, but it appeared to be "of little consequence." In Third Army's area,

---

14 *Meaning the Western Front as a whole.*
15 In order to expedite this deployment, it was decided not to detach modern units from other
    armies. Instead, Third Army was partially supplied with some older batteries that were
    intended to replace them.

artillery fire directed at XII and VII Reserve Corps was continuing without inter-ruption. Sixth Army Headquarters' follow-up report read: "General Impression: Based on the total failure of yesterday's assault, the enemy seems to have realized that his heavy barrage was insufficient for softening up our positions. The artillery bombardment itself has increased compared to yesterday, if that is at all possible."

These reports apparently still failed to exclude the interpretation that the French did not have the strength or resolve to execute an assault and were merely threatening one. At least, Falkenhayn saw no reason to make new decisions regard-ing the size or disposition of his reserves. So he continued his inspection tour. He and the Emperor arrived at Fifth Army Headquarters in Stenay. There, Falken-hayn's previous, doggedly held opinion abruptly changed. Almost simultaneously, messages arrived at the OHL from Sixth and Third Armies that erased all doubts about the gravity of the situation.

A telephone call from Third Army Headquarters to Fifth Army reported with extreme brevity: "Enemy breakthrough in the area of Souain–Somme Py. Full particulars not yet available. Request assistance from the Fifth Army Headquar-ters." However, Fifth Army was itself preoccupied with concerns about XVIII Reserve Corps and was unable to help. Instead, it submitted the message directly to the recently arrived General von Falkenhayn. Simultaneously he received a sim-ilar message from Sixth Army: "Aided by gas the enemy has broken into the posi-tions of IV Corps at Haisnes and Loos and into the positions of VII Corps west of Aubers. The entire Army Reserve and the 8th Infantry Division had to be put at the disposal of IV Corps. Further reinforcements for the army are urgently required." In the course of a telephone conversation with Third Army's com-mander, Falkenhayn received confirmation that the situation had to be considered serious and that bringing up reinforcements of "several divisions" was urgently required.

The belief that the enemy lacked the strength to mount a major offensive sud-denly evaporated, replaced by the realization that there was an enormous danger, the extent of which could not yet be ascertained. At best it was questionable whether the OHL's defensive measures would be sufficient and whether looming disaster could be averted with the few and unfavourably located combat-ready units. Falkenhayn immediately decided to travel to Mézières in order to issue the necessary instructions from there. From Stenay, he ordered the immediate trans-fer of 56th Infantry Division from Saarburg in Lorraine to Third Army and advised Sixth Army that 192nd Infantry Brigade would be readied for transfer from Sev-enth Army. In a proper assessment of the situation, he also decided that despite all concerns regarding their need for rest, the deployment of the Guard and X Corps could not be avoided. To this end he dispatched advance notice to both

Corps Headquarters that it was possible they would be moved up "in the near future."

Soon after 13:00, Falkenhayn departed Stenay by automobile on his way to Mézières.

25 September

The Attack in the Artois

Contrary to the expectations of Sixth Army Headquarters, the British attacked on their own on the rainy morning of 25 September at around 07:00. On the left flank of Bavarian II Corps and along the front of XIX (Saxon) Corps the enemy was satisfied with blowing smoke and firing smoke-generating canisters. The infantry only made feeble attempts to leave their trenches. But after exploding mines, elements of British 8th Division broke through the right flank of Bavarian 6th Reserve Division, commanded by Generalleutnant Scanzoni von Lichtenfels, and advanced to the second German line of defence. An immediate counterattack threw them back.

Indian troops used a similar strategy against the right flank of VII Corps north of Neuve Chapelle, where they also managed to occupy the first and second German lines. Local reserves of 13th Infantry Division, under Generalleutnant von dem Borne, succeeded in dislodging the enemy that evening. In front of 2nd Guard Reserve Division's sector, commanded by Generalleutnant Baron von Süßkind, the British released smoke without attacking. Farther south at Festubert and Givenchy-lez-la-Bassée, dense chlorine clouds aided by moderate westerly winds wafted over the trenches of 14th Infantry Division, commanded by Generalmajor von Altrock. British assault troops followed immediately behind the clouds; they collapsed under the German defensive fire, although not before reaching what remained of the wire obstacles. Elements of British 2nd Division temporarily broke through west of La Bassée, where the opposing trenches were in close proximity. In particular, 14th Infantry Division's farthest left flank met with strong attacks. It appeared that the units deployed there, as well as those on the flank at Haisnes, were able to master the situation.

The small local British successes north of La Bassée Canal did not significantly affect the decisions of Sixth Army's commander. His entire attention was on the area of the attack between La Bassée and Blaireville southwest of Arras. Apparently a far superior enemy—which we now know consisted of nineteen French and nine British infantry divisions and about 1,170 French and 483 British field and heavy guns—was attempting to force a breakthrough toward Douai.

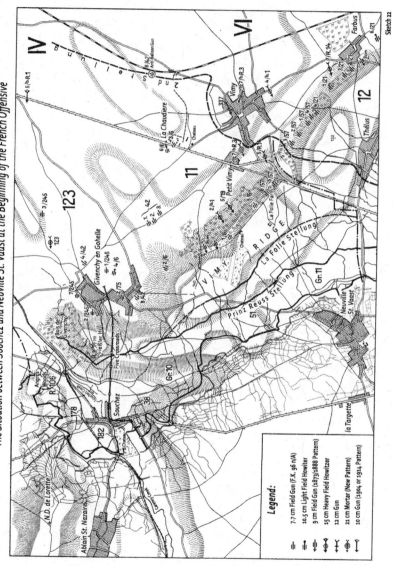

The Autumn Battle in Artois

The Situation between Souchez and Neuville St. Vaast at the Beginning of the French Offensive

Legend:

‖	7.7 cm Field Gun (F.K. 96 n/A)
⫲	10.5 cm Light Field Howitzer
⫲	9 cm Field Gun (1873/1888 Pattern)
⟟	15 cm Heavy Field Howitzer
⟟	12 cm Gun
⟟	21 cm Mortar (New Pattern)
⟟	10 cm Gun (1904 or 1914 Pattern)

Sketch 22

Facing them were only about eight German divisions with 325 field and 150 heavy guns.[16]

Elements of four British divisions attacked the sector of IV Corps' 117th Infantry Division, commanded by General der Infanterie Kuntze, which was tasked with defending a front of more than 9 kilometres. Early in the morning an intense British artillery barrage was followed by a major gas assault. Four giant clouds of smoke, each followed by a gas cloud, rolled over the German trenches at intervals of about fifteen minutes. The smoke was a dirty white, the gas a yellow-red. At the same time, the British artillery fired shells that produced much smoke and gas. Because of the weak winds, these clouds inhibited visibility, for they dissipated very slowly. At the front near the enemy, visibility was only 3 metres; at division headquarters in Wingles, some 4.5 kilometres behind the front lines, it was barely 30 metres. The effect of the gas on the defenders varied with the density of the cloud and the susceptibility of the individual, from temporary impairment to a complete eradication of combat effectiveness. Masses of British troops wearing gas masks advanced in depth through the final gas cloud. Aided by the gas's effects, and hugely superior in numbers, the British troops broke through the German positions with their first assault and advanced close to the west of Hulluch and beyond Loos. Only some elements of the defending division succeeded in holding on west of the Hulluch–Vermelles road until the evening, when they ran out of ammunition and surrendered. As a result, in 117th Infantry Division's sector, fifteen companies were destroyed and twenty-two guns lost. The division's decimated remains and reserves put up a renewed defence along the second line from the western edge of Haisnes to Hulluch–Cité St. Auguste–Cité St. Laurent, although the forces available were not sufficient to man the entire trench line. To the west, from Cité St. Laurent to the positions of the less fiercely attacked 7th Infantry Division, commanded by Generalleutnant Riedel, no continuous and defendable trench remained. On the part of the line to the left flank of 117th Infantry Division, which had been reinforced by elements of 7th Infantry Division, only the northern edges of the coal-mining towns of St. Edouard and St. Pierre allowed for organized resistance.

The situation at Loos was extremely serious. It seemed that the British forces—which had barely been kept at bay by weak infantry with little artillery support—would be quite capable of completing the breakthrough and pivoting on both sides of the gap in order to roll up the connecting German lines. Fresh British forces were reported to be already advancing toward the breach in the German line. At 09:30, Field Marshal French ordered 21st and 24th Divisions

---

16   For more about the entire artillery on both sides, refer to Appendix 2.

(deployed with the reserves at Béthune and Noeux) to begin moving. On their arrival at the front they were to be assigned to First Army. Owing to many problems with the relaying of orders, they could not commence their march until midday. The British Guard Division, which had arrived from southwest of Lillers, was sent to Noeux-les-Mines; 28th Division, which was available farther north, was also brought up; the British Cavalry Corps stood at the ready in rear of the Guard Division.

As of 10:00, Sixth Army Headquarters had not received any ominous reports about the French. Bavarian I Reserve Corps even believed that they had stopped an assault on their flank by employing surprise artillery strikes. So when IV Corps' critical situation was briefly relayed just after 10:00, Crown Prince Rupprecht ordered 26th Infantry Brigade's advance to Meurchin.[17] Soon afterwards it was assigned, along with 8th Infantry Division, to General Sixt. In the meantime, reports arrived from VII Corps indicating that its left flank had already been enveloped. Three battalions of Bavarian II Corps were brought up to Don by train in support; with that, Crown Prince Rupprecht had committed all his reserves. His request to Falkenhayn for reinforcements was approved, but these were not expected to arrive on 25 September.

The midday reports reassured the Army Commander about the situation to the north of La Bassée. However, to the south of the canal, VII Corps reported that the situation was critical: the enemy had already broken through the second lines near Haisnes and had stormed the batteries located there. Meanwhile, Bavarian I Reserve Corps reported that an attack was imminent and that attacks had already begun on VI Corps.

Infantry was being brought up by train from Douai, but the first elements of Sixt's reinforcements would reach the battlefield in the late afternoon at the earliest. It seemed hardly possible that the remainder of the decimated 117th Infantry Division would be able to hold out against the enemy's massive and already triumphant superior forces. Fortunately, the British suffered a delay caused by their heavy casualties and the intermingling of units. By noon, however, the British had revived their attacks with uncoordinated local assaults. In the north, British units entered Haisnes but were repulsed by hastily assembled forces from 14th Infantry Division. Aided by elements of 2nd Guard Reserve Division—provided by General von François—they also managed to secure a connection to 117th Infantry Division's left flank by taking the line Auchy–Haisnes. Between Haisnes and Hulluch the severely damaged 117th Infantry Division repelled additional

---

17 The brigade was to advance without one battalion, which remained with the Bavarian Regimental Command Post.

attacks on its own. The commander of 22nd Infantry Regiment, with elements of his regiment and three battalions of 7th and 123rd (Saxon) Infantry Divisions, which had been brought up by VI Corps Headquarters, stopped the advance of 15th British Infantry Division at Hill 70, which had come up from a direction southeast of Loos.

Motivated by these more favourable developments, General von Arnim unilaterally decided to counterattack with all of the reserves made available to him by Army Headquarters. Loos was to be enveloped, with 26th Reserve Infantry Brigade under Generalmajor von Dresler und Scharfenstein attacking from the northeast through Hulluch while 8th Infantry Division, commanded by Generalmajor von Hanstein, attacked from the south through Lens.

Even the events that had taken place in the meantime farther south did not change the intended deployment of the army's reserve. At 13:30 the major French infantry assault that had been expected was launched on both sides of Arras, with the main attack aimed at the 14 kilometre front between Liévin and Roclincourt. Unlike the British, the French did not disperse smoke or gas; instead they fired gas shells, mainly into the rear areas and only at recognized observation posts. Otherwise they apparently relied on the effects of their artillery, which had been ramping up to a *Trommelfeuer* since 09:00.

In the southern part of IV Corps' sector, 7th Infantry Division repelled an assault by French 43rd Division on its left flank without trouble. Two French divisions (13th and 70th) attacked the almost completely enveloped positions of 123rd (Saxon) Infantry Division. The forward trenches that protruded out of Souchez had been demolished by groundwater and by the incessant fighting of the spring, and the division had to throw both its reserve battalions into the raging battle at Loos. The French, who suddenly appeared out of the smoke cloud covering the position, overran the weakened trench garrison. It was not until the French reached the line Angres Wood–Valley Dam–Gießler Trench that their attack was contained with a counterattack by the local reserves. Subsequent French attacks were stopped with the aid of 7th Infantry Division's left flank. In the meantime, 8th Infantry Division, advancing from Loos, made one and a half battalions available to 123rd Infantry Division. On orders from the divisional commander, Generalmajor Lucius, three of 123rd Infantry Division's regiments counterattacked during the night. In the foggy early hours of the next morning they were able to gain ground despite the soldiers' exhaustion. Prisoners were taken.

Elements of French XXXIII, III, and XII Corps attacked the sector of VI Corps with great determination. The 11th Infantry Division, under Generalleutnant von Webern, was pushed back on its extreme right flank and at Neuville-St. Vaast. It could not join up with 123rd Infantry Division's left flank until it reached the

Prinz Reuß *Stellung*.[18] However, the counterattacking division repelled the enemy, who with their first assault had in places broken through to La Folie *Stellung*. By evening, after heavy fighting, the counterattackers had regained most of the original position.[19] The 12th Infantry Division, commanded by Generalleutnant Chales de Beaulieu, was overrun by XII Corps' divisions on its right flank and in its centre, where a breakthrough by the enemy's 24th Infantry Division in the area of Thélus appeared most threatening. Immediately launched counterattacks succeeded in pushing the attacker back, but the forward German trenches could not be regained. In the Prinz Reuß *Stellung* the division's right flank closed up to the left flank of 11th Infantry Division, which had also been pushed back. The enemy's penetrations in VI Corps' sector resulted in a fractured front line; in some places only the front line trenches—and in others only the Prinz Reuß *Stellung*—were still in German hands. Consequently, it became extremely difficult to control the battle.

The right flank of Bavarian 1st Reserve Division, under Generalleutnant Göringer, managed to hold the front trenches through a courageous defence against attacking elements of XII and XVII Corps. At that point an almost 5 kilometre sector on both sides of the Scarpe, held by Bavarian I Reserve Corps, had not yet come under attack. In the enveloped salient, French IX Corps launched a strong secondary attack from the town of Beaurains to the south against the fiercely bombarded position.[20] Elements of the enemy force penetrated the first line by assaulting the centre and left flanks of Bavarian 5th Reserve Division under Generalleutnant Ipfelkofer, which had been reinforced by Brigade *Hammer*. The Bavarian, Prussian, and Saxon units deployed there immediately launched counterattacks, and in the evening the position returned entirely in German hands. The 111th Infantry Division was attacked only on its right flank, where it likewise held its ground.

In the view of Army Headquarters, VI Corps and IV Corps appeared to be the most seriously threatened. As a result of air raids, the telephone lines were inoperable for lengthy intervals; thus the situation remained unclear. Reports about the condition of the troops were worrying, and the enemy advance between Souchez and Neuville-St. Vaast had grave implications. Since he had no reserves, Crown Prince Rupprecht was in no position to intervene. Opposite the British, he expected IV Corps' counterattack to succeed, so he could only order the units between Lens and Arras—which were engaged in heavy fighting—to hold their line at all costs.

---

18 *The German second line behind Neuville-St. Vaast.*

19 La Folie Stellung *was the third German line behind Neuville-St. Vaast.*

20 The IX Corps comprised the 18th, 17th, and 152nd Infantry Divisions.

However, IV Corps' counterattack did not proceed as planned. The 26th Reserve Infantry Brigade's transfer, which involved equipping the troops with close-combat weapons and deploying them in trenches that had yet to be completely cleared of British infantry, took longer than anticipated; so did the deployment of 8th Infantry Division in the maze of houses in Lens. As a consequence, the attack was repeatedly postponed. Its launch was finally set for midnight. Despite the unfavourable timing, 26th Reserve Infantry's gallant advance had achieved some success by the early morning of 26 September. In conjunction with the reinforced 14th Infantry Division's left flank, which was making headway against "Fosse 8" southwest of Haisnes, the brigade regained the largest part of the gravel pit northwest of Hulluch as well as a section of the access roads to the south.[21] The storming and subsequent defence of the gravel pit was an outstanding accomplishment. At Loos, however, 8th Infantry Division was unable to gain ground against the larger and newly deployed British forces.

The VI Corps was also engaged in fierce fighting throughout the night of 25 and 26 September. Despite valiant counterattacks, a considerable portion of the front line remained in the hands of a stronger enemy. However, by the morning of 26 September, the positions of Bavarian 6th Reserve Division, Seventh Army, and Bavarian I Reserve Corps had been cleared of the enemy through operations that resulted in heavy casualties. About 700 British and French troops had been captured. Army Headquarters was optimistic. Its only cause for concern was the "entirely insufficient supply of artillery ammunition."[22] To alleviate these concerns, the Chief of the Field Munitions Service dispatched two and a half ammunition trains for the field artillery and the same for the heavy artillery.

The Attack in the Champagne

The crisis in the Champagne was considerably more serious than in the Artois. The massed French attack was launched in rainy weather at 10:15 on 25 September. Carried out jointly and simultaneously with the British attack, its objective was to achieve a breakthrough in a northerly direction. To this end, nineteen French divisions attacked seven German divisions on the front line between Moronvilliers and the Argonne.[23] Later, prisoner reports revealed that the French

---

21 *The area under attack contained a number of gravel pits (fosses) and mines.*
22 War Diary of Sixth Army Headquarters, 25 September.
23 The following units were allotted for the assault: Fourth (French) Army—124th, 7th, 42nd, 40th, 37th, and 14th Infantry Divisions; 15th and 10th Colonial Divisions; Moroccan Division. French Second Army—28th, 27th, 22nd, 21st, 11th, 39th, and 151st Infantry Divisions; 2nd and 3rd Colonial Divisions. East of the Aisne, 128th Infantry Division of Third Army carried out a secondary attack.

The Autumn Battle in Artois
The German Positions Northwest of Hulloch

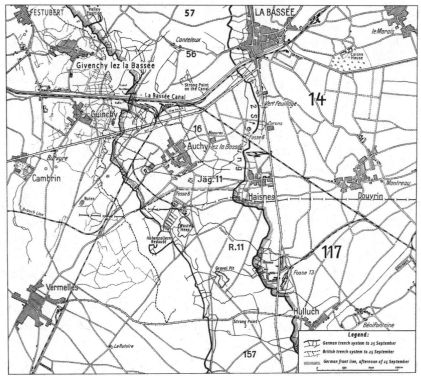

Sketch 23

units designated for the assault had been deployed several days prior to its commencement in order to allow them to become familiar with the terrain near the
front lines. Each division's assault area was approximately 1.5 kilometres wide, and
generally speaking, three regiments were deployed next to each other with the
fourth kept in reserve. Eight infantry divisions followed the assault divisions at
close intervals. Behind them, masses of cavalry—a total of seven cavalry divisions—advanced to immediately strike out behind the German lines in the event
of a breakthrough.

The attack plan was almost universal. According to German observations, the
regiments in the forward lines were staged in three battalion-sized assault waves
with an interval of about 50 metres between each wave. The first wave was preceded by specially selected bombers, who were followed close behind by "trench
clearers" (*Grabensäuberer*), whose objectives were to clear the overrun German

trenches of surviving defenders, connect the stormed position to the French trench network, and prepare flag signalling and telephone communications. The three assault waves were followed by close-ordered columns of reserves, occasionally led by mounted officers.

The first assault wave was generally obscured by clouds of gas and smoke, which prevented the German artillery from observing events in the forward area. The gas caused nausea and burning in the eyes as well as unconsciousness; it resulted in death where it permeated the dugouts.[24] Aided by favourable winds, the assault was carried forward under the protection of this cloud, even in those places where the French jumping-off trenches were more distant.

The French infantry's initial artillery support seemed to have been meticulously planned. In the attack sectors between Baconnes and the Aisne, 700 German field and heavy guns faced about 1,950 French.[25] Every target vital to the success of the assault was subjected to an overwhelming bombardment. The heavy barrage on the forward German trenches was not lifted until the first assault wave had almost reached them. In contrast to past practice, the fire that passed over to the rear areas did not abate. As a result the German infantry—which in some places were housed in deep dugouts—were taken by surprise. In the neighbouring sectors that had not been attacked, the forward trenches experienced less intense fire, but there the rear areas were subjected to increased shelling. This apparently was intended to prevent an intervention by German artillery on the flanks as well as the movement of reserves.

The German artillery, besides being vastly outnumbered and weakened by enemy action, was forced to limit its participation in the defensive battle owing to ammunition shortages. Sufficient supplies were available in the army's sector, but it was difficult to transport them to the firing positions because of a shortage of ammunition columns and the enemy's interdicting fire, which reached far into the rear. At the beginning of the attack, each battery's barrage area was already several times larger than what it could be expected to cover. In these circumstances the German artillery had restrict itself to keeping the enemy's assault positions under fire. Some heavy low-trajectory guns managed to disrupt the deployment and staging of enemy reserves; some individual batteries managed to target attack columns and artillery deployed in the open. Some French batteries were rendered inoperable using gas shells.

The XIV Corps (Armee-Gruppe *Haenisch*) was kept busy only by increased fire—especially in the sector of 29th Infantry Division—and by an assault in the

---

24 The new army gas mask, which was introduced in the autumn, was very effective but not available in sufficient quantities.

25 For more information, see Appendix 2.

area of Brimont. However, in the sector held by XII (Saxon) Reserve Corps, a strong secondary assault against the centre of 23rd Reserve Division (Generalleutnant von Watzdorf) was carried out south of Moronvilliers by 124th Infantry Division. The enemy succeeded in penetrating the lines in a number of locations; by evening, however, the division had managed on its own to regain those positions by mounting counterattacks that netted some prisoners.

On its 9 kilometre front, 24th Reserve Division, commanded by General der Infanterie von Ehrenthal, took the full brunt of the French assault. The enemy, who had initially broken through near and east of Aubérive, was thrown back by a counterattack. By early afternoon more than 1,000 prisoners had been taken. Farther east, the first attack by massed assault columns was repelled by fire; a second attack an hour later could not be stopped. The French 40th Infantry Division managed to occupy the trenches on both sides of the St. Hilaire-le-Grand–St. Souplet road. Initially there was no news from the left flank, but around noon, sporadic and sometimes strongly exaggerated or contradictory reports (mixed with his own observations) led the divisional commander to believe that the situation had become critical. He moved his recruiting depot—his last reserve—into the *R-Stellung* about 3 kilometres to the rear as reinforcements. The advance elements of the promised reinforcements would not arrive at the divisional command post north of St. Souplet until the afternoon; it was uncertain when they would be able to reach the front from there, as they had to pass through the barrage that was being directed at the Py Valley. In the meantime the enemy continued to bring additional strong forces into the attack. Enemy batteries were observed changing positions and moving forward; these were shot up by infantry and artillery, as were the mounted squadrons approaching from the area of St. Hilaire-le-Grand. The situation grew even more ominous when at 14:00 a general staff officer from the adjoining Division *Liebert* reported that it had been pushed back almost entirely into its *R-Stellung*. This position was almost 4 kilometres to the rear of 24th Reserve Division's left flank; even so, Ehrenthal was determined to hold his forward position. Reserves about the strength of a battalion arrived during the evening and were deployed with the objective of retaking the old trenches south of St. Souplet. However, at 22:00, just prior to this counterattack, General der Artillerie von Kirchbach (commanding XII Reserve Corps) ordered the division's left flank, which was steadfastly holding its position in the first line, to pull back to link up with Division *Liebert*. Based on reports received at 05:00 on 26 September, Ehrenthal was assured that these difficult-to-execute orders had been carried out. At about this time, 24th Reserve Division's right flank was firmly in control of its old position, except for one French pocket east of Aubérive. In accordance with their orders, the centre and left flanks held the Z-Stellung[26] and R-Stellung farther east. Casualties were extremely high: about 120 officers and 5,000 men, many of whom were buried alive. The enemy took fourteen field and two heavy guns as well as a few machine guns and mortars, most of which were inoperable; also, seven field and nine heavy guns were destroyed or made inoperable through excessive use. In the course of their determined counterattacks, the division's soldiers captured 21 officers and 1,780 men—in addition to several machine guns—of IV, XXXII, and VII Corps.

Adjoining 24th Reserve Division's left flank, the regiment on the right flank of the composite Division Liebert at first bravely defended its front-line positions; later, though, it was driven back to the R-Stellung. Meanwhile, the two regiments on the left wing—pieced together from various units, including some cavalry, that had replaced 85th Reserve Infantry Brigade on both sides of the Souain–Somme Py road—were unable to fight off the fierce attacks of II Colonial Corps. In the early afternoon the debilitated remnants of these units were pushed all the way back into the R-Stellung south of Somme Py. Aided by recently brought up reinforcement battalions and 16th Reserve Division's Recruiting Depot,[27] they were able to hold their ground against further attacks. Both regiments neighbouring to the east lost their front-line trenches—in part because they were overrun, in part owing to the enemy's deep penetrations, and in part because they were taken from the rear at Perthes-lès-Hurlus. That evening they slowly retreated into the R-Stellung. The separated elements on the left flank continued fighting in the front lines the next day. Due to Division Liebert's brave resistance, the enemy at first hesitated to pursue both flanks. This made it possible to recover many wounded and a lot of materiel.

Based on reports from 50th Infantry Division (Generalmajor von Engel-brechten) and the composite Division Ditfurth, at midday on 25 September, VIII Reserve Corps' commander, Generalleutnant Fleck, gained the impression that the French had taken the entire front line except at Hill 196 southeast of Tahure. So he assigned a number of battalions from 183rd Infantry Brigade to Division Liebert and 50th Infantry Division and a regiment of 5th Infantry Division to Division Ditfurth. The two remaining regiments of 5th Infantry Division were placed in army reserve in the area northeast of Somme Py. At 14:50, 50th Infantry Division reported that its right wing was holding the R-Stellung on Arbre Hill

---

26 Intermediate position (Zwischenstellung).
27 Field recruiting depots were attached to the division and accepted new recruits from the home front and returned wounded. Initial training was completed at the depots and the men allotted to their units as required. In some extreme circumstances, whole emergency battalions could be drawn from the depots for immediate service at the front. See General Staff, War Office, Handbook of the German Army in War, January 1917 (Yorkshire: EP, 1973), 15–16.

(Hill 193), that its regiment in the centre was holding the line east of the Somme Py–Tahure road, and that its left flank was holding its old positions. An hour later the report was amended to say that the division's centre and left flanks were threatened by envelopment and that their withdrawal to the *R-Stellung* had therefore become necessary. However, this report did not hold true for the left flank, which continued holding its front lines under the most difficult of combat conditions. The weak reinforcements that were only now arriving in the sector west of Tahure succeeded in stopping the enemy breakthrough. A French cavalry regiment advancing on the Souain–Tahure road was dispersed by fire.

The enemy assault had struck Division *Ditfurth*'s sector with full force. Around noon the divisional commander observed from his command post west of Ripont that large numbers of advancing French infantry had already crossed the Maison de Champagne Farm area. By committing his last reserves, it was possible to gradually push the French 39th Infantry Division back as far as the farm, to take prisoners, and to liberate the captured German batteries. However, the badly mauled Rhenish reserve regiments were unable to advance beyond the line Maison de Champagne Farm–Hill 199, 2 kilometres north of Massiges. Aided by a reverse-slope position, Division *Ditfurth*'s right flank held on to the front-line trenches. These were linked to 50th Infantry Division's left flank—which was assigned to Generalmajor von Ditfurth that evening—forming a salient in the direction of the enemy. However, the division's centre had been pushed back to the *Z-Stellung*.

The VIII Reserve Corps' losses were severe; each of the three divisions deployed lost 5,000 men. Almost all of the materiel installed in the front lines (machine guns, trench mortars, and approximately fifty artillery pieces) was lost to the enemy.

Once the situation became clear, Third Army Headquarters transferred individual battalions (partly by lorry) and batteries from the sectors that had not been attacked to the most threatened locations; meanwhile, infantry, artillery, and special units were arriving from neighbouring armies. However, these reinforcements were not sufficient to quickly and completely replace the regiments that had been partly destroyed (some had been reduced to a few companies). Nevertheless, on the evening of 25 September, Generalleutnant Wichura's 5th Infantry Division—minus one regiment—was made available to VIII Reserve Corps. It took over the eastern part of Division *Liebert*'s sector. With that, the most endangered part of the front was at least to some extent secured. The VIII Reserve Corps was ordered to hold "the *R-Stellung* and the segments of the frontlines which had not been lost at all costs," as the Army Commander expected further strong attacks.

Fifth Army's right flank became embroiled in Third Army's severe crisis when about three and a half French divisions attacked XVIII Reserve Corps (General der

Infanterie von Steuben).[28] In the days prior to the attack, in anticipation, Crown Prince Wilhelm had reinforced this corps from his own resources with one and a half heavy high-trajectory batteries and a composite infantry regiment from XVI Corps. After relentless back-and-forth fighting, 21st Reserve Division (Generalleutnant von Schwerin) and 9th Landwehr Division (Generalleutnant von Muehlenfels) were able to clear their trenches of enemy infiltrations except for a French pocket at Bois de Ville. By evening they had taken more than 500 prisoners. However, the right flank had to be retracted in order to reconnect with Division *Ditfurth* as the latter had been pushed back. This created a gap between the two divisions stretching from the "Kanonenberg" to Hill 191, just north of Massiges ("Ehrenberg"); it was barely closed by inserting the composite regiment from XVI Corps. Fifth Army Headquarters assigned additional reinforcements to XVIII Reserve Corps.

On 25 September a total of nineteen French assault divisions had launched the main offensive on the front lines in the Champagne. Yet owing to the defenders' tenacious resistance, the French commanders were unable to realize their objective and achieve a breakthrough in the German lines. The enemy's massive superiority merely pushed the German defensive lines back along a front of approximately 17 kilometres, where they re-established a new front about 13 kilometres forward of the *R-Stellung*. On the Souain–Somme Py road, where the greatest French success had been achieved, weak makeshift German forces had faced a premier French corps. This corps' deep and rapid breakthrough had been followed by an enveloping manoeuvre to the east and west that had tangible effects on the battle front. However, as a result of German fire, the infantry assault soon fragmented and the attacking troops dissolved into small groups. The French commanders appeared to have been totally neutralized. As a result, the weak German forces succeeded in inflicting heavy casualties in the intermediate trenches behind the front lines, as well as in the encampments and forested areas, and were able to stop the enemy time and again. It seems that after the successful breakthrough, the French infantry suffered casualties from their own artillery fire. The enemy forces that had advanced to the new German lines of defence were exhausted and in disarray because of the constant individual combat they had endured. They were therefore unable to mount a coordinated assault. In the evening these enemy forces dug in on the line they had reached. Owing to the characteristics of the ground, their new lines were so far removed from the German trenches that it was possible to recover a large number of abandoned German guns from between the lines.

---

28   The 3rd Colonial Division, 151st and 128th Infantry Divisions, as well as a brigade of 20th Infantry Division.

Actions of the OHL on the Afternoon of 25 September

The reports received at Fifth Army Headquarters in Stenay had apparently convinced Falkenhayn that Sixth Army was the most seriously threatened. Thus he sent it 192nd Infantry Brigade from Seventh Army. On his arrival in Mézières, at 15:00 he also ordered the transfer of the Guard Corps from its Belgian rest quarters to the rear of Sixth Army. Its advance elements were to arrive there on the morning of 26 September. The subordination of this corps to Sixth Army was ordered later that evening.

Meanwhile, new reports from Third Army suggested that it was in a perilous situation that made the deployment of large numbers of additional reinforcements a priority. The deployment of 56th Infantry Division—which had already been ordered—was not sufficient. Therefore 192nd Infantry Brigade received a change of orders at 16:00: it was to be deployed to Third instead of Sixth Army. Two hours later these instructions were supplemented with the stipulation that the brigade's advance elements were to be transported by motor convoy that night; the remainder of the brigade was to follow by train. At about 17:00, X Corps Headquarters was advised that it had been assigned to Third Army. Together with 20th Infantry Division—located north of Brussels with Third Army's battalion of heavy howitzers, half of its ammunition columns, and supply trains—it was to deploy there by train as soon as possible. Additionally, Third Army received two infantry battalions from Seventh Army, two *Musketen* battalions, and pioneer and labour units (*Armierungstruppen*).[29] By the evening of 25 September, thirty trains containing 19th Infantry Division had been unloaded in eastern Belgium, but this unit had still not received any instructions.

On 25 September a heavy field howitzer battalion from GHQ's artillery reserve that had recently arrived from the East, and that was staged in rear of Seventh Army, was assigned to Third Army. At the same time, Sixth Army received four heavy batteries. Additionally, some artillery units were already attached to the divisions deploying to Third and Sixth Army. Clearly, the major transfers of heavy artillery that had been ordered on 23 and 24 September would make themselves felt over the following days.

Although 53rd Reserve Division would have been able to deploy quickly to Sixth Army, Falkenhayn conspicuously left that division in rear of Fourth Army; apparently he was concerned about the possibility of serious British attacks in the Ypres area or landings in the sector of the Marine Corps. Already by the end of August he had pointed out to Fourth Army Headquarters that even a temporary enemy deployment on the coast could not be tolerated, whatever the cost.

---

29 Musketen *battalions were armed with automatic rifles and were about 500 men strong. Each of the battalion's ninety "Musketes" was manned by a section of four men.*

Toward evening, Third Army reported that it had found an order on a captured French officer that directed the attack to be continued day and night until the great breakthrough had been accomplished. Even without this confirmation Falkenhayn could no longer doubt that the enemy was aiming to achieve a major decision and would exert a maximum effort to achieve that goal. From an operational point of view, a successful breakthrough on the Champagne Front represented a more serious threat than in the Artois because in the Champagne the Western Army's rearward communications would be more seriously affected. Consequently the situation grew extremely tense. Third Army's report, issued around 22:30 in the evening, read in part: "VIII Reserve Corps were issued an order by army headquarters that their present positions were to be held at all costs." The army believed that if reinforcements (56th Infantry Division, 192nd Infantry Brigade, and half of X Corps) arrived on time and before the enemy could—by exerting a giant effort—break through Third Army's front, it could overcome the crisis, albeit with heavy casualties. The report concluded that 26 September would bring the decision.

On the afternoon of 25 September, after the Kaiser returned to Charleville, Falkenhayn issued a verbal report to him that conceded serious losses; but he also pointed out that a promising defence could be mounted with the deployment of strong reserves. He believed that the combat-tested competence and reliability of the German officers and enlisted men justified this opinion. Nevertheless, the uncertainty weighed heavily on the commander responsible for the entire operation—a weight made greater by the fact that he could not deny that he had deluded himself about the enemies' objectives and its will to attack.

The shattering experience of 25 September remained in his soul and was to profoundly affect his future decisions.[30]

26 September

In the Artois

In the British sector of Sixth Army's front, the morning of 26 September began with a pause in the fighting. Then a very intense enemy fire began at 11:00. During the night the British leadership had ordered that the offensive be continued, so General Haig had ordered a new attack by 21st and 24th Infantry Divisions. At noon the British attacked in dense lines in extended order on a 3 kilometre front near and north of Loos. Despite the clear weather, their batteries were

---

30   This is according to a report dated 16 June 1932 by Generalleutnant Tappen, sent to the *Reichsarchiv.*

marshalled virtually in the open north of the town; also, cavalry regiments were observed behind the advancing infantry. Supported by the left flank of 14th Infantry Division, the artillery of German 117th and 8th Infantry Divisions put these dense targets under fire, thereby weakening their combat effectiveness. However, the assault broke down only when it was subjected to close-range weapon fire. By evening, all further British assaults had collapsed here as well as farther north at the gravel pit near Hulluch. The young soldiers of British 21st and 24th Infantry Divisions retreated to (and in some cases beyond) their start lines, at first as individuals and later in large groups. There they were rounded up and reformed by the newly arrived Guard Division. The British Air Force was very busy, bombing ammunition trains in Valenciennes. The resulting explosions disrupted the railway traffic. The train station at Douai was subjected to systematic long-range fire by guns of the heaviest calibre and had to be temporarily evacuated.

After the morning of 26 September, activity in the French sector south of Arras declined considerably. Reflecting new directives issued by Foch around 21:00 on 25 September, the battle was continued mostly by the artillery. Foch felt that the emphasis had to be placed on the French army's left flank in order to build on initial successes; therefore he ordered XVII and IX Corps to cease their attacks on 26 September south of Arras. The 154th Infantry Division, which stood in reserve west of the city, was to be deployed to the rear of XXI and XXXIII Corps, both of which were to continue the offensive. In the French commander's judgment, the situation was favourable in that sector. He hoped that his left flank's advance, combined with the British successes, would result in the speedy occupation of the heights at Liévin–Vimy. Thus strong French assaults were directed at IV and VI Corps on the afternoon of 26 September. However, the enemy was able to make only minimal gains at Souchez. According to German observers, the enemy barely made it out of its trenches because of defensive fire in front of Bavarian I Reserve Corps' right flank and south of Beaurains.

At a meeting south of Amiens between Generals Joffre and Foch at 15:00 on 26 September, Joffre made a drastic decision: Tenth Army's offensive was to be halted, its ammunition expenditure limited, and one or two infantry divisions pulled out for deployment elsewhere.[31] Furthermore, these directives were to be executed in such a way that (a) the British would not gain the impression that they were continuing the attack alone, and (b) the Germans would not notice

---

31 *Foch later convinced Joffre that the extraction of two divisions from Tenth Army was unnecessary. He was only forced to give up 152nd Division, with the second division coming from Sixth Army instead.*

that the offensive had abated.[32] This order was given because the generalissimo judged the situation in the Champagne to be especially favourable. He was hoping that with the aid of the forces and ammunition to be withdrawn from the Artois, he would be able to force a breakthrough and then strategically exploit it. With that, the fighting and operations in the Artois ceased to have a decisive objective. Foch believed that he was acting in the spirit of his orders when he then had Tenth Army continue its assault on the tactically most important locations and ordered the heights at Souchez and Vimy to be taken at all costs. The battles north of Arras therefore continued with undiminished ferocity despite the Supreme Commander's intervention.

In the Champagne

On the French side, as a result of reports received on the evening of 25 September, the Supreme Commander and General de Castelnau gained the impression that the offensive was progressing smoothly. Both commanders had ordered the continuation of the attack for 26 September; additionally, Joffre announced the arrival of two new infantry divisions (16th Colonial and 157th Infantry), which were to be placed at the Army Group's disposal.

Meanwhile, on the night of 25 and 26 September, despite heavy harassing fire, the most endangered sectors of Third Army were reinforced with fresh troops and ammunition. Generaloberst von Einem therefore looked on the situation with optimism. When Falkenhayn requested information via telephone at 10:00, Third Army's Chief of Staff Generalleutnant Ritter von Hoehn reported that "all measures to block the French breakthrough are ongoing and a new crisis will arise only if the French renew their offensive with fresh forces of which there is presently no evidence."[33]

Under the pressure of unfolding events, VIII Reserve Corps' commanding general considered withdrawing his divisions to north of the Dormoise, submitting a proposal along these lines to Army Headquarters. This would have been carried out on the night of 27 September. In reply, however, he was ordered to hold his position. The guiding principle within Third Army and for the entire Western Front remained constant: not a foot of ground was to be relinquished,

---

32 According to a note in the British Official History, the text of the order read: "Stop the attacks of the Tenth Army, taking care to avoid giving the British the impression that we are leaving them to attack alone, or the Germans that our offensive is slackening off. Economize ammunition. Try, if possible, to send the Commander-in-Chief without delay two divisions, and to diminish the number of troops in the first line." J.E. Edmonds and G.C. Wynne, Military Operations: France and Belgium, 1915, II: 347.

33 This information is taken from a memorandum to the Reichsarchiv dated 8 June 1932 by General der Artillerie Ritter von Hoehn.

and any lost positions were to be retaken by counterattack.[34] To simplify the chain of command, Corps *Wichura* was formed from Division *Liebert* and 5th Infantry Division. Due to the urgency of the situation, elements of 192nd Infantry Brigade and 56th Infantry Division were moved into the combat zone, partly by motorized convoy and partly on foot, as they arrived at their points of disembarkation. The 56th Infantry Division was to reinforce VIII Reserve Corps' threatened left flank; one regiment of 192nd Infantry Brigade was made available to XII Reserve Corps. The staff and both remaining regiments of 192nd Infantry Brigade were assigned to Generalleutnant Wichura. This deployment of battalion- and regiment-sized reinforcements significantly intermixed the forces at the front—a situation that was difficult to control for the commanders involved.

To the Germans, the enemy attacks of 26 September appeared to represent individual assaults rather than a larger, cohesive enterprise. Thus, in the morning and afternoon, 24th Reserve Division's entire sector was repeatedly attacked; despite heavy casualties, it managed to hold its positions through the evening. Its artillery, reinforced in part by three heavy howitzer batteries and field artillery (the latter from the equipment reserves), quickly and successfully brought the enemy's assembled forces—including their cavalry—under fire. However, XII Reserve Corps' request for replacements for its exhausted regiments could not be granted; instead the corps was ordered to hold its positions with its existing forces.

The enemy also attacked with great force on both sides of the Souain–Somme Py road in Corps *Wichura*'s sector. Later it became apparent that five fresh infantry divisions of the second line (56th, 12th, 127th, 31st, and 53rd) had been deployed there and at Tahure. Aided by the regiments that were arriving from 192nd Infantry Brigade, Corps *Wichura* managed to hold the *R-Stellung*.

Meanwhile, VIII Reserve Corps' 50th Infantry Division repulsed five assaults, which were conducted in dense waves. This battle centred on the area around the Butte de Tahure. Stronger attacks did not develop against Division *Ditfurth*'s right flank. Nevertheless, as a result of the assaults on the heights west of the Maison de Champagne Farm and the Kanonenberg, the situation again turned perilous. With the arrival of units from 56th Infantry Division, however, the situation was restored.

---

34 In his memoirs, General von Falkenhayn writes: "As the result of a severe crisis, Third Army Headquarters considered whether a further withdrawal of the Army's entire front might be advisable; fortunately this decision was not made. Pursuant to the urgent advice of Generalmajor Knobelsdorf, the neighbouring Fifth Army's Chief of the General Staff, it was postponed until the arrival of the *OHL*, which was en route to the Western Theatre of War. Upon arrival on 25 September, a voluntary withdrawal was no longer discussed." This statement cannot be substantiated by the sources in the *Reichsarchiv* nor from the remarks of the persons involved. Neither General von Einem nor his Chief of the General Staff ever considered withdrawing any part of the army's front. See Falkenhayn, *Die Oberste Heeresleitung 1914–1916*, 141.

In XVIII Reserve Corps' sector, ferocious enemy attacks were directed pri-marily against the rear portion of 21st Reserve Division's turned flank and the Briqueterie position on both sides of the Ville sur Tourbe–Cernay en Dormois road. The French pocket at the Bois de Ville was taken, along with more than 300 prisoners.

The fighting lasted late into the night along the entire Champagne Front. During the course of the battle, prisoners were taken from 12th, 53rd, and 153rd Divisions.

The Situation at the OHL

Despite General von Hoehn's optimistic reports, Falkenhayn was troubled by the situation in the Champagne, especially in VIII Reserve Corps' sector. Apparently he feared a further loss of German positions, for around noon he decided to pro-pose to the Kaiser the subordination of Third Army to Army Group *German Crown Prince*. Consequently, Third and Fifth Armies received the following order: "In order to ensure Third and Fifth Army's optimum cooperation in the present circumstances, Third Army is assigned to the Army Group on the left flank, His Imperial Excellence the Crown Prince commanding." Generalleutnant von Hoehn, who was senior to Generalleutnant Knobelsdorf, the Chief of Staff of Army Group *German Crown Prince* (Fifth Army), was replaced by Oberst von Loßberg as the OHL's liaison officer in Mézières. As a result of these changes, Army Group *German Crown Prince* now had to support Third Army under its own power.

The balance of power on the Artois and Champagne Fronts remained very unfavourable. According to calculations made by the OHL's Intelligence Division on 26 September, in the area west of Lille (Radinghem) and Ransart, fifteen Ger-man divisions (including the Guard Corps) were facing approximately thirty-one French and British divisions, including eight that were in reserve. In the Cham-pagne between Aubérive and the Aisne, approximately seven German divisions were reportedly confronting twenty-three French divisions (including five in the second line). Although the number of German divisions in the Champagne increased with the arrival of additional forces, it was clear that more support was required. Therefore, on the evening of 26 September, Falkenhayn ordered the newly arrived 19th Infantry Division transferred from Belgium to Third Army. The latter was also assigned Carrier Pigeon Detachment Ostende in its entirety, consisting of six bomber squadrons.[35]

---

35 Each Bombenflugzeugen *consisted of six large, twin engine aircraft with pilot, observer, and gunners. See Cron,* Imperial German Army, 1914–18, *182.*

The afternoon and evening reports indicated that, for the time being, Sixth Army could manage to hold on without the support of additional reserves and that Third Army had successfully repelled the day's attacks. The fact that Seventh Army expected an attack against its left flank did not give rise to serious concerns because it was otherwise in a favourable position. Nevertheless, on the same evening Falkenhayn redeployed 185th Infantry Brigade from Armee-Abteilung *Gaede* to the rear of Seventh Army's left flank, where it was to remain at the latter's disposition.

The events of 26 September did not turn out as dangerously as Falkenhayn may have feared in the afternoon and evening of the previous day. There was no doubt that the future would bring a number of serious and strenuous battles for the army in the West and that the enemy would not soon abandon its attempts at a breakthrough; but the danger that had seemed imminent on 25 September was considered to have been averted as of the following day.

The Further Course of the Battle to the End of September

In the Artois

On the morning of 27 September, General d'Urbal was not at all satisfied with the results that had been achieved by French III and XII Corps and decided that from that point onwards the emphasis of the battle would be against the line Liévin–Souchez. Consequently, he placed 154th Infantry Division and the *Spahi* Brigade (which had been in held in reserve) at the disposal of XXI Corps and subordinated a Territorial Regiment to XXXIII Corps; he also moved a number of heavy batteries located south of the Scarpe to the rear of the army's left flank in order to place under fire the German batteries identified at Liévin and Angres. The renewed attacks of XXI and XXXIII Corps, which had been scheduled for 13:00, were delayed until 17:00. On the British side, General Haig ordered the initial withdrawal of 21st and 24th Infantry Divisions, which had suffered heavy casualties on 26 September, so that they could be reorganized in the rear. In their place, the Guard Division was directed to retake Hill 70 east of Loos, which had been lost in the course of the afternoon. Also, elements of 3rd Cavalry Division were to be deployed to the south in the city itself. The neighbouring units were to participate as much as possible, and gas was again to be discharged.

Turning to the German side, after 26 September, Sixth Army Headquarters had no doubt that a breakthrough could be averted. It reported this to the *OHL*. Nevertheless, on 27 September, elements of the Guard Corps had to be deployed on the right flank of IV and VI Corps in order to prevent a loss of ground; 1st

Guard Infantry Division was assigned to VI Corps and 2nd Guard Infantry Division to IV Corps. The VII Corps was reinforced by the last two available battalions of Bavarian II Corps and one battalion of XIX (Saxon) Corps. The VII Corps' left flank was to support the attacks of IV Corps; as a result, on 27 September the Bavarian elements assigned to 14th Infantry Division retook "Fosse 8" as well as part of the Hohenzollern Redoubt southwest of Haisnes. Because of the pouring rain, the attacking forces sank up to their calves in sticky mud. Their further advance was parried on the afternoon of 27 September by the British units' third attack. However, this attack did not nearly come close to those recently conducted in terms of strength, depth, and force. Consequently, it broke down in the German defensive fire.

Then on 28 September, 14th Prussian Infantry Division (supported by reinforcements) managed to retake the entire Hohenzollern Redoubt. No additional British attacks of consequence materialized, as the enemy required rest.

Events opposite the French now necessitated the deployment of additional elements of the Guard Corps. The enemy desperately tried to build on the initial successes around Souchez and in the ensuing days threw elements of 154th, 58th, and 130th Divisions against 123rd (Saxon) Infantry Division and VI Corps. This resulted in a very difficult contest. On 27 September the French launched unsuccessful secondary attacks at Angres, on Gießler Hill, and at Neuville-St. Vaast.[36] During the night of 27 and 28 September the situation on British First Army's southern flank became sufficiently serious to force Field Marshal French—who was almost out of reserves—to threaten to discontinue the offensive unless French Tenth Army attacked immediately and with maximum resolve. Consequently, Foch on the morning of 28 September ordered IX Corps' 152nd Infantry Division to assume control of British 47th Territorial Division's sector. At the same time, the remainder of IX Corps—after it was replaced by XVII Corps and 88th Territorial Division—was ordered to the rear of Tenth Army's left flank.

In the meantime, German VI Corps was sufficiently threatened by a southerly French thrust from Souchez that 11th Infantry Division had to be withdrawn in its entirety as far as the Prinz Reuß *Stellung*. After severe attacks on the afternoon of 28 September, the situation between Souchez and Neuville-St. Vaast became especially serious. The French stormed Gießler Hill, which was especially critical for artillery observation; 123rd Infantry Division's valiant counterattacks could only reverse this enemy thrust to a limited degree. Toward evening a report reached Sixth Army Headquarters that French assault units had taken Givenchy from the south and had already broken through the last German

---

36   *Gießler Hill was known as "the Pimple" to British soldiers.*

trenches in the La Folie *Stellung*. An immediate counterattack was unsuccessful, and elements of 11th Infantry Division and 1st Guard Infantry Division—twenty-two companies in all—were assembled for a second try. For a long time afterwards there were no reports; thus a French breakthrough at Givenchy-en-Gohelle could not be ruled out.

Reinforcements were unavailable. In the evening the *OHL* ordered Second Army to make one division available to Sixth Army in the form of a troop detachment (*Truppenabteilung*) made up of various battalion and battery elements under the command of Generalleutnant von Hartz.[37] The first trains carrying these soldiers arrived in the area of Rouvroy on the morning of 29 September. If it became necessary, Sixth Army was authorized to call on a brigade of Fourth Army's 53rd Reserve Division, but first it was to relieve 88th Infantry Brigade of XIX (Saxon) Corps near Lille in order to free it up for use against the French. Finally the army was provided with a squadron of Carrier Pigeon Detachment Metz.

By now the soldiers around Souchez were so exhausted that the intended replacement of the troops around Gießler Hill by parts of the Guard Corps had to take place immediately. Thus VI Corps had to cover the sectors of two of the exhausted regiments of Bavarian 1st Reserve Division with 11th Infantry Division as well as the remaining sector of 12th Infantry Division. This turned out to be impossible, as fierce battles raged in the Silesian Corps' sector. During the night of 28 and 29 September, 2nd Guard Infantry Division, now commanded by Generalleutnant von Hoehn,[38] successfully relieved the bloodied 123rd Infantry Division. In the meantime the entire 1st Guard Division, under the command of Oberst Eitel Friedrich, Prince of Prussia, had been fully committed to the hard-fought battle for La Folie *Stellung*. Because part of that position remained in enemy hands, the German artillery concentrated around Vimy was seriously threatened.

It was not until 29 September that Sixth Army Headquarters became convinced that the enemy had been unable to break through at Givenchy. The attackers continued to occupy the captured trench lines at and south of the town, but at least their tremendous efforts had been frustrated before they could reach their final objectives. Sixth Corps had endured great suffering in the course of these extremely hard-fought battles and had taken disproportionately severe casualties. Therefore the corps had to be gradually pulled out and reassembled little by little at Cambrai. Up until then, the commanding general of the Guard Corps, General der Infanterie Baron von Plettenberg, had commanded the mixed

---

37 The strength of this detachment was nine battalions, one cavalry squadron, eight field batteries, and two heavy batteries.
38 At the end of September, Generalleutnant Ritter von Hoehn had replaced Generalleutnant Baron von Lüttwitz as Commander of 2nd Guard Infantry Division.

elements of the Guard and VI Corps, which were located in his sector. Now the *OHL* announced that XI Corps would be redeployed from the Eastern Front with the daily arrival of thirty trains in Sixth Army's rear area; however, after its exertions and casualties in Russia, that corps was in desperate need of rest and was therefore to be quartered in and around Valenciennes. To place it more conveniently at his disposal, Crown Prince Rupprecht requested that XI Corps be staged in the area of Douai. The *OHL* also assigned the fortress of Lille to Sixth Army and transferred a mortar battery from Armee-Abteilung *Falkenhausen*. The Guard Corps was permitted to reacquire its three heavy howitzer batteries, which had been in the army's reserve. For the time being, both howitzer batteries brought along by Division *Hartz* were kept in reserve in place of those returned to the Guard Corps.

The evening of 29 September brought only a small foray at Beaurains. The prevailing opinion was that the British and French were preparing to renew their major offensive. This assessment corresponded with the facts: that morning at Lillers, Foch and Field Marshal French had agreed to a new joint attack on 2 October, which was to be launched after their forces were reorganized. In this way Foch was adhering to the orders issued by his generalissimo on the afternoon of 26 September.

By 21 September, Sixth Army had captured approximately 3,400 prisoners and 23 machine guns and had reported losses of 657 officers and around 29,000 enlisted men. The units that suffered the most were as follows:

- 117th Infantry Division, casualties of around 5,600 men
- 123rd (Saxon) Infantry Division, around 2,500 men
- 26th Reserve Infantry Brigade, around 2,200 men
- VI Corps, around 7,100 men
- IV Corps, around 3,600 men

Between 21 and 27 September the German field artillery had expended approximately 360,000 shells on the main attack front; the main calibres of the heavy artillery had expended approximately 54,000 rounds.

In the Champagne

On the French side, General de Castelnau ordered Fourth and Second Armies to continue the offensive on 27 September. Since the second German positions seemed to be "severely shaken," they were to be taken at any price, and to this end some of the heavy batteries were brought up during the night.[39] Joffre allocated three

---

39 See *French Official History*, III: 393.

new infantry divisions (48th Division from Sixth Army, as well as 15th and 129th Divisions from Army Group *East*), which were to arrive on 27 September.

By 27 September the German defensive front had been reasonably well strengthened by inserting fresh units. The Army Group reinforced Fifth Army's endangered right wing and ensured the co-operation of VIII and XVIII Reserve Corps on its threatened flanks. So as to define the command structure in the sector formerly held by VIII Reserve Corps, Generaloberst von Einem ordered the newly arrived staff of X Corps to take command of the combat sector west of a line running north from Perthes.[40] The VIII Reserve Corps Headquarters retained control of the portion to the east. He also transferred artillery and one infantry regiment each to XII Reserve Corps, Corps *Lüttwitz*, and Corps *Fleck* from the units arriving from 20th Infantry Division; meanwhile the *OHL* provided four heavy batteries from Armee-Abteilungen *Strantz* and *Gaede*. The army staff personally oversaw the construction of a new rearward position (*R2-Stellung*) behind Third Army's centre and left flank; it made use of all the available and newly arrived combat engineer and labour companies. An *R3-Stellung* along the line St. Hilaire-le-Petit–Aure was also being reconnoitred.

Captured orders told the Germans to expect that a major offensive aimed at breaking through the *R-Stellung* would begin on 27 September. In actuality, however, on that day the French attacks consisted merely of a number of uncoordinated secondary thrusts. These attacks were centred on the German forward trenches at St. Souplet, Ste. Marie à Py, Somme Py, Tahure, Maisons de Champagne Farm, and Massiges and were preceded by a strong artillery preparation during the afternoon and evening. At the focal points of the battle the French were able to achieve minor gains, especially against Division *Liebert* south of Ste. Marie à Py, where immediate counterattacks failed to restore the situation. The 24th Reserve Division's left flank, which had also been severely affected, was reinforced by one battalion from 20th and 28th Infantry Divisions; 50th Infantry Division and Division *Ditfurth* were strengthened by units from 56th Infantry Division. By evening, VIII Reserve Corps controlled three subsectors held by 50th Infantry Division, Division *Ditfurth*, and Division *Sontag*. (Generalleutnant Sontag, commanding 56th Infantry Division, had assumed the defence of the far left flank.)

In the afternoon, Fifth Army's 21st Reserve Division—adjoining to the east— also experienced fierce hand-to-hand combat, but it was able to hold on to its positions.

---

40 Generalleutnant Barron von Lüttwitz assumed command to replace General der Infantrie von Emmerich, who was ill.

Despite local advances, the enemy was again unable to achieve a significant success on 27 September. Captured diaries indicated that in some places French regiments had refused to attack, although in most places the attacks had been conducted with determination. Among the enemy soldiers captured that day were cavalry officers and non-commissioned cavalry officers tasked with reconnoitring advance routes for the cavalry units near Souain. According to a captured order the cavalry was "to take advantage of the breakthrough" on 27 September.

During the evening of 27 September, reports of a successful breakthrough west of the Souain–Somme Py road arrived at the headquarters of both French armies and the Army Group. This had a determining influence on the actions taken the next day. On the fronts of both armies, all the reserves staged close by were moved to the inner flanks; orders stipulated that they had to take advantage of the supposed success at any cost.

As a result, the afternoon and evening were occupied with fierce minor battles along the entire front between Aubérive and Massiges, where the French attacked in accordance with their orders and attempted to take the entire second German position "at any price." These attacks collapsed with high casualties. Toward evening the situation appeared serious only south of Ste. Marie à Py, where the French had managed to penetrate and push through Division *Liebert*'s *R-Stellung*. The 24th Reserve Division, which had also been ferociously attacked on its left flank, viewed the situation as sufficiently perilous to warrant the recommittal of its three totally exhausted regiments, which were in the process of being relieved, in order to excavate a switch trench at St. Souplet. By the evening of 29 September, quickly assembled units under the command of General Liebert had managed to push the enemy back into the *R-Stellung* with a gallantly conducted counterattack.[41] Almost 1,000 French soldiers of 157th Infantry Division became prisoners of war.

On the morning of 28 September the army staff assigned 20th Infantry Division (less two infantry regiments) to X Corps, keeping 19th Infantry Division (which had arrived on 27 September) around Machault in reserve. That evening, elements of this division had to be deployed to support the front. Army Group *German Crown Prince* announced that the composite 113th Infantry Division had arrived in the area west of Bouziers from Armee-Abteilung *Strantz*.

At 11:30 on the morning of 28 September, fierce fighting for Hills 191 and 199 north of Massiges—both of which had been partly lost—took place on Fifth Army's right flank. Because of severe German casualties, the Army Group's planned

---

41   These included parts of 52nd, 91st, 92nd, 184th, and 192nd Infantry Regiments and 25th Bavarian Infantry Regiment.

counterattack—which was to have used 56th Infantry and 21st Reserve Divisions—could not be executed. After fierce fighting in the last days of September, both hills had to be abandoned. Between 21 and 30 September, XVIII Reserve Corps had captured almost 1,500 French soldiers; its own losses during the same time period amounted to approximately 12,000 men.

In the Champagne, from 25 to 29 September, weak German forces retained possession of the *R-Stellung* south of Ste. Marie à Py against strong French attacks, even though the construction of this position was incomplete. In part this could be attributed to the fact that the *R-Stellung* was located on a reverse slope; thus the French artillery could not bring the position under observed fire. For the same reason, French artillery could not sufficiently support the massed enemy forces that had broken through beyond the *R-Stellung* on 28 September. The favourable topography contributed considerably to the complete success of the German counterattack on 29 September. The German army thus restored a situation that had appeared extremely threatening on 28 September.

The Situation at the *OHL* at the Beginning of October

The tremendous offensive effort in the Artois and the Champagne had come at a difficult time for the German Western Front. In the afternoon of 25 September, Falkenhayn was forced to deploy the two corps recently arrived in Belgium from the East, both of which urgently required rest. This decision ran entirely counter to his original intentions and represented an emergency measure that was necessary to deal with the unexpectedly serious threat.

Since then, however, it had been possible to deal with the situation by making relatively minor shifts in forces. Among them only the transfer of the combined Division *Hartz* from Second to Sixth Army represented a true weakening of the front in the less important area on both sides of the Oise. On 30 September the *OHL* could take the first step toward relieving entire units in need of rest through the exchange of Bavarian I Corps for VI Corps. On the morning of the same day, the first train carrying XI Corps, which was arriving from the East, passed through Liège. There was also no shortage of ammunition, and the Chief of the Field Munitions Service still had significant reserves.[42] The situation of the Western Army now seemed secure: the enemy's supreme efforts had not been able to disrupt German plans, particularly the commencement of the campaign

---

42 On 1 October the reserves of the Field Ammunitions Chief consisted of seventeen infantry ammunition trains, thirty-three and a half field artillery ammunition trains, twenty-six heavy field howitzer ammunition trains, and twenty-one and three-quarters mortar ammunition trains. In October a significant increase in munitions production was expected.

against Serbia. This represented a success with immense political and operational consequences.

Now free of a heavy mental burden, Falkenhayn began to contemplate whether it would be possible to regain the initiative and how this might be accomplished. Of course, steps toward this objective could not be taken until additional forces arrived from the East. This would present the opportunity to free up forces from quiet areas of the Western Front—something that would be out of the question until at least the second half of October. In any case, on 3 October Falkenhayn asked Knobelsdorf, Army Group *German Crown Prince*'s Chief of Staff, whether he thought it was feasible to consider "taking up the old plan for the undertaking in Alsace." These operations, which had been considered in June 1915, at which time Knobelsdorf had examined them in depth, had apparently been part of a general intention to reach a decision on the Western Front in 1915. At this point in the autumn, however, with large elements of the German Army still engaged in Serbia, it would not be feasible to initiate or conduct a decisive operation prior to the beginning of winter. Therefore Falkenhayn's question could well be interpreted to mean that he was considering whether it was possible to deliver a resounding blow to the Western enemy's far left flank using preparations that had already been completed. Such a blow could bring to an end the very difficult winter battles in the southern Vosges. If the enemy could be driven all the way to the Franco-German border, the resulting situation might afford an opportunity to launch a spring attack on Belfort.

The Renewal of the Offensive in October

In the Artois: Operations, 30 September–10 October

On the enemy's side of the Artois Front, considerable delays to the relief of the British forces' southern flank by elements of French IX Corps forced Foch (with Joffre's agreement) to further postpone the new attack planned for 2 October. After numerous meetings with the British Supreme Commander, the date for the attack was set for 6 October. Until then time was to be spent on individual operations. On that day the French Supreme Commander intended to launch new attacks in the Artois as well as the Champagne; emphasis was to be placed on the synchronization of the two operations.

In early October the impression prevailed on the German side that the French—especially opposite the Guard Corps—were being particularly enterprising in their preparations. Conversely, the British had suffered to such an extent that for the time being Sixth Army Headquarters did not expect a major attack at

The Autumn Battle in Artois
The German Attack at Loos on 8 October 1915

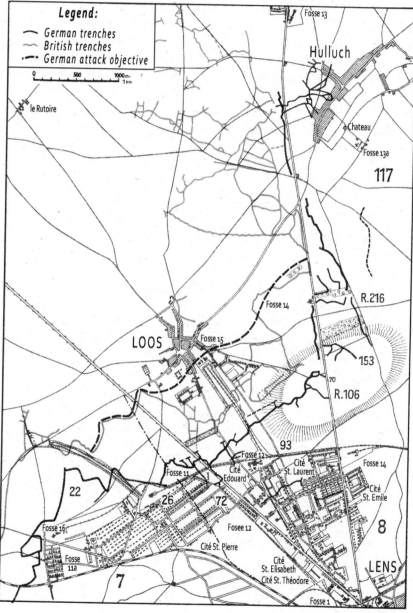

Legend:
- German trenches
- British trenches
- German attack objective

0   500   1000 m
1 km

le Rutoire

Fosse 13

Hulluch

Chateau

Fosse 13a

117

Fosse 14

R.216

LOOS

Fosse 15

153

70

R.106

93

Fosse 12

Fosse 11

Cité Edouard

Cité St. Laurent

Fosse 14

22

26

72

Cité St. Emile

8

Fosse 16

Fosee 12

Cité St. Pierre

Fosse 11a

7

Cité St. Elisabeth
Cité St. Théodore

LENS

Fosse 1

Sketch 24

Loos or to the north of the town. As of 6 October there had been a number of smaller engagements in the sectors of 123rd, 11th, and 12th Infantry Divisions, which Guard Corps Headquarters had taken over with 2nd and 1st Guard Infantry Divisions and Division *Hartz*. Fresh troops were required to retake the lost trenches as the composite 88th (Saxon) Infantry Brigade—which had been deployed on 2 October—was not up to the task on its own.[43] To free up additional forces, Army Headquarters considered a number of possibilities, concluding that the best solution was to replace Bavarian II Corps on the army's right flank with XI Corps, which was arriving from the East. This alternative did not materialize, for on the afternoon of 30 September the *OHL* ordered that the exhausted VI Corps be replaced with Second Army's Bavarian I Corps beginning on 5 October.[44]

On 1 October, Crown Prince Rupprecht visited the commanding generals of VII and IV Corps as well as the Guard Corps. General von François assessed the situation as "quite rosy [and reported that] the gradual advance in the trenches south of Haisnes was also proceeding smoothly."[45] General Sixt von Arnim was informed "that he could not count on relief and that he would have to manage with his present forces." Sixt's only concern was for the positions north of Lens, where the troops were exhausted. Also, "he expected a British attack because the enemy had redeployed his artillery which was being dealt with according to plan." Plettenberg received orders from the Army Commander that "above all else, [he was] to hold the high ground and, later, retake the Prinz Reuß *Stellung* as soon as possible." The Guard Corps then requested two fresh brigades "before it would be able to release the infantry of VI Corps ... [and reported that] their artillery was sufficient." In response the Guard Corps was informed on 2 October "that relief would be provided by transferring the southern section of the front line to Bavarian I Corps."[46] Crown Prince Rupprecht reported to Falkenhayn "that it was desirable that XI Corps, as well as the other corps returning from Russia, be deployed in a quiet sector of the front in order to acclimatize them to trench warfare." The *OHL* assigned two of Fourth Army's reserve infantry regiments for relief duties; this replaced two regiments of 123rd Infantry Division that were in need of relief. Following a period of rest, XI Corps was initially to be deployed in a quiet area.

During October the battles on the French front continued to be conducted more fiercely than those in the British sector. On the high ground west and south

---

43   This brigade was made up of 104th and 134th Infantry Regiments.

44   In the meantime Generalleutnant Chales de Beaulieu, previously commanding 12th Infantry Division, had taken command of the corps, replacing General of the Infantry von Pritzelwitz, who had fallen ill.

45   War Diary of Sixth Army Headquarters, 2 October.

46   Ibid.

of Givenchy the German forces no longer found any coherent trenches, dugouts, or access routes. This made their situation noticeably worse. Elements of the recently relieved 11th and 12th Infantry Divisions had to be deployed repeatedly to support the Guard Corps, which had suffered heavy casualties in unrelenting close combat. On the afternoon of 3 October, parts of XXI French Corps again broke through the German lines at the "Five Crossroads" west of Givenchy, advancing as far as the village's western edge. It was not until the next day that counterattacks by 2nd Guard Infantry Division managed to push them back. At this point the exhaustion of the Silesian and Guard troops required the deployment of the composite 88th (Saxon) Infantry Brigade. On 6 October the already planned relief of the Guard Corps was accomplished when Bavarian I Corps replaced IV Corps and began to take over the 600 metre sector of front from south of Gießler Hill to the northern boundary of Bavarian I Reserve Corps. By 11 October the commander of Bavarian I Reserve Corps, General der Infanterie Ritter von Xylander, had deployed his 1st and 2nd Divisions north of Division *Hartz*, which had been assigned to him as well. With this contraction of Sixth Army's portion of the front line, the German forces could now contemplate a gradual retaking of important points, especially Gießler Hill.

With this in mind, on 6 October Crown Prince Rupprecht made this report to the *OHL:*

Due to the loss of parts of La Folie *Stellung* and the Prinz Reuß *Stellung*, the situation on the heights near La Folie continues to be precarious. The defence has to be accomplished along a line which is wider than 3 kilometres and without any disposition in depth. Presently the fate of the vital crest of the ridge is based on a simple infantry trench, parts of which have had to be newly excavated. The artillery observation posts which are now located to the immediate rear of the infantry are in extreme peril. The recapture of the Prinz Reuß *Stellung*—at the very least—is absolutely essential. At present, holding the position from Givenchy to the Neuville–Thélus Road requires the strength of 1st Guard Division reinforced by five Saxon battalions and supported by elements of VI Corps. Therefore Bavarian I Corps in its entirety will be necessary to safely reacquire the lost Prinz Reuß *Stellung*. The reacquisition of the entire Gießler Hill and its forward terrain is equally important which will also take some serious fighting. To this end the Guard Corps, which is already on site and familiar with the ground, will be grouped closer together so as to make relief easier. Army Headquarters urgently requests that these relief and regrouping activities—which are recognized as being vital for the reacquisition of the lost positions by the Guard Corps—not be interfered with except in an extreme emergency. The recapture of these positions will enable us to judge if further developments permit the northward expansion of Bavarian I Corps and the complete withdrawal of the Guard Corps.

General von Falkenhayn responded that further changes to the forces that had been made available were not being contemplated at that time, although a permanent deployment of the Guard Corps to Sixth Army could not be counted on. Therefore, he continued, it would be more practical to utilize Bavarian I Corps in order to reacquire Gießler Hill, which in the opinion of the *OHL* was much more important than holding the Prinz Reuß *Stellung*. Army Headquarters, however, still considered the reacquisition of all its lost ground to be necessary; accordingly it requested that it retain control of the Guard Corps.

On the relatively quiet day of 6 October, Army Headquarters believed that the enemy might no longer be capable of a major offensive in the Artois; the transfer of enemy forces from there to the Champagne appeared more likely. Actually, both enemies still intended to execute a new combined attack. However, it had turned out that the necessary preparations could not be completed by Tenth French Army or the British by 6 October; therefore, with a heavy heart, Joffre had to forgo his planned simultaneous offensives in the Artois and the Champagne, agreeing instead to reschedule the Franco-British attack for 10 October.

In IV Corps's sector, 117th Infantry Division was assigned 26th Reserve Infantry Brigade and a reserve regiment of Fourth Army for support and relief; another reserve regiment was assigned to 8th Infantry Division. Owing to the enemy's passivity, General Sixt considered it an opportune time to launch a major undertaking of his own near Loos; this was ordered for 8 October. After a three-and-a-half-hour artillery preparation, five regiments launched an attack east and south of Loos at 17:00.[47] Elements of 7th Infantry Division joined in on the left flank, but the operation did not meet with success. Owing to poor observation in foggy weather, the artillery preparation had been insufficient. The advancing infantry was met by mostly intact wire and a well-prepared British adversary as well as French soldiers north of Hill 70. After taking around 3,000 casualties, the attackers were forced to return to their jumping-off positions. The enemy did not mount any counterattacks.

Nevertheless, the German attack had created an advantage that was not to be underestimated. The British preparations for the new attack had been so seriously impeded that the British commander informed Foch on 9 October that he could not meet the agreed-upon date and that he would only be able to launch a

---

47   The attacking troops consisted of 216th and 106th (Saxon) Reserve Infantry Regiments and 153rd, 93rd, and 72nd Infantry Regiments.

new offensive on 12 or 13 October. Because of fog, French Tenth Army also had considerable difficulties with their artillery preparations, and the attack had to be postponed again until the 11 October.

Farther north at Hulluch, it was possible to improve the new front line south of La Bassée Canal despite fierce fighting involving numerous attacks. Minor British thrusts at the Hohenzollern Redoubt and the gravel pit against disorganized Prussian, Bavarian, and Saxon units failed daily.

In the Artois: Operations, 11–13 October

On 10 October, German Sixth Army consisted of twenty-one and a half infantry divisions with 902 field guns, 200 heavy high-angle guns, and 71 heavy low-trajectory guns. These faced sixteen British and nineteen French infantry divisions.[48] Since 10 October, heavy artillery fire had been directed at the trenches of the Guard Corps; this was particularly intense on Gießler Hill in 2nd Guard Infantry Division's sector and against 1st Guard Infantry Division, under Oberst Eitel Friedrich, which was fighting to the south. Consequently, 2nd Guard Infantry Division was forced to vacate its position at the Five Crossroads west of Givenchy.

On the morning of 11 October a *Trommelfeuer* again began to fall on sectors of the Guard Corps and Bavarian I Corps. At that time, in the southern part of the area formerly held by the Guard Corps, Bavarian I Corps Headquarters was in the process of receiving orders. By 16:00, IV Corps and the Guard Corps, as well as Bavarian I Corps, were reporting that attacks were imminent. In response, Army Headquarters placed on notice three exhausted Guard regiments that were quartered as reserves around Douai; it also kept the recently relieved 88th (Saxon) Infantry Brigade (which was to be transported to the army reserve at Carvin) on the battlefield.

The French launched an attack at 17:30. Despite the raging barrage that preceded it, the attackers met with German units that were ready to defend themselves. Everywhere flares alerted the batteries that assaults were being launched. Against the positions of VII and IV Corps south of La Bassée Canal, the British merely made a foray at the Hohenzollern Redoubt while the French launched secondary assaults along the Lens–Béthune road. However, well coordinated attacks were directed against the Guard Corps' sector, Bavarian 1st and 2nd Infantry Divisions, and the right flank of Division *Hartz*. Against the Guard Corps, the attacking force, comprising elements of French XXI and XXXIII Corps, only managed to break through at Angres Wood and to the east of the Five Crossroads. French XII Corps attacked

---

48   The artillery strength of these divisions on the same day cannot be ascertained exactly.

The Autumn Battle in Artois
The French Attacks on 11 October and the British Attack on 13 October 1915

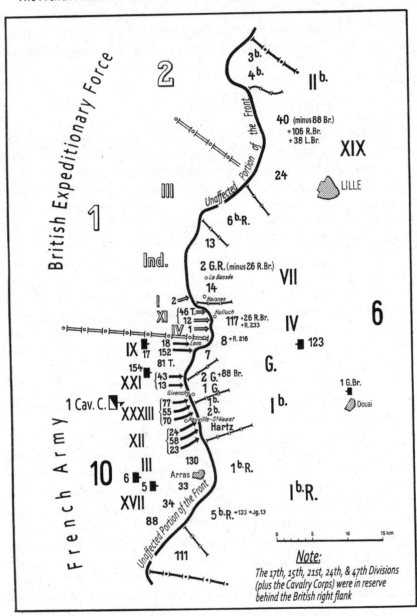

Note:
The 17th, 15th, 21st, 24th, & 47th Divisions
(plus the Cavalry Corps) were in reserve
behind the British right flank

Sketch 25

the newly arrived Bavarian I Corps in several waves but was even less successful; its attacks soon collapsed under the defensive fire. However, the counterattack ordered by General von Xylander, which was intended to retake the positions that had been lost in September by VI Corps, had to be abandoned because the enemy's positions behind the attacking forces were densely occupied. Following the barrage in the area opposite Bavarian I Reserve Corps, the enemy trenches became filled with infantry around Beaurains. However, no attack was launched.

After repeated valiant attacks on 12 and 13 October the Guard Corps managed to retake the trenches at the Five Crossroads. Despite repeated efforts, however, Angres Wood northwest of Givenchy remained in French hands.

As of 10 October, fire had noticeably increased in the Loos Salient as well. The British attack that IV Corps expected on 11 October did not materialize until 13 October. On that day the barrage started at noon and raged between La Bassée Canal and Hill 70 north of Lens. It was followed shortly after 14:00 by a gas attack. The gas was released mainly from portable containers in saps that had been driven forward from the front line. The clouds alternated between white smoke and reddish gas. The enemy artillery also fired gas shells, while the infantry threw smoke bombs. This preparation, which temporarily resulted in a complete lack of visibility, lasted for almost two hours. Due to strong winds and the influence of the sun, the cumulative effect of this major gas attack was minimal. Infantry of British 46th, 12th, and 1st Divisions attacked immediately behind the seventh gas cloud. Almost everywhere, these attacks collapsed with heavy casualties. However, the British did manage a breakthrough in the western portion of the Hohenzollern Redoubt, which had been badly contaminated with gas, and in part of the gravel pit northwest of Hulluch. Additional gas clouds were dispersed into the evening, but these did nothing to reverse the British lack of success. At the same time, British diversionary attacks were launched north of La Bassée as far as the area of Lille. Over the following days the German forces fought tenaciously and managed to gradually eliminate the small British emplacements at the Hohenzollern Redoubt and in the gravel pit.

Acceding to urgent requests from Plettenberg, on 13 October Crown Prince Rupprecht made 88th Infantry Brigade available to the exhausted Guard Corps. That same day, he also had to transfer a part of his last reserve, consisting of three Guard regiments from around Douai, to the Guard and IV Corps (each corps receiving one regiment). On 13 October at Army Headquarters in Lille, Falkenhayn brought himself up to date about the situation and promised to relieve the totally exhausted Guard Corps with Second Army's IX Reserve Corps. At the same time, he announced the arrival of XIII Corps Headquarters, together with 1st Guard Reserve and 4th Guard Infantry Divisions, at Valenciennes and Cambrai.

French support of the British attack on 13 October consisted of artillery fire only. It appeared that after these major efforts, the British and French offensive in the Artois had been broken.

During the autumn battles, Sixth Army's total losses up until the end of October amounted to almost 1,100 officers and 50,000 enlisted men. During the same period, ammunition expenditure amounted to approximately 1,200,000 field artillery rounds and approximately 236,000 heavy artillery rounds.

In the Champagne: Operations, 30 September–5 October

In the meantime, the enemy's new and formidable efforts reignited the struggle, which was now waged at full strength and fury. By 29 September, General de Castelnau was convinced that if the attacks were continued with exhausted troops, they could not be expected to succeed. Joffre had promised the deployment of additional forces and ammunition, but he concurred with Castelnau's assessment. Accordingly, on 30 September, Fourth and Second Army Headquarters were directed to hold and fortify their existing positions and to gradually pull out their exhausted units, marshal them, and move the larger cavalry units to the rear. Army Group *Centre*'s commander intended to launch a general offensive on the second German position, with fresh troops if possible.

Between 30 September and 5 October, secondary French operations began against the protruding German positions while sudden assaults were made from the breakthrough points. The French infantry proved themselves adroit at exploiting every bomb crater and remnant of trench. This same skill was apparent after they had taken portions of German trench; these were quickly reconstructed, armed with machine guns, protected by wire, and connected to the French trench network. The enemy attacks were launched mainly toward evening; attacks without artillery support were rarely made and only at dawn. The well-coordinated German artillery, which had been reinforced with seven heavy batteries, managed to stop many French attacks with concentrated fire. On 2 October, anti-aircraft guns at Rethel shot down a French airship on a reconnaissance mission and captured its crew.

During this period, reconnaissance patrols revealed that the French artillery was being redeployed. Numerous batteries were being brought up, and on 4 October approximately sixty were identified on both sides of the Souain–Somme Py road. Indeed, the French were using the pause in the battle to push their main offensive artillery closer to the German lines. Significant changes in the distribution of forces were also taking place. Both armies' Corps Headquarters—which had previously been held back—were deployed nearer to the front line. On Fourth Army's front, VI Corps moved up on the eastern side next to II Colonial Corps;

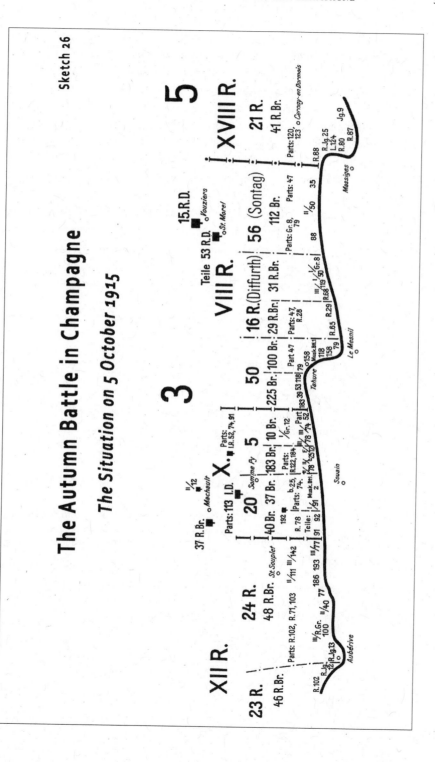

Sketch 26

The Autumn Battle in Champagne

The Situation on 5 October 1915

at Second Army, XVI Corps was inserted between XIV and XI Corps. The new attack was to be launched on 6 October using nineteen infantry divisions stationed on the front line between St. Souplet and the Aisne; both armies consisted of thirty-six and a half infantry divisions, some of greatly reduced strength.[49]

Also during this time, the commanders of German Third and Fifth Armies accelerated their efforts to re-establish a combat-ready front. Where possible, units were reorganized, reserves extracted, front and rear positions strengthened, and French preparations disrupted. Division *Liebert* was gradually replaced by 20th Infantry Division (Generalmajor Baron von Lüttwitz). The XIV Corps and VIII and XVIII Reserve Corps were preparing to relieve the threatened front by launching attacks of their own. A planned gas attack by XVIII Reserve Corps' right flank had to be scrapped when the heavy artillery bombardment prevented the installation of gas canisters. Therefore, the Army Group Commander made the Gas Pioneer Regiment—which had already been deployed—available to Third Army. Since 27 September he had also reinforced XVIII Reserve Corps with five battalions and four heavy batteries.

On 5 October, Generaloberst von Einem reported in detail on the situation and announced his intentions to the *OHL*:

> The Army Staff expects further French attacks against the 24th Reserve Division, X Corps, and the northern half of 50th Infantry Division. Opposite the Le Mesnil salient (left flank held by the 50th Infantry Division and 16th Reserve Division) the enemy has kept his distance from our frontlines. He probably recognized our existing switch and intermediate positions and he may consider an attack on these positions to be less promising. Therefore the enemy may limit himself to employing very damaging artillery fire. Simultaneous attacks against the army's left flank (56th Infantry Division) and against Fifth

---

49 On 6 October, French Fourth and Second Armies consisted of the following formations: *Fourth Army:* IV Corps (60th Infantry Division, half of 124th Infantry Division, and half of 100th Territorial Division), XXXII Corps (7th, 40th, 42nd, and half of 124th Infantry Division), VII Corps (8th, 14th, 37th, 129th, and 157th Infantry Divisions), II Colonial Corps (48th Infantry Division and the Moroccan Infantry Division), and VI Corps (12th, 51st, 56th, and 127th Infantry Divisions); 14th, 37th, 157th, and 127th Infantry Divisions were stationed behind the front and were not to be used in the attack; the Army Reserve was composed of 30th and 64th Infantry Divisions plus II Cavalry Corps and 2nd Cavalry Division. *Second Army:* XIV Corps (27th and 28th Infantry Divisions and 16th Colonial Division, the rifle group [*Schützengruppen*] of 3rd Cavalry Corps), XVI Corps (3rd, 15th, and 31st Infantry Divisions), XI Corps (21st, 22nd, and 53rd Infantry Divisions), XX Corps (11th, 39th, and 153rd Infantry Divisions), I Colonial Corps (32nd and 151st Infantry Divisions, and 2nd and 3rd Colonial Divisions); 27th Infantry Division was stationed behind the front and was not scheduled to attack; the Army Reserve was composed of 4th Infantry Division, 249th Infantry Brigade, half of 100th Territorial Division, and 3rd Cavalry Corps.

Army's right flank are considered a possibility. The Army Staff joins our soldiers in the hope that the attack will begin soon as it is being faced with confidence. The Army Staff is also convinced that our positions will be held. If we can manage to inflict heavy casualties on the attacking enemy and his attempts to break through are abandoned, we are confident that the relief forces presently staged in the army's sector (including the 37th Reserve Brigade and the infantry units from half the 53rd Reserve Division) will be sufficient. Should the enemy continue his breakthrough attempts beyond 9 October, however, the assignment of additional relief forces will become imperative.

According to estimates, at this time Third Army's losses amount to more than 40,000 men. Because of the lack of dugouts, they grow daily in the frontlines; relief units are also suffering casualties because approach trenches to the *R1-Stellung* have been lacking (they are now in the process of being constructed). In many areas of the front, observation conditions are unfavourable since the *R1-Stellung* is almost entirely located on the reverse side of the ridge and saps must first be driven forward in order to facilitate observation. The number of enemy aircraft and captive balloons (presently approximately 200 against sixty, including those provided by Fifth Army) give the French a superiority in observation which can only be eliminated over time.

An improvement of the situation in the centre of the battlefield can only be achieved through an advance to reacquire the general line Point 185 (west of Navarin-Fe)–Point 190 (Baraque)–Point 185 (north of le Trout Bricot Maison)–Point 188 (two kilometres northeast of Perthes). The soldiers know this position and like it ... Even despite the enemy's superiority in artillery, the faster our assault follows the expected French attack, the better our chances of success will be because we will be dealing with demoralised French infantry ... The Army Staff is convinced that fewer casualties will result from a strong counteroffensive than from a long-lasting defensive battle which will wear down the men and their non-commissioned officers.

Independent of this attack, a gas attack has been ordered. It is to be launched by the 35th and 36th Pioneer Regiments under the direction of XIV Corps along the line running inclusively from Fort de la Pompelle[50] to the position south of Moronvilliers. It is to be launched after 17 October, as soon as the winds prove favourable. However, this attack can only be made if the gas masks we requested—which were already needed to bring up the gas cylinders—arrive on time ... The French will thus be forced to move reserves to this location, which will then generate a relief on the actual battlefield.

---

50   *The Fort de la Pompelle, built in the early 1880s to defend Reims, was captured by the Germans early in September 1914, but was retaken by the French later in the fall. It exchanged hands several times during the war and was the scene of fierce fighting again in 1918.*

It is suggested that an attack from the army's left flank might attempt to reacquire the promontories northwest of Massiges and Hill 191 in concert with Fifth Army's right flank. However, Third Army's battlefront (from Hill 199 to the west) would then extend across a plateau which is totally dominated by enemy artillery. It is thus probably prudent to leave this for a later time when the French artillery has been moved to the rear after their large scale attempts at achieving a breakthrough have ended. In all likelihood this could then be accomplished using the combined forces of both armies.

Army Group *German Crown Prince* presented Third Army's proposals to the *OHL*, adding that it considered the attacks on Moronvilliers and Tahure to be "promising, although the timing must not be determined prematurely as they would suffer from the same barrage which is presently falling on our defensive positions."

According to information from prisoners of war and German observations, it was expected that the French offensive would resume in the near future. On 5 October the enemy's preparatory fire again grew into a *Trommelfeuer*. In the Aubérive–Aisne area, the patched-together German divisions faced twenty-nine French divisions as follows:

- Facing 24th (Saxon) Infantry Division: French 7th, 124th, 42nd, 40th, 8th, and 37th Infantry Divisions,
- Facing 20th Infantry Division: French 14th, 157th, 127th, 129th, and 56th Infantry Divisions.
- Facing 5th Infantry Division: French 15th Colonial, 10th Colonial, 12th, 28th and 31st Infantry Divisions.
- Facing 50th Infantry Division: French 27th, 22nd, 21st, and 3rd Infantry Divisions.
- Facing 16th Reserve Division: French 53rd, 11th, and 153rd Infantry Divisions.
- Facing 56th Infantry Division: French 39th, 32nd, and 2nd Colonial Infantry Divisions.
- Facing 21st Reserve Division: French 3rd Colonial, 151st, and 20th Infantry Divisions.

In the Champagne: New Major Offensive Operations after 6 October

The forty-eight-hour heavy barrage on Third Army's centre and left flank and Fifth Army's right reached its apex early on 6 October. The rear areas were cut off by gas; at times no communication was possible, even by runner. At 06:30 the French launched a major offensive against the German trenches south of the St. Souplet–Cernay en Dormois line. Increased artillery fire and forays on a smaller

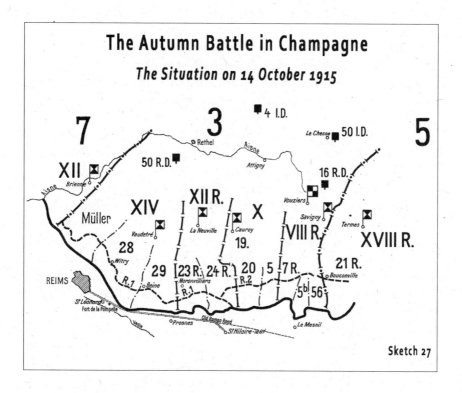

The Autumn Battle in Champagne
The Situation on 14 October 1915

Sketch 27

scale kept the neighbouring German defensive sectors occupied. The French infantry's attack strategy was not as uniform as it had been on 25 September; allegedly the units had only received their orders immediately before the attack.

The first assault collapsed entirely in front of XII Reserve Corps' 24th Reserve Division. By evening another five attacks had been brought forward with continuously renewed forces; again, these failed in the face of the brave Saxon, Baden, and Prussian units. These individual thrusts were interspersed with waves of heavy artillery fire. In some places the German artillery inundated the enemy as they assembled for the attack. Although itself inundated with gas and incendiary bombs, between enemy assaults the German artillery placed a continuous curtain barrage in front of the German lines with as much intensity as their tubes would allow. Prisoners of war reported heavy French casualties as a result of both German artillery and infantry fire.

In X Corps' sector, rising flares heralded the beginning of an enemy attack along the entire front. The vastly superior enemy broke through the German positions along the Souain–Somme Py road, although reserves quickly committed from 20th Infantry Division's sector managed to regain the lost trenches. Southeast of St. Marie à Py, Moroccan troops penetrated individual battery positions, where they killed the German gun crews. Eventually they too were pushed back. However, the enemy did manage to create a gap of approximately 300 metres on 5th Infantry Division's right flank, which was bitterly contested the following night. In summary, the first day brought the German right flank an overwhelming defensive victory.

However, the French managed to gain ground on VIII Reserve Corps' right flank. Here their attack had centred on Tahure, where, after a heavy artillery barrage, French 3rd Infantry Division took the German trenches on the Butte de Tahure on their first attempt. A counterattack temporarily restored these positions to German hands, but with fresh forces from French XVI Corps, the enemy finally managed to take and hold the Butte and the village of Tahure. A counterattack launched by units of 53rd (Saxon) Reserve Division, 50th Infantry Division, and Division *Ditfurth* failed.[51] Generalleutnant Fleck grew especially concerned when no conclusive reports about the situation at Tahure arrived during the night. As Corps Headquarters understood the situation, in the event of renewed attacks, 29th Reserve Infantry Brigade's regiments—which had steadfastly held their original trenches since the beginning of the fall offensive—would be in acute danger on their right flank as well as from the rear. To cover all eventualities, a fallback position (*Ausweichstellung*) was established. Meanwhile, Divisions *Ditfurth* and *Sontag*, which had been attacked with less intensity, managed to repulse the enemy, with heavy casualties in places as a result of hand-to-hand fighting. On 6 October, Third Army took more than 1,000 prisoners. Fifth Army's 21st Reserve Division also managed to repulse all enemy attacks.

Third and Fifth Armies had expected the enemy attack on 6 October and had staged their reserves closer to the front that morning. Over the course of the day Generaloberst von Einem provided the following reinforcements: one infantry regiment and part of 113th Infantry Division's artillery were sent to XII Reserve Corps; two of 37th Reserve Infantry Brigade's regiments were sent to X Corps and VIII Reserve Corps respectively;[52] and parts of 53rd (Saxon) Reserve Division were provided to VIII Reserve Corps. The only available regiment of the yet-to-be-deployed 15th Reserve Division (*Liebert*) was brought up to the area south of Vouziers, while Seventh Army provided fresh forces to relieve worn-out battalions. The *OHL* assigned 185th Infantry Brigade, Bavarian 5th Infantry Division,[53] and the soon-to-arrive 4th (Prussian) Infantry Division as well as three heavy batteries as

---

51 The 53rd (Saxon) Reserve Division had been assigned to Army Group *German Crown Prince* at the end of September, minus 106th Reserve Infantry Brigade, which was instead transferred to Sixth Army.

52 Assigned to Third Army at the end of September.

53 Only infantry.

reinforcements; Army Group *German Crown Prince* dispatched one infantry regiment of 53rd Reserve Division to the threatened front.

The French ceased their strong attacks against Fifth Army's right flank, but on 7 and 8 October they continued their assaults against Third Army. Their main objective seemed to be the German trenches that had been perforated by local gains at Tahure and to the west of the village. Despite valiant German counterattacks, the enemy prevailed either by advancing slightly or by holding on to the areas that had already been seized. However, all attacks against the sector held by 24th Reserve Division and the left flank of VIII Reserve Corps—where Generalmajor von Versen had assumed command of 56th Infantry Division in place of Generalleutnant Sontag, who was ill—were repulsed. There the French had been unable to make coordinated attacks because the German artillery had fired on the assembling troops in an effective and timely manner. The artillery observers in the front lines often directed fire at the pesky enemy trench mortars; they also supported the infantry by ordering curtain barrages, which became more effective as new batteries were added and the artillery concentration increased. After 25 September the artillery was reinforced to such an extent that by 7 October, Third Army had 477 field and 288 heavy guns at its disposal.

Third Army's infantry combat resources were improved as well. Under orders from the *OHL*, Armee-Abteilung *Strantz* sent one infantry regiment to each of X Corps and VIII Reserve Corps; meanwhile, the severely mauled 15th Reserve Division was withdrawn into the area around Laon, having been relieved by 7th Reserve Division.

Despite facing vastly superior forces, the German front in the Champagne had weathered the renewed offensive. Einem's expectations for 5 October had borne out. Despite superiority in numbers, the enemy had been unable to sustain its bloody attacks.

Third Army's losses from 1 to 10 October amounted to approximately 15,000 men. Due to incessant fire in the rear areas, it became ever more difficult to evacuate the wounded. Enemy aircraft remained extremely active, just as they had been prior to these combat operations. Two captive balloons fell victim to attacks in the area of X Corps. On 8 October, XIV Corps reported increased traffic in the area of Reims. The Germans thus had to expect additional French attacks.

Up to this point, the precarious situation and the only gradual availability of reserves—as well as the need to carefully and strictly husband these reinforcements—meant that as the divisions and brigades arrived, they were deployed piecemeal to the most immediately threatened sectors. Einem now asked that complete units be used as reserves. Therefore he assigned the following: 185th Infantry Brigade and the regiment provided by Armee-Abteilung *Strantz* to X

Corps; one regiment from each of Armee-Abteilung *Strantz* and 53rd Reserve Division, plus the newly arrived 7th Reserve Division, to VIII Reserve Corps.

On 10 October, army reserves were also made available. They were deployed as follows: after it was relieved by 7th Reserve Division, 50th Infantry Division was stationed east of Le Chesne; Bavarian 5th Infantry Division was deployed in the area of Leffincourt; an infantry regiment of 5th Infantry Division was staged north of Vouziers; an infantry regiment from X Corps was sent to the rear of XII Reserve Corps; two infantry regiments and three field batteries from X Corps were billeted southeast of Rethel.

Due to adverse weather and enemy forays, the planned German counterattack on both sides of Tahure was not launched until 9 October. The attacking units[54] were stopped after gaining a few hundred metres of ground, and the village of Tahure remained in no man's land, under artillery fire from both sides. The Germans dug in close to the enemy, who had clearly been planning their own attack. Considering the enemy's strength, a continuation of the attack had to be cancelled. Minor French attacks around Tahure continued from 10 to 14 October, reaching their peak on 13 October, when seven enemy assaults collapsed on both sides of the Tahure–Ripont road.

On 10 October the commander of a French squadron of twenty aircraft that had been tasked with bombing the railway buildings at Challerange, Vouziers, Attigny, and Amagne was shot down. He reported that Joffre was in Châlons, where a number of fresh divisions were waiting to continue the offensive.[55] Over the following days the enemy's attacks diminished noticeably. Corps Headquarters repeatedly reported that the enemy was increasing its entrenchment activities, which included upgrading the front line and rearward trenches. Aerial reconnaissance and other reports about strong traffic at Reims did not yet allow conclusions to be drawn about the enemy's intentions.

The losses in the Champagne were severe: in the actual autumn offensive from 22 September through 14 October they amounted to 1,700 officers and 80,000 enlisted men. On the German side alone, approximately 1,564,000 field artillery rounds and 395,000 heavy artillery rounds were expended between 22 September and the end of October. A total of 129 field and 56 heavy guns were lost, but replacing them was not a significant problem.

---

54 Elements of 73rd, 241st, and 243rd Reserve Infantry Regiments, which were later joined on the right flank by 50th Infantry Division and elements of 183rd and 158th Infantry Regiments.

55 This information proved to be incorrect.

The Enemy's Situation at the End of the Offensive

On 3 October, Joffre gave new directives: the operations in the Champagne were to be continued as a "battle of attrition" without specific operational objectives. On 7 October, he ordered the cessation of Army Group *Centre*'s offensive. On 14 October, Army Group *North* received the same orders.

The British Supreme Commander adhered to the offensive scheme a little longer. Only on 12 October did he direct British First Army to conduct operations in order to secure captured positions and to acquire individual tactically important objectives. After the failed attack of 13 October, he too ordered the cessation of the offensive.

The grandly planned double offensive had been an operational failure. Tactically, its successes amounted to limited gains in ground with a maximum depth of approximately 4 kilometres in the Champagne and 3 kilometres in the Artois. Along the entire front there had been no successful breakthrough in the German positions, while casualties had been heavy. Between 25 September and 7 October the French Armies in the Champagne (Fourth, Second, and Third) had lost 143,567 men. In the Artois, Tenth Army had lost 48,230 men between 25 September and 15 October. Between 25 September and 16 October the losses of British First Army had amounted to 56,812 men. Thus as a result of the double offensive, the Allied enemies had lost almost 250,000 men compared to around 150,000 German casualties. Certain individual units suffered especially severely. In addition to the dead and wounded, the numbers of men missing in action were considerable; in the Artois, they amounted to approximately 10,000; in the Champagne, to more than 41,000.

The enormity of their effort is best demonstrated by the number of units that were committed to battle. Until the cessation of the offensive in the Champagne, the French had deployed thirty-five infantry divisions against approximately sixteen German divisions. In the Artois, seventeen French infantry divisions fought nine German divisions. South of La Bassée Canal the BEF had deployed twelve infantry divisions against five German divisions; four additional infantry divisions had conducted secondary operations north of the canal on 25 September. By the middle of October the men who had fought in these battles were physically and emotionally exhausted and were at the end of their strength; for the most part, these men were incapable of continuing such attacks.

The consumption of ammunition sheds some light on the enemy's artillery effort. Beginning with the preparatory fire, Tenth Army's artillery had expended 1,527,500 field artillery and 254,000 heavy artillery shells by 13 October. In the Champagne, Fourth, Second, and Third Armies had expended 2,842,400 field artillery and 577,700 heavy artillery shells.

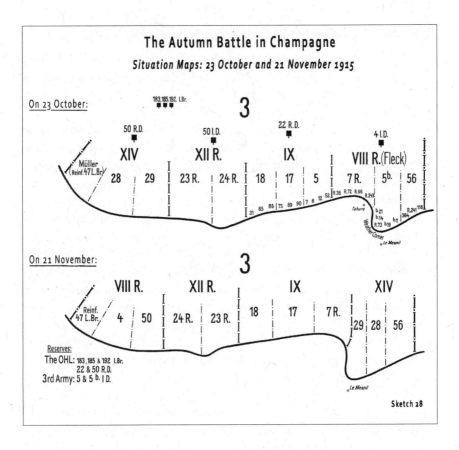

The Autumn Battle in Champagne

Situation Maps: 23 October and 21 November 1915

Sketch 28

Between 12 and 24 September, First Army's preparatory fire at Loos had used up 233,700 field artillery and 22,200 heavy artillery shells. Expenditures for the actual days of combat cannot be provided. By the end of the offensive the French and British ammunition stores had been all but exhausted; in particular, heavy artillery supplies were lacking. Also, the battles had shown that the enemy's means of attack did not yet meet the unique demands of trench warfare, which required a special style of combat.

In the circumstances, the French Supreme Command had no choice but to forgo further offensive operations. As with the British Supreme Command, its primary responsibility now was to reorganize its exhausted soldiers, replace its losses, and replenish the materiel required for an offensive, with a special emphasis on ammunition. It was obvious that this would take considerable time.

Lessons Learned from the Fall Offensive

The enemy in the West had been unable to exploit the favourable situation during July and August 1915 by mounting a major offensive on French soil in full force. The enemy also failed when attacking the German positions in the second half of September when it tried to simultaneously break through in the Artois and the Champagne. Despite extensive preparations and a numerical superiority of at least 600 battalions, the enemy had failed to achieve a success on either front. By the evening of the second day of battle there was almost no chance that the enemy would break through at any place along the German front.

In September the conditions for a breakthrough had been relatively favourable. Although the German Western Army had been reinforced so that numerically it was no longer at its lowest strength, the three divisions that had just arrived from the Eastern Front urgently required rest. This rest period was necessary to allow veteran soldiers to recuperate and to familiarize the new recruits with trench warfare in the West, as these replacements had been transferred from the home front after only a brief period of training.[56] Additionally, for reasons that are no longer discernible (but that nevertheless played a major role in their underestimation of the enemy's will to attack), the *OHL* refused to seriously consider that the enemy would attempt to break through. The *OHL* had neglected to deploy the GHQ Reserve of approximately five divisions (not counting the one and a half corps that were arriving from the East) behind the sectors of the front that were clearly under threat, instead leaving them dispersed across the Western Front. Had it properly deployed the available forces and materiel, this crisis could probably have been managed sooner and without the immediate deployment of both the Guard Corps and X Corps. The offensive did not surprise the German armies that came under attack; it did, however, find the *OHL* insufficiently prepared even though the attackers had forgone any obvious attempts at deception. The commanders and soldiers of the armies that were under attack had to compensate for the negligence of the Supreme Command. They did this with a dedication that won the victory—albeit with tremendous casualties. A great, if not crucial, part was played by the forward-looking leaders of the field railway system, which was expanded behind the German Front. This expansion permitted the quick and secure embarkation, transport, and disembarkation of large military units, which partially offset the insufficient numbers and inappropriate disposition of the available units.

---

56   For instance, the Guard Corps lost 21,000 men in Russia and a few days prior to 25 September had been assigned 8,000 recruits.

The Autumn Battle in Champagne

The Situation South of St. Souplet on 12 October 1915

Sketch 29

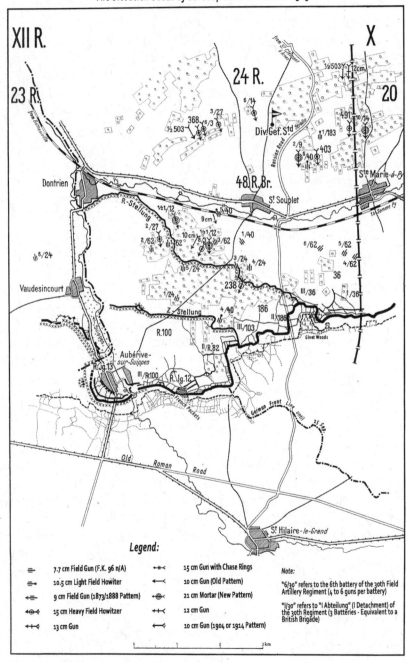

Legend:

≡	7.7 cm Field Gun (F.K. 96 n/A)	←⊪<	15 cm Gun with Chase Rings
≡⁺	10.5 cm Light Field Howitzer	←<	10 cm Gun (Old Pattern)
←≡=	9 cm Field Gun (1873/1888 Pattern)	←◉<	21 cm Mortar (New Pattern)
←◉→	15 cm Heavy Field Howitzer	←⊦<	12 cm Gun
←⊦<	13 cm Gun	←<	10 cm Gun (1904 or 1914 Pattern)

Note:

"6/30" refers to the 6th battery of the 30th Field Artillery Regiment (4 to 6 guns per battery)

"I/30" refers to "I Abteilung" (I Detachment) of the 30th Regiment (3 Batteries - Equivalent to a British Brigade)

0   1   2   3 km

AFTER THE OFFENSIVE, THE FAILURE WAS REVIEWED BY BOTH FRENCH GQG AND British GHQ. The French reports revealed that prior to the attacks, preparations for the infantry in the Artois as well as in the Champagne had not been completed.[57] The Supreme Commander recognized that the reserves had been staged close behind the front and that they had followed the first line on time. However, this is precisely what had created dangerous situations when a quick advance became difficult. In some places, especially in the Champagne, the reserves continued to push forward after the penetration of the first German line, causing massive troop concentrations and considerable casualties while dangerously impeding the lines of communication. The leadership had been unaware of the situation up front and had been unable to resolve the confusion and thus had been unable to control the situation. At the same time, the local commanders had only minimal influence on the activities of the artillery prior to and after the attack, which limited close co-operation between artillery and infantry during the course of the battle. Generally the rainy weather, obstructed aerial reconnaissance, and the soggy condition of the ground in the Artois were used to explain the fouled-up advance. All the commanders involved concluded that in all likelihood a future breakthrough would not succeed with one attempt; a series of combat operations might achieve more success. The primary challenge would be to quickly retighten the connection between artillery and infantry and to ensure the necessary reorganization of the infantry when committing the reserves.

The British report emphasized that the combat materiel—especially the heavy artillery and artillery ammunition—had been insufficient for the offensive.[58] This situation was less prevalent on the first day of combat, when gas had been effective, than over the following days, when it was more noticeable. The British artillery had failed to soften up both the German defensive emplacements on the front line and the fortifications of the second German position. Here, too, the inclement weather was singled out as a factor. An important reason for the faltering British advance was that the reserves had been staged too far *behind* the front (unlike with the French) and had not been made available to First Army Headquarters (which was responsible for conducting the battle) in a timely way. By the time the reserves got into the battle, it was too late, and even though they were eager to fight, their lack of training and experienced officers turned out to be detrimental. While the soldiers believed it was possible to force a breakthrough after

---

57   See *French Official History*, III: 545, 578.
58   See Edmonds and Wynne, *Military Operations: France and Belgium, 1915*, II: 393.

the initial success at Loos, the High Command was of the opinion that a success such as that could be achieved only by surprising the enemy using a large number of guns and a substantial expenditure of ammunition and by committing fully trained units. Even Field Marshal French harboured strong doubts and declared openly that he no longer believed that the war could be brought to a successful conclusion.

Both allied commanders agreed that the conditions of trench warfare and German technical advances in war materiel would demand a considerable increase in the deployment of their own resources. The French as well as the British saw the shortage of modern heavy artillery and ammunition as the most serious problem. The effectiveness of gas in battle had not been proven. Its deployment depended too much on the weather, and the installation of the cylinders got in the way of other attack preparations. Also, because gas was inherently dangerous, it was unpopular with the men. Nevertheless, both allied armies paid a great deal of attention to this new weapon, and a variety of experiments regarding its use were conducted behind the front as well as in their homelands.

ON THE GERMAN SIDE, THE HEADQUARTERS OF SIXTH AND THIRD ARMIES SUBmitted written accounts of the events during the double offensive.

They reported that both armies still adhered to the principle of peacetime training, which dictated that forward positions were to be defended with every ounce of strength. But this strategy had not proved entirely successful. Indeed, in many places the enemy had managed to break through and then hold on to their gains. This was explained in a number of ways. The prolonged preparatory bombardment had inflicted massive damage to the emplacements, rendering some of them indefensible. This was especially true in the parts of the line that had been severely damaged in previous battles and that could not be repaired. Also, the wire obstacles had been swept away regardless of their width. Furthermore, the British gas attack north of Loos had facilitated the attacker's penetrations in much the same way as had the German gas attack north of Ypres in April. In both cases, however, the successes achieved through subsequent use of that weapon later in the battle were far less pronounced than they had been when it was used at the opening of the offensive.

The second position had not been penetrated in either the Artois or the Champagne. Third Army's report read: "The axiom of constructing a single position in which to fight the battle will not suffice, rather the construction of a similar position behind that first line proved to be correct; so too was it proved that after breaking through the forward line the enemy would be forced to entirely reposition his artillery in order to launch an attack on the second position."[59] Not until 4 October had the enemy been able to continue the offensive by concentrating sufficient artillery in the area north of Souain. In the meantime the German defensive measures proved effective. At Loos a new British artillery deployment failed. North and south of Arras the French exhausted themselves in individual attacks on parts of the first position.

The bottom line was that even after penetrating the forward positions, an enemy offensive launched with enormous effort and preparation had been stopped by the depth of the German defensive system. The German explanation for why the attack so rapidly lost its momentum was that among compact masses of troops, order was quickly lost. According to Third Army Headquarters: "Despite adhering to the principle that the first won success had to be exploited and the advance to be kept up continuously, a coordinated attack by sectors should have been made." The report also pointed out that conclusions drawn from prisoner-of-war statements about the enemy's distribution of forces indicated that "there was hardly any talk of a methodical staging in depth for any operational breakthrough." That such a breakthrough might also be possible in the future could not be excluded.

Given the disproportionate balance of power, the German forces were insufficient for major counterattacks. On the other hand, immediate counterattacks by nearby units demonstrated that one could expect to face a weakened enemy that had just broken through the forward positions. On both battlefronts this fleeting opportunity had been exploited and the attackers had successfully been beaten back before they were able to establish themselves. A prerequisite for this, read the memorandum, was that such forces be available and that they not be depleted by too densely garrisoning the forward trenches. In their memoranda, both Army Headquarters stated that the deployment of one man for every two to three metres of the front line would be sufficient as "in some areas, sectors were actually held even where prior to the heavy artillery barrage the defending force was considerably below these figures."[60]

In addition to these significant reasons for the German defensive victory, the memoranda of both Army Headquarters listed a number of measures that had contributed strongly to success. In trench warfare these measures boiled down to close co-operation among all arms and between neighbouring sectors, particularly in exploiting flanking opportunities offered in the course of the battle. The issuance

---

59 From a memorandum titled "Experiences of Third Army in the Autumn Battles in the Champagne, 1915."

60 From a memorandum of Sixth Army Headquarters: "The Fall Offensive at La Bassée and Arras from 25 September to 13 October 1915."

of the necessary orders required that suitable observation posts be selected and secured, that reconnaissance reports be quickly and accurately transmitted, and that secure and reliable communications be established. In these respects significant improvements had been made.

A number of experiences reinforced the fact that it was indeed possible to tenaciously hold individual sectors of the defensive system against threats from the flanks and even the rear. Such defence in depth necessitated the creation of self-supporting circular strong points and points of resistance in the area between the first and second positions, as well as protection for the artillery with special obstacles. Also, these strong points and points of resistance had to be properly equipped and permanently garrisoned so that they would be capable of defending themselves and providing protection for the second position. The primary objective remained the defence of the first position; the purpose of strong points was to disperse the zone of defence so that when the enemy broke through and threatened to become overpowering, the impact of the attack could be dissipated, forcing the enemy to make a continuous series of individual thrusts. In the process, knowledge and preparation of the terrain offered considerable advantages to the defender. The value of an expanded field of fire for the infantry was relegated to second place behind the need to make each part of the position defensible, which was of greater importance. Based on specific experiences, Third Army Headquarters contended that positions on the reverse slope of a ridge provided satisfactory protection, even with an extremely limited field of fire, as they were hidden from enemy ground observation.[61] Quite apart from the enormous significance of the machine gun,[62] during hand-to-hand combat the hand grenade proved to be increasingly effective and indispensable. Training in this weapon was, therefore, required for all military personnel, including those serving with the artillery and cavalry.

Reconnaissance methods were being developed rapidly, even though equipment shortages and inadequate unit strengths prevented their thorough application. A large number of units that specialized in identifying artillery positions by measuring sound and light had already been deployed with the armies. These methods had already performed well in the ranging in of guns. Although the enemy had far more aircraft, some German aircraft had been equipped with machine guns for aerial combat. Wireless communication with pilots and photo reconnaissance techniques were improving steadily. Despite strong enemy opposition, aerial reconnaissance was being satisfactorily carried out. The losses of the British and French air forces considerably exceeded German losses.

---

61 As a matter of principle, Sixth Army Headquarters' memorandum expressed serious concerns about using such reverse-slope positions, concerns based in their own experiences.

62 During the fall battles, the Germans also used an imported automatic rifle for the first time.

No significant changes had been made to the technology or methods for con-structing field fortifications. On the other hand, the development and general use of measures that had proved useful—such as deeply excavated dugouts for the trench garrisons, and protecting batteries with camouflage and dummy defen-sive works (the effectiveness of which was observed from the air)—continued to progress.

By this time, trench warfare in the Franco-Belgian Theatre had lasted almost one year. It had been unfamiliar to the German armed forces, and as they had not had extensive peacetime training in it, commanders and their units took up this type of war with misgivings. By now, however, they had mastered it. An impor-tant contributing factor was that the enemy had only gradually intensified its efforts to break through the German lines and had done so at considerable inter-vals. The period from the fall of 1914 to the cessation of the two great defensive battles in the Artois and the Champagne was the time when the German armed forces learned trench warfare. The results of the double battle proved how well this time had been spent.

Clearly the German forces had suffered terribly in the enemy attacks on both fronts. In the days before 25 September they had endured terrible losses and expe-rienced a barrage that devastated the troops and their positions. The reserves available to the army commanders were small. Only in the final days before 25 September were a significant number of heavy batteries from the GHQ Artillery Reserve assigned. This came too late for significant countermeasures to be brought to bear prior to the offensive. As the offensive began, in addition to the bloody casu-alties, the enemy breakthrough resulted in large numbers of prisoners of war and losses of materiel. Everywhere—but especially in the Champagne on 25 and 26 Sep-tember—it had taken incredible determination and supreme sacrifice on the part of all the soldiers to stop the enemy attack in time. In comparison to this effort, the German losses in ground were insignificant; most important, the front held.

This incredible result, achieved in the face of the enemy's superiority, was absolute proof that the inner fortitude of the German commanders and soldiers had remained unbroken despite debilitating trench warfare. The higher com-mands had proved themselves in the most difficult of situations; they had also mastered the most perilous crises with admirable confidence. This was due to the exemplary dedication of the soldiers, who willingly made every sacrifice and with-stood the nerve-shattering effects of this heretofore most formidable battle of materiel. In the autumn of 1915 the German Western Army had achieved a clear—albeit costly—defensive victory in circumstances that had seemed to promise a decisive triumph for the enemy. Through their tenacity and perseverance they had won a victory reminiscent of the enthusiastic drive and the initial exuberance

The Autumn Battle in Champagne
The German Attack at Tahure on 30 October 1915

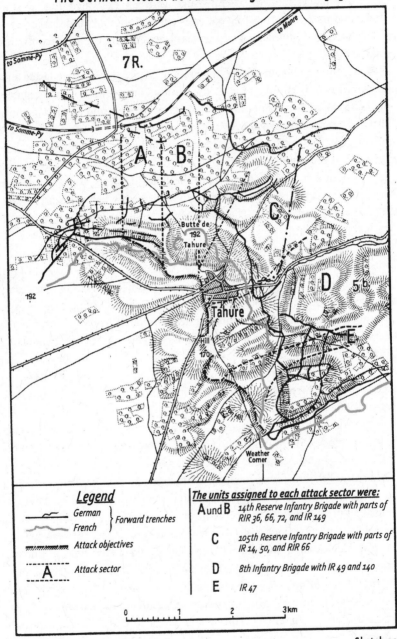

Legend

⌒ German ⎫ Forward trenches
〰 French ⎭

〰〰〰 Attack objectives

⌐ ̄ ̄ ̄ ̄ ⌐
A Attack sector
⌐ _ _ _ _ ⌐

The units assigned to each attack sector were:

A und B — 14th Reserve Infantry Brigade with parts of RIR 36, 66, 72, and IR 149

C — 105th Reserve Infantry Brigade with parts of IR 14, 50, and RIR 66

D — 8th Infantry Brigade with IR 49 and 140

E — IR 47

0   1   2   3 km

Sketch 30

that the same army exhibited during the forceful offensive of August 1914. But regardless of how things developed, there could be no expectation that an offensive could be launched with anywhere near the superiority in numbers and material that had been enjoyed by the French and British.

The Supreme Command's confidence that the German soldier was innately superior in all branches of service was enhanced—and even increased—by the way in which he had met the immense expenditure of force by the British and French in that autumn's dual offensive. Otherwise, while facing this overwhelming superiority, it would have been impossible to even contemplate hopes of a favourable military outcome in the West in the foreseeable future.

10

The Western Front to the End of the Year

Operations of the Remaining Armies to Mid-October

During the Entente's great fall offensive, even the German armies on the Western Front that had not been directly attacked were affected to one degree or another by other enemy actions, by increased firing activity, or by the dispatching of troops.

In Fourth Army's sector, the Belgians threatened the reinforced 4th Ersatz Division with an attack on 25 September. British warships pounded Zeebrugge and the German positions near Ostend from a great range but soon retreated under the fire of the German coastal batteries, which sank one of the ships. In the Ypres Salient the British launched an early-morning gas attack against the sectors of XXVI and XXVII Reserve Corps. An infantry attack followed, but this was made only by elements of 14th (British) Division against the left flank of 54th (Württemberg) Reserve Division. The British succeeded in breaching the trenches located south of the Roulers–Ypres railway line—successes that were due to the effect of the heavy barrage and impressive mine explosions. By late morning, however, they had been thrown back with considerable casualties. The 39th Infantry Division also repelled several enemy attacks after being engaged in close combat on the right flank of XV Corps. The German casualties were about 1,850 men; British losses were approximately double that number. No other attacks followed. By late September the situation near Ypres had been settled in such a way that the *OHL* was able to relocate 53rd Reserve Division—without 106th Reserve Infantry Brigade, which had been assigned to Sixth Army—to Army Group *German Crown Prince.*

During a meeting in Thielt between General von Falkenhayn and Duke Albrecht of Württemberg on 13 October, it was agreed that despite the detachment of some of its forces, Fourth Army would be capable of defending its sector. During a subsequent discussion in Ostend, which Admiral von Schroeder (Commanding Admiral of the *Marinekorps*) was invited to attend, the Chief of the General Staff of the Field Army was convinced that all the measures necessary to repel an enemy landing along the Belgian coast—which was understood to be a possibility—had been taken.

On the afternoon of 25 September, Second Army received a request for "support by infantry and field artillery" from neighbouring Sixth Army Headquarters. After a discussion with Falkenhayn it was initially decided that no reserves were to be shifted from Second Army to Sixth Army, although Third Army would have to be supported with specially designated forces. Only after an order was received from the *OHL* on the evening of 28 September did Second Army dispatch a composite division to Douai under the command of Generalleutnant von Hartz (the Commander of Bavarian 2nd Infantry Division), which was to be placed at the disposal of Sixth Army. Later, efforts by the *OHL* to deploy war-worn corps from the battlefields in the Artois and Champagne to quieter fronts and to create a stronger GHQ Reserve necessitated a number of additional changes within Second Army. Consequently, an exchange of Bavarian I Corps for VI Corps of Sixth Army began on 3 October. By the middle of the month, XVII Corps, which had arrived from the Eastern Front, had relieved XVIII Corps in its positions between Lihons and Roye. The latter was billeted in GHQ Reserve in the area to the east of Péronne.

In Seventh Army's sector, VII Reserve Corps and XII (Saxon) Corps were subjected to the heaviest French fire since 24 September. Every day until 27 September, the Army Commander, Generaloberst von Heeringen, expected the enemy to launch an attack near and to the east of Craonne. This attack, which had apparently been planned by the French, failed to materialize because of the accurate German defensive fire.[1] Despite Seventh Army's precarious situation, by the

---

1   *On 26 September the commander of French Fifth Army (which was opposite the two German corps in question) took the initiative and began to prepare a new, local attack complete with troop movements and an artillery preparation. However, after two requests for more ammunition and troops, on 28 September the Commander of Army Group East instructed Fifth Army to discontinue its preparations "little by little" as the date for the attack could not be predicted as it had to be contingent on success in the Champagne. The next day a breakthrough in the Champagne into the second German line caused the Army Group Commander to reverse his decision, and a limited artillery preparation was resumed until the night of 29–30 September, when the offensive was postponed indefinitely. The sporadic nature of the artillery fire and the sudden cessation of all preparations at the end of the month may have given rise to the German impression that their guns had broken up the attack before it could begin. See French Official History III: 428–29.*

afternoon of 25 September, 192nd Infantry Brigade and several other battalions that were staged to the army's rear in GHQ Reserve had to be moved up to Third Army. The 185th Infantry Brigade, which was brought up by the *OHL* to replace the transferred units, became the GHQ Reserve.

Over the course of October, IX Corps was eventually replaced by XI Corps, which was then arriving from the East. The 7th and 22nd Reserve Divisions were replaced by the war-worn divisions of VIII Reserve Corps, and VII Reserve Corps replaced X Corps.

Fifth Army's right flank (held by XVIII Reserve Corps) had also been affected by the large-scale French attacks in the Champagne, the adjacent XVI Corps taking the severest impact. Despite the heavy enemy fire and considerable detachment of forces, General der Infanterie von Mudra did not abandon his offensive activity, which to that point had been successful. On 27 September, 33rd Infantry Division seized the commanding positions south of La Fille Morte, which were occupied by elements of French V Corps, in the process capturing some 250 prisoners.[2] Over the next few days, several French counterattacks were repelled in bloody fighting.

The fierce French artillery and *Minenwerfer* fire that had been directed against the positions of Armee-Abteilung *Strantz* since late August only abated during the last week of September. On the orders of the *OHL* the composite 113th Infantry Division,[3] located behind the Armee-Abteilung, was sent up to Third Army on 27 September. On October 6 it was followed by the headquarters and infantry of Bavarian 5th Infantry Division and by another composite infantry brigade the following day.

The transfer of 56th Infantry Division (located behind Armee-Abteilung *Falkenhausen* in GHQ Reserve) to Third Army began on 25 September. Almost simultaneously, an unexpected lull took place along the enemy front in Lorraine. Aerial and ground patrols were immediately ordered but brought no clarity to the situation.[4] A *coup de main* conducted by Bavarian 1st Landsturm Division resulted in the seizure of some trenches south of Leintrey.

By late September the portion of the GHQ Reserve located behind Armee-Abteilung *Gaede* had been readied for entrainment on the orders of the *OHL*.

---

2 Casualties of French V Corps: 1,255 troops, 5 machine guns, and five 58 mm guns (*French Official History*, III: 428, *reports that twenty-five of the captured men were officers*).

3 Instead of 48th and 42nd Infantry Regiments, 47th and 50th Infantry Regiments of 10th Infantry Division had been assigned to 113th Infantry Division.

4 *Although five days before the beginning of the two allied offensives the French were preparing plans for a diversionary attack in Lorraine in the direction of Thiaucourt, by the end of the month the exigencies of the Champagne and Artois offensives had sapped the resources necessary to actually mount the attack. See French Official History, III: 359, 485.*

Accordingly, 185th Infantry Brigade departed on 27 September to Seventh Army, 37th Reserve Brigade of 19th Infantry Division to Third Army on 30 September, with the remainder of the division staying behind in the area around Mulhouse. To prevent enemy forces from being moved to the Champagne, the *Armee-Abteilung* began lively combat actions along the entire front line. On 12 October, Bavarian 6th Landwehr Division conducted an assault using flame-throwers and seized a French nest of resistance on the Schratzmaennele.[5] One day later, 12th Landwehr Division succeeded in seizing an advanced enemy stronghold in the Lauch Valley. On 15 October, troops of that same division used flame-throwers to penetrate the enemy trenches on the Vieil Armand, taking more than 200 prisoners. Over the next few days they systematically abandoned the captured ground so as not to sustain unnecessary casualties because of the heavy French artillery bombardment.

The Reorganization of the Western Army

The meagre results obtained by Sixth Army's counterattacks near Loos on 8 October and by Third Army's near Tahure on 9 October demonstrated that regaining considerable portions of the ground lost during the autumn battle would only be achieved with great effort and with a substantial number of casualties. The gains that could be expected from such an effort would not be proportional to the cost. In a meeting held on 10 October between Falkenhayn and the Chiefs of the General Staffs of Third and Fifth Armies, it was decided that instead of launching major offensives, the armies would complete preparations to defend against further large-scale enemy attacks with all their available means. Starting in the middle of October, the idea of temporarily suspending all major combat operations became paramount.

From this point on, the *OHL* strove to return the units that had been temporarily assigned to the two attacked armies to their original formations and to replace the exhausted divisions with well-rested ones. It also strove to equip the armies in such a way that they would be capable of ensuring an appropriate internal troop rotation. Accordingly, the *OHL* would only hold a relatively small number of reserves for itself.

On 20 October the following basic order was issued to all armies in the West:

---

5 *A mountain in the Vosges.*

The Situation in the Vosges at the End of 1915

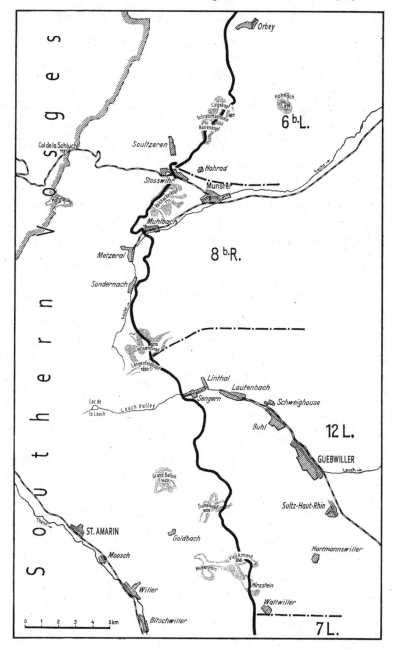

Sketch 31

With respect to the GHQ Reserve, a differentiation has to be made between:
1. The GHQ Reserves which are at the exclusive disposal of the OHL (and)
2. The GHQ Reserves which have been subordinated to the respective armies

In reference to point 1: the GHQ Reserves, which are to be at the exclusive disposal of the OHL, are to be billeted and fed by the respective army headquarters; additionally, as far as is possible, they will fall under the jurisdiction of the army headquarters.

The army headquarters will, however, not be allowed in any way to determine the disposition of these units.

In reference to point 2: the army headquarters can make use of subordinated GHQ Reserves as follows:
a) in the case of imminent danger to repel a major enemy attack—a situation which is to be reported immediately;
b) for purposes of relief by rotation. In the latter case, their deployment is to be reported to the OHL in advance. As soon as they are committed, elements of equal strength are to be extracted from the front and kept on standby where they will be at the disposal of the OHL. Furthermore, measures are to be taken to ensure that the GHQ Reserve which has been deployed can be ready to be relocated within forty-eight hours.

Figure III shows the distribution of the GHQ Reserve.

Thus all armies and Armee-Abteilungen, except for Fifth and Seventh Armies, were given elements of the GHQ Reserve of varying strength. Three divisions and the three infantry brigades (183rd, 185th, and 192nd) remained under the direct control of the OHL. The departure of the *Alpenkorps* for Army Group *Mackensen*—which was still being detrained in the area southeast of Mézières—was ordered on the same day. For the time being nearly all the GHQ Artillery Reserve units were to remain with the armies to which they had been deployed. However, a part of them were extracted from the front and placed at the OHL's disposal farther to the rear. Orders were given for all units to return to their parent armies. The 11th Landwehr Brigade was again returned to Fourth Army and was replaced in the General Government of Belgium by Armee-Abteilung *Falkenhausen*'s 7th Cavalry Division. This move began a restructuring of the Western armies, which was not fully implemented for some units until November.

On the evening of 20 October, Falkenhayn left the Western Theatre, travelling first to Berlin and then, shortly thereafter, to Serbia via Teschen. The OHL remained in Pleß.

Figure III: GHQ Reserves Made Available by the Order of 20 October

GHQ Reserve Unit	Controlling Entity
XVIII Corps	Second Army
50th Reserve Division	Third Army
22nd Reserve Division	Third Army
53rd Reserve Division	Fourth Army
XIII Corps (1st Guard Reserve Division and 4th Guard Infantry Division)	Sixth Army
113th Infantry Division	Armee-Abteilung *Strantz*
58th Infantry Division	Armee-Abteilung *Falkenhausen*
187th Infantry Brigade	Armee-Abteilung *Gaede*
19th Reserve Division	OHL (Staged in Mulhausen in Alsace and Colmar)
VII Reserve Corps	OHL (Staged Near Valenciennes)
183rd Infantry Brigade, 185th Infantry Brigade, 192nd Infantry Brigade	OHL (Staged Near Mézières)

Total: 12 Infantry Divisions and 4 Mixed Brigades

Operations from Mid-October to the End of the Year

Fourth Army

In response to a proposal from Fourth Army Headquarters, in late October the OHL agreed to conduct a new gas attack in the area east of Ypres, and a Gas Pioneer regiment was placed on standby. The commanding general of XXVII Reserve Corps, General der Artillerie von Schubert, pointed out that the proposal to seize the enemy's first line would move the troops even farther into the waterlogged terrain at a most unfavourable time of year. He proposed instead an attack that would focus on the area near Wieltje with Ypres as its objective. However, the means required for this undertaking could not be made available. So by the middle of November Generaloberst Albrecht had instead decided to install the gas cylinders along XXVI Reserve Corps' front line as well as on XXVII Reserve Corps' right flank. The rearward enemy positions were to be kept under artillery fire throughout the gas attack, but an infantry attack would not follow.

Just as in the spring of 1915, a tense waiting period began in anticipation of favourable wind and weather conditions. Finally, on the morning of 19 December, the operation was launched. Unfortunately, in XXVI Reserve Corps' area it was impossible to install the cylinders continuously due to the irregular layout of the trenches. Whether it was unfavourable winds or because the soldiers had not yet finished installing the cylinders, gas was not released everywhere, and gas-free gaps in the cloud were created. Subsequent reconnaissance patrols sent out from every company sector discovered that the enemy continued to occupy its trenches en masse in all places. These patrols had to withdraw in the face of the unbroken enemy position and thus sustained casualties. As a result, the gas attack ended without producing any noticeable success.

The units detached from Fourth Army during the autumn battle (53rd Reserve Division, two reserve infantry regiments, and Carrier Pigeon Detachment Ostend) were returned by mid-November; they were followed by the heavy batteries in December. The *OHL* began to replace the recently reunited XIII Corps—which was to become part of the GHQ Reserve—with XV Corps, which was also to have been relieved.

Sixth, Second, and Seventh Armies

Even though the heavy defensive battles in the Artois were abating, some fierce fighting did take place with the British in mid-October near Haisnes. On the evening of 15 October, and twice around noon on 17 October, the enemy tried to outflank the Hohenzollern Redoubt. After fierce fighting on both days, the enemy was repelled by troops of VII Corps.

The French also attacked once more in the second half of October on the Souchez–Neuville-St. Vaast front. A particular hotspot was the dam southeast of Souchez. At Gießler Hill, 88th (Saxon) Infantry Brigade—which on 14 October had again been deployed in place of the Guard Regiment—made only a small amount of progress in the area west of Vimy, and the main part of the heights remained in enemy hands. Bavarian 2nd Infantry Division concluded the month of October with a small success west of Vimy.

On 14 October, Crown Prince Rupprecht decided to launch a counterattack near Loos using fresh forces to push back earlier British penetrations. Bavarian II Corps, stationed north of Lille, was earmarked for this task and was to replace the exhausted 117th and 123rd Infantry Divisions. During a discussion on 15 October between Crown Prince Rupprecht and the various commanding generals, François stated that "all [his] concerns will be alleviated when II Bavarian Corps takes over the difficult sector of the Hohenzollern Redoubt." General Sixt von Arnim emphasized that this corps would get into a very difficult situation, for "the position ... first needs a lengthier period of consolidation. He added that it was his duty to declare that he deemed an attack by II Bavarian Corps to be impossible in this sector."[6] He also requested that the combat sector of IV Corps

---

6 War diary of Sixth Army Headquarters, 15 October 1915.

be narrowed in the south; this would allow him to withdraw his regiments on an alternating basis for the purposes of rest. However, the combat and weather situations precluded the opening of the planned counterattack near Loos, and the consolidation of the new positions near Hulluch and Loos thus absorbed all of the troops' resources.

In the second half of October the Guard Corps was moved to Second Army, which freed up IX Reserve Corps. On 23 October, Generalleutnant von Stetten, Bavarian II Corps' commander, took over the sector extending from VII Corps' southern boundary up to the Loos–Pont à Vendin Road, and General der Infanterie von Boehn, commanding the recently arrived IX Reserve Corps, took command of the Guard Corps' sector; 88th Infantry Brigade was moved into army reserve near Lille. The former sector of Bavarian II Corps, where 117th and 123rd Infantry Divisions were engaged, came under the command of General der Kavallerie von Laffert, the commanding general of XIX (Saxon) Corps.

On 7 November, Sixth Army Headquarters received a message from the OHL stating that enemy attacks could be expected to resume within eight to fourteen days. The following days brought clear weather, and the enemy's artillery fire and aerial reconnaissance did indeed increase considerably. After 10 November, however, observations no longer indicated an attack, and a lull set in along the British front. On the French portion of the front between Souchez and Arras, lively movements continued behind enemy lines for some time, but in this sector no major battles were fought for the remainder of the year.

By early December, according to German calculations, Sixth Army's twenty divisions were facing thirteen British and twelve French infantry divisions.[7] Adverse weather forced IX Reserve Corps to postpone its planned offensive against the Gießler Heights; Bavarian I Corps was forced to do the same in the area of Givenchy.

On 18 December the OHL ordered XIII Corps Headquarters to relocate to Fourth Army, where 1st Guard Reserve Division and 4th Guard Infantry Division—which were to remain independent divisions of GHQ Reserve—temporarily came under their command. The 50th Reserve Division, which had thus far been located behind Third Army, was assigned to Sixth Army. In exchange, the latter had to return Composite Division Hartz and other elements that belonged to different parent armies. The 50th Reserve Division assumed responsibility for the centre of Bavarian I Corps' sector.

---

7 On 24 November, Sixth Army's Chief of Staff, Oberst Baron von der Wenge Count von Lambsdorff, was transferred to Ninth Army; in his place came Generalleutnant von Kuhl, Twelfth Army's Chief of Staff.

At the end of 1915, movements and other indications in and behind enemy lines did not permit any conclusions to be drawn about coming events. However, tensions persisted all along the army's front, manifested in artillery duels and mine warfare.

In Second Army's area, the Guard Corps began arriving on 18 November from Sixth Army to replace IX Reserve Corps, which occupied the position extending from Roye to Lassigny. The adjacent 15th Landwehr Division (Division *Sack*), located to the south abutting the Oise, was also placed under the command of the Guard Corps. By late October, on the enemy's side, French troops were observed relieving the British south of the Somme.

At the beginning of December, Seventh Army took over Third Army's right flanking sector (held by the reinforced 47th Landwehr Brigade). Since bad weather prevailed for most of the time, major combat activities were precluded here as well.

Third Army

Third Army had broken up the last major enemy assault under its own strength, thus meeting the Army Commander's expectations. However, the ensuing days' fighting—which was no less heavy than what went before—drained so much of his unit's combat strength that by 6 October, additional and extensive relief had become necessary. Therefore, at around noon on 11 December, the *OHL* sent the following wire: "5th Bavarian Infantry Division and 4th Infantry Division will be placed at the disposal of Third Army. X Corps [which had been replaced by IV Corps and withdrawn to Noyon] and the 50th Infantry Division, which is also to be extracted from the front, are to be billeted ... behind the front ... and kept at the disposal of the *OHL*." Generaloberst von Einem thereupon placed Bavarian 5th Infantry Division at VIII Reserve Corps' disposal in order to relieve 16th Reserve Division. The latter was to assemble northeast of Vouziers. The 50th Reserve Division, which was in transit from the Eastern Theatre, was beginning to deploy southwest of Rethel when the first transports arrived on the morning of 12 December.

Once the French attacks had ended, Third Army Headquarters' first demand was that the German trenches be purged of all pockets of French resistance and that efforts be made to improve weak portions of the defensive front. To this end all Corps Headquarters were ordered to submit proposals for attacks with limited objectives.

On the basis of the Army Commander's instructions, on 15 October, 24th (Saxon) Reserve Division mounted a well-prepared and successful attack against a French stronghold that had held out since the September battles. All French counterattacks were repelled. The enemy sustained bloody losses, including more than 600 prisoners taken.

Up until 16 October the *OHL* had placed the units earmarked for the gas attack in XIV Corps area (which included X Corps, 50th Infantry Division, and 50th Reserve Division with nine heavy batteries from GHQ Artillery Reserve, as well as two Gas Pioneer regiments) under the command of Generaloberst von Einem to enable him to conduct extensive preparations for the attack. However, X Corps and 50th Infantry Division agreed that the combat value of their troops was inadequate owing to the shortage of junior officers and the inexperience of the newly arrived replacements. The *OHL* demanded that favourable wind conditions be immediately exploited to quickly launch the gas attack. In these circumstances the operation had to be started without X Corps and 50th Infantry Division; thus, compared to the original plan, the size of the attack was significantly reduced.

Shortly after midnight on 19 October, favourable weather conditions led the commander of XIV Corps, Generalleutnant von Haenisch, to order the attack to begin. The 50th Reserve Division, which had been inserted the day before between 29th Infantry Division and 23rd Reserve Division, had not yet completely finished its attack preparations. For this reason the attack's only defined objective was the seizure of Fort de la Pompelle southeast of Reims. Shortly after 08:00, gas was released in an area stretching from north of St. Léonard to south of Moronvilliers. On leaving their trenches the attacking German troops were met with fierce fire. Under these circumstances, Generalmajor von Trotta (also known as Treyden), the commander of 28th Infantry Division, immediately ended the attack. As a result of the heavy enemy fire, the assault detachments from 29th Infantry Division's left flank, 50th Infantry Division in the centre, and 23rd (Saxon) Reserve Division's right flank could not move forward against the enemy infantry. Only elements of 29th Infantry Division's right flank under Generalleutnant Isbert succeeded in penetrating the enemy's position south of Beine, where they captured more than 300 prisoners.

The gas cylinders that went unused on 19 October were given to 28th Infantry Division on 20 December for a renewed attack against Fort de la Pompelle. However, the fire from the enemy's trenches was so strong that again it was impossible for the assault detachments to get past the French wire. The intention of seizing the fort intact thus had to be abandoned.

In the meantime the reorganization of the army had begun. The 16th Reserve Division began departing by rail to Seventh Army on the evening of 18 October. The 4th Infantry Division moved into the billeting areas that had thereby been released and became Third Army's reserve. Falkenhayn also notified 22nd Reserve Division, which had been relieved on Seventh Army's front, that it would be deployed in GHQ Reserve behind Third Army. It was to take the place of X Corps, which was to march to Laon as soon as this fresh division arrived. On 20 October a number of moves were ordered, including the return and reintegration of 113th Infantry Division and the composite infantry brigade into Armee-Abteilung *Strantz*,[8] as well as the return of half of 53rd (Saxon) Reserve Division to Fourth Army and 37th Reserve Infantry Brigade to Armee-Abteilung *Gaede*. Three independent infantry brigades (183rd, 185th, and 192nd) were billeted in GHQ Reserve south of Mézières. Some individual regiments and parts of the artillery from the units that were being returned to their parent armies remained with VIII Reserve Corps until the conclusion of the planned attack near Tahure.

In the meantime, several French attacks were launched on 24 October at "Weather Corner" (*Wetterecke*) southeast of Tahure. The French managed to penetrate the German positions and annihilate a few Bavarian companies; however, French attacks against 7th Reserve Division failed. As a result of hand-grenade battles during the night, Weather Corner was eventually again brought under German control. The heavy casualties sustained southeast of Tahure made relief through a new attack all the more urgent. The objective of this relieving attack was the seizure of Hill 192 (the Butte de Tahure), the village of Tahure, and the hilly terrain to the south. For this purpose, 4th Infantry Division was placed under the command of Generalleutnant Fleck. The cooperation of the adjacent corps ensured that the enemy would be deceived.

The planned artillery preparation for the attack began on the morning of 30 October with *Minenwerfer*, as well as forty-five light and heavy field howitzer batteries, twelve mortar batteries, and fourteen low-trajectory heavy batteries. According to all the reports that arrived, the preparations had a good effect. The enemy's artillery responded weakly and seemingly only with field guns. At 16:00, 7th Reserve Division and Bavarian 5th Infantry Division went into the attack. The 7th Reserve Division's centre and left flanks passed the Butte de Tahure with their first assault waves. In Bavarian 5th Infantry Division's attack sector, only one regiment reached the enemy trenches; it had to retreat soon after under pressure from heavy flanking fire. Any further advance seemed to depend on the seizure of the village of Tahure, but the enveloping attack that was launched against this village during the

---

8   *This composite infantry brigade remains unnamed in the text, but it consisted of two regiments that had been deployed to Third Army from Armee-Abteilung Strantz on the orders of the OHL in the first week of October.*

night did not succeed. A renewed attack was therefore ordered for the afternoon of 31 October. In the meantime, in the hours before noon on 31 October, French artillery fire against the Butte de Tahure and the village itself intensified into a *Trommelfeuer*. After that, numerically superior enemy forces, comprised of elements of French XVI and XI Corps, counterattacked the Butte and pushed back 7th Reserve Division's centre. By 18:15 the division was even reporting that French forces had breached their defences and that major columns were advancing in a northerly direction. In response to this report, Fleck immediately brought up an infantry regiment and Army Headquarters quickly threw additional infantry forces into the threatened sector. Only some of these reinforcements actually intervened in the battle, for it was now confirmed that the Butte de Tahure remained firmly in German hands. In the evening, Generaloberst von Einem reported to the *OHL* that the attack had been abandoned because of strong enemy forces. Thus German success was limited to the seizure of the dominating Butte de Tahure and the capture of about 1,300 French troops. The casualties in Fleck's Corps were very heavy before and during this attack; their losses from 21 to 31 October were more than 7,500 men.

General Fleck's troops were ordered to mount another attack on 3 November against a hill northwest of Massiges, which was occupied by French 2nd Colonial Division. That afternoon, elements of 56th Infantry Division launched an assault supported by flame-throwers. They seized the enemy's forward trenches, which were then contested in hand-to-hand fighting over the next few days.

SINCE THE END OF OCTOBER ALL OF THIRD ARMY'S CORPS HAD BEEN REPORTING brisk movements behind the French front. German aerial reconnaissance had also noted extensive campfires in the vicinity of Châlons-sur-Marne and to the north. Given the situation's lack of clarity, Army Headquarters focused its attention on the further improvement and consolidation of its rearward positions. The entire *R2-Stellung* was to be upgraded to include a reinforced fire trench with expanded, fully developed wire as well as bombproof artillery observation posts. Also, continuous communication trenches were to be dug from the *R3-Stellung* to the front line.

The flow of supplies to Third Army was complicated because enemy shelling on the Bazancourt–Challerange railway line was disrupting regular rail transport. This shelling made the most favourably located rail depots unavailable. Because the few roads were deteriorating as a result of heavy wear, the continuation of supplies seemed questionable, particularly during the season of bad weather. As a substitute for the unusable railway line, on 5 October the Chief of the Field Railway Service ordered the construction of a new standard-gauge railway line farther to the rear.

In early November a report of the *OHL* as well as statements made by agents and prisoners indicated that the enemy offensive might resume in mid-November. Generaloberst von Einem assumed that the enemy attacks would be directed against the same sectors of the front as they had been at the start of the fall battles. Therefore, he decided to move XIV Corps, which had been least affected by the earlier fighting, up to VIII Reserve Corps' sector. The XII (Saxon) Reserve Corps had already taken similar steps by replacing the badly mauled 24th Reserve Division with 23rd Reserve Division. However, the French offensive in the Champagne did not resume because on 3 November General de Castelnau had ordered a transition to purely defensive operations for both French Fourth and Second Armies.

In line with the rearrangement of the infantry, Third Army Headquarters also reassembled the units of the heavy artillery—unless they were assigned to the GHQ Artillery Reserve—in accordance with the original order of battle. The foot artillery battalions were then collectively subordinated to the individual Corps Headquarters, where regimental and battalion commanding officers were placed in charge of giving specific combat orders to the artillery groups.

Soldiers of 23rd (Saxon) Reserve Division concluded German offensive operations in the Champagne by mounting an attack south of St. Souplet on the evening of 6 December. The attack was directed against a French observation hill, the Bois au Givet, and succeeded thanks to the careful preparation and valiant attack by the assault detachments. In conjunction with this attack, on the afternoon of 7 December the right flank of IX Corps' 17th Infantry Division rushed Arbre Hill (Hill 193), 5 kilometres southeast of Somme Py. Several counterattacks launched on 7 and 8 December were repelled.

In early December, 5th Prussian and Bavarian 5th Divisions were struck off Third Army's strength. The former returned to III Corps; the latter went back to Armee-Abteilung *Strantz*. To replace these units, 22nd Reserve Division and 185th Infantry Brigade were subordinated to Third Army with the caveat that two divisions—except for 50th Reserve Division—be made ready for entraining at forty-eight hours' notice so that they could be placed at the *OHL*'s disposal for deployment elsewhere.

On 12 December, Generaloberst von Einem briefed the *OHL* on the situation. According to his presentation, no enemy attack seemed imminent in the near future, even though the eastern half of his army still faced superior numbers of infantry and artillery. He pointed out that the seizure of the Butte de Tahure had made the situation on XIV Corps' right flank much more tolerable and that

Weather Corner, which had been endangered, had been made relatively secure by strong switch trenches.

When on 18 December the *OHL* announced that 50th Reserve Division would be departing for Sixth Army, Third Army Headquarters requested the allocation of an infantry brigade. As a result it was assigned 183rd (Saxon) Infantry Brigade.

Fifth Army

In connection with Third Army's continuation of the fighting in the Champagne, the very lively enemy artillery fire against 21st Reserve Division's sector continued into the first days of November before subsiding. After that it only periodically flared up to any great intensity, although in XVI Corps' sector German and French mines were exploded on an almost daily basis. On 26 November, VI Reserve Corps launched a gas attack. The units advancing behind the gas cloud did not succeed in penetrating the enemy trenches; even so, the enemy had obviously sustained considerable casualties.[9]

On 3 December the *OHL* ordered 27th Reserve Division (then in Serbia) to relieve XVI Corps' 27th Infantry Division. The 27th Reserve Division was then dispatched by rail to Fourth Army; 25th Reserve Division was integrated into XVIII Reserve Corps. According to an order dated 7 December, Third Army was detached from Army Group *German Crown Prince*, to which it had been temporarily subordinated.

Armee-Abteilung Strantz

In the area occupied by Armee-Abteilung *Strantz*, artillery battles and underground mine warfare remained the focus of activity in the areas of Combres, Bois d'Ailly, and Forêt d'Apremont, particularly along the front line between north of Flirey and Bois le Prêtre. The 113th Infantry Division and the composite infantry brigade, which had been attached to Third Army, were returned in mid-November,[10] while 113th Infantry Division was billeted in GHQ Reserve around Metz. On 13 November the Bavarian Ersatz Division was removed from the Armee-Abteilung and placed on standby near St. Avold–Morhange as part of the GHQ Reserve, but only after Bavarian 5th Infantry Division had been returned from Third Army.[11]

---

9 The French tallied their casualties as 50 killed and 450 wounded by exposure to gas.
10 *These had been sent to Armee-Abteilung* Strantz *on 20 October.*
11 Oberst Wild, XV Corps' former Chief of Staff, had been appointed Chief of the Staff to Armee-Abteilung *Strantz* on 3 December.

Armee-Abteilung Falkenhausen

In Armee-Abteilung *Falkenhausen*'s sector, Bavarian 1st Landwehr Division conducted an attack on 17 October but achieved only limited gains in ground. Nevertheless, it succeeded in taking about 100 French prisoners. By 25 October, 58th Infantry Division had arrived in GHQ Reserve near Saarburg. At the same time, orders came through that 7th Cavalry Division was to deploy by rail to the General Government of Belgium.

Armee-Abteilung Gaede

At the end of November the enemy's combat activity once again increased. On 21 December a fierce bombardment, which included the heaviest-calibre guns, commenced against the positions along the line Vieil Armand–Wattwiller. That afternoon the enemy launched its attack. Despite the defenders' most obstinate resistance, a reinforced brigade of French 66th Infantry Division managed to seize the fortified crest of the Vieil Armand. German reserves rushed in to establish a new defensive front line on the eastern slope of the mountain. The enemy also managed to penetrate the German trenches at Hirzstein northwest of Wattwiller.

On 22 December, 12th Landwehr Division's reinforced 82nd Landwehr Brigade mounted a counterattack. In fierce fighting that lasted throughout the day, it succeeded in retaking the Vieil Armand except for the trenches on the northern slope of the mountain, from which the enemy was finally dislodged the following day. In the process, 23 French officers and 1,530 enlisted men were taken prisoner.

On the afternoon of 24 December, 82nd Landwehr Brigade's attempt to retake the trenches at Hirzstein with the aid of flame-throwers was only partly successful. In contrast, the French succeeded in retaking some of the positions between the Vieil Armand and Hirzstein on the evening of 28 December. Counterattacks launched early on the night of 28 and 29 December and the next day, as well as an assault on 1 January 1916, restored the previously held front line. On 8 January 1916, 187th Infantry Brigade—which had been assigned to the Armee-Abteilung—retook the trenches at Hirzstein that had been lost on 21 December. In the process, 20 French officers and 1,083 other ranks were captured.

The recapture of the trenches at Hirzstein marked the conclusion of the battles for the Vieil Armand in 12th Landwehr Division's sector, with the division regaining the positions it had held before 21 December along the line Vieil Armand–Hirzstein. French losses included more than 7,000 men and 30 machine guns.[12] German

---

12 The French official history states that the casualties sustained during the period 20 December to 8 January amounted to 7,465 men (or 50 percent)

casualties since 21 December had amounted to 4,513 men. As a result of these battles, for the time being Joffre discontinued the attacks on this part of the front.

By 19 November, 37th Reserve Infantry Brigade had been returned to 19th Reserve Infantry Division. On 29 December the *OHL* approved a request to transfer 187th Infantry Brigade to Armee-Abteilung *Gaede*, where it was assigned to Bavarian 8th Reserve Division.

The Entente's Situation in the West at the End of the Year

Among the French people, the results of the fall battles and the failures at Gallipoli combined to cause significant disappointment, which was increased even more by events in the Balkans. The government and the War Ministry were subjected to fierce criticism. This led to the resignation of the Cabinet on 29 October. In Viviani's place, Briand took over as both prime minister and foreign minister. At the same time, Millerand was replaced by General Gallieni as War Minister. Some drastic changes also occurred in the higher echelons of the command structure. On 2 December the President of the Republic appointed Joffre, who thus far had commanded only the northern and northeastern fronts, the Supreme Commander of all French armies. General de Castelnau was attached to him as Chief of the Joint General Staff. Two General Staffs were established for the direct control of operations: one for the armies of the northern and northeastern fronts under General Janin, the other for the theatres of war located outside France under General Pellé. Both General Staffs were subordinated to Castelnau. Thus, Joffre received overall command and control of the war, a situation to which he had aspired. On 12 December, Fourth Army's former Commander-in-Chief, General de Langle de Cary, assumed command of Army Group *Centre*.

Owing to the large number of victims that had been claimed by the autumn battles, the manpower situation in France had become quite difficult. As of 31 December the number of casualties sustained since the start of the war had reached nearly two million men.[13] The average monthly requirement for replacements had been 145,000 men in the first half of 1915. For 1916 the War Ministry projected that the overall requirement would be 1,600,000 men. However, there were only 1,236,000 men available in the pool. The recruit classes for 1914 and 1915 had already been absorbed into the front, and the 1916 class, although they had finished training in the exercise camps inside France, were considered a final combat reserve that could not be committed prematurely to the front. The 1917 class could only be inducted in January 1916, and therefore the upper age classes had to be pushed

---

13 *See* French Official History, III: 602.

back in order to close the gaps. Accordingly, enlisted personnel of the classes up to 1895 were incorporated into active units while the men of the 1894 class were sent to territorial units.[14] The French had thereby been able to raise the size of their fighting forces from 2,576,000 men on 2 October to a total strength of 2,752,000 men by 1 January,[15] but the country's recruiting pool had been exhausted. By 23 November, thirty-three new infantry battalions had arrived from Africa and twelve from other French colonies. Even earlier, the government had decided to further incorporate the black population into war service, having issued a law on 19 October to increase recruitment in the Senegal colony.

At the front itself, the lull that had set in after the autumn battles was primarily used to undertake a major regrouping of forces, the purpose being to create reserves that could be placed at the disposal of the commanders. According to a plan prepared by Joffre on 22 October—which could be implemented only when the fighting had eased and which had not yet been completed by the end of 1915— 57 and a half of the total of 104 and a half available divisions were to be committed to the front line, 21 were to be used as army group reserves, and 26 were to be placed at the disposal of the Supreme Command. From the latter, a particularly strong reserve force was to be concentrated in the area of Amiens–Compiegne– Meaux at the start of the following year.

By mid-October the strength at the front had been decreased by two divisions, which were detached and sent to Salonika.[16]

Various changes were also made in both the organization and equipment of the French forces. In order to increase the total number of infantry divisions and thus create more reserves for the Supreme Command, the French considered adopting the German method, which involved reducing the number of infantry regiments within a division from four to three, as well as abolishing Brigade Headquarters. The extracted regiments could then be used to form new divisions. To assess the usefulness of this system, two divisions (58th and 152nd) were initially formed in such a way.

At the same time, the production of machine guns had advanced to such an extent that every infantry brigade could be equipped with a second machine-gun company. A significant reinforcement of trench weapons also occurred in December with the delivery of 400 37 mm guns, which were immediately distributed over the most important sectors of the front. The cavalry attached to the infantry

---

14 According to the French Official History, *the men of the 1900–1915 draft classes were sent to active units, while men from the 1895–1900 classes were sent to the reserves.* See French Official History, III: *603.*

15 Ibid.

16 The 57th and 123rd Infantry Divisions.

units were downsized, with each infantry division retaining only two cavalry squadrons and each territorial division one. The corps cavalry were further reduced. In order to better utilize larger cavalry formations in positional warfare, one "regiment on foot" was formed in each cavalry division and one "light division on foot" was formed in each cavalry corps; these were equipped with rifles and light machine guns.[17] This was, however, only a temporary measure that was to be suspended in the event of a return to a war of movement. Regarding field artillery, those guns that had been taken out of action because of barrel damage had not yet been fully replaced. By the end of 1915 only the territorial divisions were still equipped with the old 90 mm gun. However, the Supreme Command's plan to equip each infantry division with three artillery detachments could not be realized for the time being because of a shortage of guns. The heavy artillery was also being restructured with the objective of creating twenty-five regiments that would each be composed of three detachments. Normally two of these detachments would be assigned to the corps, with one retained in the army's reserve. For the time being only older-type guns were available and only a few batteries were equipped with rapid-firing guns. Motorized transport was to be used extensively in place of draft horses for both field and heavy artillery. A request by Joffre that the War Ministry increase the production of ammunition yet again met with considerable difficulties. As a result, the quantities of ammunition he was demanding could not be provided. In the aviation and balloon corps, too, the increases demanded by the Supreme Commander took time to achieve because of production problems.

In accordance with the experiences gained during the autumn battles, the defensive works along the front were further improved, particularly in the rearward areas. Since the High Command expected a German counterattack soon in the area of Fourth Army (located in the Champagne), the defensive works there were to be significantly reinforced. By late December the construction of a new line of defence behind Army Group *East*'s right flank was also under way. These defences were intended to repel a possible German attack from across the Swiss border.

In England, dissatisfaction with the present course of operations had become prevalent in wider circles. One could not ignore the fact that the battles of 1915 had not produced any significant progress in France, but rather had resulted in heavy losses in human life, all without breaching the German front line or even substantially degrading the enemy's strength. The Commander-in-Chief of the BEF, Field Marshal French, pointed to insufficient reinforcements and assistance from

---

17 *The* French Official History *uses the terms "regiment à pied" and "division légère à pied."*

the homeland as one of the main causes for this lack of success; however, important figures in the government expressed doubts as to whether the now sixty-three-year-old Field Marshal, given his frail health, would continue to be able to meet the demands of his position. In mid-December, Prime Minister Asquith notified the Field Marshal that he was to be replaced and asked that he initiate the first steps toward this end himself. Sir John agreed, resigned his command on 17 December, and was appointed—after receiving the title of Viscount—Commander-in-Chief of all British Home Forces. His successor was First Army's former commander, Sir Douglas Haig. At the same time, the Chief of the General Staff of the British Army, General Robertson, assumed the function of Chief of the Imperial General Staff in London. In the BEF he was replaced by Lieutenant General Launcelot Kiggell, a former director at the War Office.[18] The Commander-in-Chief of British First Army became General C.C. Monro,[19] and Sir E.H.H. Allenby[20] took command of Third Army. The Indian Corps, the personnel of which could not bear the cold and wet winter weather in France, had been withdrawn from the front by early November and dissolved as a formation on 8 December.[21] During December the Indian troops departed France by sea; the majority were transported to Mesopotamia.

Responding to Serbian calls for assistance, the British government felt compelled to expeditiously dispatch troops to Salonika. To this effect, four of the infantry divisions committed in France[22] were deployed to the Balkans in late October and November.[23]

---

18 Kiggell had been Director of Home Defence at the War Office. While a figure of immense importance, the best published sources on Kiggell remain biographies of his immediate superior and friend, Sir Douglas Haig.

19 At the time, General Charles Carmichael Monro was in the Dardanelles, and Lieutenant-General Henry Rawlinson was temporarily placed in command.

20 The original text incorrectly reads "E.A. Allenby."

21 The contemporary British view of Indian troops and their suitability for both the climate of northern Europe and as adversaries for the Germans is reflected in Edmonds and Wynne, Military Operations: France and Belgium, 1915, II: 402–4. On the racial and sexual construction of the Indian soldier on the Western Front, see Jeffrey Greenhut, "Race, Sex, and War: The Impact of Race and Sex on Morale and Health Services for the Indian Corps on the Western Front, 1914," Military Affairs 45, no. 2 (1981): 71–74. The perspective of the Indian soldier is examined in David Omissi, "Europe through Indian Eyes: Indian Soldiers Encounter England and France, 1914–1918," English Historical Review 496 (2007): 371–96. For the broader context, see Gregory Martin, "The Influence of Racial Attitudes on British Policy towards India during the First World War," Journal of Imperial and Commonwealth History 14, no. 2 (1986): 91–113.

22 The 27th and 28th Infantry Divisions as well as 22nd and 26th of the newly arrived Kitchener divisions.

23 The most comprehensive English operational history of the Franco-British campaign in Macedonia remains Cyril Falls, Military Operations: Macedonia, 2 vols. (London: HMSO, 1933–35).

In view of the somewhat unfavourable overall situation of the Entente at the end of 1915, the need to more closely co-operate in all theatres of war took on increased importance. Once again the French Supreme Commander made an attempt to achieve this goal. On his initiative all Allied powers were invited to an Inter-Allied Conference at Chantilly. The conference was held from 6 to 8 December; its main result was an agreement that a joint offensive in all theatres of war was envisaged only for the following June. Should the Germans attack one of the Entente powers before that date, all other allies pledged to provide extensive assistance. France and Britain also decided to evacuate the Gallipoli peninsula, thereby terminating the Dardanelles operation. The evacuation began just prior to the end of 1915.

The Situation at the *OHL* in November and December[24]

After the divisions that had been freed up in Russia arrived on the Western Front and the fighting forces in the West had been reorganized, the *OHL* grew certain that the potential for a new Franco-British attempt to breach the German front line was great. When the *OHL* received credible information in early November regarding a new and imminent offensive by both enemies, on 4 November the following directive was sent to the headquarters of the Western Armies:

> Information available from various sources suggests with a high degree of probability that our Western opponents intend to repeat their attempts to launch a large-scale offensive in the next few weeks or possibly within the next fourteen days. I think I will find general consent when I state that such a development would be very welcome to us.[25]

Two days later, Falkenhayn notified these headquarters that, according to a report from a reliable source, Briand's new ministry wanted to resume the offensive in the West "within eight to fourteen days." In fact, by that time the enemy had abandoned any intention of launching an offensive.

See also Alan Palmer, *The Gardeners of Salonika: The Macedonian Campaign 1915–1918* (London: André Deutsch, 1965); *and* Alan Wakefield and Simon Moody, *Under the Devil's Eye: Britain's Forgotten Army at Salonika 1915–1918* (Stroud, UK: Sutton, 2004). *For an analysis of the strategy behind the campaign, see* David Dutton, *The Politics of Diplomacy: Britain and France in the Balkans in the First World War* (London: Tauris, 1998).

24 The discussion of General von Falkenhayn's decisions ends on 7 December 1915 as fundamental changes were made during the next few weeks, which will be described in the next volume of the series.

25 In reality, the information received by the *OHL* was not true.

By late December, divisions that were no longer required for the Serbian campaign began to arrive behind the Western Army. They were either placed directly
at the disposal of the *OHL* or assigned to the various armies.

In the meantime, Falkenhayn again embraced an idea that had already been
repeatedly considered in various forms and that had been repeatedly postponed: an
operation to clear the Upper Alsace (presumably in preparation for a large-scale
offensive in the West that he intended to launch in the spring of 1916). According
to a directive issued on 24 August, under the supervision of the headquarters of
Army Group *German Crown Prince*, Armee-Abteilung *Gaede* was to give detailed
consideration to such an attack. Besides improving the ground by constructing battery positions, depots, and communication roads, these preparations were to address
questions of initial deployment, and so on. On 11 October, General von Knobelsdorf, after a conference in Mézières, noted: "The *OHL* will release four corps for
'Operation Belfort,' which should not be affected by current developments. After the
artillery has gone into position, infantry forces will arrive on 120 trains and will
immediately begin the assault." In late November, Headquarters *Gaede* submitted
proposals for the attacks to its army group and reported that about eight weeks
would be required to complete the necessary preparations. In addition to the troops
of Armee-Abteilung *Gaede*, the draft plan called for the commitment of eight
infantry divisions from the *OHL*. The attack would be launched between the southern foothills of the Vosges Mountains and the Swiss border; not including the
artillery already in place, it would be supported by seventy-two heavy batteries supplied in part by the GHQ Artillery Reserve and by the newly arriving infantry divisions. Additionally, twelve of the heaviest-calibre guns and two 38 cm naval guns
would be made available. By the close of the year, the ammunition situation was satisfactory, as the Chief of the Field Munitions Service had an extensive reserve at his
disposal. Special measures therefore had to be taken for its protection.

But it seems that by the end of November it was still undecided whether the
operation to clean up the Imperial areas of Upper Alsace should be limited in
scope, or whether it should be directly linked to an attack on Fort Belfort.[26] Since
the beginning of the month, Headquarters *Gaede* had been pushing for a decision
that would consider the fact that it was impossible to close on the Imperial border under the fire of the guns of Fort Belfort.

On 29 November Falkenhayn arrived in Mézières for a short visit. He returned
to Pleß on 2 December. In addition to a conference with the various General Staff

---

26   In a letter to the *Reichsarchiv* dated 11 February 1931, General der Infanterie von Knobelsdorf
     reported that in his detailed exploration in the preparations for this attack, he found that
     twenty-nine infantry divisions would be necessary. This is not confirmed by the documents.

chiefs of the Western Armies, he had a briefing with General von Knobelsdorf regarding the preparations for the Upper Alsace offensive. The meeting resulted in a significant expansion of the original objectives. Now, two attacks were to be conducted in Alsace: the already prepared attack in the Sundgau (codenamed *Schwarzwald*), and a second in the southern Vosges (codenamed *Kaiserstuhl*). Alongside, but separated by distance, a third attack was to be launched in the Argonne (codenamed *Waldfest*). Clearly, the requirements in men, heavy artillery, and ammunition would have to be considerably increased.[27]

Falkenhayn informed the Kaiser of his intentions on 3 December in Pleß. He planned to conduct a decisive strike in the West that would bring an end to the war. The attack was to be in the direction of Belfort; the offensive in Upper Alsace would be thereby determined. All the necessary available forces would be provided.

The next day, Fifth Army Headquarters received an executive order that began "The execution of Schwarzwald [i.e., the attack through the Sundgau toward Belfort] is in view." The order continued:

1. "Schwarzwald" is to be jointly conducted with the other operation, the name of which has yet to be communicated.[28] The option of simultaneously launching a mock attack in a third place will be reserved.

2. For both operations, the required forces may be provided at any time starting on 10 January. For "Schwarzwald," two additional infantry divisions will be kept at the ready.

3. Surprise, which is absolutely necessary, can only be achieved by maintaining the most stringent secrecy in all preparations up to the start of the initial deployment; thus the initial deployment must be conducted with all possible speed and must be followed by an immediate start to the operation.

4. The artillery will be brought up in twenty-four hours, the other troops over the following seventy-two hours.

On 5 December, Falkenhayn supplemented his instructions by adding that he was willing to place III Corps Headquarters at the army group's disposal "for the preparation of 'Schwarzwald' ... provided that at the appropriate time, the

---

27 In a letter to the *Reichsarchiv* dated 6 July 1931, General der Infanterie von Knobelsdorf reported that all the measures taken in connection with the Upper Alsace undertaking were merely designed to deceive. General von Falkenhayn made a similar assertion in his memoirs. See Falkenhayn, *Die Oberste Heeresleitung 1914–1916*, 188.

28 Which of the other two operations—the one in the southern Vosges or in the Argonne—was meant here cannot be easily determined. However, Fifth Army High Headquarters mentioned "Waldfest" and thus clearly linked "the other operation" to the attack in the Argonne.

command of the assault group is given to General von Lochow." The III Corps Headquarters was made subordinate to the army group "for special purposes" on 7 December. At the same time, Third Army's subordination to Army Group *German Crown Prince* was suspended.

On 5 December a decree was sent to "all army headquarters in the West, Army Group *Mackensen* and the headquarters of the GHQ reserve units." It read:

> His Majesty expects that the commanders of the GHQ Reserve units will make maximum use of the time which is available to them in order to prepare the units under their command to be efficient not only in static warfare, but also in a war of manoeuvre. It need not be mentioned that a tightening of military discipline will increase pride and attentively maintain a sense of honour, which is an indispensable foundation for our activities and the basis of all our efforts.

The planned distribution of the GHQ Reserve, which had not yet been fully deployed, is shown in Figure IV.

The GHQ Artillery Reserve immediately available at this time in the Western Theatre consisted of the following: eighteen horse-drawn heavy field howitzer batteries of the new type and three without draft horses; two mortar batteries; seven 10 cm gun batteries, of which three were horse-drawn; five gun batteries of the 12 cm and 15 cm calibres without draft horses; and four more batteries equipped with captured guns.

Figure IV: GHQ Reserves—Western Front, December 1915

In the area of Fourth Army	53rd Reserve Division, XV Corps
Sixth Army	XIII Corps Headquarters with 1st Guard Reserve Division and 4th Guard Infantry Division, VII Reserve Corps
Second Army	XVIII Corps
Seventh Army	III Corps
Third Army	183rd Infantry Brigade, 192nd Infantry Brigade, 50th Reserve Division
Fifth Army	27th Infantry Division
Armee-Abteilung *Strantz*	113th Infantry Division, 121st Infantry Division, Bavarian Ersatz Division
Armee-Abteilung *Falkenhausen*	58th Infantry Division
Armee-Abteilung *Gaede*	19th Reserve Division
Belgian General Government	26th Infantry Division

A total of 19 infantry divisions and 2 independent infantry brigades

Note: Additionally, XXII Reserve Corps, 11th Bavarian Infantry Division, 105th Infantry Division, and 107th Infantry Division were located in the area of Army Group Mackensen.

The bulk of the GHQ Artillery Reserve remained with the armies for the time being. In terms of modern equipment, it included approximately twenty heavy field howitzer batteries, twenty-six mortar batteries, fourteen 10 cm gun batteries, six 13 cm gun batteries, four heavy 15 cm gun batteries, and two 38 cm naval gun batteries.

In Army Group *Mackensen*, four heavy field howitzer batteries, two mortar batteries, and two 10 cm gun batteries were available on short notice.

On the home front, five high-trajectory gun batteries, each of the heaviest calibres (30.5 cm and 42 cm), were also available.

THUS IN EARLY DECEMBER 1915, FALKENHAYN BEGAN THE OPERATION WITH which he intended to decide the war in the West. His plan entailed a concentrated, large-scale, surprise strike in Upper Alsace. For that purpose, he had about twenty divisions directly subordinated to him in the Western Theatre, as well as an abundance of heavy artillery stocked with an ample supply of ammunition. The reserves available to Army Group *Mackensen* could be called on quickly to augment these forces as their commitment to Russia was easily suspended.

11

The Central Powers' Situation at the End of 1915

WHILE THE FIGHTING RAGED IN THE CHAMPAGNE AND THE ARTOIS, THE CEN-
tral Powers met with success on other fronts. On 6 September a new alliance between
the Central Powers and Bulgaria was concluded for the campaign against Serbia.
On 7 October a combined German and Austro-Hungarian offensive struck Serbia
simultaneously across the Sava and the Danube. The Austro-Hungarian Third
Army and German Eleventh Army pushed the Serbian troops southwards away
from Belgrade and Negotin toward Nis. On 12 October the Bulgarian attack began:
First and Second Armies drove westward from the border toward Nis and the retreat-
ing Serbian Army. By the end of the month the main Serbian forces had been split
and isolated. Once Nis fell on 6 November the supply route to Turkey was open
and the remnants of the Serbian armies retreated into the mountains. Except for
an unsuccessful French foray up the Vardar River in November, the campaign for
Serbia was effectively over. In December, 140,000 Serbian soldiers and 50,000 civil-
ians began a long retreat to the Adriatic port of Durazzo, where on 23 February 1916,
133,000 were evacuated from the coast.[1]

---

1 *DW* IX: 196–286.

Meanwhile on the Italian Front, two more Italian offensives across the Isonzo ended in failure. On 18 October, twenty-five Italian divisions supported by 1,363 guns attacked an Austrian army of twelve divisions and 634 guns. By the end of the offensive on 4 November, the Italians had again suffered enormous casualties: 67,000 men, including 2,115 officers. By comparison the defenders lost 42,000 men, including 7,200 missing. The Fourth Battle of the Isonzo, which began a week later on 10 November, was equally unsuccessful and equally costly. By the time it ended in mid-December the Italians had lost a further 49,000 men for a total of 116,000 during the two autumn battles. By comparison, the Austro-Hungarians, who were out numbered more than two to one, lost 71,000 during the Third and Fourth Battles of the Isonzo.[2]

The Central Powers' greatest success came against Russia. By the middle of July the two earlier offensives toward the San and in Eastern Prussia had created a huge salient in Russian Poland. On 13 July the German and Austro-Hungarian troops advanced along a continuous line. The Russians fell back in a general retreat. Warsaw fell on 4 August, Kovno on 18 August, and Brest-Litovsk on 24 August.[3] *By the end of the year the Russian armies had lost more than 2.2 million men, including 1 million missing.*[4] *Thus at year's end the Central Powers faced 1916 from a position of strength rather than insecurity. As Robert Foley writes, at the end of 1915 the Central Powers stood at the height of their success.*[5]

THE TREMENDOUS FORCE OF THE ENTENTE'S GREAT OFFENSIVE IN THE WEST caught General von Falkenhayn in the middle of his preparations for the Serbian campaign. Initially it appeared that it would not be possible to continue to implement plans for offensive operations against Serbia as it seemed that the dangerous situation in the West might require a shift in strategic emphasis. However, he

---

2 *DW* IX: 327–34.
3 Foley, *German Strategy and the Path to Verdun*, 147–51; Stone, *The Eastern Front 1914–1917*, 174–91.
4 *DW* VIII: 596.
5 Foley, *German Strategy and the Path to Verdun*, 151.

pursued his operational objectives with a remarkable steadfastness and did not allow the tense situation in the French Theatre to dictate his actions during the Entente's offensive in the West. Pursuant to an urgent request by Generaloberst von Einem, only 5th Infantry Division—which was about to begin its departure for the Danube on 24 September—was made available to Third Army. The *OHL*'s remaining directives during the fall battles in the Artois and the Champagne dealt primarily with the deployment of reserves that had already been staged on the Western Front or that had previously been designated to depart for that theatre.

Otherwise the preparations for the Serbian campaign were not affected by the Franco-British attacks and reconnaissance. Preparations for crossing the Sava and the Danube continued without interruption. The significance of this should not be underestimated: a change in the Serbian operations could well have jeopardized Bulgaria's co-operation at the final hour. Additionally, the defensive victories of the German Western Army were instrumental in at least partially reinvigorating the morale of the Central Powers and counteracting the unfortunate outcome of the Austro-Hungarian offensive in eastern Galicia and Volhynia[6] and its effect on those Balkan states which were not yet participating in the war. This was of particular significance, especially during the commencement of operations against Serbia.

In this campaign, Falkenhayn's main strategic objective was the opening of the long awaited land connection with Turkey. For General Conrad, however, the political goal of resolving the Balkan question once and for all by subjugating Serbia and Montenegro was of primary importance. The antagonism between the two General Staff chiefs was becoming more and more evident during the Serbian campaign; this antagonism arose primarily from their differences in opinion.

After his main objective in the Balkans had been achieved, Falkenhayn as before intended to free up all expendable forces for deployment to the West, where he aimed to achieve a quick decision in the war. Conrad, however, hoped to use the German forces on the Serbian Front to realize his far-reaching plans in the Balkans. In order to bring clarity to the situation, on 3 November the German General Staff chief queried Conrad through the Foreign Office's envoy, Treutler:

> After the conclusion of the Serbian campaign which was conducted by us with great sacrifice, but predominantly in Austria's interest, General von Falkenhayn would like to be informed as to which degree he has command over the German forces in order to bring the entire conflict to a conclusion

---

6 An area in modern-day Ukraine located between the Bug and Prypiat Rivers, known in German as "Wolhynien."

as soon as possible. Complete clarity is required as to the peace terms that are to be imposed unconditionally on Serbia.

When Conrad was informed on 5 November of the negotiations between the foreign policy leaders in Berlin and Vienna over Serbia's future, he demanded on behalf of his government that the subjugation of the Serbian people be the objective of the war. Contrary to his request, at their conference on 10 and 11 November in Berlin, the Central Powers' foreign ministers decided that Serbia and Montenegro should continue to exist as sovereign states and that only a few border areas would be annexed by the Dual Monarchy. This coincided with Falkenhayn's wishes, but it did not in the least satisfy the aspirations of the Austro-Hungarian Chief of the General Staff and thus did not help resolve the existing differences between the allies' two military leaders. The situation was further aggravated by the fact that Conrad did not trust the Bulgarians, who apparently had their own designs on Serbia—designs that were not compatible with the interests of the Dual Monarchy. With the withdrawal of German units across the Danube—a move that was seen by the *AOK* as a rejection of their plans—these differences increased during November.

By 24 November, Generalfeldmarschall von Mackensen believed that he had succeeded in "decisively defeating the Serbian Army and opening a secure connection with Constantinople via Belgrade and Sofia." Although the peace that was hoped for with the defeated enemy had not yet been realized, great things had been accomplished: not only had a land connection to Turkey been restored, but with Bulgaria aligned within the German sphere of influence, a central European block (*Mitteleuropa*) that stretched from the North Sea to the Red Sea and almost to the Persian Gulf had been created.

AFTER THE SERBIAN CAMPAIGN REACHED A CONCLUSION AT THE END OF NOVEMber, there was initially a consensus among the victorious powers that they would continue combined operations to secure Montenegro and Albania and to expel the Franco-British forces that had landed at Salonika. However, these operations presented difficulties: first of all, there was no rail network, and more important, there were political consideration regarding Greece. As before, the Central Powers focused on making it easier for the Greek government to maintain its neutrality. The Franco-British forces had penetrated the Greek border just as Serbian soil was being evacuated, so in the opinion of Falkenhayn there was no compelling reason to execute the operation in Salonika, although he admitted that it would be significant for morale if the enemy were to be driven from Greek soil as well.

The question of continuing the larger operations was addressed in a conversation between Falkenhayn and Enver Pascha in Orsova on 24 November. The Turkish Vice-Generalissimo suggested that a combined operation be mounted by all the Allies in the French or Russian Theatre, and he emphasized his willingness to deploy Turkish forces under German command for its execution. On 26 November, Treutler reported this meeting to the Foreign Office: "Falkenhayn told me about the meeting with Enver whose generosity he truly admired. Enver expressed his conviction that the war had to be concluded with a major operation in Russia or in France and for that he offered von Falkenhayn the Turkish Army." The Central Powers thus faced a number of prospects for the continuation of the multi-front war in the Balkans and the Middle East. The opportunity to achieve a decision on the northern portion of the Eastern Front by attacking the Russians on their flanks and interior line—an opportunity that had been missed in the summer because of the impending Serbian campaign—could now be seized through the subjugation of the Rumanians and the creation of new threats to southern Russia. However, Treutler reported, the Chief of the General Staff had turned down Enver Pascha's offer because he did not believe that the Turkish Army was suited for deployment to the European Theatre given its climate. Moreover, the expertise and equipment of the Turkish Army was indispensable to regaining Gallipoli and defending Syria and Baghdad. The report closed: "Enver finally acceded to Falkenhayn's proposals and again emphasized that the German General Staff should lead the Great War; and that he intended to entirely subordinate himself." One wonders whether political consideration for Bulgaria, whose territory would have to be crossed by Turkish forces moving against Rumania, was instrumental in Falkenhayn's decision to turn down Enver Pascha's offer.[7]

Falkenhayn's decision did mean that Rumania's ambiguity continued to be a concern. Both King Ferdinand and Prime Minister Bratianu had declared that they would vouch for Rumania's neutrality and that they were committed to preventing Russian forces from crossing Rumanian territory by force of arms; even so, there were indications that Bucharest was leaning toward the Entente. On 18 November during an audience with the German military attaché, Ferdinand declared that owing to the public's great "sympathy" for the French and their "animosity" toward Hungary, for the time being it was impossible for Rumania to align itself with the Central Powers. It was evident that the connection between Bucharest and St. Petersburg remained tight, for shipments of war materiel from Russia to Rumania continued despite extreme shortages in Russia.

---

7 The documents are insufficient to answer this question.

Considering this situation, Major Bronsart von Schellendorff, the German military attaché in Bucharest, insisted that decisive action be taken against the government in Bucharest. In a memorandum dated 13 December and addressed to the Chief of the General Staff, he emphasized that Rumania would join the Entente when the moment was right. Instead of waiting for a point in time that would be adverse for us, he wrote, it would be preferable to use the presently favourable situation for an attack on Rumania. Bronsart concluded that the occupation of Rumania would generate considerable strategic, political, and economic advantages. Given his fundamental mindset toward the Eastern question, Falkenhayn could not agree with this reasoning. He felt it was sufficient to demand that an aggressive position be taken with Rumania, and with this in mind he directed a communication to Foreign Minister Jagow on 15 December: "I believe that we must understand that we cannot expect Rumania to join us in the foreseeable future. However, we can attempt to gain her actual neutrality by forcing her to abstain from her frequent chicanery and to enter into normal trade relations with us instead." In his response of 20 December, Jagow warned against "engaging in intimidating and threatening politics with Rumania"; in correspondence of the same day he pointed out that for the time being Germany depended on grain imports from Rumania and, therefore, also on her good will.

Throughout the year, Falkenhayn had clung tenaciously to the belief that victory had to be reached on the Western Front as soon as circumstances permitted. Therefore it was not difficult for him to dismiss the suggestion that the Rumanian question be resolved quickly. As before, for him operations in the other theatres were merely ancillary and were to be handled with the least amount of effort and the least possible investment of time. Based on this, he presented his intentions to the Kaiser on 3 December. A memorandum written by Generaloberst Pleßen on the same day read: "General von Falkenhayn presents His Majesty with a serious picture of the war and the bottom line is that a decision can only be reached with a blow in the West for which all available forces must be staged!—he wants to attack Belfort because there he has the best protection on the flanks—he did not say when." Generalmajor Tappen noted: "On the occasion of his presentation to His Majesty, the offensive in Alsace became a settled matter."

After Falkenhayn's presentation to the Emperor on 3 December, operations on the Southeastern Front declined in importance at the *OHL*. The weight of the war had again shifted to the Western Front.

DURING 1915 THE SITUATION AT SEA DID NOT CHANGE SIGNIFICANTLY.[8] IT WAS important for the conduct of the land war that the German Fleet maintain naval supremacy in the Baltic, thereby preventing Russia from receiving the weapons and ammunition it urgently required.

At the beginning of the year the Chief of the Admiralty received a directive from the Kaiser that was intended to secure more freedom of action for the Fleet Commander than had previously been the case. He received the authorization to

undertake frequent forays into the North Sea with the objective of cutting off forward enemy formations and to attack if he has superiority. Engaging vastly superior enemy formations is, however, to be avoided if it is at all possible. Given the overall situation at present, the deep sea fleet is of increased significance and is an important political instrument in the hands of the Kaiser and thus an adverse battle at sea would have particularly grave consequences.

These directives placed demands on the commanders that were difficult to fulfill.

Based on a plan that had been developed prior to the issuance of these new orders, on 23 January the Chief of the Fleet dispatched large as well as small cruisers and torpedo boats to Doggerbank, where British patrol boats had frequently been sighted. The enemy got wind of this plan in time and on 24 January attacked with superior forces. During the battle that developed, the heavy cruiser *Blücher* was lost.

Over the course of the year, Admiral von Pohl, the former Chief of the Admiralty Staff who had been appointed Chief of the Fleet in February 1915, undertook seven forays during which the fleet never crossed the centre of the North Sea. Because of the reticence of the British Fleet, they met only enemy mines and submarines.

In the Baltic the fleet did not engage in any naval battles because the major elements of the Russian Fleet had taken a defensive posture, opting to protect the Gulf of Finland and St. Petersburg.

As a result of the spring offensive on the left flank of the German Army in Kurland, the Baltic Fleet gained new bases with the capture of Libau and Windau.[9] In seeking to continue the Eastern Army's offensive operations over the course of

---

8 For more on the history of German naval operations in 1915, see Marinearchiv, *Der Krieg zur See 1914–1918: Der Krieg in der Nordsee Band 3—Ende November 1914 bis Anfang Februar 1915* (Berlin: E.S. Mittler & Sohn, 1923); idem, *Der Krieg zur See 1914–1918: Der Krieg in der Nordsee Band 4—Anfang Februar bis Dezember 1915* (Berlin: E.S. Mittler & Sohn, 1924); idem, *Der Krieg zur See 1914–1918: Der Krieg in der Ostsee Band 1—Kriegsbeginn bis Mitte März 1915* (Berlin: E.S. Mittler & Sohn, 1921); idem, *Der Krieg zur See 1914–1918: Der Krieg in der Ostsee Band 2—Kriegsjahr 1915* (Berlin: E.S. Mittler & Sohn, 1929).

9 *Liepāja and Ventspils.*

the summer, *OberOst* suggested that naval operations be mounted in the Gulf of Riga in order to "tie up the Russian forces on the other side of the Daugava River." Although the promised quick advance from the army's left flank on Riga did not materialize, Grossadmiral Heinrich Prince of Prussia, Commander of the Baltic Fleet, decided to send naval elements into the gulf anyway. This decision was premised on his hope that the Russian Fleet would put to sea and that a battle with its covering forces would ensue. It was also precipitated by a suggestion from Falkenhayn that a demonstration outside or within the Gulf of Riga would be very welcome. The German Fleet fought its way through the minefields and on 19 August entered the gulf, advancing as far as Pernau.[10] There it blocked the port with scuttled ships and, as planned, returned to its home ports.

Significant participation in operations on the Russian Front by the navy would only have been possible along the Baltic coast in the direction of St. Petersburg. Because of the overall situation and the great distances involved for the Field Army, however, such a combined operation could not be seriously considered. The forces required for such an undertaking, if they could have been mustered at all, would have been out of proportion to the possible advantages.

Protecting shipping from Nordic countries to Germany was the most important task performed by the Baltic Fleet. Of these shipments, the iron ore obtained from northern Sweden was of a special significance for the German armament industry and the army's fighting ability.

During 1915, commercial warfare by submarine, which had been initiated with the "war zone declaration" of 4 February, was unsuccessful from the outset in curtailing neutral sea traffic owing to the limited number of submarines. The sinking of the British passenger vessels *Lusitania* and *Arabic* in May and August 1915, which had resulted in the death of American citizens, led to ominous protests by the United States and presented the German leadership with the difficult question of how far to accede to the demands of a major neutral power without endangering important military interests. With regard to this issue, no satisfactory agreement between the government and the naval commanders materialized. The discussion ended with a compromise: for the time being, commercial warfare by submarine would be discontinued entirely in the waters around Great Britain. This order was issued on 18 September to the High Seas Fleet and the *Marinekorps*. When they were told to carry on the submarine war in the North Sea only according to the Prize Code, they discontinued it entirely.[11] Only the submarines in the Mediterranean,

---

10 *Pärnu.*

11 *The Prize Code* (Prisenordnung) *of 1909 and Prize Courts Ordinance* (Prisengerichtsordnung) *of 1911 established the rules of search and seizure on the high seas for German captains. It read in part: "1. During a war the commanders of His Majesty's ships of war have the right to stop and*

where conditions differed from those around Great Britain, and the mining submarines of the *Marinekorps*, continued their activities without interruption. By
the end of 1915 the German U-Boat fleet consisted of forty-one vessels, including
those in the Mediterranean, the Dardanelles, and the Baltic.[12]

DESPITE ALL THE MILITARY SUCCESSES, THE CUMULATIVE OPERATIONAL RESULTS
of 1915 were not entirely satisfactory. Important issues such as a secure connection
with Turkey and Bulgaria's entry into the war on the side of the Central Powers
had been resolved; but the final defeat of Russia in the East—which would have
allowed a final decision to be achieved in the West—had not been accomplished.
This goal had not been realized even though the rear and flank of the Eastern
Army had been protected in selfless defensive battles waged by Germany in the West
and by Austria on its Italian Front. The Russians' strength had suffered greatly as
a result of the large combined offensive in the summer of 1915, but the question
lingered: Was the remaining time and manpower sufficient to reach a decision in
the West? The possibility that a rejuvenated Russia would soon reappear on the
battlefield had also to be considered.

The Central Powers were unable to appear in any of the various theatres
with sufficient superiority. The end of 1915 saw the enemy's armed forces evenly
distributed in force on all fronts except in the Balkans, where they were inferior
in numbers. On the Western Front, 113 infantry divisions faced 150 of the Entente;
in the East, 88 German and Austro-Hungarian divisions stood against 126 Russian divisions; on the Italian Front, 24 and a half Austro-Hungarian divisions
faced 38 and a half Italian divisions. Thus on the whole, 225 and a half divisions
of the Central Powers faced 314 and a half enemy divisions. Furthermore, approximately twelve German and Austro-Hungarian divisions were tied up in the
Balkans.

---

search enemy and neutral merchant vessels, and to seize—and, in exceptional cases, to destroy the
same, together with the enemy and neutral goods found thereon; 2. The law of prize does not apply
to public vessels of a neutral state. Public vessels of the enemy are confiscable under the laws of
war, without further proceedings. Public vessels comprise ships of war as well as ships used in the
public service of, and subject to the command of, the state. Other ships, the property of the state,
are placed in the same category." For more on the history of German prize law see, Charles Henry
Huberich and Richard King, "The Development of German Prize Law," *Columbia Law Review*
18, no. 6 (1918): 503–38.

12 During 1915 nineteen submarines were lost.

NONE OF THE ENEMIES DISPLAYED ANY DISPOSITION TOWARD PEACE. THE LONDON Treaty of 4 September 1914 firmly united the countries of the Entente, a unity strengthened by the admission of Japan on 19 October 1915 and of Italy on 30 November.[13] As shown by a number of private advances, even the badly defeated Russians and Serbians were rejecting overtures for a separate peace. For the time being, an end to the war was not in sight and the danger was growing that Germany would be entirely cut off from overseas supplies. While thus far it had been possible to handle economic problems with anticipatory measures, and although these problems had not exerted a direct influence on the conduct of the war and the maintaining of the army's will to fight, the longer the war lasted, the more the economic situation would become a threat. At the same time, the longer the war lasted, the more the Entente would be able to bank on the fact that the Central Powers would exhaust themselves militarily and economically. Time favoured the enemy in an alarming, ominous way.

Despite concerns about the overall situation and the horrible sacrifices in blood that had been made to that point, the mood on the front and at home remained optimistic. Based on the clear military successes that had been achieved on the battlefield, the German people remained unshaken in their trust that the war would be brought to a positive conclusion. The initial enthusiasm for war that had been witnessed in the summer of 1914 had been replaced by tenacious determination. As 1915 made way for 1916, the will to prevail was unbroken.

THE LOSS OF ALL GERMAN COLONIES EXCEPT FOR GERMAN EAST AFRICA WAS significant for the overall situation. Aside from the fact that this threatened to isolate Germany from the rest of the world, the enemy had now gained an important political and economic bargaining chip, one that to a certain extent balanced the value of the territories that had been occupied by the Central Powers in Eastern and Western Europe. But at the same time, the weak German forces in the colonies had managed to pin down considerable enemy forces. Their heroic resistance forced the Entente to commit a large number of men to this secondary theatre.[14]

---

13 *"The London Treaty" was an agreement between France, Great Britain, and Russia which stated that no power would seek or accept a separate peace.*

14 *There is a large body of literature on the campaign in Africa. For an excellent overview see* Hew Strachan, *The First World War in Africa* (Oxford: Oxford University Press, 2004). See also Ross Anderson, *The Forgotten Front: The East African Campaign 1914–1918* (London: Tempus, 2007); *and* Byron Farwell, *The Great War in Africa, 1914–1918* (New York: Norton, 1986).

The same applied to the cruisers and auxiliary cruisers that had been located on the world's oceans at the beginning of the war. By the summer of 1915 they had been sunk or they had had to enter neutral ports because of lack of fuel. At the turn of the year there was only one German auxiliary cruiser left in the Atlantic.[15]

In the final analysis, the military situation of the Central Powers was strained at the end of 1915. One thing was certain: time was short, and a military decision in favour of the Central Powers had to be forced, for otherwise an end to the war could not be foreseen. In working toward this goal, if there was to be any expectation of success, it was vital that circumstances be created in which this great decisive battle could be risked—circumstances that would only be realized by pooling all available forces.

---

15   *For an overview of the cruiser war, see* Paul Schmalenbach, *German Raiders: A History of Auxiliary Cruisers of the German Navy, 1895–1945* (Annapolis, MD: Naval Institute Press, 1979).

APPENDICES

Appendix 1

Comparison of German, British, and French Artillery in the Spring Battles in the Artois

At the Beginning of May	Calibre: 6.8 to 9.9 cm	Calibre: 10 to 14.9 cm		Calibre: 15 to 19.9 cm		Calibre: Over 20 cm		
	Flat trajectory	Flat trajectory	High Angle	Flat trajectory	High Angle	Flat trajectory	High Angle	Total
German	582	36	156	16	83	0	20	893
French	824	96		88	70		12	1,090
British	450	28	100	4	36		13	631
						French and British Guns Combined		1,721

At the End of May	Calibre: 6.8 to 9.9 cm	Calibre: 10 to 14.9 cm		Calibre: 15 to 19.9 cm		Calibre: Over 20 cm		
	Flat trajectory	Flat trajectory	High Angle	Flat trajectory	High Angle	Flat trajectory	High Angle	Total
German	16	72	184	18	160		49	893
French	904	111		74	68		12	1,169
British	450	28	100	4	36		13	631
						French and British Guns Combined		1,800

Appendix 2

Comparison of German, British, and French Artillery in the Autumn Battles in the Champagne and Artois

Champagne 25 Sept. 1915	Calibre: 6.8 to 9.9 cm	Calibre: 10 to 14.9 cm		Calibre: 15 to 19.9 cm		Calibre: Over 20 cm		
	Flat trajectory	Flat trajectory	High Angle	Flat trajectory	High Angle	Flat trajectory	High Angle	Total
German	376	54	90	28	132	1	52	733
French	1,293	275		117	164	4	106	1,959

Artois 25 Sept. 1915	Calibre: 6.8 to 9.9 cm	Calibre: 10 to 14.9 cm		Calibre: 15 to 19.9 cm		Calibre: Over 20 cm		
	Flat trajectory	Flat trajectory	High Angle	Flat trajectory	High Angle	Flat trajectory	High Angle	Total
German	637	68	168	20	144	1	52	1,090
French	789	172		97	77		48	1,183
British	654	35	172	13	36	2	31	943
					French and British Guns Combined			2,126

Appendix 3

Comparison of German Forces at War's Beginning and the End of 1915

	August 1914	At the End of 1915		August 1914	At the End of 1915
		I. Formations			
Armies	8	13[1]	Cavalry Corps	4	11
Corps	40	53[2]	Cavalry Divisions	4	11
Infantry Divisions	92[3]	161[4]			
Independent Brigades	24[1]	21			

II. Units (Stated in Approximate Numbers)

1. Infantry (Including *Jäger*)			2. Cavalry		
Battalions	1,330[5]	2275	Squadrons	610[6]	720[6]
Machine Gun Companies and Detachments	360[5]	950	Machine Gun Platoons	–	80
Cyclist Companies	18	70			

3. Field Artillery			4. Pioneers		
Batteries	940[5]	1735	Companies	260[7]	590[8]

5. Foot Artillery					
			Searchlight Companies	27	175
Batteries	335[9]	1085	*Minenwerfer* Companies	–	100
Survey Sections	–	100	*Minenwerfer* Detachments	–	90[10]

6. Aerial and Anti-Aircraft Troops			7. Intelligence Troops		
Reconnaissance Detachment	33	80	Army Telegraph Detachments	9[11]	21
Artillery Detachment	–	15	Lines of Communications Telegraph Directorate	8	18[12]
Bombing Squadrons	–	6	Corps Telephone Detachment	40	71
Flak Batteries	–	10	Divisional Telephone Detachments	–	62
Flak Platoons	–	165	Wireless Stations (Heavy and Light)	53	92
Single Flak Guns	18	80			

Appendix 3 *(continued)*

	August 1914	At the End of 1915		August 1914	At the End of 1915
8. Railway Troops			**9. Mechanized Troops**		
Military Railway Directorate	2	8	Lines of Communications Motorized Transportation Columns	68	117
Military Traffic Detachments	6	8	Light Motorized Transportation Columns	27	138
Railway Traffic Companies	21	72[13]			
Railway Construction Companies	63[14]	105			
Railway Labour Companies	4	4			

---

1   Excluding *Armee-Abteilungen* and *Armee-Gruppen*.
2   Including the *Marinekorps.*
3   Including the main fortress reserves.
4   Including the Alpenkorps and the 2nd Marine Division.
5   Including mobile troops and fortress garrisons.
6   Three cavalry detachments equals a squadron.
7   Heavy artillery of the Field Army and Siege Artillery.
8   Including the mobile companies of the fortress garrisons and the park companies.
9   Including park and mining companies.
10   Excluding the un-established *minenwerfer* platoons.
11   Single motorized telephone detachment of GHQ.
12   Single telegraph director at GHQ.
13   Including six field railway traffic companies, excluding eighteen aerial railway units.
14   Including Landwehr construction companies.

Appendix 4

Overview of German Powder and Munitions Production from War's Beginning to the End of 1915

I. Monthly Output

	Guaranteed Maximum	August 1914	Actual Production December 1914	December 1915
Powder (Excluding Black Powder)	1,400 tons	1,240 tons	2,170 tons	4,000 tons
Infantry Ammunition	150,000,000 cartridges	130,000,000 cartridges	150,000,000 cartridges	213,000,000 cartridges
Field Gun Ammunition	200,000 shells	170,000 shells	1,200,000 shells	2,100,000 shells
Light Field Howitzer Ammunition	70,000 shells	65,000 shells	414,000 shells	800,000 shells
Heavy Field Howitzer Ammunition	60,000 shells	26,000 shells	266,000 shells	684,000 shells
Mortar Ammunition	12,500 shells	3,000 shells	19,000 shells	104,000 shells
10 cm Gun Ammunition	5,000 shells	2,000 shells	19,000 shells	145,000 shells

II. Total Output

	From War's Beginning to the End of 1914	From the Beginning to the End of 1915
Powder (Excluding Black Powder)	7,500 tons	43,300 tons
Infantry Ammunition	725,000,000 cartridges	2,200,000,000 cartridges
Field Gun Ammunition	3,200,000 shells	21,500,000 shells
Light Field Howitzer Ammunition	1,300,000 shells	8,200,000 shells
Heavy Field Howitzer Ammunition	618,000 shells	6,500,000 shells
Mortar Ammunition	66,000 shells	850,000 shells
10 cm Gun Ammunition	52,000 shells	1,180,000 shells

Appendix 5

Falkenhayn's Standing Orders for the Defence in the West, 1914

Chief of the General Staff of the Field Army
GHQ, Mézières
11 November 1914
Top Secret!
Written by an Officer (draft handwritten by Generalmajor Wild von Hohenborn)

General Remarks

1. For the near future, it is most important that the present line be held. At the same time the offensive spirit cannot be lost; rather, every convenient opportunity to seize the terrain in front must be taken. Even minor forays foster the offensive spirit, counteract slackening, and never fail to make an impression on the enemy. The precondition for a successful operation is always thorough preparation; unsuccessful operations encourage the enemy to the same extent to which they negatively affect our own troops.

The experience gathered everywhere during the course of the war has shown that the enemy always attempts to retake lost positions with intensive counterattacks, therefore each position that is taken is to be immediately and strongly fortified. What has been taken must always be held.

2. Generally, the front line of our positions must be retained. When they have been created merely for tactical reasons, they may be useless for a continuing defence in some areas. In those instances improvements should be made forward to that line, relinquishing minor portions of the terrain is justified only where the former is not possible. Here it must be kept in mind that even our relinquishment of totally useless objectives is considered a major accomplishment by the enemy and is then exploited accordingly.

3. To absolutely ensure that we can hold our positions, the front lines are to be further reinforced with all available resources. In addition to the deployment of the most effective obstacles in front of the location, secure shell-proof protection against hostile artillery fire must be built. Strongly covered shelters, completely covered means of communications as well as concealed batteries must be constructed at this time, if that has not been accomplished already. Special attention must be paid to the artillery observer posts; the provision of armoured plates for them has already begun. Portable infantry shields and armoured shields for the machine guns, which will be effective even against infantry fire at close quarters, will also be provided. Emphasis is placed upon protecting the forward guns by inserting

effective obstacles in front of them. The more fortified the front lines, the more troops can be spared and either moved to the rear or possibly freed up for deployment elsewhere. It must constantly be a priority to spare troops from the front lines by reinforcing the stationary obstacles.

The fact that front-line troops generally do not like working on defensive installations, and since the importance of the fortifications makes it necessary, their superiors must personally act to enforce the work and motivate them.

4. In addition to fortifying the front lines, the upgrading of the rear positions must take place at the same time. The experience of the campaign demonstrates that to effectively prevent an enemy breakthrough, it is not important to create large, continuous, standardized positions, but rather an incremental defence of numerous closely spaced successive terrain points with strong obstacles and good flanking installations. This means of defence is new to us and numerous voices express concern that the presence of rear area [defensive] lines may exert an unfavourable influence on the perseverance of the troops on our front line. Our experiences with the enemy are sufficiently convincing for us not to miss the advantages posed for us of lines situated closely behind each other. Therefore it is recommended that we create a system of defensive positions and concealed batteries that favour tenacious resistance closely behind the front line. These positions are also meant to securely accommodate the reinforcements for the front line. The importance of flanking all positions with installed artillery pieces and machine guns must be emphasized.

5. The previous remarks do not preclude the construction of any already planned, or perhaps completed, extensive positions independent of both the front lines and the ancillary fortifications connected to them which would be intended for the rear area reserves. It must be noted that caution is required regarding their effect on the mood of friend and foe alike.

6. Furthermore, emphasis is placed on thoroughly building up an effective telephone system, especially between the various weapons positions. Where possible, the current, as well as captured cables, are to be buried to a shell-proof depth. This primarily refers to the cables of the advance artillery observation posts which are vital and generally in particular danger.

7. In addition to carefully planning the defence arrangements by installing obstacles when constructing the rearward shelters, and in order to avoid unnecessary casualties, as well as to grant the troops sufficient rest through an increased sense

of security, care must be taken to protect the troops against long-range hostile artillery fire. A continuous effort must be made to protect the house fronts of rear-area accommodations facing the enemy, which are thus still exposed to hostile artillery fire. They should be reinforced with sandbags and earth berms, and underground shell-proof living quarters should also be constructed at the same time in basements by filling the first floor with dirt, or something similar, thus achieving a maximum level of security—especially for the commanders. Experience teaches us that many a casualty could have been avoided if appropriate measures had been taken.

8. Protecting all positions in the rear, particularly since the defoliation of the trees, against aircraft, will not be easy; however, it must be categorically demanded. In this situation the commanders have a lot of room for imaginative creativity. Securely accommodating the many horses will demand thorough consideration as well.

9. We suggest a three-step rotation for the entire duty roster: front line, standby, total rest.

10. An all-out effort must be made to maintain the positive mood of the troops. In addition to their physical welfare, sports activities for the troops stationed in the rear may be a consideration. For the troops in the rear, manoeuvers in the field not only serve as additional training, but also add an invigorating element to their duties. That discipline should be stabilized and reinforced by way of occasional drill exercises goes without saying—special attention must be given to maintaining the spirit of our officers. When after months of daily combat, there is a prevailing impression that their emotional vigour will falter, in certain instances even a short leave to one of the larger cities in the base area or in one of the Red Cross sanatoriums has proven to be very beneficial.

11. For the foreseeable future our situation in a sense is akin to Combat Winter Quarters. Therefore installing a variety of stoves, issuing wool blankets and warm underwear, keeping the snow (and melting snow) out of the trenches and dugouts—in short: every conceivable protection against the impact of winter must be the constant concern of the personnel responsible for such matters. However, in this context it is again emphasized that even during this time in winter quarters the will to advance should not become dormant (see point one). Should this happen, the danger of losing the war could become real.[1]

---

1   This last sentence was personally added by Falkenhayn.

12. The extraction of strong reserves should be a priority. The Corps Reserves serve the purpose of ensuring that the corps' position will be held either by way of reinforcements or counterattacks. Army reserves are given the task of preventing major enemy attempts at penetration or to serve in offensive undertakings ordered by the Army Commander. The GHQ Reserves are the *OHL*'s flexible reserves and can assume the task of the Army Reserves or, as is their main mission, to be available for special major operations. In the first case, they are at the disposal of the Army Group commanders. The more forces the army headquarters provide to the *OHL* after expanding their positions and replenishing their corps, the more significant the benefit of the *OHL* reserves will be for the whole!

SELECTED
BIBLIOGRAPHY

~~~

Afflerbach, Holger. *Falkenhayn. Politisches Denken und Handeln im Kaiserreich.* Munich: R. Oldenbourg, 1994.

Anderson, Margaret Lavinia, "A German Way of War?" *German History* 22, no. 2 (2004): 254–58.

Anderson, Ross. *The Forgotten Front: The East African Campaign 1914–1918.* London: Tempus, 2007.

Asprey, Robert B. *The German High Command at War: Hindenburg and Ludendorff and the First World War.* New York: Warner, 1994.

Bethmann Hollweg, Theobald von. *Betrachtungen zum Weltkriege, Teil II: Während d. Krieges.* Berlin: Hobbing, 1921.

Bucholz, Arden. *Hans Delbrück and the German Military Establishment: War Images in Conflict.* Iowa City: University of Iowa Press, 1985.

Bundesarchiv. *Der Weltkrieg 1914 bis 1918: Die militärischen Operationen zu Land, Band XIII–XIV.* Berlin: E.S. Mittler & Sohn, 1956.

Burdick, Charles. "Foreign Military Records of World War I in the National Archives." *Prologue* (Winter 1975): 212–20.

Carver, Field Marshal Lord. *The Turkish Front, 1914–1918.* London: Sidgwick and Jackson, 2003.

Cecil, Lamar. *Wilhelm II: Emperor and Exile, 1900–1941, Volume II.* Chapel Hill: University of North Carolina Press, 1996.

Chickering, Roger. *Imperial Germany and the Great War, 1914–1918.* New York: Cambridge University Press, 2004.

Chickering, Roger, and Stig Förster, eds. *Shadows of Total War: Europe, East Asia, and the United States, 1919–1939.* New York: Cambridge University Press, 2003.

Churchill, Winston. *The World Crisis: 1915*. New York: Scribner, 1928.

Citino, Robert Michael. *The Path to Blitzkrieg: Doctrine and Training in the German Army, 1920–1939*. London: Lynne Reinner, 1999.

Colville, H.E. *History of the Sudan Campaign*. 2 vols. London: Intelligence Division, War Office, 1890.

Cook, Tim. "Canadian Official Historians and the Writing of the Two World Wars." Ph.D. diss., University of New South Wales, 2005.

———. *Clio's Warriors: Canadian Historians and the Writing of the Two World Wars*. Vancouver: University of British Columbia Press, 2006.

Corrigan, Gordon. *Sepoys in the Trenches: The Indian Corps on the Western Front 1914–15*. Staplehurst, UK: Spellmount, 1999.

Cramon, August von. *Unser österreichisch-ungarischer Bundesgenosse im Weltkriege*. Berlin: E.S. Mittler & Sohn, 1922.

Cron, Hermann. *Imperial German Army, 1914–18: Organization, Structure, Orders of Battle*. Solihull, UK: Helion, 2002.

Demeter, Karl. *Das Reichsarchiv: Tatsachen und Personen*. Frankfurt: Bernard und Graefe, 1969.

Doughty, Robert A. *Pyrrhic Victory: French Strategy and Operations in the Great War*. Cambridge, MA: Harvard University Press, 2005.

Dutton, David. *The Politics of Diplomacy: Britain and France in the Balkans in the First World War*. New York: Tauris, 1998.

Echevarria, Antulio J. "Heroic History and Vicarious War: Nineteenth-Century German Military History Writing." *Historian* 59, no. 3 (2007): 573–90.

Edmonds, Sir James E. *Military Operations: France and Belgium, 1915, Volume 2*. London: Macmillan, 1928.

Edmonds, Sir James E., and G.C. Wynne. *Military Operations: France and Belgium, 1915, Volume 1*. London: Macmillan, 1927.

Evans, Richard J. *In Defence of History*. London: Granta, 1997.

Falkenhayn, Erich von. *Die Oberste Heeresleitung 1914–1916*. Berlin: E.S. Mittler & Sohn, 1920. (English trans.: *The German General Staff and Its Decisions, 1914–1916*. New York: Dodd, Mead, 1920.)

Falls, Cyril. *Military Operations: Macedonia*. 2 vols. London: HMSO, 1933–35.

Farwell, Byron. *The Great War in Africa, 1914–1918*. New York: Norton, 1986.

Fischer, Fritz. *Krieg der Illusionen: die deutsche Politik von 1911 bis 1914*. Düsseldorf: Drost, 1969.

———. *War of Illusions: German Policies from 1911 to 1914*. New York: Norton, 1975.

Foley, Robert. *German Strategy and the Path to Verdun: Erich von Falkenhayn and the Development of Attrition, 1870–1916*. New York: Cambridge University Press, 2005.

Fosten, Donald S.V., and Robert J. Marrion. *The German Army, 1914–1918*. Oxford: Osprey, 2005.

Fotakis, Zisis. *Greek Naval Strategy and Policy 1910–1919*. London: Routledge, 2005.

French, David. *British Economic and Strategic Planning, 1905–1915*. London: Routledge, 2006.

————. *British Strategy and War Aims, 1914–1916*. Oxford: Oxford University Press, 1995.

————. "'Official but not history'? Sir James Edmonds and the Official History of the Great War." *Journal of the Royal United Services Institution* 131 (1986): 58–63.

————. "Sir James Edmonds and the Official History: France and Belgium." In *The First World War and British Military History*, ed. Brian Bond. Oxford: Clarendon, 1991.

Freytag-Loringhoven, Hugo Friedrich von. *Menschen und Dinge, wie ich sie in meinem Leben sah*. Berlin: E.S. Mittler & Sohn, 1923.

Friedeburg, Friedrich von. *Schlachten des Weltkrieges: In Einzeldarstellungen bearbeitet im Auftrages des Reichsarchiv Band 2: Karpathen- und Oniester-Schlact 1915*. Oldenburg: Stalling, 1924.

Friedrich, Wolfgang-Uwe. *Bulgarien und die Mächte 1913–1915*. Stuttgart: Steiner, 1985.

Gallwitz, Max von. *Meine Führertätigkeit im Weltkriege 1914–1916*. Berlin: Berlin: E.S. Mittler & Sohn, 1929.

Gardner, Brian. *Allenby*. London: Cassell, 1965.

General Staff, War Office. *Armies of the Balkan States, 1914–1916*. London: HMSO/Battery, 1996.

————. *Handbook of the German Army in War, January 1917*. Yorkshire: EP, 1973.

Goltz, Generalfeldmarschall Colmar Baron von der. *Denkwürdigkeiten*. Berlin: E.S. Mittler & Sohn, 1932.

Gooch, John. *Army, State, and Society in Italy, 1870–1915*. New York: St. Martin's, 1989.

————. *The Plans of War: The General Staff and British Military Strategy, 1900–1916*. London: Routledge and Kegan Paul, 1974.

Goodspeed, Donald James. *Ludendorff: Soldier, Dictator, Revolutionary*. London: Hart-Davis, 1966.

Green, Andrew. *Writing the Great War: Sir James Edmonds and the Official Histories 1915–1948*. London: Frank Cass, 2003.

Greenhalgh, Elizabeth. *Victory Through Coalition: Britain and France during the First World War*. Cambridge: Cambridge University Press, 2006.

Greenhut, Jeffrey. "Race, Sex, and War: The Impact of Race and Sex on Morale and Health Services for the Indian Corps on the Western Front, 1914." *Military Affairs* 45, no. 2 (1981): 71–74.

Grey, Jeffrey, ed. *The Last Word? Essays on Official History in the United States and British Commonwealth*. London: Praeger, 2003.

Großer Generalstab, *Kriegesgeschichtliche Abteilung, Der deutsch–französische Krieg, 1870–1*. 8 vols. Berlin: E.S. Mittler & Sohn, 1874–81.

Gudmundsson, Bruce I. *Stormtroop Tactics: Innovation in the German Army, 1914–1918*. New York: Praeger, 1989.

Guinn, Paul. *British Strategy and Politics, 1914–1918*. Oxford: Clarendon, 1965.
Guth, Ekkehart. "Der Gegensatz zwischen dem Oberbefehlshaber Ost und dem Chef des Feldheeres 1914–15: Die Rolle des Major von Haeften im Spannungsfeld zwischen Hindenburg, Ludendorff, und Falkenhayn." *Militärgeschichtliche Mitteilungen* 35 (1984): 113–39.
Haber, Fritz. *Fünf Vorträge aus den Jahren 1920–23*. Berlin: Springer, 1924.
Hall, Richard C. *The Balkan Wars, 1912–1913: Prelude to the First World War*. London: Routledge, 2000.
———. *Bulgaria's Road to the First World War*. Boulder: East European Monographs, 1996.
Hamilton, Richard F., and Holger H. Herwig, eds. *The Origins of World War I*. Cambridge: Cambridge University Press, 2003.
Hanslian-Bergendorff, Rudolf. *Der chemische Krieg*. Berlin: E.S. Mittler & Sohn, 1925.
Herrmann, Matthias. *Das Reichsarchiv 1919–1945*. Ph.D. diss., Humboldt Universität, 1994.
Herwig, Holger H. "Clio Deceived: Patriotic Self-Censorship in Germany After the Great War." *International Security* 12, no. 2 (1987): 5–44.
———. *The First World War: Germany and Austria-Hungary 1914–1918*. London: Arnold, 1997.
———. *German Naval Officer Corps: A Social and Political History, 1890–1918*. Oxford: Oxford University Press, 1973.
———. *"Luxury" Fleet: The Imperial German Navy, 1888–1918*. London: Ashfield, 1987.
Hickey, Michael. *The First World War: The Mediterranean Front, 1914–1923*. Oxford: Osprey, 2002.
Higham, Robin, ed. *Official Histories: Essays and Bibliographies from Around the World*. Manhattan: Kansas State University Library, 1970.
———. *The Writing of Official Military History*. Westport, CT: Greenwood, 1999.
Hindenburg, Paul von. *Aus Meinem Leben*. Leipzig: Hirzel, 1920. (English trans.: *Out of My Life*. New York: Cassell, 1920.)
Hoffmann, Max von. *Die Aufzeichnungen des Generalmajor Max von Hoffman*. 2 vols. Berlin: Verlag fur Kulturpolitik, 1929.
Horne, John N., and Alan Kramer. *German Atrocities 1914: A History of Denial*. New Haven, CT: Yale University Press, 2005.
Huberich, Charles Henry, and Richard King. "The Development of German Prize Law." *Columbia Law Review* 18, no. 6 (1918): 503–38.
Hussey, John. "Kiggell: A Second Opinion." *Army Quarterly and Defence Journal* 124, no. 4 (1994): 464–71.
Indian Intelligence Branch, *The Second Afghan War, 1878–80*. London: HMSO, 1908.
Institute for Balkan Studies. *Greece and Great Britain during World War I: First Symposium*. Thessaloniki: Institute for Balkan Studies, 1985.
James, Lawrence. *Imperial Warrior: The Life and Times of Field Marshal Viscount Allenby 1861–1936*. London: Weidenfeld and Nicolson, 1993.

Janssen, Karl-Heinz. *Der Kanzler und der General: Die Führungskrise im Bethmann Hollweg und Falkenhayn.* Göttingen: Musterschmidt, 1966.

Jarausch, Konrad H. *The Enigmatic Chancellor: Bethmann-Hollweg and the Hubris of Imperial Germany.* New Haven, CT: Yale University Press, 1973.

Johnson, Alexander L.P. "Military Histories of the Great War." *Journal of Modern History* 3, no. 2 (1931): 266–86.

Kalm, Oskar Tile von. *Schlachten des Weltkrieges: In Einzeldarstellungen bearbeitet im Auftrages des Reichsarchiv Band 30: Gorlice.* Berlin: Stalling, 1930.

King, Jere Clemens. *Generals and Politicians: Conflict between France's High Command, Parliament, and Government, 1914–1918.* Berkeley: University of California Press, 1951.

Kirchbach, Arndt von. *Kämpfe in der Champagne, Winter 1914–Herbst 1915 (Der grosse Krieg in Einzeldarstellungen, heft. 11).* Oldenburg: Gerhard Stalling, 1919.

Kitchen, Martin. *The Silent Dictatorship: The Politics of the German High Command Under Hindenburg and Ludendorff, 1916–1918.* London: Holmes and Meier, 1976.

Kitromilides, Paschalis M., ed. *Eleftherios Venizelos: the Trials of Statesmanship.* Edinburgh: Edinburgh University Press, 2006.

Kriegsgeschichtliche Forschungsanstalt des Heeres. *Der Weltkrieg 1914 bis 1918: Die militärischen Operationen zu Land, Band X–XII.* Berlin: E.S. Mittler & Sohn, 1937–39.

Kuhl, Hermann von. *Der Weltkrieg 1914–1918, Band I und II.* Berlin: W. Kolk, 1929.

Leontaritis, George B. *Greece and the First World War: From Neutrality to Intervention, 1917–1918.* Boulder, CO: East European Monographs, 1990.

Litzmann, Karl. *Lebenserinnerungen, Band I.* Berlin: Eisenschmidt, 1927.

Liulevicius, Vejas G. *War Land on the Eastern Front: Culture, National Identity, and German Occupation in World War I.* New York: Cambridge University Press, 2000.

Löbel, Uwe. "Neue Forschungsmöglichkeiten zur preußisch-deutschen Heeresgeschichte." *Militärgeschichtliche Mitteilungen* 51 (1992): 143–49.

Ludendorff, Erich. *Meine Kriegserinnerungen, 1914–1918.* Berlin: E.S. Mittler & Sohn, 1919.

Lundeberg, Philip K. "The German Naval Critique of the U-Boat Campaign, 1915–1918." *Military Affairs* 27, no. 3 (1963): 105–18.

Luvass, Jay. "Military History: Is It Still Practicable?" *Parameters* (Summer 1995): 82–97.

Macleod, Jenny, ed. *Gallipoli: Making History.* London: Frank Cass, 2004.

Marinearchiv. *Der Krieg zur See 1914–1918: Der Handelskrieg mit U-Booten Band 1–3.* Berlin: E.S. Mittler & Sohn, 1931–34.

———. *Der Krieg zur See 1914–1918: Der Krieg in der Ostsee Band 1–2.* Berlin: E.S. Mittler & Sohn, 1921–29.

———. *Der Krieg zur See 1914–1918: Der Krieg in der Nordsee Band 3–4.* Berlin: E.S. Mittler & Sohn, 1923–24.

Martin, Gregory. "The Influence of Racial Attitudes on British Policy Towards India during the First World War." *Journal of Imperial and Commonwealth History* 14, no. 2 (1986): 91–113.

Meyer, Gustav. *Der Durchbruch am Narew, Jui–August 1915 (Der grosse Krieg in Einzeldarstellungen, heft. 27–28)*. Oldenburg: Gerhard Stalling, 1919.

Miller, Geoffrey. *Straits: British Policy Towards the Ottoman Empire and the Origins of the Dardanelles Campaign*. Hull: University of Hull Press, 1997.

Ministère de la Guerre, État-Major de l'Armée, Service Historique. *Les Armées françaises dans la Grande Guerre, Tomes II and III*. Paris: Imprimerie Nationale, 1922–37.

Mombauer, Annika. *Helmuth von Moltke and the Origins of the First World War*. Cambridge: New York University Press, 2001.

Morgen, Curt von. *Meiner Truppen Heldenkämpfe*. Berlin: E.S. Mittler & Sohn, 1920.

Mortlock, Michael J. *The Landings at Suvla Bay, 1915: An Analysis of British Failure during the Gallipoli Campaign*. Jefferson, NC: McFarland, 2007.

Nowak, Karl Friedrich, ed. *Die Aufzeichnungen des Generalmajors Max Hoffmann, Band I und II*. Berlin: E.S. Mittler & Sohn, 1929.

Omissi, David. "Europe through Indian Eyes: Indian Soldiers Encounter England and France, 1914–1918." *English Historical Review* 496 (2007): 371–96.

Otto, Helmut. "Der Bestand Kriegsgeschichtliche Forschungsanstalt des Heeres im Bundesarchiv-, Militärisches Zwischenarchiv Potsdam." *Militärgeschichtliche Mitteilungen* 51 (1992): 429–41.

Palmer, Alan. *The Gardeners of Salonika: The Macedonian Campaign 1915–1918*. London: André Deutsch, 1965.

Philpott, William. *Anglo-French Relations and Strategy on the Western Front*. New York: St. Martin's, 1996.

Pöhlmann, Markus. *Kriegsgeschichte und Geschichtspolitik: Der Erste Weltkrieg. Die amtliche deutsche Militärgeschichtsschreibung, 1914–1956*. Schöningh: Paderborn, 2002.

———. "Towards a New History of German Military Intelligence in the Era of the Great War: Approaches and Sources." *Journal of Intelligence History* 5, no. 2 (2005): 25–54.

———. "Yesterday's Battles and Future War: The German Official Military History, 1918–1939." In *Shadows of Total War: Europe, East Asia, and the United States, 1919–1939*, ed. Roger Chickering and Stig Förster. 223–38. New York: Cambridge University Press, 2003.

Poincaré, Raymond. *Au Service de la France*. 10 vols. Paris: Plon, 1926–33.

Redern, Hans von. *Die Winterschlacht in Masuren (Der grosse Krieg in Einzeldarstellungen, Heft 20)*. Oldenburg: Gerhard Stlling, 1918.

Reichold, Helmut, and Gerhard Granier, eds. *Adolf Wild von Hohenborn: Briefe und Tagebuchaufzeichnungen des preussischen Generals als Kriegsminister und Truppenführer im ersten Weltkrieg*. Berlin: H. Boldt, 1986.

Reichsarchiv. *Der Weltkrieg 1914 bis 1918: Die militärischen Operationen zu Land, Band I–IX*. Berlin: E.S. Mittler & Sohn, 1925–34.

Renzi, William A. "Great Britain, Russia, and the Straits, 1914–1915." *Journal of Modern History* 42, no. 1 (1970): 1–20.

————. *In the Shadow of the Sword: Italy's Neutrality and Entrance into the Great War, 1914–1915.* New York: P. Lang, 1987.

Röhl, John. *The Kaiser and His Court: Wilhelm II and the Government of Germany.* Cambridge: Cambridge University Press, 1994.

Roskill, Stephen. *Churchill and the Admirals.* New York: Morrow, 1978.

Rudenno, Victor. *Gallipoli: Attack from the Sea.* New Haven, CT: Yale University Press, 2008.

Rupprecht von Bayern, Kronprinz. *Mein Kriegstagebuch.* Berlin: Deutscher National, 1929.

Salandra, Antonio. *L'intervento 1915.* Milan: Garzanti, 1930.

Samuels, Martin. *Command or Control? Command, Training, and Tactics in the British and German Armies, 1888–1918.* London: Frank Cass, 1995.

Sanders, Liman von. *Fünf Jahre Türkei.* Berlin: A. Scherl, 1919.

Saxena, Shyam Narain. *Role of Indian Army in the First World War.* Delhi: Bhavna Prakashan, 1987.

Schmalenbach, Paul. *German Raiders: A History of Auxiliary Cruisers of the German Navy, 1895–1945.* Annapolis, MD: Naval Institute Press, 1979.

Schulte, Bernd F. *Vor dem Kriegsausbruch 1914: Deutschland, die Türkei, und der Balkan.* Düsseldorf: Drost, 1980.

Sondhaus, Lawrence. *Franz Conrad von Hötzendorf: Architect of the Apocalypse.* Boston: Humanities, 2000.

Stone, Norman. *The Eastern Front 1914–1917.* New York: Penguin, 1998.

Strachan, Hew. *The First World War in Africa.* Oxford: Oxford University Press, 2004.

————. *The First World War: Volume I: To Arms.* Oxford: Oxford University Press, 2001.

Symons Barrow, George de. *The Life of General Sir Charles Carmichael Monro.* London: Hutchinson, 1931.

Thorne, I.D.P. "Kiggell." *Army Quarterly and Defence Journal* 119, no. 4 (1989): 439–41.

Tirpitz, Alfred von. *Erinnerungen.* Leipzig: Verlag K.F. Koehler, 1919. (English trans.: *My Memoirs.* New York: Hurst and Blackett, 1919.)

Torrey, Glenn E. "Rumania and the Belligerents 1914–1916." *Journal of Contemporary History* 1, no. 3 (1966): 171–91.

————, ed. *Rumania and World War I.* Iasi: Center for Rumanian Studies, 1998.

Trumpener, Ulrich. *Germany and the Ottoman Empire, 1914–1918.* Princeton: Princeton University Press, 1968.

————. "The Road to Ypres: The Beginnings of Gas Warfare in World War I." *Journal of Modern History* 47, no. 3 (1975): 460–80.

Tschischwitz, Erich von. *Schlachten des Weltkrieges: In Einzeldarstellungen bearbeitet im Auftrages des Reichsarchiv Band 3: Antwerpen, 1914.* Berlin: Gerhard Stalling, 1925.

Tucker, Spencer C., ed. *The Encyclopaedia of World War I.* 5 vols. New York: ABC-Clio, 2005.

U.S. War Department. *Histories of 251 Divisions of the German Army Which Partici-pated in the War, 1914–1918*. Uckfield, UK: Naval and Military Press, 2001.

Verhey, Jeffrey. *The Spirit of 1914: Militarism, Myth, and Mobilization in Germany*. New York: Cambridge University Press, 2000.

Wakefield, Alan, and Simon Moody. *Under the Devil's Eye: Britain's Forgotten Army at Salonika 1915–1918*. Stroud, UK: Sutton, 2004.

War Office General Staff. *Official History of the Operations in Somaliland, 1901–4*, 2 vols. London: HMSO, 1907.

Wavell, Archibald Percival. *Allenby, a Study in Greatness: The Biography of Field-Mar-shal Viscount Allenby of Megiddo and Felixstowe*. Oxford: Oxford University Press, 1944.

Wegener, Wolfgang. *The Naval Strategy of the World War*. Annapolis, MD: Naval Insti-tute, 1989.

Weiss, Dieter J. *Kronprinz Rupprecht von Bayern (1869–1955): Eine politische Biografie*. Augsburg: Pustet Friedrich, 2007.

Wheeler-Bennett, John W. *Hindenburg: The Wooden Titan*. London: Macmillan, 1936.

Wietzker, Wolfgang. *Giftgas im Ersten Weltkrieg: Was konnte die deutsche Öffentlichkeit wissen*. Ph.D. diss., Heinrich-Heine-Universität, 2006.

Wilhelm, Crown Prince. *Meine Erinnerungen aus Deutschlands Heldenhampf*. Berlin: E.S. Mittler & Sohn, 1923.

Wilson, Keith. "Historical Engineering." In *Forging the Collective Memory: Governments and International Historians through Two World Wars*, ed. Keith Wilson. 1–28. Providence: Berghahn, 1996.

Wilson, Michael. *Destination Dardanelles*. London: Cooper, 1988.

Winter, Jay, and Antoine Prost. *The Great War in History: Debates and Controversies, 1914 to the Present*. New York: Cambridge University Press, 2005.

Woodward, David R. *Lloyd George and the Generals*. London: Frank Cass, 2004.

Yalman, Ahmed Emin. *Turkey in the World War*. New Haven, CT: Yale University Press, 1930.

Zandek, I., and H. Böhm. *Bestand RH 61—Kriegsgeschichtliche Forschungsanstalt des Heeres*. Freiburg: Bundesarchiv-Militärarchiv, 2002.

Zuckerman, Larry. *The Rape of Belgium: The Untold Story of World War I*. New York: New York University Press, 2004.

Zwehl, Hans von. *Erich von Falkenhayn, General der Infanterie: Eine biographische Studie*. Berlin: E.S. Mittler & Sohn, 1926.

INDEX

408   INDEX